The Forsaken Realm of Tolkien.

(Tolkien and the medieval tradition)

by

Alex Lewis & Elizabeth Currie.

Medea Publishing

Medea Publishing
medea@micro-plus-web.net

This edition 2005
1 2 3 4 5 6 7 8 9 10

First Published by
Medea Publishing 2005

A catalogue record for this book
is available from the British Library

ISBN 0-9543207-1-9

Printed and Bound in Great Britain
by Intype Libra

Contents.

The Forsaken Realm of Tolkien.

	Title	Page
	Introduction	i
	About the Authors	ii
Chapter One:	Gondolin Analysed; The Fall of a City.	1
Chapter Two:	The link between Troy and Gondolin.	30
Chapter Three:	Lost Tales, Found Manuscripts.	77
Chapter Four:	The Tale of Tuor & Eärendil.	107
Chapter Five:	A Tale of Two Cities; Troy and Minas Tirith.	144
Chapter Six:	Heroes and villains; Achilles and his counterpart.	182
Chapter Seven:	What It Isn't; Gondolin & Famous Fallen Cities.	203
Chapter Eight:	Eärendil's Fellow Voyagers.	218
Chapter Nine:	Quenya - the Concept.	241
	Bibliography:	255
	Index:	259

Cover Art: Ruth Lacon:
'Tholos [Tomb f] sidechamber, Potamos Elias, Thera: 1916.'

To

Franco Manni for faith

Ted Nasmith for belief

Christopher and Priscilla Tolkien for Insight

and

J.R.R. Tolkien for inspiration

Introduction.

2005

What readers might ask when they first see this book is why did we choose the title *Forsaken Realm of Tolkien* for our second volume of Tolkien studies. The reason is encapsulated in the sub-title: 'Tolkien and the medieval tradition'. There is a realm of documents out there forsaken from the middle of the twentieth century onwards. Literature of the period from the pre-Christian era through to the end of the nineteenth century which seems to have disappeared off the collective horizon of most people. It encompasses the medieval period. It is important to note that within this forgotten literature lie some of Tolkien's main sources of inspiration for both *The Lord of the Rings* and *The Silmarillion*. What we found in our current studies has brought us to a much deeper understanding of the development of both of Tolkien's major works and the way in which certain characters within LotR came into being. To summarise, we are examining a time when Homer was less well known than Dares or Dictys. When there were links in literature between the eastern end of the Mediterranean, northernmost parts of Scandinavia, and everywhere in between - documents which Tolkien would have been very conversant with.

The material we deal with in this volume can by its very nature be very difficult to approach, and some of the explanations are dense and closely argued. We have striven at all times to present the material in as stimulating and interesting a format as we might and tried to make it as easy to digest as we could. If we have even partly succeeded in doing so, it will be satisfying for the authors. The subject matter in this volume was originally thought to be sufficient to fill perhaps a couple of chapters in this second book, but 'the tale grew in the telling' as more and more insights led to further research and important findings. Thus there is a large body of material originally meant for this volume which has been left out and which should be presented in due time in further volumes of Tolkien studies.

We would like to thank many people without whose encouragement and support over the years since *The Uncharted Realms of Tolkien* appeared, this volume might never have seen the light of day. First and foremost we must give our gratitude to Christopher Tolkien and other members of the Tolkien family for their unfailing interest in our studies. Secondly, to Franco Manni of Brescia, Italy who has been a great friend and supporter. Thirdly we would like to thank Ted Nasmith of Toronto, Canada for unstinting help and encouragement over the last few years. Our thanks to Susanne Stopfel for help translating the *Orendel* story which was only available in German. Others too have been very kind with their praise for what we achieved with The Uncharted Realms of Tolkien and pressed us for more. This is in part a response to those requests. If we have done our job correctly and diligently, the reader might well discover that re-reading of LotR and QS will be done thereafter in a new light and with a new and far broader appreciation of the genius of J.R.R.Tolkien. We would like to thank our publishers for their support. We thank HarperCollins Publishers for permission to quote from various of their works.

About the authors:

Alex Lewis was born in Oxford. He attended a Public School in Oxford with some links to Tolkien. During the 1960's he lived within a one minute walk of the house where Tolkien wrote most of his important works - 20 Northmoor Road. He holds a Batchelor of Science and Master of Science degrees as well as Postgraduate qualifications and he has worked abroad extensively. He has taught on the Dale Carnegie Management Course and was a member of staff at Manchester University. He was Chairman of the Tolkien Society 1988 to 1992, presented a paper at the 1992 Tolkien Centenary Conference, and helped to inaugurate the annual Tolkien Seminars. He is co-author of the important study: *The Uncharted Realms of Tolkien*, published in 2002. He has presented many papers on Tolkien at seminars, and has had articles and letters published in Mallorn, Amon Hen, the Radio Times, the Oxford Mail as well as BBC Music Magasine. He has spoken about Tolkien on local and national radio stations in several countries. His articles and stories have been published and translated into French, German, Italian, Greek, Czech, and Polish. In 2002 - 2004 he was Guest Speaker at the Italian Tolkien Conference, Brescia, Italy and has spoken at many other international conferences. Alex Lewis also founded Nigglings, the writers special interest group of the Tolkien Society and is editor of its publications. Alex writes fiction novels and composes music.

Elizabeth Currie was born in Scotland and has been a longstanding member of the Tolkien Society, co-author of *The Uncharted Realms of Tolkien* in 2002, and contributing articles and stories to its publications and papers to its seminars on many occasions. She holds two degrees - one in the Arts the other in the Sciences - is widely read, and travels extensively.

The two authors between them have over fifty years combined experience and research into JRR Tolkien, his writings and the environment of his time.

About the method of writing:

This book was even more a total team effort than *The Uncharted Realms of Tolkien*. Both authors had an input into all aspects of the work, it was discussed at length and modifications suggested by both parties. It is not possible to start to assign parts of it to any one author. The old adage "two minds are better than one" would seem to serve admirably. Translations of the Middle-english texts in this volume were made by Elizabeth Currie. Analysis of Greek words by Alex Lewis.

Disclaimer:

Chapter One:

Gondolin Analysed; The Fall of a City.

Most readers and scholars of Tolkien expect to find the sources of Tolkien's major stories in Northern mythology and legend. Tom Shippey for instance sets LotR in a northern bedrock when he says: 'As for Gandolf, that is an Italian miscomprehension, familiar from Browning's poem 'The Bishop Orders His Tomb', but *wildly inappropriate* to a work which *does its best to avoid Latinisms*' (p4. Road to M-e). And as for QS: 'Though Tolkien meant *The Silmarillion* to fill a gap in English tradition, he does indeed seem to have drawn mostly on *Old Norse or Icelandic* literature for its main themes.' (p.244 Author of the century). Humphrey Carpenter in his Biography of Tolkien (part 3, p.97) quotes from a letter written years later (Letter 131 to Milton Waldman from late 1951): 'I had a mind to make a body of more or less connected legend... It should possess the tone and quality that I desired, somewhat cool and clear, be redolent of our 'air' (the clime and soil of the North West, meaning Britain and the hither parts of Europe; *not Italy or the Aegean,* still less the East...' Yet even Carpenter puts his finger on an important fact (p.104): '... one may detect certain literary influences [in the Children of Hurin]; the hero's fight with a great dragon inevitably suggests comparison with the deeds of Sigurd and Beowulf, while his unknowing incest with his sister and his subsequent suicide were derived quite consciously from the story of Kullervo... But again these 'influences' are *only superficial*... [it achieves] a degree of dramatic complexity and a subtlety of characterisation not often found in ancient legends.' (our italics in text)
This then is the problem - the influences which we can find amongst northern sources are only superficial when they are not missing entirely. Taking the Kalevala for instance, it supplies only a bare and unsatisfactory thread onto which Tolkien had to twine episodes from other legends, then transform the whole in order to weave a grand story. For other stories there were no visible parallels at all within Northern European legend. Indeed, even in the stories cited, the 'Soup' is a very tiny component of the overall tales. Did Tolkien just invent outright to fill in the major gaps? That is what most readers have assumed until now. But from all we understand of Tolkien's methods if we accept he was being honest in his essay *'On Fairy Stories'*, it is very hard to reconcile the level of outright invention with what we know of his writings. So where else can we look to find Tolkien's sources?

This is an area which has led to major miscomprehension, some of which Tolkien himself was very aware of. For instance, in his study of Homeric women in LotR, Fenwick (M.Fenwick, Mythlore 81, 1996, p.17-23) introduces his theme with a talk given by W.H. Auden in 1966 to the Tolkien Society of America, where he claimed:

'Tolkien is fascinated with the whole Northern thing,' he said, 'People seem to divide - they're attracted by either the Northern thing or the Southern thing, by Scandinavia or the Mediterranean - and for Tolkien north is a sacred direction.' This from someone who was an old student of Tolkien's and a friend of his in later years (he wrote a review for LotR). It moved Tolkien to respond thus:
'Auden has asserted that for me 'the North is a sacred direction'. That is not true. The North-west of Europe, where I (and most of my ancestors) have lived, has my affection, as a man's home should. I love its atmosphere, and know more of its histories and languages than I do of other parts; but it is not 'sacred', nor does it exhaust my affections. I have, for instance, a particular love for the Latin language, and among its descendants Spanish. That it is untrue for my story, a mere reading of the synopses should show. The North was the seat of the fortresses of the Devil. The progress of the tale ends in what is far more like the re-establishment of an effective Holy Roman Empire with its seat in Rome than anything that would be devised by a 'Nordic'.'
(Letters, No.294, p.376) (emphasis ours)
Therefore Tolkien is nowhere near as 'Northern' as most critics would suggest.

In his essay *Tolkien and the Appeal of the Pagan* in Chance 2004, Shippey creates an opposition between 'classical' writing and 'Northern myth', in which he comes down in favour of the latter, and argues that this difference is critical to Tolkien's preference for the 'Northern' over the 'Classical':
'The very familiarity of these stories has, however, overlaid the shock effect that they had on the literary world when they first began to appear in print. They introduced an entirely new mythology, which had been completely forgotten everywhere except in remote outposts like Iceland. To someone brought up on classical epic and biblical story, they furthermore introduced an entirely new worldview, or mind-set, or as Tolkien might say, literary 'flavour'. And yet, on further inspection, English readers might start to think it was not so absolutely unfamiliar after all. Snorri's readiness to treat themes of the utmost importance, such as old age and death and the end of the world, with a pervasive humour, while strange to and indeed forbidden by classical literary theory, was just what Shakespeare had been accused of by generations of French critics. Snorri's Old Icelandic still translates very easily into colloquial modern English. Perhaps the worldview had not gone away after all; it had just been dropped by the literary caste, the media people, the teachers and arbiters of literature - people who, as Tolkien would readily have agreed, had consistently rejected any form of native popular culture, whether *Grimm's Fairy-Tales* or Shakespeare or Tolkien himself, coming around only slowly and reluctantly in a whole series of rearguard actions. What, we should ask, were the surprising or shocking novelties in Snorri's matter and method?...

Tragedy was high style and comedy was low style, and the two should be carefully separated (his failure to do this was one of the French arguments against Shakespeare, while later on Dickens remained in the critical wilderness for generations because comedy could not be taken seriously). but Norse writers seemed to have no feeling for decorousness. As mentioned above, Snorri was ready to combine themes of the utmost importance with a pervasive humour. And this too is a part of the heroic temperament and the "theory of courage". Indeed, everything that has been said here about Snorri can be seen as part of a coherent philosophy. The laconism [Shippey has earlier mentioned the 'habitual use of understatement' in Norse writing] connects to the fatalism; if things are fated, there is no point in talking about them. Both connect further with the cult of "naked will": the hero cannot be defeated, even by fate, if he refuses to give up or yield..."

(T.A. Shippey in Chance 2004, 'Tolkien and the Invention of Myth', part III, ch.9, pp.145-162)

It has to be said that most of what Shippey says against the 'classical' appears to stem from sheer unfamiliarity with the works in question. For a start, it is vitally important not to confuse 'classicism in literature' with 'Classical literature' - and this, unfortunately, is what Shippey with his references to French critics is doing. French criticism of the 18th century and after was derived from the Greek and Roman literary criticism which bedevilled many Roman writers and was resurrected in the Renaissance to baleful effect, having a most unfortunate impact on the whole Western literary-critical tradition. However, it cannot be emphasised too much that many of the greatest Classical authors lived before these critical ideas were developed, and many more simply ignored them. Aristotle's treatise on Tragedy, which has been the bane of many a post-Renaissance playwright, includes criticism of every single dramatist then living or recently dead. None of the 'great names' now held up as shining examples, such as Euripides and Aeschylus, escape being marked down for one fault or another. Homer had no more idea of the Greek literary-critical definition of Proper Epic Poetry than did the *Beowulf* - poet; he lived some three or four hundred years before anyone got around to splitting those particular hairs and almost certainly composed orally rather than on papyrus anyway. Not that this kept Classical commentators from criticising Homer for not writing a better *Iliad* !

Translators from the 17th century onward have a lot to answer for in 'taming' Classical literature, as understood by most European readers. We can be quite certain that Tolkien knew the relevant works in the original; and that is a different matter entirely to even the best recent translations. In particular, the 'decorousness', the over-seriousness, the absence of comedy and the absence of anything 'indelicate', which is sometimes called Classical, is an artefact of translators willing to change their text to suit the tolerable limits of thinking in their own day. Homer is hard enough (there are bits in the *Odyssey* which are exceedingly serious yet as funny as they are untranslatable in polite company); and some other Classical writers almost defy translation even today. A very good example is the great Athenian playwright Aristophanes. His works are an amazing mix of scalding political satire on the most serious issues up to and including war (and produced, it might be added, in the middle of the Peloponnesian War between Athens and Sparta - it is absolutely certain that no British government in the 20th century would have tolerated such criticism during time of war); broad bawdry that (Aubrey Beardsley's misinterpretations notwithstanding) rarely turns truly obscene; wildly fantastic invention; and genuinely funny comedy. Anything less 'classical' in the critics' sense is hard to imagine. Trying to split European literature into the southern, classical, over-lavish and humourless and unTolkienian, and the northern, medieval, laconic (itself a Greek term!) humorous and Tolkienian, simply will not wash.

Even Verlyn Flieger, respected medievalist, finds it impossible to consider Tolkien as being influenced by non-Northern material. She begins in an essay with an open enough mind:
'It can be argued that other European mythologies besides that of Arthur might fit Tolkien's general description...Many so-called mythologies are made up of different kinds of narrative composed over centuries, and are the accumulated work of many hands. Another example is that of the combined mythologies of Greece and Rome.' But she then falls back on Auden's statement:
'However, while this mythology is certainly a body of "more or less connected legend," I would eliminate it as an influence on the grounds that Tolkien had no particular affinity for what he called "Southern" myth, greatly preferring the Eddas and sagas of Iceland and Scandinavia. Moreover, Greek and Roman myth can hardly be said to be "redolent" of the air of Britain and North West Europe.'
(Flieger, V., Mythlore 87, 2000, Vol.23.1, pps. 47-59)

To search for Tolkien's sources, we need to look much further afield and avoid Auden's, Flieger's and Shippey's mindset of "Northern things' and 'Southern things' being mutually exclusive. This is an exploration that has stretched across two volumes, of which this is the first. We decided to start 'at the beginning' and look at the first story that Tolkien completed within his work that encompassed Middle earth: *The Fall of Gondolin*, which was written according to Tolkien in Letter 165 (1955): '...the mythology first began to take shape during the 1914-1918 war. *The Fall of Gondolin* (and the birth of Eärendil) was written in hospital and on leave after surviving the Battle of the Somme in 1916.' In wondering what antecedents *The Fall of Gondolin* might have we looked far and wide, finding little if anything in Northern European myth or legend that looked at all plausible. Eventually we realised that the story of Gondolin draws on two main sources, the story of Troy and the story of Eärendel. In this chapter we will be looking at the unexpected connection between the stories of Gondolin and of Troy; in following chapters we will explore the links between the Tale of Eärendel and that of Gondolin.

Many people might be surprised at the thought of J.R.R. Tolkien borrowing anything from any classical writer, given what he wrote above in his long letter to Milton Waldman in 1951, and especially from Homer's Iliad and Odyssey. Homer, however, is something of a red herring in this inquiry. If all we had was Homer to go on, then indeed one might conclude that there was little to link the Trojan Wars to The Fall of Gondolin. The real breakthrough was the discovery that there are not one but two versions of the story of Troy. Firstly there is the Classical story, which is the one most people are taught about nowadays. It is the only one that is easily available in good translations from almost any bookstore. Secondly and much more importantly, there is the medieval version, which we now believe is the one that inspired Tolkien and became the source for one of the two major strands in the story of Gondolin. The reason that it has been overlooked is that it is simply not easy to obtain. It has effectively disappeared off the horizon of collective modern consciousness, something that seems to have happened in the middle of the 20th Century as far as we can ascertain - because it has been shown to be later than originally believed and thus less reliable as a source of the legend. There are five very important points which we wish to make here about this almost forgotten medieval Troy legend. Firstly, it favoured the Trojans and presented them as the heroes and the Greeks as the villains, whereas the familiar Classical story has the Greeks as the heroes. Secondly, it was popular; it exists in many variations and each one was reproduced both in manuscript and early print many times. Thirdly, it existed alongside and intertwined with the other areas of medieval storytelling, influencing them to an astonishing degree. Fourthly, in the time when the literature and languages which Tolkien studied were alive, and especially in high medieval Europe, these versions were thought to be the 'true tradition' of Troy while Homer was seen as an unreliable source. Fifthly, and very importantly, we can be absolutely certain that Tolkien knew the medieval Trojan legend well.

I: The Medieval Version of the Tale of Troy

a; Who's the Hero?

The medieval version of the Tale of Troy does not descend from Homer, who was known to Europe in the Middle Ages only through a poorly-translated and heavily abbreviated Latin version of the *Iliad*. Instead, medieval writers drew on two Classical works that purported to be historical accounts of the Trojan war, the 'Journal of the Trojan War' of 'Dictys the Cretan' and the 'History of the Fall of Troy' of 'Dares Phyrgius' (both available in English translation in R.M. Frazer 1966, 'The Trojan War; the Chronicles of Dictys of Crete and Dares the Phyrgian', Indiana University Press). Both these works had been written in the first place to fill a perceived need. As far back as the Classical Greek 'fathers of history', Thucydides and Herodotus, historians had doubted that Homer told the true story of the Trojan War, but there seemed to be no independent evidence. Inevitably, two people decided to fill that gap, whilst at the same time addressing contemporary issues of their own. 'Dictys' and 'Dares' were quickly accepted and became perhaps the most successful historical forgers of all time - they were not disproved until the beginning of the 18th century. Both were probably written in Greek; fragments of a Greek version of 'Dictys' have turned up on papyrus in Egypt, and it is generally accepted that 'Dares' has a Greek original too. 'Dares' and 'Dictys' both probably date to the 1st or 2nd century AD. However, unlike the *Iliad*, whose status as near-Holy Writ of Classical culture probably made translation a rather pointless exercise, both these works were translated in full into Latin. As a result, it was this version of the Tale of Troy that became influential in medieval Europe. To the medieval west, Homer wrote bad poetry, whereas Dares and Dictys wrote history. Homer lied, and the truth of the Trojan war lay in Dictys and Dares.

There was one other very important result of Europe's loss of the *Iliad*. The overwhelming majority of the surviving material on Troy known to medieval authors in Western Europe was pro-Trojan. Firstly there was Dares the Phyrgian's 'History of the Fall of Troy', an account of the war by someone representing themselves as Trojan, viewed from and favouring the Trojan side. Secondly there was Virgil's *Aeneid*, which tells the story of the fall of Troy in its first few books through the eyes of a Trojan survivor, Aeneas, whose family goes on to found Rome. Virgil was one major representative of a whole pro-Trojan Roman attitude, and during the medieval period the general points that Virgil makes about the Trojan origins of Rome would be even more influential than his actual story. Thirdly, Dictys of Crete regards the Trojans as barbarians - but 'his' greater theme of 'war is hell and imperialism is worse' means that by the end, the Greeks are as bad as if not worse than the Trojans. By 1160, when Benoit de Saint-Maure wrote one of the first French romances on a Trojan theme, a distinctive pro-Trojan medieval narrative had emerged. In this story, as in Tolkien's tale of Gondolin, it is the besieged people inside Troy who are the Good Guys and the heroes, and the besiegers outside Troy who are the villains. Indeed, the common saying 'beware of Greeks bearing gifts' is a paraphrase from Virgil's *Aenid*: 'Timeo Danaos et dona ferentes' (I fear the Greeks even when they bring gifts) (Aenid II, 49) - and was taken as a pejorative statement about Greeks in general based on the sentiments of that pro-Trojan stance.

It is well worth pointing out that much medieval writing on Troy was effectively historical, even though it was written in verse. There were straightforward 'romances' either on the whole subject (like the French *Roman de Troie* of Benoît de Saint-Maure - all 30,300 lines of it! - and the Middle English *Seege or Batayl of Troye*) or on particular sections, such as Boccacio's *Il Filostrato*, 'the one prostrated by love' about the Trojan prince Troilus and his faithless lady-love, the maiden Cressida. By far the most influential sequence of works, however, tells the story as actual history. From Guido delle Colonne's *Historia Destructionis Troiae* through its three Middle English translations (the alliterative 'Destruction of Troy', the Laud 'Troy Book' and John Lydgate's 'Troy Book'), to Caxton's translation of the *Recuyell of the Histories of Troye*, these works are about the Tale of Troy as history. They are certain that these events really happened; they present the facts and play down the things the romances bring to the fore - the supernatural, the marvellous and the love interest. These works are trying to make the story they have to tell relevant and interesting for their audience, but they also insist on its truth. In modern terms, these poems are the equivalent of the BBC/History Channel co-production, not the blockbuster Hollywood film. This distinctive medieval 'historical' approach to legends is also the one picked up and used by

J.R.R. Tolkien in his works. He avoids the magical and the clearly supernatural as much as possible throughout his published writings. Galadriel's Mirror in *The Lord of the Rings* works by probability, not foresight; Tolkien does not allow his Elves to appear and disappear at the drop of a hat, as such creatures often do in medieval romance. Gandalf's 'magic' is all of a practical and explainable variety, and Galadriel talks in realistic terms about the nature of magic with Frodo and Sam in Lothórien. The Trojan legends are not the only place where Tolkien could have seen this attitude at work in medieval writing, but since they offer romances and histories on the very same subject they are certainly one of the best examples.

So that we might draw upon these stories in detail to compare them with *The Fall of Gondolin*, we shall give a broad summary of the story as it is told by Dares and Dictys first. We will then begin to delve deeper in order to show the many points at which the source material links to Tolkien's own writing. In this medieval version of the Trojan War (summarised here from the Laud 'Troy Book' and the alliterative 'Destruction of Troy') there is pride and folly on both sides, but the Greeks are the ones who consistently turn a bad situation into a worse one. In the beginning, sailing in search of the Golden Fleece, Jason and his companions land on a remote beach in search of water and rest, rather than sailing into Troy's harbour openly. As a result, Laomedon King of Troy understandably thinks they may be raiders, and sends out a strong company of knights to tell the Greeks to leave at once or face the consequences. Jason sails onwards, but Hercules feels insulted and wants revenge. When he returns to Greece after Jason's quest has succeeded, Hercules calls on several Greek kings to aid him. They summon their armies and fleets and sail for Troy. There, Laomedon is killed in battle; the city is sacked and demolished; the inhabitants are killed or enslaved; and the king's daughter Hesione is given to the Greek lord Telamon, the first to enter the city, who shamefully keeps her as his concubine rather than marrying her. Only one of Laomedon's sons survives, Priam, who happens to be away conducting a border skirmish when the Greeks arrive. He returns as soon as he hears what is happening, but it is too late. Troy has fallen, and its destroyers have already sailed for home. Priam then spends many years rebuilding Troy, restoring the kingdom to prosperity and military strength, creating a new web of alliances, and building a new city of Troy, larger, stronger and fairer than before, with a marvellous palace at its heart.

When Priam finally gets round to thinking about the Greeks, he begins with a low-key and sensible approach. He wants his sister back, but he is prepared to forego vengeance for his father, let bygones be bygones and make friends with the Greeks if they will only return Hesione; and he sends one of his most trusted lords, Antenor, to tell this to the Greek kings. The Greeks respond to this overture with pride, arrogance and threats of violence; Antenor barely escapes with his life. He is at so much risk in his last port of call that he sails out into the beginning of a storm that almost sinks his ships before he returns to Troy. Priam is understandably upset, calls his council and gets approval to send an invasion fleet to Greece to teach its kings a lesson. His eldest son Hector is offered the command but does not want it; he points out that the Greeks are still vastly stronger than the Trojans, and provoking them is sure to have a bad end. Next in line is Paris, who thinks Hector is being overcautious, but still does not think an invasion is the right answer; he wants to lead a raid to capture some great Greek lady, ostensibly to exchange for Hesione, and he is sure of success because Venus has told him he will have the fairest lady in Greece, after he gave that goddess the prize when asked to judge between her, Juno and Minerva. The third brother, Deiphobus, agrees with this strategy, but the fourth, Helenus, prophesies destruction for Troy if Paris goes on such an errand. The others are stunned into silence until the youngest brother, Troilus, insultingly asks what Helenus (a priest) knows about war, declares that no-one can know the future or the gods' will, and supports Paris's idea. Fatefully, Priam adopts the idea of a raid, though he is twice more told that it will lead to his death and his city's fall, once by a philosopher on his council, and again by his daughter Cassandra who is also foresighted. He ignores the prophecies of doom. Paris sails for Greece and arrives at the island of Cythera with its famous temple of Venus, making himself out as a princely pilgrim. Learning of this, Helen comes to visit the temple, ostensibly to worship, actually to meet this foreign prince of whom she hears so much. It is love at first sight; Paris carries her off, together with her ladies and the temple treasure. Once they reach Troy all thought of an exchange for Hesione is forgotten and Paris and Helen are married as soon as possible.

The Greeks assemble a vast army and sail for Troy, while the Trojans call in their allies. An attempt at negotiation fails due to Greek arrogance, and the war begins. The medieval writers work their way forward through a precise series of battles and truces, from the landing of the Greeks to the final fall of Troy. This can seem interminable and boring to modern readers, a gory version of the sports section in the news. However, in the hands of a master like the 'Destruction'-poet, who has a real grasp of pacing, incident, character and variation, this section can become not only readable but interesting. Almost certainly, too, these long poems were never meant to be read as a whole; they would have been intended to be taken in like a television serial, in a series of sessions in which one or more 'books' of the piece were read aloud at a time. Performed by a skilled reader, the bad versions would be improved and the good ones would be superb.

It is the Trojans who are made out to be heroes in the medieval version; Hector is a perfect knight whose very courtesy accidentally throws away the one real chance for his side to win (much like the supposedly 'Northern' characteristic of *ofermod* or overmastering pride of the Anglo-saxon Ealdorman Beorhtnoth at the Battle of Maldon, which Tolkien criticised in his poem *The Homecoming of Beorhtnoth Beorthelm's Son*. Here we see it in action centuries before it was described for the Anglo-Saxon nobleman); Paris is a brave man though he still prefers the bow to the lance; and little brother Troilus is Hector's true heir, his people's last hope. By contrast Achilles, Homer's main hero, is made out to be cruel, cowardly and treacherous. His retiral from the fighting is not due to an insult from Agamemnon, but rather to Achilles considering whether or not to betray the Greeks in return for Priam's daughter Polyxena and a handsome dowry. Achilles kills neither Hector nor Troilus in fair fight. He sneaks up on Hector and attacks while the Trojan prince is distracted by having taken a Greek lord prisoner. Troilus is mobbed by a thousand of the Myrmidons, and their lord Achilles only moves in when the Trojan prince is wounded, exhausted, and unable to put up a fight. Achilles compounds his dishonourable behaviour by dragging Troilus' body like that of a traitor, head-down at his horse's tail. Finally, when all the princes of Troy are dead and hope is gone, the Greeks use negotiation as a mask to take advantage of internal treachery. Two Trojan lords, Antenor and Aeneas are willing to betray their city in return for their own safety, and hopes of ruling whatever survives. With the treacherous twosome as deceitful go-betweens, the Greeks begin a negotiation they have no intention of honouring. Priam and his counsellors agree a peace and pay a vast sum in gold, silver and wheat as an indemnity; but the Greeks still use the Horse to sneak a group of men into the city, open the gates, and sack and destroy Troy, killing King Priam and most of the population of the city.

This is not the end, however, for one of Priam's sons survives, the saintly and foresighted Helenus. Hector's wife Andromache and her young son Laomedon also live through both siege and sack; Andromache is spared by the Greek kings in council because she argued that the body of Achilles should be returned for honourable burial after he was killed by the Trojans, and at her pleas and those of Helenus her young son is spared too. Neoptolemus/Pyrrhus, Achilles' son, is sufficiently in love with Andromache to take her and the boy to Greece, even though he had voted to kill young Laomedon. After some time Neoptolemus deserts Andromache, being smitten with love for Hermione, the daughter of Helen and Menelaus, who is inconveniently married to Orestes, Agamemnon's son, here ruling at Athens. Neoptolemus carries Hermione off and marries her instead, but he has already fathered a child on Andromache. In short order, Neoptolemus gets his comeuppance, killed by Orestes in a surprise attack when he has gone on pilgrimage to Apollo's shrine on 'Delphos' (probably a mistake for the island of Delos). While her husband is away, Hermione tries to have Andromache killed, calling in her father Menelaus to get rid of her rival and secure the kingdom for herself. Andromache escapes the palace with her son and the people rally to her; Achilles' father Peleus carries her and young Laomedon to another city, where her second child is born. Orestes meanwhile reclaims his errant wife, and Peleus and Andromache are left in charge of Thessaly as regents for Neoptolemus' son Achillides. This young lad, however, turns over the kingdom to his elder half-brother Laomedon, so that Priam's grandson, the heir of Troy, comes to rule Thessaly where all the trouble started - since in this version Jason of the Golden Fleece is from the same family as Achilles. Laomedon frees the surviving Trojan prisoners, while Achillides eventually gains a throne elsewhere in Greece. So in the medieval version, the whole war turns out to be futile; for within a generation Greece itself is ruled by princes who are partly or wholly Trojan by blood.

It is worth pointing out that whilst nowadays we tend to think we are taking the story of Troy 'straight from Homer', we are still doing no such thing. The '*Iliad*' is a long poem (the Oxford World's Classics translation runs to 443 pages) but its focus is relatively narrow. There are allusions to many things outside the strict run of the story Homer is telling, but these in themselves make it clear that even when the *Iliad* was composed, it was one version of one story within a mass of tales about the Trojan War. It is only chance that has led Homer alone to survive intact from the large number of poems on the subject which we know existed in the Classical period, and much that we think of as being essential to the story - such as the Wooden Horse - was found in those other poems, not Homer. Any retelling of 'the story of the Trojan war' has to refer to works other than the '*Iliad*' and '*Odyssey*'. So, since we too have to reach beyond Homer to tell the Tale of Troy, we should not blame medieval writers for making use of all the material at their disposal. This is especially true because much of the time they were trying to write history, not romance, an exercise for which Homer is as unfitted now as he was in the eyes of the Greek historians such as Herodotus and Thucidides. We have an unfair advantage over the medieval writers; we have the results of a hundred and fifty years of archaeological discovery to hand if we want to write a 'history of the Trojan War'. They sincerely believed that Dares and Dictys were real contemporary documents, and they used them as well and honestly as they could. In that light they were 'source-legends' for much that came after throughout Europe.

b; The Popularity of the Trojan Legends

The medieval Troy legend was not merely the preserve of a small number of people. It was one of the most popular sets of stories in circulation. Large numbers of surviving manuscripts and early printed books contain these stories; many more are mentioned in, for example, wills, such as those cited by R.M. Wilson for a completely different reason in chapter 8 of 'The Lost Literature of Medieval England'. Translation and rewriting spread the Troy legend from Italy to Iceland: versions exist in Latin, the international language of the Middle Ages (the 12th-century poems *Ilias* of Simon Chevre d'Or & the anonymous *Historia Troyana Daretis Frigii*, and from the last quarter of the 13th century the very important prose *Historia destructionis Troiae* of Guido delle Colonne); in Middle High German (13th-century *Liet von Troie* of Herbort von Fritzlar and *Trojanerkrieg* of Konrad von Würzburg); in Old English (a summary in the translation of Orosius' *History Against the Pagans* made for Alfred the Great) and in Middle English (alliterative *Geste Hystoriale of the Destruction of Troye*, stanzaic *Troy Book* of John Lydgate, among others); in Anglo-Norman (Benoît de Sainte-Maure's *Roman de Troie* of c.1165) and in French, in Spanish, Portuguese and Norse (*Trojumanna Saga*), and many more (list assembled from: Scherer, 1963, Wood, 1985, & Schlauch, 1934). Troy would have dominated and filled the medieval mind when it sought for legend. As we have stated, Troy as told by Dares and Dictys and with hints from

Virgil seems to be the point of origin of much of the writing that followed. In complete contrast, since the Second World War, the medieval Trojan legend seems to have done as effective a vanishing trick as Bilbo with his magic ring - if one looks for modern translations and studies of these texts, one looks for them in vain. There seem to be no academic institutions in Britain that offer any opportunity to study the medieval Trojan legend, and beyond these shores - as far as we are able to ascertain - the situation is much the same. This has meant that, since the popularity of LotR began in the mid 1960's and events such as the publication of the *Silmarillion* in the late 1970's, no one has examined the medieval Trojan legends seriously with respect to Tolkien's writings.

c; The Soup of Story

The Trojan legends did not exist in isolation from other areas of medieval life. These stories were intimately interlinked with both legendary and historical material of many kinds.

Let us look first at the use which medieval writers made of the Trojan legends in writing the history of later times and peoples. The first known case of this occurred when the late Roman writer Cassiodorus fabricated a genealogical link to Troy and therefore a cousinship to the Romans, for his employer Theodoric the Great when he was writing up the history of the Goths (Scherer 1963, Notes, s.v. p.51). This link was made through Telephus son of Hercules, a former foe of the Greeks (he was the adopted heir of Teuthras, King of Mysia, an ally of Priam) who was won over to their side and became a friend of Achilles, and a Trojan princess, perhaps a daughter of Priam (all this outside Homer but appearing in influential - though mostly lost - poems of the Classical era). Cassiodorus used the old idea, that all the sons of Hercules had emigrated north out of Greece, to settle Telephus and his bride in far Scandinavia where they could join the ancestors of the Goths. By doing this Cassiodorus created a situation where Theodoric could present himself to his Roman subjects as a long-lost cousin, a rightful heir and renewer rather than a barbarian destroyer of Rome's culture and political power. Thus the matter of Troy is being used for political ends at the start of the medieval period, just as Virgil had used it for political as well as creative purposes in his *Aeneid* back in the 1st century BC.

Two other examples are worth a brief mention. The Franks claimed descent from a Trojan prince, Francio or Francus (a story already known when it was elaborately described to Henry I in 1127); therefore the Tale of Troy lurked in the background of the Charlemagne cycle and related works. This idea was still valid in French high culture after the impact of the Renaissance; in the 16th century the French poet Pierre de Ronsard wrote the *Franciade*, an epic poem which glorified Francus and traced his 'history' just as Virgil had glorified Aeneas as ancestor of the Romans and traced his story in the Aeneid (Scherer 1963 Introduction, p.xvii; Appendix A, section '16th century'). In the twelfth century in England, Geoffrey of Monmouth's *Historia Regum Britanniae*, which is usually thought of only as the source of Arthur (and perhaps Lear and other legendary figures) actually opens with an extended account of Brutus, the great-grandson of Aeneas of Troy (Geoffrey trans. Thorpe, 1966; Part One). Geoffrey's account of Brutus's rescue of other descendants of the Trojans who are living as slaves in Greece, and their migration to Britain, is a neatly-written and exciting story in and of itself. More than this, it links the 'unknown' history of pre-Roman Britain to the 'known' history of the Classical world, and this idea was important right through until Tudor times. So 'historical' Trojan links are not unimportant, or a passing fad; they could lie at the heart of how a nation's elite (and even many of its people) saw themselves.

Probably the most important instance of Trojan legends being linked with seemingly unrelated material, given our context of looking at the sources for J.R.R. Tolkien's works, appears in Snorri Sturluson's *Edda*. This book, written in Iceland in the 13th century, is one that our readers may well know as one of the most important sources for Norse mythology. What is not usually mentioned is that Snorri makes skilful use of the Trojan legends to get around his biggest problem, which was that he was writing about poetry irredeemably steeped in pagan religion, for a Christian audience. Iceland was a recently converted country, and many of its churchmen would have bitterly opposed any attempt to take the 'old faith' seriously; that might confuse people, and confusion over religious matters could not be tolerated. Snorri found two solutions. One was to make his own position clear, stating firmly that readers should not take what he was talking about as worthy of belief even if it was useful in poetry. The second was a far more inventive and wide-ranging answer to the problem. This was to make the Norse gods into clever mortals, the descendants of refugees from Troy, who were able to rule over the primitive north by reason of their superior skills and knowledge; in time, the real story was forgotten, history became myth and men became gods. This material appears in Snorri's *Prologue*, at the end of the following section, *Gylfaginning*, and in the Epilogue of the third section, *Skaldskaparmal*. It thoroughly defuses the stories of the old gods which have just been told, reminding readers of the right religious direction and providing acceptable answers to the obvious question of what these 'Aesir' were. In the first two instances Snorri links the northern 'gods' with the descendants of the nobility and royalty of Troy; in the third instance, Snorri makes a far more daring equation between principal characters in the tale of Troy and the Aesir of Scandinavian myth. In this account Ragnarok becomes the Trojan war, Hector is Thor, Pyrrhus/Neoptolemus the son of Achilles is the Fenris-wolf (because he acts like an outlaw or wolfshead) and Priam's surviving son Helenus is Ali (dropping the 'h' as most medieval writers do improves the comparison of names), the Ás who survives Ragnarok, and so on.

It is worth noting also that Snorri Sturluson links the legendary with the linguistic at the end of his *Prologue*, where he says:
'These Aesir found themselves marriages within the country there, and some of them for their sons too, and these families became extensive, so that throughout Saxony and from there all over the northern regions it spread so that their language,

that of the men of Asia, became the mother tongue over all these lands. And people think they can deduce from the records of the names of their ancestors that those names belonged to this language, and that the Aesir brought the language north to this part of the world, to Norway and to Sweden, to Denmark and to Saxony; and in England there are ancient names for regions and places which one can tell come from a different language from this one.' (Sturluson/ Faulkes 1987, Prologue, p.5)

As a piece of philology-before-the-fact, which moreover seems to skate close to the idea of Indo-European languages, this passage would almost certainly have appealed strongly to Tolkien. [see Note 1] It could well have encouraged him to take Snorri's *Edda* as a model, not in its poetics or even its systematization of Norse myth and legend (though that may well have been useful to Tolkien), but first and perhaps most importantly in its wide-ranging mixture of sources and its specifically medieval attitude to the story of Troy. Note also the idea of some spark of divinity residing within the bloodlines of the ruling families, the nobility of northern Europe: This is a concept not all that far removed from Tolkien's idea of the bloodline of Lúthien Tinúviel, the thin thread of not only Elvish but angelic, Maiarin blood (for Lúthien's mother was the Maia Melian and her father the elf-king Thingol) that comes down through the line of the Kings of Númenor and Arnor to Aragorn in the Third Age of Middle-earth in LotR.

Since many readers may be asking why medieval writers bothered to make such links between their own native story-sets and the Matter of Troy, it is perhaps worth explaining the background a little. In the medieval period, such uses of the Trojan legends were not just a literary or even academic game - this was a highly political act. It seems very probable to us that these uses of Trojan legends were the literary expression of a bid for recognition of these peoples as cousins and therefore heirs of Rome. The existence of the Roman empire was remembered as an historical fact thanks to Christian writers such as Isidore of Seville (who also went into some detail on the colonisation of Europe by the Trojans - Colonne/ Meek 1974 p.xxvi) or Saint Augustine of Hippo, even if almost everything else about the Classical world was forgotten. In the early medieval period, to be a rightful heir of Rome was to be a legitimate ruler in lands which had after all mostly been Roman provinces. By the time that ceased to be an important political and cultural factor, Rome's heirs had become the founder-members of the international club called Christendom. At this time, the Trojan legends still had uses beyond just being good, popular entertainment. As one among an array of devices for linking local to Biblical history, the story of Troy offered ways of making non-Classical, local pagan cultures into something respectable enough to survive in a new, Christian environment when many people might not want this to happen. Even in Iceland, many - perhaps most - churchmen were against any custom or story which they thought contained some element of heathenism, as Margaret Schlauch points out in the first chapter of her book 'Romance In Iceland' (1934).

Snorri Sturluson was not a churchman; he was a wealthy layman with interests in politics, history and literature, who was assassinated in 1241 due to his involvement in Norwegian political affairs. For him to link the Icelandic legends to the Tale of Troy was firstly, to try to salvage enough of his people's pagan past to offer hope for a cultural future connected to that past. The popularity of the later *riddarasögur* and *lygisögur*, Icelandic versions of the international literature of medieval Europe, might suggest that Snorri failed. However, in actual fact the survival of any works dealing with Norse myth and legend represents an unmatched triumph for Snorri Sturluson and those of the same mind, for nothing like them appears elsewhere in Europe. A great deal of writing often said to be 'mythological' is in fact no such thing, as with most 'Celtic Myth', and there are peoples and language-groups about whose pre-Christian beliefs we know virtually nothing, such as the Angles and Saxons and their relatives on the Continent. The only pagan deities we find in Britain are of the kind exemplified by Nodens of whom we know virtually nothing and which was a name Tolkien took great interest in on a philological, but perhaps also mythological - level. Shippey tells us: 'In 1928 excavations on a site near Lydney in the west of England had revealed a temple devoted to some kind of mystery cult and still flourishing in the fourth century... The temple was eventually abandoned... the Lydney temple fell into disuse - but not completely into oblivion.... in the story and the place-name one can hear the echo of a hopeless resistance... all ending in forgetfulness with even the memory of the resisters blurred, till recovered by archaeology - and philology. For Tolkien's job was to comment on the name 'Nodens' found in an inscription.' (Shippey, 1992, ch.2, p.32-33)

Secondly, in linking Icelandic tradition to the Tale of Troy, Snorri was asserting the right of an island often seen as distant, poor and marginal, to full membership of Christendom. When Snorri Sturluson was writing, this link mattered a great deal, because those on the edge of Christendom, those who in one way or another did not quite fit, were liable to be attacked by official forces linked to Rome under the guise of removal of heretics. Never mind poor benighted pagans like the Prussians; the conquest of the Byzantine Empire by the redirected Fourth Crusade (1204), the purges of Gnostic Christian communities or the international approval for the English Kings' attacks on Ireland (from the 1160's onward) were object lessons in what could happen, and Snorri is almost certain to have known of all these events. Robert Bartlett's book *The Making of Europe; Conquest, Colonisation and Cultural Change*, 950-1350, (1993, Penguin) is probably the best source for anyone wishing to investigate this phenomenon further. Iceland actually had extremely wide-ranging international connections, along the Viking trade-routes to the Black and Caspian Seas as well as south to Western Europe, but those very links brought in suspect people and ideas that could prove to be a real danger when they were interpreted by Rome and its allies. In an era when the Greek Orthodox church was regarded as schismatic and the Byzantine Empire as dangerously half-hearted if not outright treacherous to the Crusaders, having Orthodox priests arrive in the far north (as mentioned by Ursula Dronke in her paper in R.R. Bolgar (ed) 1971) was not a mere curiosity; it set alarm bells ringing from Iceland all the way to Rome and caused a great deal of trouble.

The story of Troy was not just literature in medieval eyes, it was history, and as such it could be called in as useful propaganda. It appears that both the Western lords who sacked Constantinople and conquered much of the surrounding lands in the misdirected Fourth Crusade, and the ultimate destroyer of the same Byzantine empire, the Ottoman sultan Mehmet the Second, called the Victorious, employed 'revenge for the fall of Troy' as useful propaganda to help make their actions understandable and acceptable (Gerritsen and van Melle 1998 s.v.Hector for the former, Wood 1985 ch.1, p.38, for the latter). Claiming links to Troy for Scandinavia in general and Iceland in particular is likely to have been seen by Snorri Sturluson as a useful insurance policy, not just a literary conceit; it removed in advance one argument that could have been used against him and his people in any possible offensive. The habit of medieval writers of inventing links between their own countries and peoples and Troy, then, was not just an example of confusion over history, or inspired by some wish to ignore native cultures and origins in favour of the Classical world, or to include the latest bestseller in their repertoire. Of course it could be the result of any or all of these motives; but it could also have some usefulness, often unstated perhaps but just as real, in the strange world of medieval politics.

If there is one group of legends that embodies historical reality, Classical creativity and medieval belief, it is the Tale of Troy. This is a story that lies at the bedrock of European history and legend as nothing else does. It is first in point of time; it is foremost in application. French writers may have taken their Charlemagne legends very seriously, as English writers were serious about Arthur, but no claim based on either legend would easily be accepted outside those countries where the tales were rooted. Scottish writers, for instance, accepted that Arthur was probably historical, but contested hotly the English accounts of his conquests (which included Scotland), in pursuit of their own independence. The Trojan legend was different. It lies behind almost everything in the medieval period; accepted, unchallengeable, continually renewing itself.

There are conclusions which are very important for Tolkien and his work in all this. For two hundred years through the Age of Reason, roughly the 18th and 19th centuries, the clear majority of scholarly opinion was that the Tale of Troy was a myth in the sense of being a lie. It never happened; there was no such place, nor did people like that ever live. The discoveries of Heinrich Schliemann and his successor in Aegean archaeology proved just how wrong that idea was. A city did stand where Troy was said to; it was destroyed, not once but several times, so a Trojan War really could have happened; people like Agamamnon, Priam and Odysseus were believable reflections of a lost age. But the archaeologists and the scholars who listened to them were not the first people to think this way. Ask Snorri Sturluson, and he would have said that Troy was real - that Homer wrote fiction based on fact, and the facts had survived in Dares and Dictys. Ask the Classical Greek historian Thucydides and he, too, would have been certain that the Trojan War really happened; Homer had not told the whole story, certainly, any more than the Athenian playwrights did, but it was all based on facts. There were the ruins at Mycenae and Tiryns to prove *that*. And Snorri and Thucydides would have been right.

Now, J.R.R. Tolkien is well known for taking his myths and legends seriously. Ever since Shippey's great study, *The Road to Middle-earth*, was first published, this has been taken simply as a result of Tolkien being a philologist. Shippey says:

'... the thing which was perhaps eroded most of all was the philologists' sense of a line between imagination and reality. The whole of their science conditioned them to the acceptance of what one might call '*-' or 'asterisk reality, that which no longer existed but could with 100 per cent certainty be inferred.'

And:

'...stripped of its layers of scholarly guardedness, the essence of Tolkien's belief was that 'the word authenticates the thing'. This was a belief grounded on philology.'

(Shippey 1992, ch.1, p.19 & ch.3, p.51)

So, if Tolkien takes European legend and folklore seriously, he is doing it only for philological reasons according to Shippey. We believe that this is right as far as it goes; words *did* matter, immensely. But it is only half the truth; story and history mattered too. It would not have taken Tolkien long to discover, once he reached Oxford as a young undergraduate if not indeed before, that some things which were being hailed as radical new discoveries of history behind myth and legend, of which the clearest examples were the discoveries at Troy and Mycenae, were things which had before the 'Age of Reason' been regarded as unquestionably historical *as well as* great creative inspiration. The lesson is clear - trust your sources, *believe* what the stories say; and that was exactly what Tolkien proceeded to do, with Troy as with other tales. [Note 2] This is the first part of the reasons for why, as we believe, Tolkien chose to rework the medieval Trojan legend.

Secondly, the medieval Trojan legend provided a ground base of history/ story underlying later developments; it created a unity underlying diversity. This is exactly what *The Book of Lost Tales* and later *The Silmarillion* were intended to be; fictional, written later, yet reimagining what *might* have been - what, given both Troy and philology, could and perhaps even *should* have been. Such a layer of tales functions in respect of later myth and legend just as proto-Indo-European relates to medieval and modern Indo-European languages. This idea, as we have seen was not quite as original to the philologists as they might have liked to suggest in their pride at being a 'science'; Snorri Sturluson almost got there first in the 13th century. This is the second lesson that it appears Tolkien drew from the medieval Trojan legend - that in story as in language, there could be background, a rootstock (a first bowlful of stock into the Soup-pot, in Tolkien's terms) from which new shoots could arise and onto which other branches could be grafted. There could be not only asterisk-language but asterisk-legend. Sigurd was a Frank (thus R.W. Chambers in the 1921 edition of *Beowulf: an Introduction* , and he states it so matter-of-factly as to make it certain the theory was raised long before), the Franks were descended from Troy - so even there in the apparently impeccably northern European Volsung saga, a new story is *linked in* to the old pattern. These are two important conclusions to start with; that the medieval Trojan legend could have provided a clear model for Tolkien's strategy of writing theorised 'originals', the Great Tales whose echoes resound through later storytelling; and that it would have been the biggest single object lesson in trusting your sources that he is likely to have met. Later we will be exploring in far more detail the connections between this medieval Trojan legend and Tolkien's writings.

First, though, we need to examine the use of these legends by medieval authors who were creating fiction rather than history, and writing stories that we might not expect to be connected to Troy any more than we would look for such a connection in Tolkien's work. Some of these links were intentional and arose from the 'historical' connections. Thus, occasional references to the legends of Troy occur in Middle English Arthurian writing, sparked by Geoffrey of Monmouth's work which starts in Troy and ends with Arthur and the Anglo-Saxon conquest. For instance, there is a mention of Aeneas's 'treachery' to Dido in the well-known alliterative poem 'Sir Gawain and the Green Knight' (Penguin Classics, Trans. with intro by Brian Stone, 2nd Ed. 1974), while the later and much slighter 'Syr Gawayne and the Grene Knight' opens with a direct invocation of the Trojan legend:

'*Since the siege and the assault ceased at Troy -*
The town battered and burnt to embers and ashes -
The knight who there wrought the coils of treason
Was tried for his treachery, the most thorough on earth
It was Aeneas the nobleman and his high kinsmen
That since then have seized lands, and masters become
Of well-nigh all the wealth in the western isles

(Quoted from the Introduction to the Early English Text Society edition of the 'Geste Hystoriall of the Destruction of Troye', p.xl) After a start like that one expects to be confronted with the Trojan story, not a piece of Northern English Arthuriana! Yet it echoes Geoffrey of Monmouth's history, which begins in Troy and climaxes with Arthur, and therefore this section was included by the poet for that reason, however much it may confuse us modern readers.

On the other side of the Channel, the anonymous French or Norman author of Le Roman de Thebes includes passing references to a sword forged by both Wayland and Vulcan (lines 1557-64 - with three goddesses and three 'fairies' doing the tempering and engraving) and to the story of Roland (1675-8) in his ostensibly Classical tale (Coley 1986). A much more thorough-going fictional crossbreeding was achieved by the 15th-century Italian poet Matteo Maria Boiardo, who managed to mix the stories of Troy, Charlemagne and Arthur into his sprawling romance *Orlando Innamorato*, 'Roland in Love' - which was perhaps understandably left unfinished at his death (Scherer 1963 Appendix A, section '15th century'). And Roland/Orlando is not that far linguistically removed from Orendel, who shall be examined in a later chapter.

Besides authors who deliberately set out to create links between the Trojan legend and other stories, whether in a historical or fictional framework, there was also a great deal of casual and accidental contact going on between the various stories told and written in the medieval period. Within their own sphere the Trojan legends were seen as part of a set of tales from the Classical world, sometimes loosely grouped as 'The Matter of Rome'. These stories included the tale of Troy proper, the story of Aeneas (reworked from Virgil's Latin epic *Aeneid*), the story of the Greek city of Thebes, and the fictionalised life of Alexander the Great. There were works which grouped several of these stories under a single title, as well as compilations which put several separate stories within the same set of covers. The habit of copying or binding material together whether the works were related or not could accidentally bring very different stories into near contact. The sole surviving manuscript of *Beowulf*, for instance, is bound together with part of the Old English version of the Classical novel 'Apollonius of Tyre' and a version of the Alexander-romance as well as an old English poem on the Biblical heroine Judith (Doody, M.A., True story of the Novel, 1998, Pt.1, ch.1, p.29 & Pt.2, ch.9, p.182). In addition to such accidental collisions on parchment, there must have been a great deal of cross-fertilisation on the minds of people who read, heard, composed and wrote stories as all the great tales would have been told concurrently. Despite occasional attempts to classify stories into groups (such as the famous threefold division into Matter of Britain, Matter of France and Matter of Rome made by the French writer Jean Bodel at the end of the 12th century), the reality was much more that a large number of tales existed in a nebulous cloud of 'story', some obviously linked together, some much less clearly associated. Many tales fitted nowhere in particular despite the natural tendency to associate less-well-known heroes with better-known figures. The human attraction to find links between things both natural and man-made would provide the driving force to that unifying provide the driving force to that unifying tendency. Given all of this, we can say for certain that the medieval experience of literature was not compartmentalised in the way that modern scholarship dealing with the same material is. If, in Tolkien's terms, stories come from the Soup, almost the first stock in the pot was Troy. This is the second lesson of the medieval use of the Trojan legend. No story is an island, no people live in primal isolation telling only their own tales. Stories are part of a web, and the most seemingly unlike tales may actually be close relatives. This, of course, is exactly what we see in Tolkien's *Silmarillion*, where stories with wildly diverging sources are brought comfortably together as successive parts of a single overarching plan - an idea going right back to the work's beginnings in the *Book of Lost Tales*.

Furthermore, original languages and settings were no barrier to the spread of stories during the medieval period. Latin for one thing was a learned unifying language throughout the known civilised world. As always, a good strong tale could interest people far beyond its original homeland. We tend to forget that, difficult as travel was, people did move around a lot in medieval times. Trade, war and pilgrimage took people far from their homes, and the people they met were as interested in new stories as 'news' in our sense of the word. This resulted in whole tales being moved around to be translated or recreated in a new language (a very common medieval literary activity) and in the creation of stories which reflected this mobile and multilingual situation. Thus, for example, someone whose native tongue was Middle Dutch could have access to both translated and original Arthurian romances (of which *Percheval* and *Walewein ende Keye* are examples respectively), to stories about Charlemagne and other heroes associated with the Matter of France (*Roelantslied* (translated) and *Madelghijs* (original)), to tales about Classical heroes from the Trojan War (*Historie van Troyen,*) to Alexander the Great (*Alexanders Geesten*), and stories from the Germanic heroic sphere (*Nievelingenlied*). There were tales of saints which included as much adventure as holiness, such as the native *Sint Servaes*, whose hero encounters Attila the Hun, and a version of the Irish Saint Brendan story, *De reis van Sinte Brandaan*. There were also unclassifiable works both serious, such as the tale of the Seven Sages of Rome (*Van den VII vroeden van binnen Rome*), and light-hearted, such as the stories about Reynard the Fox (*Van den Vos Reynaerde*). Many of these stories have wide geographical scope; a good example of this is the tale of *Bevis of Hampton*, probably originally written in Anglo-Norman, the action of which moves from England to Egypt via France. Almost unknown today, this once highly popular story was translated into Middle Dutch, Old French, Italian, Welsh, Irish and Yiddish (among many others), and remained in print in one country or another right up to the Second World War. No doubt people had preferences, but the important point is that a wide range of stories were available to readers, hearers and authors, and any one piece could have an effect on the next new version of something else.

Overall, medieval storytelling was an international business. This is most obvious in the high and late medieval periods, roughly from 1000 to 1500, but it went right back to the beginning - R.W. Chambers pointed out in his 1912 edition and commentary of the Old English poem *Widsith*, that the form in which Alexander the Great and the Greeks appear in the poem implies that they were borrowed into the Germanic legends at a very early date, well before the fall of Rome. If the names were there, almost certainly the stories were known too. So even though Tolkien's main interests were with the earlier medieval era, the image of the 'web of story' reaching right across Europe is still valid. Tolkien had very old models for using Classical stories right alongside Northern European ones in his own creative work.

The supposedly 'Classical' legend of Troy was not lost in the Late Roman period and only recovered in the Renaissance as some modern readers might assume; it continued as a living part of storytelling in the Middle Ages, albeit in a pro-Trojan and often pseudohistorical form that is now very unfamiliar. It did not exist in isolation, but was an active part of medieval European culture, linked with other legends and even having practical political and ideological applications. Nor did the Renaissance fundamentally alter the situation. The medieval version of the Trojan story did not sink out of sight at this time. Homer might have reappeared, but the medieval story had always been more history than legend. As such, it could coexist surprisingly comfortably with a renewed interest in the *Iliad* and the *Odyssey*. Homer was seen as one poetic version of the Trojan legend, not a sole source for what happened. Only when the whole idea of the Trojan

War as an historical event was challenged from the 17th century onwards, would Dictys of Crete and Dares Phyrgius be demoted first to fiction and then forgery, making the pro-Trojan medieval version of the Tale of Troy academically unrespectable - though publishers of chapbooks and other cheap histories and entertainments continued to use it until the end of the 18th century (Gerritsen and van Melle 1998 s.v.Hector).

It is often forgotten or regarded as uninfluential, but J.R.R. Tolkien had as much early interest in the Classics as in medieval Northern European literature. Humphrey Carpenter's *Biography* describes how on his return to King Edward's school, Tolkien began to learn Greek:

'Of his first contact with this language he later wrote: 'The fluidity of Greek, punctuated by hardness, and with its surface glitter captivated me. But part of the attraction was antiquity and alien remoteness (from me); it did not touch home.'

(Carpenter, 1977, Part 2, ch. 2, p.35)

Despite this, Tolkien was interested enough for Carpenter to say later:

'Already when beginning to learn Greek he had entertained himself by making up Greek-style words.' (ibid, ch. 3, p.44)

Garth goes further into the first quote above, citing Tolkien as saying: 'and with its surface glitter captivated me... and I tried to invent a language that would embody the Greekness of Greek...' (Garth, 2003, Great War, Pt. 1, ch.1, p.15)

At King Edward's school, Carpenter confirms (our emphasis given below): 'Clearly Ronald Tolkien had an aptitude for languages - his mother had seen that - and King Edward's provided the ideal environment in which this aptitude could flourish. The study of *Latin and Greek was the backbone of the curriculum*, and both languages were taught particularly well in the First (or senior) Class, which Ronald reached shortly before his sixteenth birthday. The First Class was under the bright eye of the headmaster, Robert Cary Gilson, a remarkable man with a neat pointed beard who was an amateur inventor and an accomplished scientist as well as a skilled teacher in the classics... When teaching, he encouraged his pupils *to explore the byways of learning and to be expert in everything that came their way*: an example that made a great impression on Ronald Tolkien.' (ibid, Pt. II, ch.3 p.41-2)

Secondly, when describing Tolkien's discovery of Gothic, Carpenter quotes Tolkien as saying that when he opened Joseph Wright's *Primer of the Gothic Language* he experienced 'a sensation at least as full of delight as first looking into Chapman's *Homer* ' (Carpenter 1977, Part II, ch. 3, p.45). What this tells us is that at some point in his life, Tolkien's enthusiasm for Homer matched or even exceeded his known enthusiasm for Gothic, which is normally seen as one of the wellsprings of his interest in languages. It is very important to emphasise that it was Classics that Tolkien went up to Oxford to study as an undergraduate and which he studied during the first two years of his four years at Oxford.

Following on from this, we can be absolutely certain that Tolkien knew the medieval Trojan material well, because one of his papers in his Schools or Final examinations was on Chaucer's *Troilus and Criseyde*, a version of one story from the medieval Matter of Troy (Garth 2003, Great War, ch.3, p.63). It would be flatly impossible to study this story at university level without looking at three basic questions; first, how does Chaucer, writing before the Renaissance, tackle a 'Classical' story at all; secondly, how has a story wholly absent from Homer arisen; and thirdly, how does Chaucer's treatment relate to other medieval literature. The answers to such questions inevitably lead to the whole body of medieval Trojan legend, starting in Middle English with the alliterative *Destruction* and the Laud *Troy Book*, and leading all the way to Geoffrey of Monmouth and Snorri Sturluson (Benson 1983, Hist. Troy in M-e Lit, Part 3, ch.VI, section 1). Tolkien scored a First in his final exams, and this tells us several things. Firstly, his 'Honour Moderations' in which he barely scraped a Second, counted towards his degree; so he must have done extremely well in his Schools to counterbalance his earlier problems. Secondly, his final exams included papers on authors Tolkien was less confident in dealing with, such as Shakespeare and Johnson (Garth 2003 ch.4, p.81); to get a First he must have done well even on these, but his marks in areas he was good at must have been astonishing. Thirdly, to get a First in a discursive subject such as English, you have to do much more than trot out the 'right answers'; you have to show wide-ranging knowledge of your field and an ability to connect the seemingly unrelated into a convincing whole. It is worth repeating what Carpenter said about Tolkien's education at King Edward's school: 'The First Class was under the bright eye of the headmaster, Robert Cary Gilson... a skilled teacher in the classics... When teaching, he encouraged his pupils *to explore the byways of learning and to be expert in everything that came their way*: an example that made a great impression on Ronald Tolkien.' (Carpenter 1977, Pt. II, ch.3 p.41-2) One should note that this Headmaster Robert Cary Gilson was the father of Tolkien's close friend Rob Gilson of the TCBS. So, that First Class degree tells us that Tolkien was aware of everything we have just been discussing, in depth and in detail. Lastly, it is reasonable to suggest that Tolkien would have been excited and inspired by discovering the existence of bridges between the two areas he was so interested in, the Classical and the medieval, in the shape of the medieval Trojan legend. This legend had a great deal to offer him. In general, it suggested an underlying unity behind the disorganised surviving legends which connected up all the fragments, and it taught a clear lesson about trusting medieval sources rather than later critics. In specific, the medieval Trojan legend offered a distinctive version of the longest lived story in Europe and opened up the possibility of treating such legends creatively rather than regarding them as untouchable monuments. These bridging stories might well have been suggested by his tutors as suitable for his transition from the Classics to English midway through his undergraduate studies - they would have contained the familiar in terms of the Classical story and the languages of the north which Tolkien had such a facility for. In simple terms, the road from Homer to Beowulf lay for Tolkien through the works of Dares, Dictys and Guido delle Collone and associated tales.

d; Modern Context

The chapbooks and penny-dreadfuls were not quite the end for the medieval Trojan legends, however. In the 19th century, the Pre-Raphaelite painters turned as much to the medieval version of the Tale of Troy as the Classical one for inspiration. Most importantly, perhaps, their associate William Morris worked with the Trojan material in a way which was much influenced by the medieval versions of the story. According to M. Scherer:

'... William Morris began a group of Trojan poems, but left it unfinished. Disenchanted with the industrial age he turned to the romances and planned a long, connected series based on a central theme, in which Troy became once more a medieval city and its heroes knights of chivalry. Only six poems and the rough drafts of a few more were completed, but these contain some of the legend's most poignant and personal nineteenth-century interpretations. The poems had their artistic counterpart in the paintings of Edward Burne-Jones and a few of Rossetti's paintings and drawings.'

(M.Scherer 1963, Introduction, p.xvii)

According to Scherer's 'Appendix 1; Works of Literature and Music' and 'Notes', Morris's poems were published in 1915 in Vol.24 of *The Collected Works of William Morris* as 'Scenes from the Fall of Troy'. The individual pieces dated to between 1857 and 1865 and their titles were: 'Helen Arming Paris'; 'The Defiance of the Greeks'; 'Hector's Last Battle'; 'Hector brought Dead to Troy'; 'Helen's Chamber'; 'Achilles' Love Letter'; 'The Descent from the Wooden Horse'; and 'Helen and Menelaus'. In an Introduction to that volume of *Collected Works*, the author's daughter May Morris gave her father's list of projected Trojan poems; the project was also discussed in J.W. Mackail's *The Life of William Morris*, published in 1907 (Vol.I, pp166-78, cited in the *Notes* to Scherer 1963 under Page xvii).

In fact, although both M. Scherer and May Morris called them 'poems', these 'Scenes from the Fall of Troy' are just that - dramatic scenes, with a setting indicated and occasional 'stage directions', in which characters speak to each other and actions take place. There is poetry in the sequence, but the bulk of it is 'verse' only as Shakespeare's plays are sometimes misdescribed as such. Indeed, Morris's 'poems' read a lot like Shakespeare's dialogue. In 'The Descent from the Wooden Horse', for example, the beginning reads as follows:

Troy: *In the Wooden Horse.*

Agamemnon, Menelaus, Diomedes, Ulysses, Nestor, Ajax
Telamon, Teuce, Ajax Oileus, *and others.*

AJAX to ULYSSES
Now may we speak? are they not gone away?
It must be dead night now. I am nigh dead:
By the gods their stupid singing of loud hymns
Nigh made me mad, nigh was I screaming out.

TEUCER
And we heard Helen we have fought about
These ten years: sickening for a caged man
To hear her speak and not to see her face -
Gods how I burn with fever!

ULYSSES
                                        Hist, heroes -
No words. (*listening*)
[   ]   What is it, Prince of Ithaca?
[*One sings from without*]
        O my merchants, whence come ye
        Landing laden from the sea?

ULYSSES
Sinon I hope, but wait what followeth.
(W. Morris 1915, p.41)

It is worth noting that unfinished as this work is, Morris completed enough and left enough notes to make it clear that he is indeed following the medieval pattern. Hector dies early in the war and Achilles falls in love with Priam's daughter Polyxena, just as in the medieval versions. It is not particularly clear whose side Morris is on, if anyone's. What we can say is that we know that Tolkien rated William Morris highly as an author, and it is fairly probable that he would have wanted to read new works by Morris if he knew that they were in the new volume of Morris's *Complete Works*. The inclusion of another unpublished piece, Morris's 'The Wooing of Swanhild' - his version of the medieval legends which gathered around the great Gothic king Ermanaric - in the same volume, might well have helped interest Tolkien in it. Again, it is quite likely that any review of the book, or any comments by readers, would have included all this important information. There is a good chance, then, that Tolkien would have known of Morris's Trojan poems, which would have brought Tolkien's attention to the medieval version of the Tale of Troy at exactly the right time and place for him to investigate further and think about using it himself - if, indeed, Tolkien had not already been reading about it anyway. As has been mentioned, he moved from Classics to English in the early stages of his undergraduate studies at Oxford University, and reading the Middle English versions of the tale of Troy would have been a good halfway house between the two subjects. Oxford University's Bodleian Library would have obtained these books so Tolkien need not have gone out and bought them for himself.

William Morris was also responsible for perhaps the oddest translation of Homer's *Odyssey* ever set before the British public. Morris began the project in the early 1880's after translating the *Volsungasaga*, which may account for some of the peculiarities of the work. It follows Homer's story exactly, but is written throughout in verse, in a distinctively medievalising manner:

'Tell me, o Muse, of the Shifty, the man who wandered afar,
After the Holy Burgh, Troy-town, he had wasted with war;
He saw the towns of menfolk, and the mind of men did he learn;
As he warded his life in the world, and his fellow-farers' return,
Many a grief of heart on the deep-sea flood he bore,
Nor yet might he save his fellows, for all that he longed for it sore.
They died of their own souls' folly, for witless as they were
They ate up the beasts of the Sun, the Rider of the Air,
And he took away from them all their dear returning day;
O Goddess, O daughter of Zeus, from whencesoever ye may,
Gather the tale, and tell it, yea even to us at the last!'

(Homer/Morris 1912, p.1, lines 1-11)

This work was first published in 1887 in two volumes. It was reprinted four times before appearing as part of two multivolume editions, first the set of Morris's works printed in the Golden Type of his own Kelmscott Press (Vol.V, 1901), and then in the Collected Works series with introductions by May Morris. For all its oddities, William Morris's version of the *Odyssey* was important, as Michael Wood points out:

'But it was in the nineteenth century that Homer came into his own as a popular 'classic', the most influential of all the attempts being William Morris's *Odyssey* (1887), part Norse saga, part Tennyson, and Andrew Lang's strangely effective late Victorian *Iliad*, which was reprinted eighteen times between 1882 and 1914.' (Wood 1985, ch.1, p.34)

In content, this translation has nothing to do with the medieval Troy-stories. In style, it certainly aims to evoke the same sort of time. It is by no means unlikely that Tolkien would have encountered this translation of the *Odyssey* in the school library that was the inspiration and first meeting-place of his 'TCBS' group of friends if it were not actually suggested to him as reading matter by his Headmaster Robert Cary Gilson. For according to Garth: 'For his final four years at King Edward's Tolkien was in the senior or First Class under the headmaster, Robert Cary Gilson, who encouraged him to look into the history of Latin and Greek.' (Garth, 2003, Great War, Pt.1, ch.1, p.16)

Another development around the turn of the 19th and 20th centuries was the making of comparisons between the Greek 'Heroic Age' and other periods supposed to be similar to it. The book most worth noting in this respect is H.M. Chadwick's 'The Heroic Age' of 1912, which is 474 pages of comparison of the Mycenean Greeks and their Homeric afterlife, with 'the heroic age of the Teutonic peoples', by a very distinguished academic writer. As the Preface puts it:

'The type of poetry commonly known as heroic is one which makes its appearance in various nations and in various periods of history. No one can fail to observe that certain similar features are to be found in poems of this type which are widely separated from one another both in date and place of origin. In view of this fact it has seemed worth while to attempt a comparative study of two groups of such

poems with the object of determining the nature of the resemblances between them and the causes to which they are due. Occasional illustrations have been taken from other groups of poems belonging to the same type.'
The resulting collision between *Beowulf* and the *Iliad* may now be out of academic fashion, but the mere fact of its existence, at a time when it could easily have been regarded as important reading for someone who like Tolkien was moving from Classics to English Language, is noteworthy.

Another point worth making is that from roughly 1800 to 1950, 'Classics' in general, Greek in particular and Homer in specific were at the centre of British culture in a way we can hardly imagine now in our modern multicultural society. Anyone with much of an education was likely to have been introduced to Latin - as the mother of one of the authors did in the 1940's, even though she came from a working-class family and left school with fairly simple qualifications to take up a secretarial career. Go much further up the ladder of education and status, and Greek made an appearance. Latin was a pre-requisite for entry to a British University up until the middle of the 20th Century, and Oxbridge only dropped the requirement for a Latin GCE O Level in 1970. For a number of reasons, Homer was the one Greek text that everyone who studied the language would know; Homer was regarded as a 'classic' even in the Classical period, he could be interpreted in ways that fit with the prevailing mindset of the day, and he fitted in reasonably well with ideas about what schoolboys could and could not be allowed to read. Many other Greek authors were far more problematical. What was seen as Homer's stern morality, however, could easily be persuaded to fit in with ideals of stiff upper lips and courage, the importance of games, and 'gentlemanly' quasi-aristocratic behaviour. Helped along by Virgil's ideas of manifest destiny and imperialism, Homer could become the base text for the British Empire. Add in a little Plato, and heroic action in the field of battle was converted to equally heroic service by enlightened rulers, Guardians in Plato's terms, on behalf of the Great Unwashed. Whether read in the original or in translation, no other text (except perhaps the Bible) leant itself to so many fruitful rereadings or sat so near to the preoccupations of the Victorian, Edwardian and Between-Wars worlds.

On a broader front, the influence of the Classics was inescapable. Reworked Classical architecture was a style that was always in favour, particularly for institutions of learning or government. It is worth noting that of all the projects for the rebuilding of the Houses of Parliament, only the one actually chosen was 'medieval'; all the rest were Classical in style. Town halls, theatres, museums, art galleries, concert halls were all frequently built in Classical style.On the Albert Memorial, Shakespeare sits at the feet of Homer; literature, it was generally thought, owed everything worthwhile to the Greeks. Interest in the likes of *Beowulf* or Morris-style medievalism was limited, whereas interest in the Classics was extremely widespread. It was generally thought that the basis of good taste in all the arts was the Greek achievement, in which Rome's distinctive contribution was submerged. In the field of history, ideas of 'Germanic origins' and 'Saxon democracy' covered three rough spots in the general adulation of the Classics.

Firstly, they expressed a distinctive British identity as successors and surpassers of Rome, which had fallen into decadence and been overtaken by the youthfully vigorous Northern peoples; secondly, they expressed an 'auld alliance' with German against an even more rabidly Classics-worshipping nation, France (it took two World Wars to demolish that one); thirdly, it got around the problem that the British political system was like nothing the Classical world ever saw. Yet Rome's ideals - or ideals said to be Roman - were the guide-star of late-19th and early-20th century imperialist British thinkers (Hutton 1999, ch.1, pp.11-17; Jenkyns 1980 & 1991; Wood 1985 ch.1 p34-5).

Importantly, this was not just a secular response; it also had an impact on religious thinking. Excellent examples of this are found in the works of Cardinal J.H. Newman, who founded the Birmingham Oratory that was so important to Tolkien and his family, and who taught many of the men who in turn taught Tolkien. Newman followed the likes of St Augustine of Hippo when he worried that, even though he was a Christian priest, he still loved his classics and their 'scenes of heathen fame'. He managed to reconcile the two by coming to the opinion that pagan mythology, literature and philosophy were but a preparation for the Gospel - an idea that casts a long shadow over much of Tolkien's writing and thought. Indeed, in Letter 181 (1956) and note to Letter 212 Tolkien: 'a good man would or should *die* voluntarily by surrender with trust *before being compelled* (as did Aragorn). This man have been the nature of *unfallen* Man; though *compulsion* would not threaten him; he would desire and ask to be allowed to 'go on' to a higher state. The Assumption of Mary, the only *unfallen* person, may be regarded as in some ways a simple regaining of unfallen grace and liberty...'
Newman himself was a writer of both poetry and prose; the words to Elgar's oratorio *The Dream of Gerontius* are Newman's, and he wrote at least one novel. His *Callista* of 1855 is a tale of North African Christians standing firm through a persecution led by the depraved and hypocritical priests of 'Eastern cults' such as that of Astarte, while the priesthood and devotees of the traditional Roman cults, presented as dignified and moral, lack the power to intervene (Hutton 1999, ch.1, pp.11-17; Jenkyns 1991). It is very likely that Newman was a most important model for Tolkien, for the acceptable use of creativity, for an attitude to myth, and for a distinctive Christianised Classical, Neoplatonic philosophy. With this in the background, and given firstly that Tolkien was good enough to win a place at Oxford to study Classics (and got an A+ in Greek philology as well as a Second Class at Hons Mods. - the equivalent today of an upper second class honours level pass in what were effectively part one examinations towards his degree), and secondly that whilst at school he had actual experience of using the languages and literature creatively (Carpenter mentions giving speeches in Greek and taking part in a production of a Greek play, p.57, ch.4), it would be surprising indeed if there were no classical motifs in Tolkien's later fictional writing.

Note 1:

The usual approach to Tolkien's sources is via his interest in *Beowulf*. In *Beowulf: the Monsters and the Critics* (Tolkien, 1983, ch.1, p.24-5) Tolkien gives a view of the differences between northern and southern mythologies:

'But we will now return once more to the monsters, and consider especially the difference of their status in the northern and southern mythologies. Of Grendel it is said: *Godes yrre bær*. [he bore the anger of God] But the Cyclops is god-begotten and his maiming is an offence against his begetter, the god Poseidon... In Virgil, whatever may be true of the fairy-tale world of the Odyssey, the Cyclops walks veritably in the historical world. He is seen by Aeneas in Sicily... as much a perilous fact as Grendel was in Denmark....

we may with some truth contrast the 'inhumanness' of the Greek gods, however anthropomorphic, with the 'humanness' of the Northern, however titanic. In the southern myths there is also rumour of war with giants and great powers not Olympian... But this war is differently conceived. It lies in a chaotic past. The ruling gods are not besieged, not in ever-present peril or under future doom. Their offspring on earth may be heroes or fair women; it may also be the other creatures hostile to men. The gods are not the allies of men in their war against these or other monsters. The interest of the gods is in this or that man as part of their individual schemes, not as part of a great strategy that includes all good men, as the infantry of battle. In Norse, at any rate, the gods are within time, doomed with their allies to death. Their battle is with the monsters and the outer darkness. They gather heroes for the last defence....

This may make the southern gods more godlike - more lofty, dread and inscrutable. They are timeless and do not fear death. Such a mythology may hold the promise of a profounder thought. In any case it was a virtue of the southern mythology that it could not stop where it was. It must go forward to philosophy or relapse into anarchy.'

The first thing to ask is: when did Tolkien write this, and for what audience. Christopher Tolkien tells us that it was written in 1936 for the Sir Israel Gollancz Memorial Lecture to the British Academy. Tolkien was, basically 'selling' the values of *Beowulf* to his audience - and he did a very good job. So he ought to, being a very persuasive debater. He started debating at King Edward's school. 'In the Lent Term of 1910... he devoted much time to the Debating Society.' '...where in his last year in 1911 he became the Secretary of the Debating Society.' (Carpenter, 1977, Part 2, ch.4, p.56-7) He continued his involvement with debating at Oxford: 'He also took part in the Stapledon, the college debating society.' (ibid, ch.5, p.61). The function of a debater is to put forward a case in the strongest possible way; one minimises any contrary arguments as much as is possible. It can be seen how persuasive he was in his famous debate with C.S. Lewis, after which Lewis moved from being an agnostic to being Christian.

Secondly, if we examine the claims that Tolkien makes above for northern and southern gods, it is clear at once that he is knowingly understating the background to the two sets of mythologies. The Classical matter of the gods was written in a pagan polytheistic background where gods could be celebrated as part of a vibrant culture. The northern mythologies as received by us however (see chapter 1) are written in a post-Christian era, and in order for them to be allowed to survive, to be acceptable by the Church as something other than heresy or dangerous reversion to paganism, the gods must be 'diluted' - Snorri Sturluson turned the gods into clever men from the south who were worshipped by the simple northerners. Tolkien certainly knew this, for Snorri had written about this explicitly several times over in the collection known as his Edda.

Michael Drout in his analysis of the much larger text underlying Tolkien's famous paper '*Beowulf; the Monsters and the Critics*', shows that the original lectures were far more wide-ranging in concept:

'The old Gods disappeared - partly because they were strong and still connected with religion not solely with a world-mythology, partly because, as I shall suggest, their going was nonetheless not disastrous to the theme - and the heroic figures, the men of old... remained and not only were not ousted by Moses... or by St. Matthew or St. Andrew, but transmuted and recoloured the conception of Christian tradition....There is probably a truth in a generalisation which contrasts the inhumanness of the Greek deities with the humanness of the Northern - remember that we may well paint in what is left us of later mythologies that do not exactly fit; alive though we may be to the danger of accepting late Norse mythological traditions as any parallel or illustration of the lost English ones...' (p.65)

This seems to echo the published text, though he is showing that the northern myths 'transmuted and recoloured' the conception of Christian tradition - in which case, the same may be said in reverse - they were 'recoloured' by Christian beliefs and sentiments. Indeed, Drout goes on to quote from Tolkien:

'Of pagan English eschatology we know nothing - except our guess that the similar heroic temper cannot have had a fundamentally different background of mythology, however different the details, from the Scandinavian. What little we know of the latter is, however, difficult enough to estimate as a picture of Scandinavian imaginative beliefs - paganism is rarely a unified system, it is variable locally and in time; and its fragments in the North reach record in tattered form from times of confused or faulty memories, the periods of decay, or periods long after such things had become only conventional trappings of poetry and the amusements of antiquarians like Snorri - almost as far from real paganisn as an 18th century Jove or Mars.' (p.67)

(Drout 2002, ''Beowulf' and the Critics' by J.R.R. Tolkien)

Tolkien would have been well aware that there were major historical differences between the 'North and the 'South'. He would also have known well that the two areas of Scandinavia and the Mediterranean were not simply opposites, but facets of a polytheistic 'truth'. They were linked by a variety of peoples more or less influenced by their 'Northern' and 'Southern' neighbours. Scandinavia proper was never part of the Roman Empire and there is little sign of trade between the two - thus influence per se had to be indirect. Further South, the ancestors of the Angles and Saxons were connected to the Empire by trade and raid, and their culture was subject to a degree of Classical influence, as were their myths and legends. Importantly, they were still able to choose what they wished to be influenced by. Further South, along the Rhine and in the 'German' provinces of the Empire, there was even more of a mixture of 'Classical' and 'Germanic'. Here, North and South met forcibly - but proved to be far from irreconcilably different. The two pantheons 'collided' and were fused into a single working system accepted by locals and incomers alike, where a god such as Mars Thingsus was not at all unusual (M. Todd 1992, 'Early Germans', ch.6, p.104). Britain (which was invaded by the Romans in 43 AD) was like the 'German' provinces in that it saw a deep and thorough fusion of native and imported cultures, myths and religions. For example, the native Celtic and incoming Classical patron goddesses of the hot spring at Bath were fused into a new entity, Sulis-Minerva. The difference in Britain was that a version of Classical, Christian culture expanded beyond the old imperial borders after the theoretical 'Fall of Rome', leading to the great flowering of Early Medieval Ireland and Scotland, whereas throughout the 'Germanic' areas, the old beliefs and legends flourished. To add to the problem in Britain, the Norman Conquest in 1066 initiated a further phase of 'denaturalisation' - something Tolkien was extremely alive to. As a result, in Britain both the Romano-British and the Anglo-Saxon heroes of the Dark Ages have been forgotten or been changed beyond recognition. Shakespeare did not write 'plays' about Hengist and Horsa, or Arthur or Ambrosius Aurelianus. After all, William Tyndale had only fifty years before translated the Bible into English, which then raised its status. Therefore, distinguished though the Middle English tradition was, earlier texts were not able to survive as 'literature', nor were they considered as such. By contrast, in France, Germany and the Scandinavian countries, Dark Age legends thrived throughout the Middle Ages and therefore survived to a far greater extent.

So 'Northern European' polytheistic gods were not incompatible with 'Southern European' deities, and religion served the same functions in both societies. Tolkien would have known this, too. What Tolkien claimed in 'Beowulf; the Monsters and the Critics' was not the entire compass of his knowledge of the relationship between the Classical and Norse gods, but only what was necessary to the purpose of his lecture. When he had more space (and less need to convince quickly) he was more detailed and more accurate.

Note 2:

Indeed, this idea of trusting the reality behind myth is part of the rationale Tolkien used to convert C.S. Lewis from agnosticism to Christianity. As Carpenter relates:
'*But*, said Lewis, *myths are lies, even though lies breathed through silver.*
No, said Tolkien, *they are not.*
... just as speech is invention about objects and ideas, so myth is invention about truth.
We have come from God (continued Tolkien), and inevitably the myths woven by us, though they contain error, will also reflect a splintered fragment of the true light, the eternal truth that is with God. (Carpenter, 1977, Part 4, ch.4, p.151)

Chapter Two:

The link between Troy and Gondolin.

I;Patron Gods

a; Lord of Waters

To paraphrase Gandalf at the Council of Elrond: 'There is indeed a wide waste of time between the Fall of Troy and the Fall of Gondolin, between the loss and the finding. But the gap in the knowledge of the Wise has been filled at last.' (FotR, Book II, ch.2, p.263).
Just like Gandalf in The Shadow of the Past we are able to add in paraphrase: 'the Story passed out of knowledge and legend; and even so much of its history is known now to only a few, and the Council of the Wise could discover no more. But at last we can carry on the story, we think.' (FotR, Book 1, ch.2, p.61-2)
For this, we must return to our original pair of 'reporters' of the true events - Dictys of Crete and Dares the Phyrgian. How do they treat the matter of Troy?

Dictys and Dares virtually remove the fantastic and the supernatural from their accounts of the Trojan War - Dares does not even have the Wooden Horse. Troy does however have a major and complex association in Classical writings with the sea-god Poseidon. In 'The Legends of Troy in Art and Literature' (1963), M. Scherer cites the *Iliad* for the failure of Laomedon, Priam's father, to pay the disguised Apollo and Poseidon for building the walls of Troy (Scherer ch.1, p24). This mistake led Poseidon, angry at the breach of faith, to send Hercules to sack the city in order to obtain Laomedon's horses - or, variably, to send a sea-monster which could only be appeased by the sacrifice of Laomedon's daughter Hesione. In that version the sea-monster was killed by Hercules in return for a promise of the horses which Laomedon (who had obviously not learned his lesson!) did not keep. This in turn led Hercules to go to Greece and ask his friends for help, then return to Troy with an army to take and sack the city. The only survivors of the Trojan royal family were Priam, who succeeded to the throne, and his sister Hesione, who was given to one of Hercules' close friends and carried off to Greece. Variations on these stories appear, according to M. Scherer, in Pliny the Elder's *Natural History* (which dates to the 4th century BC), Ovid's *Metamorphoses* and Diodorus of Sicily's *Historical Library*. The latter two authors linked Hercules' problems at Troy with his having sailed past the city with Jason and the Argonauts. Most medieval versions rationalise the whole episode by having Hercules' dispute with Laomedon arise from Laomedon's refusal to let the Argonauts land to seek water or buy provisions; but the story of Hercules and Hesione's rescue does appear in Raoul Lefevre's version and therefore in Caxton's *Recuyell*.

Tolkien inverts this relationship, making his Vala Ulmo, Lord of Waters, into the virtual patron of Gondolin rather than its antagonist. In doing so, however, he is still following medieval precedent. The Middle English poem, the *Destruction of Troy*, adds Neptune at a point where Guido delle Colonne merely has 'in the name of the gods' because Neptune is referred to elsewhere in Guido's work as the principal deity of Troy (Benson 1980, Part 2, ch.III, p.53, referencing line 6094 of the '*Destruction*'). Ulmo sends the dream which makes Turgon go in search of a hollow vale wherein to build a secret citadel:

'Ulmo coming up the river laid a deep sleep upon them and heavy dreams; and the trouble of the dreams remained after they awoke, but neither said aught to the other, for their memory was not clear, and each believed that Ulmo had sent a message to him alone. But unquiet was upon them ever after, and doubt of what should befall, and they wandered often alone in untrodden lands, seeking far and wide for places of hidden strength; for it seemed to each that he was bidden to prepare for a day of evil, and to establish a retreat, lest Morgoth should burst from Angband and overthrow the armies of the North.' (QS, 1977, ch.13, p.135), and: 'And in the next year Ulmo himself appeared to him, and bade him go forth again alone into the Vale of Sirion; and Turgon went forth, and by the guidance of Ulmo he discovered the hidden vale of Tumladen in the Encircling Mountains, in the midst of which there was a hill of stone. Of this he spoke to none as yet, but returned once more to Nevrast, and there began in his secret counsels to devise the plan of a city after the manner of Tirion upon Túna, for which his heart yearned in exile.' (ibid, p.136).

It is Ulmo, also, who promises to send a messenger when Turgon is in most danger, and who arranges for tokens to be left that will prove the identity of the rightful carrier of the sea-lord's word. There is an important omission at this stage in the story, for there are no parallels in Tolkien's account of the founding of Gondolin to Poseidon's strange appearance in disguise as a master-builder, or Laomedon's foolish reneging on a bargain, even though this is a story paralleled in folklore and legend across much of Europe, not least in the story of the building of the walls of Asgard, the citadel of the Norse gods. Here, then, Tolkien certainly seems to be following medieval rather than Classical sources and is being less fantastical, more realistic.

In Book I of the *Aeneid*, Aeolus, God of the winds, whips up a tempest at Juno's request to wreck Aeneas and his Trojan refugees on the shores of North Africa; Neptune, the god of the sea, is angry with Aeolus for causing this storm and calms the waves, allowing the refugees to reach land safely (Virgil trans. D.West, 1990/2003, The Aeneid, Penguin). M Scherer (1963) reproduces some splendid illustrations of this episode in her ch.6, 'The Aeneid', p.184-5. This Classical dispute between a greater and a lesser deity parallels Tolkien's depiction of the disagreement between Osse, Maia of the waves, and Ulmo, Vala of water. Osse is acting on the instructions of the other Valar, who are exceedingly angry with the Noldorin Elves, when he wrecks the last of the ships that Turgon king of Gondolin sent in search of Valinor and tries to strike at Tuor. Ulmo is following his own memories of the Music of the Ainur when he protects Tuor and saves the elvish sailor Voronwë to be his guide on the road to Gondolin:

'And Ulmo spoke to Tuor of Valinor and its darkening, and the Exile of the Noldor, and the Doom of Mandos, and the hiding of the Blessed Realm. "But behold!" said he, "in the armour of Fate (as the Children of Earth name it) there is ever a rift, and in the walls of Doom a breach, until the full-making, which ye call the End. So it shall be while I endure, a secret voice that gainsayeth, and a light where darkness was decreed. Therefore, though in the days of this darkness I seem to oppose the will of my brethren, the Lords of the West, that is my part among them, to which I was appointed ere the making of the World... And now the Curse of Mandos hastens to its fulfilment, and all the works of the Noldor shall perish, and every hope which they build shall crumble. The last hope alone is left, the hope that they have not looked for and have not prepared. And that hope lieth in thee; for so I have chosen." ' (UT, 1980, Part One, ch.1, p.29)

Ulmo's power over rivers as well as the sea is unparalleled in mythology *per se*, but there is a passage in the *Aeneid* which comes close to suggesting something similar. When Aeneas is trying to reach Italy after leaving Queen Dido's realm in North Africa, Venus begs Neptune to allow the Trojan refugees' fleet safe passage, and he replies in the following words:
'Then Neptune, son of Saturn and master of the ocean depths, answered in these words: 'O Venus of Cythera, it is wholly right that you should put your trust in the sea, which is my kingdom, for you were born from it. I also have deserved your trust, for I have often checked the wild fury of the sea and sky, and my care for your Aeneas has been no less on land - I call the rivers Xanthus and Simois to testify to this. During Achilles' pursuit of the broken army of Troy, when he was driving them against their own walls and killing them in their thousands, when the rivers were choked and groaning with corpses and Xanthus could find no way to roll down to the sea, there was Aeneas standing against the might of Achilles, his strength not equal to it and the gods opposed, and it was I who caught him up in a hollow cloud, although my own desire was to take these walls that I had built with my own hands for the treacherous Trojans and turn them over from top to bottom.' (Virgil trans.West, 1990/2003, book 5, p.112)
Here the rivers seem to be presented as subordinate to Neptune. However, there are many other reasons why Ulmo should be lord of all waters, not just the sea, and this one, unclear passage should not be taken as a sole or even a major source.

Something which is emphasised in this passage and missing from Tolkien's account is that of the enmity which arises between sea-god and city. While Turgon does decide not to follow Ulmo's advice, there is no evidence that Ulmo in some way withdraws his protection from Gondolin thereafter, or that he is actually angry with the people of Gondolin because of their king's foolishness. In the 1950's version, Tolkien introduced the idea that Gondolin only falls after Ulmo is no longer able to protect it:
'Yet Doom is strong, and the shadow of the Enemy lengthens; and I am diminished, until in Middle-earth I am become now no more than a secret whisper. The waters that run westward wither, and their springs are poisoned, and my power

withdraws from the land; for Elves and Men grow blind and deaf to me because of the might of Melkor. And now the Curse of Mandos hastens to its fulfilment, and all the works of the Noldor shall perish, and every hope which they build shall crumble.' (UT Part One, ch.1, p.29)
This idea, that Ulmo wants to help but is increasingly unable to, looks very much as if it echoes but reverses the idea of Poseidon/Neptune's wrath against Troy (similarly, the totally unexplained failure of the Eagles of Manwë to warn the people of Gondolin of the approach of Morgoth's army looks like an echo of the anger of Zeus/Jupiter, with whom such birds were closely associated). Oddly enough, in the earlier version of *the Fall of Gondolin* (BOLT vol.II) Ulmo's powers in the river Sirion seems undiminished, and it is the fact that the refugees from Gondolin are far from water that causes them to become lost and hardship from thirst, disease and so on. This would link in with a general degrading of the powers of the Valar in Middle-earth from the earliest times when they were referred to as 'Gods' to the later 'Powers'.

It is worth pointing out here that we have been able to find only a tiny handful of correspondences between the *Aeneid* and anything in Tolkien's writings; the possible significance - or lack of it - of this fact is discussed below.

b; Immortal Love

A second point which fits here is that the *Iliad 's* depiction of relationships between mortals and immortals is in some respects closer to Tolkien's than is that of other material. Folktales the world over depict the devastation of a mortal deserted by an immortal lover. The fictional depiction of the concern of immortals for mortals is different and much rarer. There is however one very good example of it, and this is in Homer's *Iliad.* In that poem the immortals - the gods and especially the goddesses - may be casual about their relations with mortal lovers, but they are deeply concerned with the fortunes of their demi-god offspring. For example, Thetis, the sea-nymph mother of Achilles, knows that he is going to die in the Trojan War, *but not exactly when* ; well before he falls she is distraught, continually afraid for him, mourning in advance and torn by every twist of events, still hoping against all reason that *maybe* she can save her precious son. The suffering inflicted on the gods themselves by the discovery of just how much, emotionally, they have invested in their mortal though partly godly children, and of how terribly vulnerable those children are in the mortal world, is enough to make the quarrelsome, interventionist Olympians doubt the wisdom of meddling with the affairs of mortals. For a motif of such sophistication to appear in a work as early as the *Iliad* is more than a little surprising; it implies that in the background is someone who had applied a fair amount of thought to the philosophy as well as the course of events and literary style in the poem they were creating.

The echoes of this idea in Tolkien's depiction of elf-human marriages are quite clear. Unlike the situation in folklore, where the pattern is that mortal husbands lose immortal wives through carelessness or culpable action, Tolkien follows a pattern of immortal women facing the inevitable loss through death of mortal men. Someone is going to be left behind when the mortal partner dies; and the grief of the immortal partner will be both deep and terribly long-lasting. Even the end of the world may not re-unite such a couple, depending on what Eru has in mind for both groups of His Children at that point. This idea is set out most clearly in LotR, in the terrible choice that Arwen makes and the price that Elrond sets on that choice, in Arwen's parting from her father and in her farewell to Aragorn on his deathbed:

"Nay, dear lord," she said, "that choice is long over. There is now no ship that would bear me hence, and I must indeed abide the Doom of Men, whether I will or I nill: the loss and the silence. But I say to you, King of the Númenoreans, not till now have I understood the tale of your people and their fall. As wicked fools I scorned them, but I pity them at last. For if this is indeed, as the Eldar say, the gift of the One to Men, it is bitter to receive."

"So it seems," he said. "But let us not be overthrown at the final test, who of old renounced the Shadow and the Ring. In sorrow we must go, but not in despair. Behold! we are not bound forever to the circles of the world, and beyond them is more than memory, Farewell!"

"Estel, Estel!" she cried, and with that even as he took her hand and kissed it, he fell into sleep.

... 'But Arwen went forth from the House, and the light of her eyes was quenched, and it seemed to her people that she had become cold and grey as nightfall in winter that comes without a star.' (RotK, Appendix A, pp. 343-4).

Note that Arwen is the one most affected by this sundering, even though in theory she ought to be wise enough to understand and accept death after such a long life, being 2899 years old at the time (calculated from RotK, Appendix B Tale of the Years). This exactly parallels the expressions of grief shown by Thetis, the sea-nymph mother of Achilles.

This pattern is also present in both of the elf-human marriages of the *Silmarillion* tradition, though not quite from the beginning. In *The Book of Lost Tales* both Lúthien and Beren are elves, and both choose mortality as the price of return to the world; Lúthien fades first, following the folkloric pattern (as is fitting in this story - something to be explained in the next book) and Beren afterwards dies. Later, in the more familiar version, Lúthien's desperate love and care leads her to choose mortality rather than be parted forever from Beren. One is tempted in both the case of Lúthien and Arwen to suggest that their love is so all-consumingly possessive as to rival that of a Bearer for their Ring of Power. Neither elf-lady is willing to accept death as a loss or defeat without a fight. Lúthien manages to effect a stay of execution for Beren. Arwen on the other hand is left bitter and desolate without her mortal lover - just as Frodo is left desolate without the Ring. But for Arwen unlike Frodo, as Tolkien contrasts, there is no ship to bear her across the sea. By contrast Tuor and Idril face the Classical dilemma right from the start. In the BOLT outlines for the *Tale of Eärendel*, Tuor is said to sail west and leave Idril behind, stricken with desperate grief (much as Arwen is); in one outline she is desperate enough to swim after him and even succeeds, revealing her sea-nymph links (of which more later). This also goes some way towards the Lúthien solution. Briefly, in this version, Tolkien had them both appear in Tuor's ship 'going swift down the wind at dawn or dusk' apparently pre-empting Eärendel as the Sailor Star. In the 1926 *Sketch* and 1930 *Quenta Noldorinwa*, both Tuor and Idril sailed west together and simply vanished; later, as in the 1977 *Silmarillion*, Tuor 'alone of mortal Men was numbered among the elder race, and was joined with the Noldor, whom he loved; and his fate is sundered from the fate of Men.' (QS, ch.23, p.295) Here in a sense Idril goes 'one better' than Lúthien and has her man and the Undying Lands as well. This is a striking philosophical inconsistency, for Tolkien is usually very clear about Men being mortal and unable to change the fact. Tuor seems somehow to be granted both eternal life and eternal youth, as are heroes translated to Olympus in Classical legend. Similarly, when the story-element appears that both Eärendil and Elwing reach Valinor together, he tells her to stay aboard ship, but she jumps into the foam to join him, preferring to share his peril than be sundered from him forever. This would seem to only be derivable from the Classical sources as far as we can tell.

II;Names and Geography

a; Names

There are definite connections to be found with names between the medieval tradition and Tolkien's writings. Examining the seven names of Gondolin from BOLT, we are told:

"'Tis said and 'tis sung: Gondobar am I called and Gondothlimbar, City of Stone and City of the Dwellers in Stone; Gondolin the Stone of Song and Gwarestrin am I named, the Tower of Guard, Gar Thurion or the Secret Place, for I am hidden from the eyes of Melko; but they who love me most greatly call me Loth, for like a flower am I, even Lothengriol the flower that blooms on the plain.' Yet," said he, "in our daily speech we speak and we name it mostly Gondolin."

(BOLT vol.II, ch. 3, p.158).

Now Gondobar occurs in the poem The Happy Mariners in a revised version probably dating from 1940 (BOLT vol.II, ch.5, p.275, line 24) and refers to a place beyond the Twilit Isles somewhere near Valinor. The two elements Gond - stone and bar - dwelling give us the meaning, and by extension Gondothlimbar does follow. It can be suggested that the city that Priam built was a city of stone by definition. They rely upon the heavy walls for their defence - and they hold fast for the ten years of the siege, and only treachery allows the enemy inside. In the medieval versions of the Trojan legend, the fine stonework of the city is heavily emphasised.

Gondolin itself appears from the beginning so far as we can tell, at a date when Tolkien's languages were in extreme flux - not much touched since he left Oxford, with 'proto-Quenya' stranded half-way between Gothic and Finnish and proto-Sindarin/Gnomish doubtfully in existence. Though accommodated to successive developments in the 'Elvish' languages, Gondolin may in origin not have sprung from any careful use of invented words. In the appendix to BOLT vol. 1 this name is broken down as: Gonn- (stone) followed by Dolin (song). The earlier name list for Quenya does not give Gondolin at all. However, in the Appendix 'Elements in Quenya and Sindarin names' in QS, we have the split: Gond- and -lin. Gond now means 'stone', whereas the -lin root as used in Gondolin has two possible meanings (QS, Appendix, p.434). One is 'sing, make musical sound', but the second is 'pool, mere'. It may not be coincidental that in the *Iliad*, that city was famous for having two springs under the walls, one hot and one cold in which people of the city did their washing.

The Quenya form of Gondolin, Ondolindë, is potentially even more significant, since there is a very high chance that it is a meaningful word in Classical Greek. We have ονθος - the nearest form to 'ondos' - meaning dirt, and the close form ονγος / ονκος - means lump or knot (Morwood & Taylor, 2002). We can also compare this with ορος - meaning mountain, range of hills or even frontier (Lidell & Scott, 1871). So 'ondos' is most likely to be hillock or stony outcrop. Note that the dictionaries we were able to consult were very limited in their range. Thus if the 'Lindë' component stood for a place such as perhaps 'Lindos' an ancient city on the island of Rhodes, we would have 'Hill of Lindos'. John Garth points out that 'ond', stone, is a word which was once regarded as a sole survivor from the pre-Celtic languages of Britain (Garth 2003 'Great War' ch.5, p.98). From the above, the pre-Celtic language may have been influenced by early Greek. And Ond, of course, is the name that Tolkien first gives to the realm that eventually becomes Gondor in LotR (*Return of the Shadow*, HOME Vol.VI Index, p.488) - we shall return to Gondor and to Rhodes in a later chapter.

Gwarestrin can be split down as follows: 'Gwareth' is 'watch, guard or ward', and 'estirin' is 'pinnacle or tower'. These elements are early (BOLT vol.II, Appendix) and do not occur in the QS Appendix of elements of names. This of course provides us with a direct link through to the meaning of the name Minas Tirith, which means Tower of Guard. This, as will be seen later, is very significant. Gar Thurion, or the Secret Place, appears not to come from anywhere in the given lists BOLT vol.II, ch.3, p.158) . Thurin means the secret one in the Tale of Turin in Unfinished Tales. However, Thurion and Gar are both Classical Greek words. Gar is a preposition with a wide range of meanings; it is given as 'for, since, as, why, what, if only!' (Morwood & Taylor, 2002). Thurion is of a common form: θυρ οω - means to shut, to close; θυρα - means the fold of a door, gate, palace, royal court, entrance, threshold, table, board or even raft; θυρεοσ - means a large shield or a door stone. (ibid) The idea of closure, of shields and of guard is conveyed by the Classical Greek words, and this comes across in the meaning that Tolkien assigns to this name of Gondolin, but even more to the overall idea of the city itself.

The name Loth means flower and Lothengriol means 'lily of the valley'.

Coming from the other side, Troy's alternative name of Ilios bears a strong resemblance in form to the Greek word for 'sun', elios (the usual 'h' is Latin decoration and in original intent soundless). Whether or not this is philologically tenable, formally the likeness is interesting; so too is the common Greek habit of rededicating sites once sacred to Apollo Helios to the Old Testament prophet Elias, often Ilias in modern Greek spelling (Severin, 1987, citing P.L. Fermor in ch.12, p.213). This material should be considered against Tolkien's depiction of a rayed Sun as one of Turgon's principal devices (BOLT vol.II, ch.3, p.172: Hammond and Scull, 1995, ch.6, p.194), and the persistent association of Turgon with sun and moon symbols - in the later 'Tuor' the last gate of Gondolin built before the Nirnaeth is that of the Sun. The possibility that the 'Golden Flower of Gondolin' is also a solar reference should not be ruled out either. Add to that the principal defining characteristic of Priam's Troy is that of the massive stone walls, built in the finest quality (said to have been built by two Gods, Apollo and Poseidon) that serve to defend the Trojans through ten years of siege - truly a city of stone, and this is borne out by the archaeological excavations of Schliemann and those who followed him at the site of Troy in Asia Minor. Thus we have two cities of stone in Troy and Gondolin.

Another point worthy of note is the matter of the titles which Tolkien used for his story. The title actually written on the cover of the books which contain the first (pencil) and second (ink) versions of the story in its BOLT form is *Tuor and the Exiles of Gondolin (which bringeth in the great tale of Eärendel)* . When the piece was read to the Exeter College Essay Club in 1920, however, it was already being referred to as *The Fall of Gondolin*, and J.R.R. Tolkien would consistently refer to it afterwards by this name, as pointed out by Christopher Tolkien in the introduction to the piece in BOLT vol.II (ch. 3, p.146). The version of the story which appears in 'Unfinished Tales' was retitled 'Of Tuor and his Coming to Gondolin' by Christopher Tolkien with the laudable aim of not confusing readers, since the story never reaches the fall of the city, but this too was known to J.R.R. Tolkien himself by the old title (UT, Introduction). This is significant because several of the medieval versions of the story of Troy emphasise the fall of the city in their titles, such as Guido delle Colonne's *Historia Destructionis Troiae*, 'History of the Destruction of Troy' and the Middle English 'Geste Hystoriall of the Destruction of Troy'. In the 20th century, William Morris's Troy-poems had appeared under the title 'Scenes from the Fall of Troy'. Tolkien is thus keeping surprisingly close to a traditional title in his altered scenario.

A small point worth mentioning is that John Lydgate's short 15th-century versified chronicle of Guy of Warwick includes a list of of cities chastised by God; specially picked out as particular examples are Nineveh, Rome, Carthage and Troy. (The Legend of Guy of Warwick, V.B. Richmond, 1996, Garland Publishing). Tolkien uses a closely similar list in the BOLT Tale of Gondolin:

'Glory dwelt in that city of Gondolin of the Seven Names, and its ruin was the most dread of all the sacks of cities upon the face of the Earth. Nor Bablon, nor Ninwi, nor the towers of Trui, nor all the many takings of Rûm that is greatest among Men, saw such terror as fell that day upon Amon Gwareth in the kindred of the Gnomes; and this is esteemed the worst work that Melko has yet thought of in the world.' (BOLT vol.II, ch.3, p.196)

In the notes on 'Changes made to names in *The Fall of Gondolin* ' (BOLT vol.II, ch.3, p.203), Christopher Tolkien points out that:

'*Bablon, Ninwi, Trui, Rûm* The original text of Tuor A had *Babylon, Nineveh, Troy*, and (probably) *Rome*. These were changed to the forms given in the text, except *Nineveh* > *Ninwë*, changed to *Ninwi* in Tuor B.'
John Lydgate, though probably little-known at best to most of our readers, was one of the major figures of English literature in his day (he lived c.1370-1449). A near contemporary of Chaucer, he wrote and translated both romances and didactic works. Since Tolkien studied Chaucer's Trojan story *Troilus and Criseyde* for his final examinations, and Lydgate wrote a *Troy Book*, it is very likely that Tolkien knew Lydgate's work well. A short, digestible piece on a theme such as *Guy of Warwick* which was then as well-known as it is now forgotten would have made a good introduction to Lydgate's style. Nor should we forget that during the war years the city of Warwick was to play a large part in Tolkien's personal and imaginative life, as is shown by the various mentions of the place in *The Book of Lost Tales*, vols. I & II. Much of the rest of Lydgate's work is on the grand scale, running to many tens of thousands of lines, whereas his *Guy of Warwick* is a short and snappy 565 lines. There is a reasonable chance, then, that Tolkien's choice of examples of famously destroyed cities is not random. This is examined in more detail in a later chapter in this book.

One last small point about names is worth making. 19th and early 20th century maps of the Troad show an area entitled 'Lisgar - Marsh and Bushes' alongside the River Mendere (the Classical Scamander) a little way above its mouth (c.f. the map reproduced as a fold-out at the back of Leaf 1912, more accessibly reproduced as the plate on p.43 of Wood 1985). Names similar to Lisgar appear in association with the mouth of the river Sirion in the Gondolin story. In the BOLT 'Fall of Gondolin', we are told that:
'Nor was this without Ulmo's devising, and that night the Noldoli came to him and he arose from sleep. Guided by their blue lanterns he found a way beside the river border, and strode so mightily inland that when dawn filled the sky to his right hand, lo! the sea and its voice were far behind him, and the wind came from before him so that its odour was not even in the air. Thus came he soon to that region that has been called Arlisgion "the place of reeds", and this is in those lands that are to the south of Dor Lómin and separated therefrom by the Iron Mountains whose spurs run even to the sea.' (BOLT vol.II, ch. 3, p.153)
This region, like the Lisgar of the Trojan plain, lies well above the river mouth and is a freshwater reed swamp. It is noted in 'Changes made to names in *The Fall of Gondolin*' that 'This name was added later to *Tuor B* ' which suggests it may date with other revisions carried out by Tolkien when he was preparing to read 'The Fall of Gondolin' to the Exeter College Essay Club in the spring of 1920. It is therefore quite possible that this addition of a 'Lisgar'-like name was a deliberate if sidelong reference, since by that stage Tolkien would have had access to his own books and possibly (since he was working for the Oxford English Dictionary), to the Bodleian Library as well. In the 1950's version of Gondolin, 'Arlisgion' becomes 'Lisgardh', moving closer to its original in name (which fits with a number of other changes that introduce new but Trojan motifs) but changing its location away from the likely model, becoming 'the land of reeds at

the Mouths of Sirion' (UT Part 1 section I, p.34). This name does not appear in the 1977 'Silmarillion', though the mouths of Sirion are often referred to.
By itself the appearance of this name would be only coincidence, but in view of all the other evidence presented in this chapter we think it is worth considering that there is a definite link.

b; Geography

If we examine the early descriptions of Gondolin in BOLT, it is clear that the city is not completely isolated behind a continuous ring of tall mountains. Gondolin lies within 'the Encircling Hills', but these seem to be a complex piece of topography; hills, peaks, mountains, forests and heaths are all mentioned as being part of the range (BOLT vol.II, ch.3, pp. 165-73). This compares well with the alliterative *Destruction* 's only description of the land around Troy, as the Greeks make ready for an evening council in Agamemnon's tent:

'All darkened were the mountains and moors round about [Note 1]
(Panton & Donaldson 1968, alliterative Destruction, bk.XVII, line 7350)
'Moor' can mean 'marsh' as well as 'heath', and this is significant, because there is actually a place which is a very good match for the early geography of Gondolin. In their 1897 book *The Mycenean Age*, the Greek archaeologist C.Tsountas and the American historian J.I. Manatt included an appendix on recent discoveries in the north of Greece. The draining of the great wetland of Lake Copais had revealed earlier water-control work going right back to Mycenean times. Exploration of former islands resulted in the discovery of a very large and important fortress on one rocky isle (Tsountas and Manatt's Gha, now called Gla and thought to be Homer's Arne) which is described as follows:
'The island of Gha lies about half a mile from the eastern shore of Copaïs... It is a great rock springing directly out of the lake, and on the northwest, where the face is almost perpendicular, it rises to a height of some 70m. above the plain. From this point the ground gradually falls away on the west and south to half that altitude, and still more sharply to the east, the north gate being only some 12m. above the plain. Following the very edge of the rock, so as to economise every inch of space, runs the fortress-wall - a mighty rampart about 20 feet thick, and about three quarters of a mile in circuit. It is thus the largest circumvallation of the Mycenean Age.'
(Tsountas and Manatt 1897, Appendix B, p.375)

This is an excellent match for Tolkien's rock of Amon Gwareth, on which Gondolin is sited, rising steeply - and on one side precipitously - from the extensive level plains round about. Tuor and Voronwë have 'a day's light march' from the passage through the hills to the city. The plain of Gondolin itself is so extensively reworked as to suggest the effort put into the levels of Copaïs. Furthermore, like Gla, Gondolin is set to the side rather than in the centre of the flat ground. The hills and mountains which enclose the Copaïs basin are also a good match for the early description of Gondolin. Now, we have been arguing that Tolkien was basing Gondolin upon Troy; so why should he use a mainland Greek site as the basis for the physical form of his city? The answer is firstly, that at this early date there is not much sign of Tolkien using the actual geography of Troy in any way; and secondly, Tolkien may have changed the description deliberately, to avoid an obvious Trojan reference, since at this time the excavations at Troy were so well-known. We will be looking in detail at why he might have made such geographical changes in Chapter 3.

By the 1950's, with *Of Tuor and His Coming to Gondolin*, the situation is different. Now Gondolin is isolated by impassable mountains, as described in *Unfinished Tales* :

'...they climbed out then onto the east bank, and they had now come into the tumbled hills that lay at the feet of the mountains. And looking up Tuor saw that they towered up in a fashion other than that of any mountains that he had seen; for their sides were like sheer walls, piled each one above and behind the lower, as were they great towers of many-storeyed precipices.' (UT, Part 1, ch.1, p.43)

This is almost certainly the result of development within the tale itself, with little reference to any external source. It is however worth noting firstly that in the medieval *Alexander* - romance, a text which likely provided Tolkien with the idea of Trees of the Sun and Moon, there is a city isolated behind near-impassable mountains. This idea went on to a long career in medieval romance as the setting for the court of the fabulous Eastern Christian monarch Prester John, near if not in the Earthly Paradise at a great height and among mountains. Secondly, *Of Tuor and his Coming to Gondolin* was written after the appearance of the film *Lost Horizon*, based on the book of the same name by James Hilton, in which the 'earthly paradise' of Shangri-La lies isolated behind near-impassable peaks in the Himalayas. We have no idea if Tolkien knew either book or film, but both were highly successful and it is not impossible that he had read or seen one if not both versions. The *Lost Horizon* tale draws on a combination of Eastern legend and the same Western stories that created the Prester John tale, so Tolkien might have found either the book or the film interesting enough to take mental note of the setting. The growing power and menace of Morgoth within the confines of Beleriand within his *Silmarillion* stories would have given the development of a fence of tall mountains behind which to hide a city and its people logical causality.

It has to be noted that in *The Hobbit* (which had been written in the late 1920's and early 30's), there is no mention of Gondolin being a 'hidden' city; indeed, it seems to suggest that Gondolin was well-known:

'They knew the sword at once. It had killed hundreds of goblins in its time, when the fair elves of Gondolin hunted them in the hills or did battle before their walls. They had called it Orcrist, Goblin-cleaver, but the goblins called it simply Biter. They hates it and hated worse any one that carried it.' (TH, ch.4, p.63)

There are three points we would make about these comments in *The Hobbit*. Firstly the elves of Gondolin are said to have hunted the goblins in the hills - not mountains - surrounding their city. Secondly the elves 'did battle before their walls'; this indicates a prolonged period of warfare, not the one or two day event that the fall of Gondolin is portrayed as in BOLT. Indeed, <u>there is no continuous fighting outside the walls</u> in BOLT, only a siege. The people of the House of the Hammer of Wrath led by Rog attack the balrogs outside the gates - but they fought with great maces like hammers, not swords. For a sword to be 'recognised' and become 'infamous' also requires more than a day's exposure in battle (even allowing for the battle of the Nirnaeth many years before the city's fall in later versions). Thirdly, the text seems to suggest that Orcrist had many bearers - that is how we would interpret 'hated worse any one that carried it'. Although it can be said that *The Hobbit* is a trivial and not serious work of Tolkien's, he was importing into it ideas such as Gondolin wholesale, and that included their settings.

The idea of such famous swords appearing in a hoard, not in the ruins of the city they came from or in a tomb, could echo a point made by the Greek archaeologist C.Tsountas and the American historian J.I. Manatt:

'On the other hand, it is a surprising fact that not a sword nor a trace of one has been found in any of the prehistoric settlements at Troy... and Heilbig... notes there "an almost complete absence of weapons which correspond to the ordinary notion of a sword." (Tsountas and Manatt 1897, ch.VIII, p.198-9, note 6)

Tsountas and Manatt's account of the Copaïs basin also suggests some other parts of Tolkien's geography. The idea of a vast basin with no surface outlet of water to the sea, and a central lake hidden among vast marshes, can be found in Tolkien's writings from *The Book of Lost Tales* onwards, with the hollow land of Mithrim, later Nevrast. More directly, Tsountas and Manatt describe the way by which water does escape from the Copaïs area:

'The lake has no outlets save by subterranean rifts in Mt Ptoon on the north and east. There are 23 of these *katabothrae* (as the Greeks call them), through which the waters reach the Euboean channel at Larymna, and at least two other points. The largest of the them (near Kokkino) has "an entrance upwards of 80 feet high, and vaulted over by a precipitous overhanging cliff." Into this great fissure one can make his way some 175 paces before the rock-walls close in upon him, leaving only narrow, dark rifts for the water...

...from one of the *katabothrae* - namely, that of Binia - ancient engineers undertook to tunnel through to the Bay of Larymna. Over the low Pass of Kephalari, in a line of 2,230 m., they sunk 16 shafts from 18 to 63 m. in depth, and for a distance of 500m. they had actually tunnelled from shaft to shaft, thus seeking to secure a more certain and regular discharge of the waters than the natural rifts alone could guarantee.' (Tsountas and Manatt 1897, 'Mycenean Age', Appendix B, p.375)

Compare this with Tolkien's descriptions of the Gate of the Noldor. In *The Book of Lost Tales* it is a tunnel made by the Elves:

'Thereafter 'tis said that magic and destiny led him on a day to a cavernous opening down which a hidden river flowed from Mithrim. And Tuor entered that cavern seeking to learn its secret, but the waters of Mithrim drove him forward into the heart of the rock, and he might not win back into the light. and this, 'tis said, was the will of Ulmo Lord of Waters at whose prompting the Noldoli had made that hidden way.

Then came the Noldoli to Tuor and guided him along dark passages amid the mountains until he came out into the light once more...'

(BOLT vol.II, ch.3, p.149-50)

In the 1950's *Of Tuor and His Coming to Gondolin*, the old idea of the subterranean river is retained, but somewhat changed:
'But even as dim dusk came on the third day of his journey, Tuor found before him a wall of rock, and there was an opening therein like a great arch, and the stream passed in and was lost.' Again, the river runs through great tunnels towards the sea, and Tuor is able to follow it. This is like the situation at Lake Copaïs in the wall and arched cave-mouth, unlike it in having a clear passage all the way through to the sea. Tolkien seems to be altering the underground waterway to better suit the geography of Beleriand as it has developed by this later date, but still retaining elements of the original source as much as possible.

III; The Gates of the City

Here there is some of the most compelling evidence for the links between the medieval tradition of Troy and Tolkien's own works. It comes up in two major manifestations. Troy has six named gates (the Antenorean, the Dardanian, the Ilian, the Scaean, the Thymbraean and the Trojan - Frazer 1966, Dares, p.137) which have passwords (Frazer, Dares, p.165), while in Dicty's version what is effectively a 'seventh gate' is added when a hole is made in the walls of Troy to admit the Wooden Horse (Frazer, Dictys, p.112-3). These six gates reappear in the 13th-century Latin prose of Guido delle Colonne;
'From the surface of the earth up to the top of the city, the ramparts were built up in an amazing arrangement of walls two hundred cubits high on all sides. The surface was inlaid with marble stones of many different colours, so that they pleased the sight of those gazing at them On the crown of these encircling walls, there were towers, one not far distant from the next, which rose high above and overhung the walls. Entrance to and exit from this city was provided for by six gates, the first of which was called the Dardanian, the second the Thymbraean, the third the Ilian, the fourth the Scaean, the fifth the Trojan, the sixth the Antenorean. Each of these gates was fortified by strong towers along the sides and adorned with carvings of marble images on all sides. Each of these permitted peaceful entrance to friends wishing to enter and threatened the fierce and bold attacks of proud resistance to any enemies. The outer side of these walls was also protected along the circumference by a deep trench with hidden pitfalls, and a broad plain widened the distance between the trench and those walls.'
(Colonne/Meek 1974, bk.5, lines 116-132, p.45)
Now let us examine Tolkien's first reworking of the Trojan model - Gondolin:
In the early *The Fall of Gondolin*, there are no actual gates mentioned on the passage through the hills, although its entrance and exit are described as 'gates' but have no doors or guards. There is mention of what are termed 'the gates of Gondolin' (BOLT vol.II, ch.3, p.159), but one might suppose that this is one grand pair of gates leading into the city on the hill:
'Now is there a sally from the gates of Gondolin and a throng comes about those twain in wonder..." (ibid, p.159), and this is backed up by : 'Tuor saw that they

[the gates] were of iron and of great height and strength...' (ibid, p.160). One cannot, of course, assume that merely because other gates were not mentioned at this point, no other gates existed. But the matter will remain uncertain.
However, in Unfinished Tales in Of Tuor and his Coming to Gondolin we are given a very detailed description of Tuor and Voronwë's passage through the seven gates. It is very interesting to note that Gondolin began life with six gates to which one was added after the Nirnaeth Arnoediad (p.46 -50), summarised here:
'Thus they came at length to a wide arch with tall pillars upon either hand, hewn in the rock, and between hung a great portcullis of crossed wooden bars, marvellously carved and studded with nails of iron.... 'You have passed the First Gate, the gate of Wood,' said Elemmakil...
In the wall was a great archway above the road, but it seemed that masons had blocked it with a single mighty stone. As they drew near its dark and polished face gleamed in the light of a white lamp that hung above the midst of the arch. 'Here stands the Second Gate, the gate of Stone,' said Elemmakil....
After a little space they came to a wall yet higher and stronger than before, and in it was set the Third Gate, the Gate of Bronze: a great twofold door hung with shields and plates of bronze, wherein were wrought many figures and strange signs. Upon the wall above its lintel were three square towers, roofed and clad with copper....
Thus at last they drew near the Fourth Gate, the Gate of Writhen Iron. High and black was the wall, and lit with no lamps. Four towers of iron stood upon it, and between the two inner towers was set an image of a great eagle, wrought in iron, even the likeness of King Thorondor himself... But as Tuor stood before the gate it seemed to his wonder that he was looking through boughs and stems of imperishable trees into a pale glade of the Moon... there was not one grill but three in line...
... and Tuor saw beside the way a sward of grass, where like stars bloomed the white flowers of *uilos*, the Ever-mind that knows no season and withers not; and thus in wonder and lightening of heart he was brought to the gate of Silver.
The wall of the Fifth Gate was built of white marble, and was low and broad, and its parapet was a trellis of silver between five great globes of marble; and there stood many archers robes in white. The gate was in shape as three parts of a circle, and wrought of silver and pearl of Nevrast in likenesses of the Moon; but above the Gate upon the midmost globe stood an image of the White tree Telperion, wrought of silver and malachite, with flowers made of great pearls of Balar...
... they entered upon a long white road, that ran straight towards the Sixth Gate; and as they went the grass-sward became wider, and among the white stars of *uilos* there opened many small flowers like eyes of gold.
So they came to the Golden gate, <u>the last of the ancient gates of Turgon</u> that were wrought before the Nirnaeth; and it was much like the Gate of Silver, save that the wall was built of yellow marble, and the globes and parapet were of red gold; and there were six globes, and in the midst upon a golden pyramid was set an image of Laurelin, the Tree of the Sun, with flowers wrought of topaz in long clusters upon chains of gold. And the Gate itself was adorned with discs of gold,

many-rayed, in likenesses of the Sun, set amid devices of garnet and topaz and yellow diamonds...
... the way was short to the Seventh Gate, named the Great, the Gate of Steel that Maeglin wrought after the return from the Nirnaeth, across the wide entrance to the Orfalch Echor.
No wall stood there, but on either hand were two round towers of great height, many-windowed, tapering in seven storeys to a turret of bright steel, and between the towers there stood a mighty fence of steel that rusted not, but glittered cold and white. Seven great pillars of steel there were, tall with the height and girth of strong young trees, but ending in a bitter spike that rose to the sharpness of a needle; and between the pillars were seven cross-bars of steel, and in each space seven times seven rods of steel upright, with heads like the broad blades of spears. But in the centre, above the midmost pillar and the greatest, was raised a mighty image of the king-helm of Turgon, the Crown of the Hidden Kingdom, set about with diamonds...' (UT, Part 1, ch.1, pp.46-50)

It is our belief that somewhere there may well be a medieval text we have as yet not examined with details of seven gates leading up through a mountainous region towards a city given somewhat as above from which Tolkien drew his inspiration. The most likely place to seek this would be in the stories about the Earthly Paradise, the Christian kingdom of Prester John in the East - as per *Mandeville's Travels*, amongst others where the Earthly paradise sits high up in a mountain range from where the four great rivers of the world issue. This also links in with legends of Shambala, or Shangri La - which was in all likelihood a small remote Himalayan realm in a fertile valley surrounded by mountains that had both Nestorian Christian and Buddhist influences, visited by a Portuguese explorer Antonio Do Andrade in 1624 (Michael Wood - In Search of Myths and Heroes, Programme 2, BBC 2 Friday 11th February 2005, and forthcoming book by Michael Wood). He published his book of his travels in Lisbon in 1626 (Novo Descobrimento do Gram Cathay, ou Reinos do Thibet).

Another Greek city which figures in medieval romance is Thebes, onetime home of Oedipus (the luckless legendary king who gave his name to Freud's 'Oedipus complex' by killing his father and marrying his mother), and afterwards bitterly disputed between his sons Eteocles and Polynices. Thebes does have seven gates, and the story would have been available to Tolkien in Middle English in John Lydgate's *Siege of Thebes* ; it is also found in summary form in Chaucer's *Troilus and Criseyde*, though this is primarily a Trojan story. However, these seven gates are each associated with the king and the six counts of the city, and they give onto seven principal streets, whereas Gondolin has twelve noble houses, and the number of streets is nowhere mentioned. Given these points, and also the general lack of other resemblances between the Theban story and that of Gondolin, compared to the number of points at which the stories of Troy and Gondolin coincide, it seems very unlikely that the Theban legends were a major source for Tolkien (John Coley (trans.), 1986, Le Roman De Thebes, lines 5173-5256).

Returning to the Gates of Gondolin, the decoration of the *tholos* tombs at Mycenae may be of some interest. Part of this is now in the British Museum, courtesy of Lord Elgin and the slightly later British nobleman Lord Aberdeen (Wood, 1985, ch.5). The original doors of these tombs were of wood decorated with bronze; there were also bronze plaques lining the interior of at least one of them. Surrounding these doors were fine carved decorations of white, blue, green and red marble. The main structure of the tombs and their sloping entrance-ways was of the local dark limestone, well-cut in blocks which are of astounding size. The lintel of the 'Treasury of Atreus' is about 30 feet long, 16 feet wide and 3 feet thick; it weighs no less than 120 tons, and crowns a door three times the height of a man. It is also worth noting that there has long been speculation that the missing heads of the lions above the Lion Gate at the citadel of Mycenae were either of gold or at least gilt. This shows that the fulsome description of the Seven Gates of Gondolin is not completely fantastic and is based upon actual existing artefacts. The second manifestation of the model of Troy is in Minas Tirith in LotR with its seven circles and seven gates within the city itself. This is fully discussed in a later chapter as it has great significance of its own.

IV; Warnings Ignored

There are prophecies in both the Trojan legends and Tolkien's tale of Gondolin. In the medieval versions of the Tale of Troy, Priam is three times warned that the city will fall if he carries on with his plan to send Paris to Greece with the aim of taking some noble lady captive and exchanging her for his sister Hesione. The passages appear in Guido delle Colonne's sixth book, and also in the alliterative 'Destruction of Troy'. First, in a family discussion, Priam's eldest son Hector is reluctant to support his father's first idea, a full-scale invasion. Paris, next in line, take the opportunity to suggest a raid instead, and his third son Deiphobus supports him, but when he finishes talking the fourth in the family, Helenus (variously called priest by Guido and bishop by the less historically-minded Destruction-poet) prophesies disaster:

'You have yourself assessed truly before,
That I never told you a tale in times that have passed
But you have found it come out exactly as I said it would
Therefore put off this purpose; let Paris not go
For any reason in the world, because of woe that may befall
I tell you with certainty, and it will happen
That if Paris is sent out to do as he wishes
To strike against Greece, and do grim work there
Solemnly I tell you, this city will then cease to exist
By the Greeks it shall be dashed to the ground and trampled under foot
And we shall be exiled forever; this chance shall befall.

(Panton & Donaldson 1968, bk.VI lines 2489-99) [Note 2]

The youngest of Priam's legitimate sons, Troilus, scoffs at this and urges them to follow Paris's plan. He is decidedly impolite to his brother Helenus, saying:

'Oh noble men of good fame, what troubles your hearts?
Why are you worried now, and speechless?
And moved so much, all for a mad priest
That knows nothing of knighthood but scolds [like a woman] in church?

(Panton & Donaldson 1968, bk.VI lines 2526-9) [Note 3]

Secondly, Priam takes the matter to his full council and is again warned that keeping to this course will bring destruction, by one Protheus son of Eusebius, both philosophers; but everyone else mocks this, just as Troilus mocked Helenus. Lastly, Priam's daughter Cassandra tries to persuade her father that this can only lead to disaster, but also fails.

'Yet I may say truly, and hold it as certain
Had the counsel of the knight Hector been taken
And the earnest speech afterward of Helenus the bishop
Cassandra's fears considered with all
And the prophecy of Protheus, put into his heart
Then Troy with its towers had been a noble town yet
And lasted in glory until the world's end.

(Panton & Donaldson 1968, bk.VI lines 2711-5) [Note 4]

In *The Book of Lost Tales* version of Tolkien's tale of Gondolin, Tuor arrives in the city with messages rather than a clear warning from Ulmo; the sea-Vala first asks Turgon to make ready to fight, and then when Turgon refuses to set his people and their city at such risk, asks him to send messengers to Valinor; but Turgon has been doing just this with no success, and will support no more such ventures. By the 1926 *Sketch of the Mythology*, the idea of a warning is explicit: 'This Ylmir does because he knows that ere seven full years are passed the doom of Gondolin will come through Meglin' (*The Shaping of Middle-earth* , HOME vol.IV, ch.II, section 16 and commentary). This idea would be still further expanded with the introduction of the scene where Ulmo tells Turgon to leave arms and armour for a messenger whom Ulmo will one day send.

It is given in short form in the published *Silmarillion* :

'And Ulmo warned Turgon that he also lay under the Doom of Mandos, which Ulmo had no power to remove. 'Thus is may come to pass,' he said, ' that the curse of the Noldor shall find thee too ere the end, and treason awake within thy walls. Then they shall be in peril of fire. But if this peril draweth nigh indeed, then even from Nevrast one shall come to warn thee, and from him beyond ruin and fire hope shall be born for Elves and Men. Leave therefore in this house arms and a sword, that in years to come he may find them, and thus shalt thou know him, and not be deceived' And Ulmo declared to Turgon of what kind and stature should be the helm and mail and sword that he left behind.'

(QS, ch.15, p.150)

The arms are found and claimed by Tuor in the 1950's version in UT, and in note 6 Christopher Tolkien refers to the above QS passage. However the QS passage is a late addition, contemporary to, or later than the version given in UT.

The idea of armour being left to identify the messenger whom Ulmo promises to

send to Gondolin is not present in any of the versions prior to the 1950's Tuor - that is, the 1926 or 1930 versions ('A Sketch of the Mythology' or 'The Quenta Noldorinwa'), nor was it critically given in the 1937 Quenta Silmarillion.
In all the versions of the story it is Idril who realises doom is near and tries to save, if not her city, then at least some of its people. In the BOLT version, Idril is shown to be foresighted: 'Know then that Idril had a great power of piercing with her thought the darkness of the hearts of Elves and Men, and the glooms of the future thereto - further even than is the common power of the kindreds of the Eldaliё; therefore she spake thus on a day to Tuor: "Know, my husband, that my heart misgives me for doubt of Meglin, and I fear that he will bring an ill on this fair realm, though by no means may I see how or when - yet I dread lest all that he knows of our doings and preparations become in some manner known to the Foe, so that he devise a new means of whelming us, against which we have no defence." (BOLT vol.II, ch. 3, p.167)

Comparing this to the medieval Troy-tales, Idril can be seen to occupy Cassandra's role, though with the major exception that she receives a warning only once, late in the day and, instead of telling everyone and getting nowhere, she tells only her husband and succeeds in taking precautions that ultimately save her and her son and husband as well as a tithe of the people of Gondolin from the ruin. Once more Tolkien is reversing the run of story from the source. Tuor himself combines three roles; as a counsellor he resembles Protheus, as a bearer of divine warning he resembles Helenus; and as the man who later marries Turgon's daughter and become his effective heir, he resembles the cautious Hector. One might also suggest that Voronwё represents Protheus, for he is as convinced as Tuor of the veracity of the warning. As Maeglin urges the king to ignore the warning (from the 1926 *Sketch* onwards), he plays the roles of both Troilus and Paris in the family debate; later, as traitor, he takes on the roles of Antenor and Aeneas. It seems almost certain that this drastic reduction in the number of characters and combination of roles is the result of the very much smaller scale of the BOLT *The Fall of Gondolin* compared to the medieval works. The later 'Silmarillion' versions are mere summaries, and the 1950's 'Tuor' never reaches this stage, so we have no idea if Tolkien would have changed this and had more of a debate in Gondolin over what to do, when he had more room to work with.

V; The Glory that was Gondolin

a; Trees

The medieval writers of romances added many marvels to the picture of Troy, most of them inspired by accounts of the contemporary 'city of wonders', Constantinople. While the writers of 'historical' versions tried to cut down on such elements, one at least survived their efforts to keep to the facts. This was a tree which was said to stand in King Priam's palace, either in the hall where his throne was set (alliterative *Destruction*), before its doors (the Laud *Troy Book*) or

in the middle of the palace courtyard (Guido delle Colonne). Both the Laud book and Guido's account place the description of the tree in the passage where Greek ambassadors arrive just before the start of the siege of Troy (Guido's book 12), not in the main description of the city and palace (Guido's book 5).
The alliterative *Destruction of Troy* describes this tree as follows;

'Yet they marvelled more that in the middle of the hall
Was a tree that was the best, all of real gold
Great and marvellous for men to see
The trunk was of shining gold, set in the middle of the hall
It was larger than a laurel-tree and taller as well
Twelve cubits by measure was its clear height
And all most well formed even to the noble boughs
The breadth of those branches was as wide as could be seen
Thick and long and shining like the sun
From the dais to the doors spread abroad
And on all sides filling the circuit of the hall
The branches were thick, some of bright gold
Some of silver in truth, most beautiful of colour
With leaves most lovely, made of [both] the same [metals]
With buds above , bright to look upon
And fruit on it formed in the fairest of shapes
Of many kinds that were white, fixed above [to the branches]
That shimmered as sheer as any shining stones'

(Panton & Donaldson 1968, book XII lines 4958-74). [Note 5]

In the Lydgate *Troy Book* this tree is described as having:

'...rich branches and the leaves so fair
Twined each with other to make a pair,
One leaf of gold, with one of silver sheen
And scattered through with stones both white and green.'

(quoted in modernised spelling in Scherer 1963, ch.1, p.52)

While in the Laud *Troy Book* the tree stands outside:

'Before the door was set a tree
That fair and proper was to see
The tree was all of fine gold
From the ground to the top
And all the branches of that plant
Were silver & gold, no lie to tell
For every one of silver bright
Another [was] of gold that shone clear.
There was never fruit that ever grew
But they hung there of proper colour
And all were silver and gold within
This work was made with cunning skill.'

(Laud Troy Book, lines 9529-40) [Note 6]

In Tolkien's 'Fall of Gondolin' we find not one but two marvellous trees. The 'Book of Lost Tales' version says that they were living things: 'On either side of the doors of the palace were two trees, one that bore blossom of gold and the other of silver, nor did they ever fade, for they were shoots of old from the glorious Trees of Valinor that lit those places before Melko and Gloomweaver withered them: and those trees the Gondothlim named Glingol and Bansil.' (BOLT vol. II, ch. 3, p.160)

In the published 'Silmarillion' these trees reappear, but now as artificial creations: 'There shining fountains played, and in the courts of Turgon stood images of the Trees of old, which Turgon himself wrought with elven-craft; and the Tree which he made of gold was named Glingal, and the Tree whose flowers he made of silver was named Belthil.' (QS, ch.15, p.151)

In UT, the two trees are fixed to the fifth and sixth gates in 'Of Tuor and his Coming to Gondolin': 'The wall of the Fifth Gate was built of white marble, and was low and broad, and its parapet was a trellis of silver between five great globes of marble; and there stood many archers robed in white. The gate was in shape as three parts of a circle, and wrought of silver and pearl of Nevrast in likenesses of the Moon; but above the Gate upon the midmost globe stood an image of the White tree Telperion, wrought of silver and malachite, with flowers made of great pearls of Balar...'

'So they came to the Golden gate, the last of the ancient gates of Turgon that were wrought before the Nirnaeth; and it was much like the Gate of Silver, save that the wall was built of yellow marble, and the globes and parapet were of red gold; and there were six globes, and in the midst upon a golden pyramid was set an image of Laurelin, the Tree of the Sun, with flowers wrought of topaz in long clusters upon chains of gold. And the Gate itself was adorned with discs of gold, many-rayed, in likenesses of the Sun, set amid devices of garnet and topaz and yellow diamonds...' (UT, Part 1, ch.1, p.49)

The idea that the Trees of Gondolin are artificial first appears when they are described as 'images' made by Turgon, in notes to the last pre-LotR 'Silmarillion' writings, as given in *The Lost Road* , HOME vol.V, Part 2, ch.VI, section 2. This idea reappears and is elaborated in the post-LotR works, the 'later Quenta Silmarillion' and the 'Grey Annals', given in *The War of the Jewels* , HOME vol.XI. In the former work, the description extends beyond that in the published QS: '...and the light which sprang from them filled all the ways of the city.' (HOME vol.XI, Part 2, section 12, p.200) This is reminiscent firstly of the original lightgiving Two Trees and their living offshoots in Gondolin, and secondly of the Heavenly Jerusalem of Revelations 21: 19-23 where 'And the city has no need of the sun nor yet of the moon to shine upon it; for the glory of God illuminates it and the Lamb is its lamp.' (The Complete Bible in Modern English, trans. F. Fenton, 5th edn 1913) We have here created legends basing themselves upon older legends, much as Tolkien would have experienced with the Trojan legends and their offspring throughout Europe - so the two trees in Gondolin are legendary, but are based upon the older legend of the Two Trees of Valinor. The wondrous nature of the real living Trees is pushed back to the unreachable realm of Valinor and artifices put in their places, still full of wonder, but at one remove from the original, more amazing source.

Incidentally, two trees (the Cherry of the Left and the Orange of the Right) also stood in front of the palace of the emperors of Japan during the Heian period, roughly 750-1150 AD (Morris 1964). It is worth remarking upon the fact that Japan can seem decidedly 'elvish': its location on maps made before Columbus corresponds closely to that of Tol Eressëa in Tolkien's maps; the aboriginal people are the Ainu, a name which is very close in form to Tolkien's Ainur; Heian Buddhism had a chronological system -of three 'ages of the world', each lasting about two thousand years, which was rather like Tolkien's eventual time-scheme; the astounding painstaking craftsmanship that does not concern itself with how much time anything takes to be fashioned (including arms and armour - think of Gandalf's sword Glamdring) - as if they might live forever - and the importance of taste; even the importance in historical politics of clan unity and clan disunity; these are all points of resemblance. It is also true that after the opening up of Japan in the 1860's, there was a great deal of interest in the country in the West in the late 19th and early 20th centuries. Unfortunately, attractive as these similarities are, there is absolutely no evidence of Tolkien's ever having shared this interest in Japanese history and culture. It seems most likely that Japan's imperial Two Trees must be set down to a particularly delightful coincidence, though the possibility ought to be borne in mind that both the early medieval Japanese and the high medieval Europeans came up with the idea of two trees outside a palace from a common source somewhere along the Silk Road.

Of course, there is a tree in the court of the white tower in Minas Tirith that will remind us of Troy once again. The heraldry of Gondorian Kings is also very suggestive of a Trojan link, with its white tree. The connections with Minas Tirith will be discussed in a later chapter.

b; Heraldry and linguistic games

We find links between the disposition of the houses of the peoples of Gondolin and those in the medieval Trojan stories and indeed in the heraldic devices described. In the BOLT 'Fall of Gondolin', the twelve noble houses of the city are enumerated; 1) the house of the King; 2) the followers of Tuor; 3) the folk of Meglin; 4) the Swallow; 5) the Heavenly Arch; 6) the Pillar; 7) the Tower of Snow; 8) the Tree; 9) the Golden Flower; 10) the Fountain; 11) the Harp; 12) the Hammer of Wrath (BOLT vol.II, ch.3, p.175).

The same number appears prominently in a similar context in connection to Troy in Snorri Sturluson's *Edda* :

'Near the middle of the world was constructed that building and dwelling which has been the most splendid ever, which was called Troy. We call the land there Turkey. This place was built much larger than other and with greater skill in many respects, using the wealth and resources available there. Twelve kingdoms were there and one high king, and many countries were subject to each kingdom.

In the city there were twelve chief languages. The twelve rulers of the kingdoms were superior to other people who have lived in the world in all human qualities.'
And again:
'Odin found the conditions in the country attractive and selected as the site for his city that place that is now called Sigtunir. He also organised rulers there on the same pattern as had been in Troy, set up twelve chiefs in the place to administer the laws of the land, and he established all the legal system as it had been in Troy...' (Both quotes: Sturluson trans Faulkes 1987, Prologue)
Furthermore, when the alliterative *Destruction*'s account of Troy's allies, which is given in Book XIII at lines 5432-5547, is looked at in detail, it gives twelve named countries and twenty-four kings or lords. We think it is almost certain that Gondolin has twelve noble houses because Troy is said to have had the same number of lords, in a source -Snorri's *Edda* - which we can be absolutely sure that Tolkien would have known. This would be backed up by the twelve allies of Troy in the alliterative *Destruction* , which does not give a list of the lords actually living in the city. As a comparison, there may also be twelve tribes of Israel, but the number apart, there are no other points of similarity with any of Tolkien's stories. If there was an influence, then it might be a Biblical one upon the medieval writers of the reworked Trojan legends.

The idea that each lordship arose from a different people with a different language is quite possibly reflected in the phonetic variance of the names of the lords of those houses given in BOLT, which vary far more than the 'standard' situation of one or two elvish languages found in the 1977 *Silmarillion* would suggest. These names are; 1) Turgon; 2) Tuor; 3) Meglin; 4) Duilin; 5) Egalmoth; 6) & 7), Penlod; 8) Galdor; 9) Glorfindel; 10) Ecthelion; 11) Salgant; 12) Rog. Several of these names have no explanation in the system of elvish languages that Tolkien developed after writing the initial versions of the 'Lost Tales', much less any later vocabulary (so far as these are currently known). 'Penlod' has a distinctly Welsh sound to it. 'Egalmoth' and 'Ecthelion' are jagged phonetic cousins, and the latter at least could easily be Greek. His name stands alongside other possibly Greek or Hellenised names in Tolkien's work such as Tirion and Túna, and is itself close to the Mycenean Greek name Ekhelawon (found on Linear B tablets - Wood 1985, ch.7, p.216). 'Salgant' looks as if it could be medieval German (compare Sifrit for Siegfried in the Nibelungenlied) or even French. Lastly, 'Rog' by Tolkien's later standards would make a good name for an orc! (it could be related to the Middle English version of modern 'rough'; however, it could also be Gothic in origin, as 'balrog' appears to derive from *balwa-reiks, 'torment-mighty' - Wright 1910 Glossary, s.v's balwjan & reiks (1), aj.). Other names may well have inspired parts of Tolkien's language-system to account for them, the explanations being far later, rather than being made according to any existing pattern. For example, 'Turgon' appears in the *Lost Tales* version from the start, but is not given a meaning in the name-lists and dictionaries attached to these stories. The name is explained as 'commander of power' or 'valorous lord' in the late 1920's or even 1930's; in the very late account in *Peoples of Middle-earth*, the Quenya meaning is the same but in Sindarin 'would have conveyed... 'Master-shout'', the second element being 'command' in the sense of 'issue orders, call out' (HOME vol.XII, Part Two, ch.XI, pp.345 & 362). It is possible that 'Turgon' originated as an epithet, 'Of the Commanding Voice', matching the alliterative *Destruction* 's description of Priam of Troy as having 'of furse stevyn', a fierce or brave voice, rendered as commanding in the editors' marginal note (Panton & Donaldson 1968, Book VIII, line 3865). This name could well be Greek in origin, since the element 'gon' could correspond to 'Γο'ον' - meaning to wail, groan or lament, just as in *Peoples*, Sindarin *caun* is 'outcry, clamour' with special reference to lamentation. So it looks very much as if Tolkien has invented Turgon's name and only after that found an 'Elvish' meaning for it. There is another echo of the idea of multiple languages in Gondolin in the suggestion that 'Eärendel' 'was a name wrought of some secret tongue among the Gondothlim, and that has perished with them from the dwellings of the Earth.'(BOLT vol.II, ch. 3, p.165). However we know that it originates outside Tolkien's own stories and is a name in its own right.

The 'prehistory' of Tolkien's invented languages is a matter of formidable complexity which is virtually unstudied as yet. Carpenter's *Biography* mentions several 'phases', with very different backgrounds. There is Greek: 'Already when beginning to learn Greek he had entertained himself by making up Greek-style words.' There is Spanish: 'His guardian spoke Spanish fluently and Ronald had often begged to be taught the language, but nothing came of it, though he was given the freedom of the books. Now he looked at them again and began work on an invented language that he called 'Naffarin'. It showed a great deal of Spanish influence, but it had its own system of phonology and grammar.' There is Gothic/ Germanic: 'He was not content simply to learn the language, but began to invent 'extra' Gothic words to fill gaps in the limited vocabulary that has survived, and to move on from this to the construction of a supposedly unrecorded but historical Germanic language.' (Carpenter 1977, Part 2, ch.3, p.44). According to John Garth, this invented language was called 'Gautisk' and may have been an attempt to reconstruct Geatish, the language Beowulf would have spoken (Garth 2003 'Great War', ch.1, p.17, note). There is Finnish, which certainly had a major effect, but probably only in certain areas, for Tolkien himself says in *Letters* no.163 (1955);

'...Most important, perhaps, after Gothic was the discovery in Exeter College library, when I was supposed to be reading for Honour Mods, of a Finnish Grammar. It was like discovering a complete wine-cellar filled with bottles of an amazing wine of a kind and flavour never tasted before. It quite intoxicated me; and I gave up the attempt to invent an 'unrecorded' Germanic language, and my 'own language' - or series of invented languages - became heavily Finnicized in phonetic pattern and structure.'

There is also Welsh, which Tolkien had been intrigued by before he encountered Finnish (Carpenter says, 'He managed to find books of medieval Welsh, and he began to read the language that had fascinated him since he read a few words of it on coal-trucks.' - Part 2, ch.5, p.64), and which he appears to have remained interested in long after Finnish had lost its appeal. In the same letter he goes on to say: 'That of course is long past now. Linguistic taste changes like everything else, as time goes on; or oscillates between poles. Latin and the British type of

Celtic have it now, with the beautifully co-ordinate and patterned (if simply patterned) Anglo-Saxon near at hand and further off the Old Norse with the neighbouring but alien Finnish. Roman British might not one say? With a strong but more recent infusion from Scandinavia and the Baltic. Well, I daresay such linguistic tastes, with due allowance for school-overlay, are as good or better a test of ancestry as blood-groups.' (Letters no.163, 1955)
As far as invention goes, the 'Gnomish lexicon' which is the source for part of the material in the name-lists to the two volumes of BOLT implies that Tolkien had been using Welsh extensively at some point before 1917.

With all this in the background, Tolkien would have been well able to find names of differing phonetic 'taste' to reflect a multilinguistic situation in Gondolin, based on Snorri Sturluson's idea of a Troy where twelve languages were spoken. It is a pity that there has been no extensive investigation of themakeup and development of Tolkien's invented languages, which would make it possible to look more closely at the names of the lords of Gondolin. It is still worth noting that only some of these names reappear in later writing. These are Glorfindel, Ecthelion and Egalmoth. Glorfindel appears to have been a chance reuse of no significance; Tolkien tied himself, as well as readers and critics, in knots over the question of whether there were one or two characters of the name. Ecthelion by contrast reappears in a context which is potentially very significant, as the name of two Stewards of Gondor closely associated with the White Tower of Minas Tirith; we will be looking at the Trojan connections of this section of LotR in more detail later. Egalmoth, the nearest apparent phonetic relative of Ecthelion, also turns up in the list of the Stewards. So, overall, the names of the lords of Gondolin appear to reflect a linguistic situation of far greater diversity than Tolkien usually shows. This can be accounted for if, like the basic concept of twelve noble houses, it came from Snorri Sturluson's account of Troy in his *Edda*. The reappearance of some of these names elsewhere in Tolkien's work is also likely to be significant.

Another aspect of the noble houses of Gondolin which may well link them to the Trojan legends is Tolkien's use of lavish heraldic descriptions in connection with them. The king's household carried variously the moon and sun or a Scarlet Heart; Tuor's following had White Wings of swans or seabirds; Meglin's people had no sign or emblem, only blank black shields; the folk of the Swallow bore an arrowhead on their shields; the folk of the Heavenly Arch had a multicoloured roundel representing a rainbow; there were the folk of the Pillar and of the Tower of Snow; the folk of the Golden Flower carried a rayed sun; there were peoples of the Fountain and of the Harp; the folk of the Hammer of Wrath had for sign the Stricken Anvil, and had a hammer set about with sparks on their shields.

There is not much heraldry associated with Troy by Guido delle Colonne. Describing the battalion led by Troilus, Guido mentions that the prince's own shield is 'all azure with three gold lions depicted on it'. Secondly in the same account of the Trojan arrangements for the second battle of the siege, the nameless king of Cisonia is said to have arms which were 'green or yellow without any device.' Lastly there is Hector's shield, 'a field all gold or yellow and in the middle one red lion was painted'; but this is not constant - elsewhere Guido gives Hector, like Troilus, three lions (Colonne/Meek 1974, bk.15, lines 49, 65-6, 142-3, p.124-7, respectively; and bk.14, ll.243-4, p.121). These match none of Tolkien's descriptions and therefore cannot be his source. It is possible that a work more influenced by the highly decorative accounts in Benoit de Sainte-Maure's 12th-century French *Roman de Troy*, such as the Middle English *Seege or Batayle of Troy*, (which we have not been able to obtain), might be a more likely source for such descriptions.

Tolkien's heraldry does find some parallels in manuscript paintings of the Nine Worthies, such as one from c.1390 illustrated as plate 47 by Scherer. Here the central figure, presumably King David, carries a harp upon his shield; to the left, the three pagan Worthies Hector, Alexander and Julius Caesar, carry respectively an enthroned lion, a scraggy doubleheaded eagle looking far more like a tree, and a lion waving an axe. The other two Jewish Worthies, Joshua and Judas Maccabeus, have a dragon and a songbird, while of the Christians Arthur has three crowns, Charlemagne three fleurs-de-lis and an eagle, and Godfrey de Bouillion carries the gold-on-silver Cross of Jerusalem. More of this particular connection shall be discussed in our next book of Tolkien studies.

Out of these designs, several can be compared at once to the 'Gondolin' descriptions. David's Harp is obvious; Alexander's blundered Eagle/Tree is subjective but possible; Joshua-or-Judas's unpredatory bird could refer to either the Swallow or the Wing; Charlemagne's fleurs-de-lis suggest the name of the Golden Flower while Godfrey's cross gets so complex on his banner as to approach 'a rayed sun' by default.

The sevenfold gem of the Heavenly Arch, composed of rubies and amethysts and sapphires, emeralds, chrysoprase, topaz and amber (and added to with an opal on the helmet) is reminiscent of the breastplate ascribed to the Jewish High Priests, with its nine gems of ruby, topaz and diamond, ligure, agate and amethyst, amber, onyx and pearl (Exodus 28: 17-20 - The Complete Bible in Modern English, F. Fenton 5th edn 1913). This could well be associated with one of the Jewish Worthies somewhere. There is also a faint resemblance to the Heavenly Jerusalem (Revelations 21: 19-21); 'The foundations of the wall of the city were decorated with every precious stone. The first course, jasper; the second sapphire; the third, chalcedony; the fourth, emerald; the fifth, sardonyx; the sixth, sardius; the seventh, chrysolite; the eighth, beryl; the ninth, topaz; the tenth, chrysoprasus; the eleventh, jacinth; the twelfth, amethyst. As so often, Tolkien's version is more concise than its parallels, and actually makes more sense. His seven gems are all clearly identifiable and distinct from one another, whereas the two Biblical lists have puzzled commentators for millennia.

The middle English *Geste Historyall of the Destruction of Troy* includes a comment about a Greek leader that may well have influenced Tolkien's depiction of Salgant;

'Polidarius was pimply as a fat porker
Full great in the fundament, huge with grease
So swollen was his body, that burden enough had
The feet of that fellow to haul him about
Or stand up straight for his strong charge.'

(Cited Benson 1980 Part 2 ch.III, p.51) [Note 7]

By comparison, in BOLT vol.II we have Salgant described thus:
'Behind them came the host of the Harp, and this was a battalion of brave warriors; but their leader Salgant was a craven, and he fawned upon Meglin. They were dight with tassels of silver and tassels of gold, and a harp of silver shone in their blazonry upon a field of black; but Salgant bore one of gold, and he alone rode into battle of all the sons of the Gondothlim, and he was heavy and squat.'
(BOLT vol.II, ch. 3, p.173-4)

VI; Trojan Women (and others)

a; Dancing Feet

We have a definite descriptive link between the Trojan legends and Tolkien's main female character in the Fall of Gondolin which seems so unusual as to defy any other explanation. The unusual detail first comes in Dares' description of Priam's daughter Polyxena;
'Polyxena was fair, tall and beautiful. Her neck was slender, her eyes lovely, her hair blond and long, her body well-proportioned, her fingers tapering, her legs straight, and ***her feet the best***. Surpassing all the others in beauty, she remained a completely ingenuous and kind-hearted woman.' (Frazer, Dares, p.143) (emphasis ours).
Dares gives a list of 31 physical descriptions of Trojans and Greeks, and only that of Polyxena mentions feet. With this account of Polyxena we can compare the descriptions of Idril, princess of Gondolin. In chapter 15 of the published *Silmarillion* she is described thus:
'But fairer than all the wonders of Gondolin was Idril, Turgon's daughter, she that was called Celebrindal, the ***Silver-foot*** , whose hair was as the *gold* of Laurelin before the coming of Melkor.' (QS, ch.15, p.151)
In the BOLT 'Fall of Gondolin', Idril is described as follows:
'Fair indeed was she and brave thereto; and the people called her Idril of the **Silver Feet** [editor's note reads: faintly pencilled above in *Tuor B* ; *Idril Talceleb*] in that she went ever barefoot and bareheaded, king's daughter as she was, save only at pomps of the Ainur...'
The 'earliest 'Silmarillion' ' of 1926-30 (*Shaping of Middle-earth* , HOME vol. IV Part 2, section 16) and the following 'Quenta Noldorinwa' of c.1930 both retain the idea that Idril's epithet arises from her preference for going barefoot; 'Very fair and tall she was, well nigh of warrior's stature, and her hair was a fountain of

gold. Idril was she named, and called Celebrindal, Silver-foot, for the whiteness of her foot; and she walked and danced ever unshod in the white ways and green lawns of Gondolin.' (ibid, sections 16 & 17, second version of the QN). Unfortunately the 1950's text 'Of Tuor and his Coming To Gondolin' does not reach far enough to offer any detail on this point. The dating thereafter is singularly hard to unscramble, but probably contemporary with or slightly later than 'Of Tuor..." are the texts in the so-called 'later Quenta Silmarillion' and the 'Grey Annals', as presented in *The War of the Jewels* , HOME vol. XI. This comes closest to the 1977 version: 'But fairer than all the wonders of Gondolin was Idril Turgon's daughter, she that was called Celebrindal for the whiteness of her unshod feet, but her hair was as the gold of Laurelin before the coming of Melkor.' (ibid, Later QS section 12, p.200)

While Polyxena is the likely source of a lady with lovely feet among the Trojans, the actual epithet 'silver-footed' belongs to the sea-nymph Thetis, the mother of Achilles. This name appears in the *Iliad* in, for example:

'At this they vanished in the offshore swell,
and to Olympus Thetis the silvery-footed
went once more, to fetch for her dear son
new-forged and finer arms.'
(Homer/Fitzgerald 1998 book XVIII, lines 52-5, p.325)

It is likely that Idril has acquired this by-name because Thetis herself is in one version of the Greek legends (Ovid, p.257 Peleus and Thetis) a 'fairy bride' whose would-be husband, Peleus of Thessaly, has to hold her fast through a whole series of changes of shape until she gives up and consents to wed him, in a manner very closely analogous to the disenchantment of Tam Lin in the Scottish ballad of the same name (Hartland 1925 ch.IX, p.242: Chadwick 1912 ch.XIII p.264 note 3). Later in this version of the story, Thetis tries to make her son Achilles immortal by anointing him with ambrosia by day and putting him in a fire to burn out his mortality by night. Finding out about this but not understanding why Thetis is acting so strangely, Peleus speaks harshly to her, upon which Thetis abandons her husband and not-quite-immortal son (Hartland 1925 ch.XI, p.317). As an elf who marries a mortal, Idril parallels Thetis in one respect; as the inheritor of Polyxena's lovely feet, she can be regarded as a more logical bearer of the name 'silver-footed' than Thetis herself. Obviously, there are major differences in Tolkien's story. Firstly, Idril differs from Polyxena in that she has married and borne a son before the fall of the city, which she survives, whereas Polyxena is unmarried and survives the fall of Troy only to be killed on Achilles' tomb by his son Neoptolemus/Pyrrhus. Secondly, Idril differs from Thetis in that she does not require to be disenchanted in order to be married, she has no need to try to make her son immortal by magical means, and she neither abandons her family nor subsequently brings supernatural aid to her son. At all these points, Tolkien's version resembles medieval romance rather than folklore or Classical legend. This shows that Tolkien is working in a highly original way with his source materials.

b; The Accidental Destroyers.

Let us turn now to the two women in the Trojan story who cause the destruction of the city, Helen and the much-less-well-known Hesione, Priam's sister, and their analogues and parallels in Tolkien's Tale of Gondolin. Helen is the most famous of all the female characters in the tale of Troy. In the account of Dares Phyrgius, Helen is carried off whilst away from home, visiting the Temple of Venus/Aphrodite on the island of Cythera, and she is at first said to be 'not unwilling', only later having regrets (Frazer, Dares, p.141). This parallels the story of Aredhel who is taken captive and married by Eöl whilst wandering away from Gondolin. Tolkien says of her that 'It is not said that Aredhel was wholly unwilling, nor that her life in Nan Elmoth was hateful to her for many years' (QS, ch.16, p.160) Only later does she come to regret her choice to leave Gondolin and stray abroad, just as Helen comes to dislike Troy after the death of Paris Alexander, when she is married to his brother Deiphobus (Frazer, Dictys, p.101). Some ideas normally associated with Helen of Troy appear to have been displaced in the collision between the Tale of Troy and the Tale of Eärendel which created *The Fall of Gondolin*, Helen is very much associated with water-birds; she was the daughter of Leda, Queen of Sparta, who was seduced by Zeus in the shape of a swan. As a result, Helen and her sister Clytemnestra, and their brothers Castor and Pollux, were all hatched from eggs. In Tolkien's story there *is* an important character who has similar waterbird connections, but this is Elwing, wife of Eärendel and daughter of Dior son of Lúthien, who comes in a generation down the line and in a different place, the Havens of Sirion. In the very early phases of the Tale of Eärendel, Elwing was said to have been carried off, like Helen in reverse, by Melko/Morgoth's army when they sacked the Havens. The first change was to have her attempt suicide in order to evade capture, only to be turned into a white bird or a seabird by Ulmo; the second was to shift responsibility for the sack of the Havens of Sirion from orcs to elves, in the shape of the Sons of Fëanor. This idea would be Tolkien's view, so far as we can tell, for the rest of his life. Possibly it was the practical reflection that if Helen was hatched rather than born, her mother should have been the one transformed into a bird, not her father, that persuaded Tolkien to attach the motif to a woman. We will be looking again at Elwing's transformation later in the book. So there are echoes of Helen of Troy in the story of Gondolin, but some of them have been moved around within the tale to unexpected places. This is completely in line with what Tolkien does with characters he invents in stories like LotR during their development from original conception to eventual appearance in print.

Going back to the Trojan legends, Hesione, Priam's sister, is unlike Helen and Aredhel in that she is definitely carried off against her will. However, Hesione does resemble Aredhel in a different respect. In the medieval versions, it is Hector's excessive courtesy, giving up a successful attack in deference to a cousin, that ultimately leads to the fall of Troy - for he has thrown away their only real chance to drive off the Greeks. This cousin is Ajax Telamonius, Hesione's son. He of course would be the analog to Maeglin in the *Fall of Gondolin*. The son of the king's sister in both cases causes the fall of the city. The alliterative 'Destruction' describes the incident in detail (Panton & Donaldson 1968 bk.XV lines 7073-7124), but Guido delle Colonne has the essentials:

'On the Greek side he met his first cousin, the son of Hesione and the son of Telamon, who was called by the name of Ajax Telamonius, and who was advancing against him in a hostile fashion with great courage in fighting, since he was a man who was very powerful on account of his strength, and was a very bold warrior. These two who were so bold began to battle with determination, but as they were fighting each other they exchanged words, and Hector recognised the son of his aunt and that they were related by blood ties. Hector accordingly became very happy at that point, and when he had laid down his arms, he softened towards him [Ajax Telamonius] with great affection and promised to please him in all things, and advised and asked him to come to Troy to see the large family of his kinsmen. He [Ajax] refused, however, and not neglecting the safety of his Greeks and his country, asked Hector, if he had such great affection for him, to manage it and bring it about that the Trojans would cease to fight further and would not pursue the fleeing Greek further, but that they would go back to Troy, sending the Greeks away in peace on that day. The unfortunate Hector promised. He at once, by a blast on the trumpet, ordered it and brought it about that all the Trojans retreated and ceased fighting. The Trojans had already set fire to the Greek ships and were already setting all the ships adrift, but at the voice and command of their leader, they desisted completely from everything and greatly disturbed and disappointed, went back to the city and entered it. This was the trivial cause for which the Trojans on that day ceased from obtaining their victory which they never afterward were able to reach, because the fates opposed.' (Colonne/Meek 1974, bk.15, lines 671-696, p.141)

We can see that Ajax Telamonius resembles Maeglin in three ways. Firstly and least importantly, Ajax Telamonius is a man of notable prowess, and Maeglin is consistently described as 'no weakling or coward' He is said to have fought well in the Nirnaeth: 'Wise in counsel was Maeglin and wary, and yet hardy and valiant at need. And that was seen in after days: for when in the dread year of the Nirnaeth Arnoediad Turgon opened his leaguer and marched forth to the help of Fingon in the north, Maeglin would not remain in Gondolin as regent to the King, but went to the war and fought beside Turgon, and proved fell and fearless in battle (QS, ch.16, p. 166). Secondly, the excessive favour shown to Ajax as his kinsman by Hector matches Turgon's favouring of Maeglin. Thirdly and most notably, Ajax Telamonius is the son of Hesione, King Priam's sister, by a foreign lord bitterly opposed to the Trojans, just as Maeglin is the son of Aredhel, the sister of King Turgon, by a foreign lord, Eöl, who is bitterly opposed to the Noldor, Turgon's people (and is slain by them in Gondolin). The development of the story of Aredhel and Maeglin, as detailed in the various volumes of the HOME series, is long and complicated. As C.J.R. Tolkien points out in *The Shaping of Middle-earth* :

'the story of Maeglin in *The Silmarillion* is one of the latest elements in the book.' (HOME IV, ch.2, commentary on section 16, p.193).

Naturally, since it had been worked on over a long span of time, Maeglin's story reflects many changes in opinion by J.R.R. Tolkien himself. In some ways the early changes increased the likeness between Maeglin's story and that of Ajax Telamonius. In the BOLT version, 'Meglin' is wholly Noldorin; 'Now that Gnome was come of an ancient house, though now were its numbers less than others, but he himself was nephew to the king by his mother the king's sister Isfin; and that tale of Isfin and Eöl may not here be told.' (BOLT vol.II, ch.3, p.164-5) By the 1926 Sketch , we have 'Meglin son of Eöl and Isfin sister of Turgon was sent by his mother to Gondolin and there received, although half of Ilkorin blood, and treated as a prince' (*The Shaping of Middle-earth* , HOME vol.IV, ch.2, section 16). On the other hand, later changes moved in a far more independent direction, making the story less like that of Hesione in its later stages, though retaining some essential features. It can therefore be seen that there are definite links between the female characters in the Trojan legends and Tolkien's *Tale of Gondolin*.

VII; Of Balrogs and Heroes

During the sack of Gondolin, one of the city's great lords, Ecthelion of the Fountain, meets one of Morgoth's mightiest servants, Gothmog Lord of Balrogs. Though already wounded, Ecthelion kills Gothmog, but is himself slain.

A similar event occurs in the medieval Trojan legend when, according to Dares, Paris Alexander and Ajax meet in a great battle towards the end of the war, where each kills the other: 'Alexander, using his bow with frequent success, pierced the unarmed Ajax' body; Ajax, however, though wounded, pursued and finally killed his assailant. Then, as the wound had exhausted his strength, he [Ajax] was carried back to the camp, and there, though they drew out the arrow, he died.' (Frazer, Dares, p.161)

In Guido delle Colonne's version, this Ajax is none other than Ajax Telamonius, the son of Hesione sister of King Priam of Troy. In the alliterative *Destruction*, the relationship between this incident and Tolkien's combat between Gothmog and Ecthelion becomes even clearer:

'The Death of Ajax by Paris slain.'

'Paris by pain was cut to the heart
To see his men so marred by wounds and murderously slain
By the force of his bow and with a strong arrow
That was steeped in poison, Paris pierced Aiax' armour
Rent through his ribs, tore him inside
[So that] all his blood was blackened, and his complexion changed
Then felt/knew well the fellow [Aiax] that he was doomed
And would die of that stroke before the day was over.'

'The Death of Paris by Ajax slain.'

'He pressed through the fight to Paris in his foaming anger
And as he fought in the field, to that fellow [Paris] he said
"Paris, you have swiftly brought me to my death
And shattered me with one shot of your sharp gear

Yet before I die of your stroke, and sink swiftly into hell
You shall first go before me and seek out our way!
It is right and proper return for your headlong love
That you part now with pain from your good lady Helen
Who is the cause of this trouble and this cold anger
And the death of many a doughty duke and knight."
Then he drove to the warrior [Paris] with a long sword
Dashed through the helmet and the hard cheek-pieces
And he [Paris] fell to the ground and yielded up his ghost [died]
Even dead of that one stroke, and suffered no more
Then Aiax also, exceedingly swiftly
Fell off his horse, flat to the earth
And from the pain of his deadly wound passed from this life
Even died of that stroke, and to sorrow went.'

(Panton & Donaldson 1968, book XXVI, lines 10700 - 10726) [Note 8]

This compares with the fight between Gothmog and Ecthelion in three ways. Firstly, it is the most notable mutual killing in the whole poem; no other pair of such important heroes kills each other. Secondly, Aiax is hit 'between liver and lights' according to the same episode in the Laud Troy Book, which compares very well with Gothmog being struck in the midriff by the spike of Ecthelion's helmet. Thirdly, the fall of both Ecthelion and Gothmog into the well in the King's Square is a neatly reworked rendition of 'damp (dump, fall swiftly) into helle' of line 10713 - see note 7. Mortally wounded and unable to stand, Gothmog takes Ecthelion with him, and they sink together into the depths in a literally damp, watery place, which erupts in steam as the fiery Balrog heads for a different sort of Underworld to the burning hell envisaged by the medieval writer.

VIII; Treachery, Low Cunning and Cowardice

a; Who's the Traitor?

We have more connections between Gondolin and Troy in the means by which both cities are brought down. In Dares' account, Troy is betrayed from within, by a conspiracy headed by a lord named Antenor:

'During the same day, Antenor, Polydamas, Ucalegon, and Dolon met in secret. They were amazed at the stubbornness of the king, who, when surrounded by the enemy, preferred to die rather than sue for peace, thus causing the destruction of his country and people. Antenor had a plan for solving their problems, and if the others would swear their allegiance, he would reveal it.

When all had sworn as he wished, he first sent word to Aeneas, and then told them his plan. They must, he said, betray their country, and in such a way that they might safeguard themselves and their families. Someone must go - someone that no-one could suspect - and tell Agamemnon. They must act quickly. He had noticed that Priam, when leaving the council, was enraged because he had urged him to sue for peace; and he feared that the king was devising some treachery.

All promised their aid and immediately chose Polydamas - he would arouse least suspicion - to go in secret and see Agamemnon...'

After some to-ing and fro-ing to prove Polydamas's offer is real, involving the giving of a password to the Greeks that they use successfully, the Greeks agree to Antenor's offer:

'Then the members of the council, binding themselves on oath, promised that if Troy were betrayed the next night, no harm would come to Antenor, Ucalegon, Polydamas, Aeneas, and Dolon, or to any of their parents, or indeed to their children, wives, relatives, friends, and associates, or to any of their property.

When they had sworn to this promise, Polydamas gave them instructions. At night, he said, they must lead the army to the Scaean gate - the one whose exterior was carved with a horse's head. Antenor and Aeneas would be in charge of the guard at this point, and they would open the bolt and raise a torch as the sign for attack.'(Frazer, Dares, p.164-5)

(NB, Ucalegon's odd name is close to 'Ancalagon', which Tolkien uses as the name of a dragon in the War of Wrath)

Everything goes to plan: the Greeks break into Troy and 'During the whole night the Greeks did not cease wreaking slaughter and carrying off plunder.'(Frazer, Dares, p.166). Afterwards, the assembled Greek army agrees to honour the kings' promise to Antenor and the other traitors. Antenor thanks them, and begs for the lives and freedom of Priam's son Helenus and daughter Cassandra, which Agamemnon grants. Subsequently Antenor remains as lord of the ruins of Troy, but Aeneas and all his people are driven out, because they tried unsuccessfully to hide Priam's youngest daughter Polyxena from the Greeks.

According to Dares, this princess was seen by Achilles when she went outside the walls during a truce to tend the grave of her brother Hector on the anniversary of his death. For love of Polyxena Achilles first offered to take himself and his Myrmidons out of the fight, then tried to persuade the whole Greek army to give up the war and leave Troy in peace, and finally stayed out of the fighting even when the Greeks were in trouble for several months. However, after Achilles returned to the fray, the queen of Troy made a false offer of a meeting to negotiate again for Polyxena's hand, at which Achilles was ambushed by Paris/Alexander and his men, and killed.

In the later medieval accounts of Guido delle Colonne and his followers, Antenor is actually captured by the Greeks, and his son's attempt to rescue him fails (Benson 1980 part 2, ch.IV, p.93).

Gondolin is also betrayed from within, by Maeglin. Son of Turgon's sister Aredhel, Maeglin arrived in Gondolin with her and he 'prospered and grew great among the Gondolindrim, praised by all and high in the favour of Turgon... Wise in counsel was Maeglin and wary, and yet hardy and valiant at need... Thus all seemed well with the fortunes of Maeglin, who had risen to be mighty among the princes of the Noldor, and greatest save one in the most renowned of their realms.'(QS, ch.16, p.166-7) Maeglin always had an unstated grudge over his

father's death - when Eöl was cast from the precipice at the command of Turgon - for when the King allows Huor and Hurin to leave Gondolin, breaking one of his own laws (and thereby in fact endangering the city's secrecy - it was Hurin shouting outside the Encircling Mountains that drew Morgoth's suspicions to that region, which resulted in Maeglin being captured), Maeglin was angered at the King's decision:
'But Maeglin, the King's sister-son, who was mighty in Gondolin, grieved not at all at their going, though he begrudged them the favour of the King, for he had no love for any of the kindred of Men; and he said to Húrin: 'The King's grace is greater than you know, and *the law is become less stern than aforetime*; or else no choice would be given you but to *abide here to your life's end*.' ' (QS, ch.18, p.191; our emphasis). For when it came to it, the decision offered to Eöl the Dark Elf, Maeglin's father, by Turgon, was to dwell in Gondolin. But he refused to accept the King's law and demanded that he leave with his son, if his wife was minded to abandon him. When that was denied, he tried to kill Maeglin and by accident killed Aredhel instead.
Maeglin's dislike for Men was fuelled further by Turgon's agreement to allow his only daughter Idril to marry Tuor the son of Huor. Maeglin nursed an unnatural love for his first cousin, and thus was thwarted in love and by one who he considered unworthy. But somehow Turgon held Maeglin high in his esteem and he was one of his most trusted advisors. Likewise in the account of Troy by Dares, Antenor was one of Priam's most trusted friends and helpers - so much so that one of the gates of Troy was named for him when it was rebuilt after the first sack of the city by the Greeks, in which Priam's father Laomedon died (Frazer, Dares, p.136-8). This in turn parallels Maeglin's addition of a seventh gate to the original six gates of Gondolin after the disaster of the Nirnaeth Arnoediad, which Turgon and the army of Gondolin only narrowly escaped. Tolkien picks up on the motif of Antenor being captured by the Greeks and has Maeglin taken captive by Morgoth's forces; but in the altered situation, this is far more serious and hopeless for the victim.

In the *Silmarillion* it has a short version: 'Maeglin was no weakling or craven, but the torment wherewith he was threatened cowed his spirit, and he purchased his life and freedom by revealing to Morgoth the very place of Gondolin and the ways whereby it might be found and assailed.' (QS, ch.23, p.292).
In the earlier *Book of Lost Tales*, the treachery goes further - and Meglin is far more proactive in his betrayal - and just as with Antenor, Maeglin gives Morgoth not only the location but the method by which the city might be taken:
'But evil came into the heart of Meglin, and he said to his captors: "Know then that I am Meglin son of Eöl who had to wife Isfin sister of Turgon king of the Gondothlim." But they said: "What is that to us?" And Meglin answered: "Much is it to you; for if you slay me, be it speedy or slow, ye will lose great tidings concerning the city of Gondolin that your master would rejoice to hear." ' (BOLT vol. II, ch.3, p.168)
Meglin then suggested that he be taken to Melko. '... the rede that Meglin gave to Melko was that not all the hosts of the Orcs nor the Balrogs in their fierceness

might by assault or siege hope ever to overthrow the walls and gates of Gondolin, even if they availed to win unto the plain without. Therefore he counselled Melko to devise out of his sorceries a succour for his warriors in their endeavour. From the greatness of his wealth of metals and his powers of fire he bid him to make beasts like snakes and dragons of irresistible might that should overcreep the Encircling hills and lap that plain and its fair city on flame and death.' (ibid, p.169) This of course was exactly the situation that the Greeks faced before Troy. They won the plain of Troy but not all their hosts by assault or siege could ever hope to overthrow the walls and gates of Troy. Only by the use of 'technology' as suggested by Antenor did they trick their way into the city and sack it.
Reversing the Achilles/Polyxena motif, the woman Maeglin wants is one of his own, the king's daughter Idril Celebrindal, whom Maeglin cannot honourably marry because they are too closely akin. Morgoth promises to give Maeglin Idril's life and hand after Gondolin falls. Maeglin is also promised rule over the remnant of the people of Gondolin after the conquest, again paralleling the story of Antenor.

b; Wooden Horses and Bronze Dragons

The method of bringing about the downfall of both Troy and Gondolin is by means of a 'constructed animal'. In the case of Troy it is a horse and in the case of Gondolin, it is hollow metal dragons. Indeed, one might add to that the breaking of the gate of Minas Tirith at the siege was achieved by the use of a battering ram in the shape of a ravening wolf which was named Grond, in memory of the Hammer of the Underworld of old. This will be covered in a later chapter.
In Dictys of Crete's account of the fall of Troy, it is Priam's son Helenus who tells the Greeks to construct the wooden horse:
'We must, he said, offer a wooden horse to Minerva; this gift would prove fatal to Troy. The horse must be so large that the Trojans would have to break their walls; Antenor would urge and advise them to do this.' (Frazer, Dictys, p.111)
Earlier, Helenus had fled from Troy because Paris/Alexander had committed sacrilege, ambushing and killing Achilles in the temple of Thymbraean Apollo, in a sacred grove where Greeks and Trojans had mingled freely (ibid, p.98). The horse is only a device to get the Trojans to breach their own walls, which Dictys calls 'those walls which had stood for centuries unharmed, and which, as tradition told, were the masterwork of Neptune and Apollo' (ibid, p.112)
In Guido delle Colonne and the alliterative *Destruction*, it also a Trojan defector who suggests the stratagem of the horse, but the person responsible is not Helenus. Instead it is one Calchas the priest, who came over to the Greeks at the very start of the war because he was commanded to do so by the god Apollo. This is reflected in the fact that Maeglin betrays Gondolin to Melko/Morgoth, who was originally one of the Valar or Gods, and counsels him about how to take the city, reversing Calchas' being counselled by Apollo. This reversal of roles is typical of Tolkien's method of working as we have shown on previous occasions.
In the BOLT version of the story of Gondolin, it is 'Meglin' who tells Melko/Morgoth how to break through the impenetrable defences of Gondolin:

'From the greatness of his wealth of metals and his powers of fire he bade him make beasts like snakes and dragons of irresistible might that should overcreep the Encircling Hills and lap that plain and its fair city in flame and death.' (BOLT vol. II, ch.3, p.169)

This is of more significance than is at first obvious, because medieval versions of the Tale of Troy turned the wooden horse into a *bronze* one. As M.Scherer summarises it: 'The change came about gradually. Dictys mentioned briefly that the horse was made of wood. Dares reduced it to a horse's head above the Scaean gate, through which the Greeks entered by night. Benoit implied that his audience knew the material but did not specify it. So far as is known Guido delle Colonne was the first to say that the Greeks made 'a horse of bronze, *equm ererum*, big enough to hold a thousand men'. With but few exceptions later romancers followed Guido.' (Scherer 1963 ch. 'The Fall of Troy', p.115-6)
Scherer points out that tales of marvellous automata had long been filtering through to medieval Europe from the east, fuelled by accounts of real marvels such as the roaring bronze lions, singing gilt birds and flying throne of the Byzantine emperors. These stories were picked up and embroidered still further by writers of fiction. Some medieval accounts of the fall of Troy kept to the original idea that the Horse held only a small company of commandos, who opened one of Troy's gates and lit a fire to act as a signal to the main Greek army (preserved for them in Virgil's 'Aeneid'). Others followed Guido delle Colonne and had the Horse hold a thousand men who are primarily responsible for the sack of Troy, though they do still summon the rest of the army. A missing section in the manuscript deprives us of the 'Destruction'-poet's version of the making of the horse, but it can hold a thousand men and is made of brass; the Laud-poet trims the scene of the construction of the horse considerably, but keeps the main points of its being able to hold a thousand men, and being made of brass (Benson 1980 Part 2 ch.IV, p 92; Laud lines 17995-18004).

A bronze horse is obviously closer to Tolkien's bronze and iron dragons than a wooden one, and the medieval versions have two further possible consequences relating them to Tolkien's version. Firstly, on purely practical grounds, it is easier to imagine a large number of people being accommodated in something dragon-shaped, which would resemble a railway train in arrangement, than in something horse-shaped. Like the medieval Troy-poets, Tolkien most often introduces an unexpected level of realism rather than relying on the marvellous or supernatural, so this motive for the change should not be ruled out. Secondly, a horse can under certain circumstances be equated to a dragon. In the second chapter of 'White Horses and Other Hill Figures' (first published 1949, reprinted Alan Sutton Publishing 1981), Morris Marples gives examples of dragon place-names associated with the Uffington White Horse and describes the intermittent debate as to whether the creature depicted on White Horse Hill is a horse or a dragon; one of his citations is from 1886, and we can be fairly certain that Tolkien knew the Uffington area with its famous horse.
Shippey points out that: 'As for the 'white horse on the green field' which is the emblem of the Mark you can see it cut into the chalk fifteen miles from Tolkien's

study, two miles from 'Wayland's Smithy' and just about on the borders of 'Mercia' and Wessex, as if to mark the kingdom's end.' (Shippey, 1992, ch.4, p.111-112) It would therefore be fairly easy for the medieval 'horse of brass' to become Tolkien's dragons: 'Those dragons of fire and those serpents of bronze and iron that fare already about the hill of the city...' (BOLT vol.II, ch.3, p.176)

It has often been suggested that these metallic dragons at the fall of Gondolin are a direct reflection of the dramatic and widely publicised early appearances of tanks in the First World War. However, there are major problems with this identification. Great War tanks carried only a tiny fighting crew; and few if any appear to have carried flamethrowers as weapons. Muzzle-blast from the main gun will not do, for two reasons; First World War tanks were turretless, carrying their weaponry in side-mounted bays; and dragons breathe fire, rather than spitting rocks. Furthermore 'armoured personnel carriers' would not appear until much later, after the Second World War in fact. Since the leading characteristics of Tolkien's dragons are that they are fiery and carry large numbers of orcs, they can hardly be tanks. Nor does the emphasis on their coiling and writhing movement suggest an armoured vehicle of any vintage. Even modern fast-moving tanks do not carry this kind of python-like suggestion; they are too compact, too blocky, more the armoured dinosaur than the snake. Early in the 20th century, descriptions of pythons and boas were a staple in boys' adventure tales set in Africa or South America; nor should we forget that Britain has two native snakes, and Tolkien's early acquaintance with the Lickey Hills and the coasts of Cornwall and Devon could easily have included an encounter with a snake. Plus being born in Bloemfontein, South Africa, his personal interest in the flora and fauna of that country and continent ought not to be dismissed too lightly - it has to be remembered that one of his earliest memories was of being bitter by a spider (Carpenter, 1977, Part 2, ch.1, p.21). Overall, then, it is far more likely that Tolkien's metallic dragons represent a steady imaginative extension of the 'brazen horse' idea through the practicalities of seating many people, by way of ideas about snakes, than that they are connected to tanks.

IX; The Fall of the City

a; Dates

Tolkien has the fall of Gondolin begin on the day of a seasonal festival, the Gates of Summer (BOLT vol.II, ch.3, p.172 and QS, ch.23, p. 292). This is highly unlikely to have been a random choice. A Classical chronological inscription, the so-called Parian marble, included an exact date for the fall of Troy before it was damaged in the English Civil War in the 17th century. Luckily, it had already been copied, so we know what its anonymous compiler had calculated. Working from astronomical calculations, and from synchronisms between Homer & the other epic poets and the legendary genealogy of the kings of Athens, the Parian Chronographer stated that Troy fell on a date equivalent to 5th June 1209 BC (Wood 1985 ch.1, p.28). Looked at from a British point of view, the beginning of

June is also effectively the beginning of summer, thanks to the skewed relationship between seasons and astronomy in North-Western Europe. So,Tolkien placed the date of the Fall of Gondolin at a time of year notably close to the date of the Fall of Troy. This is unlikely to be coincidence, because no other event in the 'Silmarillion' tradition has such a seasonal date. Every other event has only a year-number in one of the 'Annals' texts if it has a date at all. This is so even after we can be sure that Tolkien had invented the detailed Elvish calendars which appear in *The Lord of the Rings* and would allow more exact dating. The link between the fall of Gondolin and the Gates of Summer is, then, significant, and very probably does represent a link between Gondolin and Troy. By itself this is a small piece of evidence, but it is worth putting forward as one more link in the chain.

b; The Craven King

The behaviour of Turgon, King of Gondolin, when faced with the imminent disaster of the approach of Morgoth's armies, is also significant. He gives up the fight at a critical point: As is told in detail in BOLT: 'Then said the king: "Great is the fall of Gondolin," and men shuddered, for such were the words of Amnon the prophet of old, but Tuor speaking wildly for ruth and love of the king cried: "Gondolin stands yet, and Ulmo will not suffer it to perish!" Now were they at that time standing, Tuor by the Trees and the king upon the Stairs, as they had stood aforetime when Tuor spake the embassy of Ulmo. But Turgon said: "Evil have I brought upon the Flower of the Plain in despite of Ulmo, and now he leaveth it to wither in the fire. Lo! hope is no more in my heart for my city of loveliness, but the children of the Noldoli shall not be worsted for ever." Then did the Gondothlim clash their weapons, for many stood nigh, but Turgon said: "Fight not against Doom, oh my children! Seek ye who may safety in flight, if perhaps there be time yet: but let Tuor have your loyalty." But Tuor said: "Thou art king": and Turgon made answer: "Yet no blow will I strike more", and he cast his crown at the roots of Glingol. Then did Galdor who stood there pick it up, but Turgon accepted it not, and bare of head climbed to the topmost pinnacle of that white tower that stood nigh his palace.' (BOLT vol.II, ch.3, p.184-5)

In the medieval Trojan legends, a point arrives when Priam locks the gates of Troy and refuses to fight any more, because of the losses his people and his allies have suffered. The alliterative *Destruction* tells us that:

'Priam, for sorrow over his fine sons
Had no will to fight and no wish to pass the walls
He determined to wait for two months before taking any further action
[and] He swiftly commanded that the gates be guarded
The Trojans in that time, as the book says
[went] with great sorrow through the city, crying piteously
[They] had no hope of their finding safety; then their hearts failed
And they drooped with sorrow as if they would die
Agamemnon, by skilful men, sent word to the great [Priam}
Often, in truth, in that same time

Told him to send forth his soldiers, assemble on the field
and make ready for battle; or else yield his city
The noble [Priam] would not answer, for fear of what might happen
He had fallen into a deep dread of taking such chances, since his destiny seemed miserable
and in fear that his people would be utterly destroyed in battle
and also because he had hope of help soon
Of Amazons adventurous that followed their queen
That came to the city at the last moment [barely in time]
To help honourable Hector in war.'

(Panton & Donaldson 1968, bk.XXVII, lines 10788-10806) [Note 9]

This is one of three occasions at the end of Book XXVI in the middle of Book XXVII and at the start of Book XXVIII when Priam is said to despair in the alliterative *Destruction of Troy*. This matches Turgon's three refusals to lead the people of Gondolin at the height of the crisis (see above). The Middle English poets were translating from Guido delle Colonne's Latin, and they took various attitudes to this decision of Priam's, remarking on it as any historian might on someone's actions. The Laud-poet makes Agamemnon challenge Priam directly over his conduct, accusing him of cowardice and shameful behaviour:

'For such a king should ever despise
Such a display of cowardice
And lie not there like a pig in a sty
Acting like a villein.'

(Laud lines 15919-22, cited Benson 1980 Part 2 ch.IV, p.79) [Note 10]

Turgon's actions follow the pattern of Priam's inaction, but are more serious (and more spectacular) because Gondolin's gates have already been breached when Turgon refuses to continue to rule. He is in effect deserting the people of Gondolin in their hour of greatest need, whereas Priam still has his walls intact, and some hope of help. This scenario find a far more exact echo in Tolkien's work in the siege of Minas Tirith, which we will be discussing in detail in a later chapter.

c; The Toppling Tower of Gondolin

One of the notable events during the fall of Gondolin is the collapse of Turgon's tower: 'Yet even as they spake a great noise and a yelling rose form that place of anguish. Behold, the tower leapt into a flame and in a stab of fire it fell, for the dragons crushed the base of it and all who stood there. Great was the clangour of that terrible fall, and therein passed Turgon King of the Gondothlim, and for that hour the victory was to Melko.' (BOLT vol.II, ch.3, p.187)

This tower matches elements in the medieval descriptions of Troy. Guido delle Colonne says that:

'But King Priam, however, for the location of his dwelling and a site for his own mansion ordered the great and famous Ilium, as his great palace was called, to be constructed in a higher place of the city out of the towering native rock in the city. and the master fortress of great security which was hewn by force from this native

rock was glorious Ilium. From its foundation to the highest point which roofed it over in the shape of a sphere, its height reached a summit five hundred feet above the tops of the towers not far from it on the ramparts, which were themselves far higher than that same height.'
(Colonne/Meek 1974, bk.5, lines 170-183 & 202-211, pp.46-7)

Where Colonne has domes, the alliterative *Destruction* has towers:

'Enclosed by a separate wall thickly set all about with towers
perfectly circular like a ring richly made
full five hundred feet was their height.'

(Panton & Donaldson 1968, bk.V, lines 1634-6) [Note 11]
Tolkien's simplification to one tower appears to follow Homer, who refers on more than one occasion to 'the great tower of Ilion'. Something that was excitedly identified as this very tower was located by Schliemann's old assistant Dörpfeld when he took over excavations at Troy from 1893 onwards. The find was the remains of a massive and very well-built tower, next to the south gate of the city. It had also been a shrine to the gods of Troy, echoing a scene in Homer when Andromache goes to the tower instead of the temple of Apollo to pray for Hector's safety (Wood 1985 ch.2 p.89, & ch.4 p.143). The idea will reappear in *The Lord of the Rings*, in the White Tower of Ecthelion (itself a name from the tale of Gondolin) which crowns the Citadel of Minas Tirith. This is discussed in detail in a later chapter in this book.

Nothing like the toppling of Turgon's tower appears in the medieval versions of the Trojan story that we have looked at. Guido delle Colonne has a tower but it is not apparently destroyed in his version. A very similar set of events does however occur in Virgil's *Aeneid*. In Book 2, when Aeneas is describing the Fall of Troy to his Carthaginian hosts, he says that when he reached Priam's palace: 'The Trojans for their part were tearing down their towers and the roofs of their buildings. They saw the end was near, and these were the weapons they were preparing to defend themselves with in the very moment of death, rolling down on the heads of their enemies the gilded beams and richly ornamented ceilings of their ancestors. Down on the ground others were standing shoulder to shoulder with with drawn swords blocking the doorway. My spirit was renewed and I rushed to bring relief to the palace of our king, to help its defenders, to put heart into men who were defeated.

There was a forgotten entrance at the rear, a secret doorway entering into a passage which joined the different parts of Priam's palace. While the kingdom of Troy still stood, poor Andromache often used to come this way unattended to visit Hector's parents, taking her son Astyanax to visit his grandfather. I slipped through this door and climbed to the highest gable of the roof, from where the doomed Trojans were hurling down missiles. There was a tower rising sheer towards the stars from the top of the palace roof, from which we used to look out over the whole of Troy, the Greek fleet and the camp of the Achaeans. We set about this tower and worked round it with iron bars where there was a joint we could open up above the top floor of the palace. Having loosened it from its deep bed in the walls, we rocked it and suddenly sent it toppling, spreading instant destruction and crushing great columns of the Greeks. But others still came on and the hail of rocks and other missiles never slackened.

In the portico in front of the palace, on the very threshold, Pyrrhus, son of Achilles, whom men also call Neoptolemus, was rampaging and the light flashed on the bronze of his weapons. He was like a snake which has fed on poisonous herbs and hidden all winter in the cold earth, but now it emerges into the light, casts its slough and is renewed. Glistening with youth, it coils its slithering back and lifts its breast high to the sun with its triple tongue flickering from its mouth.' (Virgil trans West, 1990/2003, Book 2, p.37-8)

Aeneas is alone; he can bring little 'relief' to the defenders of the palace, whereas in Tuor's case he brings real help for the defenders in the shape of both his troops and Ecthelion's. In Virgil's poem, it is the Trojans themselves who overturn their tower, whereas Tolkien has the tower brought down apparently by the enemy, but the result is the same; many of the enemy are killed, though it is already too late to make a difference. Tolkien's dragons are real, even if metallic, whereas Virgil's serpent is figurative, but the same motif appears in the same place in the *Aeneid* as in *The Fall of Gondolin*. Virgil's references to the bronze of Pyrrhus/Neoptolemus' weapons, and to the high-coiling snake reaching skyward, are also echoed in Tolkien's description.

d;The Women of Gondolin

It is worth noting further in this connection that Virgil emphasises the plight of the women in the palace: '...inside all was confusion and lamentation, and deep into the house the hollow chambers rang with the wailing of women, and their cries rose to strike the golden stars. Frightened mothers were wandering through the great palace, clinging to the doorposts and kissing them... I saw Hecuba with a hundred women, her daughters and the wives of her sons.' (Virgil trans West, 1990/2003, Book 2, p.39)

Ovid too uses the women of Troy as potent symbols of the city's plight:

'...Dragged by the hair
Apollo's priestess [Cassandra] stretched her hands to heaven
In vain appeal. Embracing while they might
The statues of their country's gods, the wives
Of Troy crowded the burning shrines, until
The Greeks in triumph carried them away,
Their bitter prize.
(Ovid/Melville/Kenney 1986, bk.XIII, lines 410-16)

This motif of the piteous state of the women is also a major element in Tolkien's description of the parallel scenes in Gondolin:

'Thereby he rescued many bands of captives and gathered no few wandering and driven men, and so got to the King's Square with hard fighting; and men were fain to greet him for they had feared him dead. Now are all the women and children that had gathered there or been brought in by Egalmoth stowed in the king's halls, and the ranks of the houses made ready for the last...

Then did men speak of a sally, and were of two minds. Many held that it were impossible to burst through, nor might they even so get over the plain or through the hills, and that it were better therefore to die about the king. But Tuor might not think well of the death of so many fair women and children, were it at the hands of their own folk in the last resort, or by the weapons of the enemy, and he spake of the delving and the secret way...

Then because of the wailing of the women in the halls of the palace and the greatness of his pity for that sad remainder of the peoples of Gondolin, he gathered all that rueful company, maids, children and mothers, and setting them amidmost marshalled as well as he might his men around them.'

(BOLT vol. II, ch.3, pp. 183 & 185-6)

On the one hand, it must be a near certainty that after his grammar-school education with its emphasis on the Latin and Greek 'classics' (which were after all the subject that won him his undergraduate place at Oxford University), Tolkien knew the *Aeneid* so well that the odd reminiscence is almost unavoidable. On the other hand we have scrutinised the *Aeneid* closely and the number of points at which it resembles anything in Tolkien's work is very small. Yet most of those points are of potentially considerable significance: the passage relating to the fall of Turgon's tower; the passage which seems to adumbrate the dispute between Ossë and Ulmo, and indeed Ulmo's dispute with the other gods; the swans that Venus mentions when she is trying to cheer up Aeneas on his way to Carthage which could be taken as a source for Tuor's swans; the escape and further adventures of Helenus son of Priam. This leaves us with the awkward situation of having a book which Tolkien was not using very often at all, yet which when it does crop up is important. Such a situation is certainly not inconsistent with the possibility that Tolkien might have been using the *Aeneid* from memory, and specifically, from his recall of particular passages that caught his attention and stuck in his mind, not necessarily even with their author's name attached to them. Another possibility which ought to be raised that these ideas are also to be found elsewhere, in some work which could be acting as a common source for Virgil and Tolkien, such as the Greek 'Epic Cycle' of poems about Troy. Though these 6th/7th century BC pieces have survived to modern times only in summaries, the process might just have preserved exactly those 'high points' which Tolkien and Virgil seem to share (Scherer 1963, Appendix I). It is undeniably simpler however to assume direct if exceedingly scanty influence of the *Aeneid* on Tolkien.

e; The Children of Heroes

The towers of Troy reappear in another passage relating to the fall of Gondolin, this time from Ovid's *Metamorphoses* :

'Astyanax was hurled
Down from the turret whence he'd often watched
(His mother pointing) his great father fight
To save the ancestral city and himself.'

(Ovid/Melville/Kenney 1986, bk.XIII, lines 416-19)

Astyanax was the son of Hector and Andromache in Homer and most classical sources, which said that the boy was killed by the Greeks after being taken captive in the fall of the city, and that he was thrown from the walls of Troy. Ovid shifts the scene specifically to a tower, from where mother and son had often watched the battles before Troy. There are very probably two influences of this idea in the Tale of Gondolin. First, the house of Tuor and Idril was:

'built for him [Tuor] upon the southern wall. for he loved the free airs and liked not the close neighbourhood of other dwellings. There it was his delight often to stand on the battlements at dawn, and folk rejoiced to see the new light catch the wings of his helm...' (BOLT vol. II, ch. 3, p.164), echoing the idea of a mother and son watching events from the tower or turret upon the walls of Troy.

Secondly, Maeglin intends to kill Eärendil by throwing him from the walls of Gondolin. Idril says to Tuor: 'Lo! I dreamed on a night that Meglin builded a furnace, and coming at us unawares flung therein Eärendel our babe, and would after thrust in thee and me; but for that sorrow at the death of our fair child I would not resist.' (ibid, p.167)

However, in Tolkien's story Eärendil does not die as does Astyanax, but is saved in the nick of time by Tuor, and it is Meglin who is hurled to his death - mirroring the death of his own father Eöl:

'Now then Meglin had Idril by the hair and sought to drag her to the battlements out of cruelty of heart, that she might see the fall of Eärendel to the flames; but he was cumbered by that child, and she fought, alone as she was, like a tigress for all her beauty and slenderness. There he now struggles and delays amid oaths while that folk of the Wing draw nigh - and lo! Tuor gives a shout so great that the Orcs hear it afar and waver at the sound of it. Like a crash of tempest the guard of the Wing were amid the men of the Mole, and these were stricken asunder. When Meglin saw this he would stab Eärendel with a short knife he had; but that child bit his left hand, that his teeth sank in, and he staggered, and stabbed weakly, and the mail of the small coat turned the blade aside; and thereupon Tuor was upon him and his wrath was terrible to see. He seized Meglin by that hand that held the knife and broke the arm with the wrench, and then taking him by the middle leapt with him upon the walls, and flung him far out. Great was the fall of his body, and it smote Amon Gwareth three times ere it pitched in the midmost of the flames; and the name Meglin has gone out in shame from among Eldar and Noldoli.' (ibid, p.178)

In this scene, Tolkien is following the medieval Trojan legend in which the son of Hector survives, rather than the Classical story in which the child perishes.

X; The Exiles' Tale

We would like to take some time to consider who survives the fall of Troy and also the fall of Gondolin.

In the *Aeneid*, it is Aeneas himself, his father Anchises and his son Iulus who escape; his wife Creusa is lost in the flight from the city and though he goes back, he cannot find her; only her ghost appears and tells him to carry on with his life. Helenus son of Priam escapes in unstated circumstances and spectacularly repairs his fortunes by becoming a king in Greece; Andromache wife of Hector survives being enslaved and taken as a concubine by Pyrrhus/Neoptolemus son of Achilles, to whom she bears three children while his Greek wife is barren; after Pyrrhus /Neoptolemus dies, Andromache marries Helenus.

In the medieval Trojan versions, Aeneas, Antenor and all their households survive - being traitors whom the Greeks have agreed to spare. From Priam's family, the priest and prophet Helenus, Andromache wife of Hector, and her young son Laomedon the Less all survive; Laomedon subsequently becomes a king in Greece and frees the enslaved Trojans there.

From the sack of Gondolin there are survivors, and some who are kin to the king of the city just as in the Trojan legends. Neither pattern is an exact match for the escape of Tuor, his wife Idril and their son Eärendil from Gondolin; the second case is somewhat closer in that it is members of the royal family including the direct and indirect heirs to the throne who escape the fall of the city. There are also reminiscences of the *Aeneid* however, when Tuor has to go looking for Idril just as Aeneas searches for Creusa, and when after the escape proper, Tuor sees Eärendil being carried on the shoulders of one of his companions (and in danger of being left behind when they are attacked) just as Anchises is carried on Aeneas' shoulders.

'Behold then at the clearing of the airs they saw, but a few furlongs off, a knot of men that fled on foot, and these were pursued by a strange cavalry, for on great wolves rode Orcs, as they thought, brandishing spears. Then said Tuor: "Lo! there is Eärendel my son; behold, his face shineth as a star in the waste... for the wolfriders were scattering them piecemeal, and the child was upon the shoulders of one Hendor, a house-carl of Idril's, and he seemed like to be left with his burden.' (BOLT vol. II, ch. 3, p.190)

It is the exiles who escape from Gondolin who transmit the knowledge of the fall of that city - from Tuor to Eärendel to his son Elrond who tells Bilbo Baggins at Rivendell, and so we have the 'Translations from the Elvish' in the Red Book of Westmarch. This may be compared to the account of Dares Phyrgius in the Welsh which appears in the Red Book of Hergest.

The sons of the survivors of Troy found kingdoms; Ascanius son of Aeneas in Italy; Laomedon son of Hector in Thessaly. Tolkien appears to break this pattern, for in the 1977 *Silmarillion* it is Elros son of Eärendil who is the first king of Númenor, not Eärendil himself. However, in *The War of the Ring*, in one of the drafts for the 'Ithilien' chapters of LotR, Tolkien says: '... and Earendel himself, the half-elven, first king of Westernesse.' (HOME vol.VIII, Part Two, chV, p.155). Tolkien said the same thing again later (ibid, p.158 & n.26 p.168) and subsequently changed it to the more familiar form with Elros as first king. It is most unlikely that this is an inadvertent slip, as the commentary suggests, since Earendel as first king of Númenor is an exact match for the Trojan pattern. He could have been both guiding star and king for his people.

Geoffrey of Monmouth has the people of Britain derive from the Trojans - and therefore the tale of the Fall of Troy is integral to the history of the peoples of

Britain. There would seem to be a set of parallels that run as follows:
Gondolin - Havens of Sirion - Tol Eressëa
Troy - Italy - Britain
In BOLT, Tol Eressëa and Britain become the same place, doubling and paralleling the story of Britain's Trojan founders as told by Geoffrey of Monmouth and by Guido delle Colonne;
'Afterward certain other provinces received from among the Trojans an enduring settlement. Such is England, which we read was settled by the Trojan, Brutus, which is why it is called Britain.' (Colonne/Meek 1974, bk.2, ll.28-31, p.10)
It is passages like this that make it to be greatly regretted that we have been unable to obtain a copy of the one edition of Guido's work which Tolkien could certainly have read before writing the *Book of Lost Tales*, Caxton's *Recuyell of the History of Troy*, (an English translation of a French translation, which might itself introduce the sort of distinctive mistakes that, if picked up by the next author in a chain, can identify sources and create new ideas in the bygoing) which was edited and published in the early 20th Century. Delle Colonne's book itself, though there had been numerous editions and translations from the 15th-17th centuries, was not given modern publication until 1936. It would be exceedingly interesting to try to work out how much Tolkien might have taken from Guido delle Colonne and how much from Geoffrey of Monmouth, but without the *Recuyell* this simply cannot be done.

If Troy may be equated with Gondolin, who would be the equivalent of the saviour figure Eärendil who survived the Fall of the city and brought the help of the Valar to Beleriand? If one follows the logic of Geoffrey of Monmouth, then one might draw the conclusion that it would be King Arthur. This whole matter will be revisited in a later book.

A final point about the battle for the cities that can be made is this: The anonymous poet of the 'Laud Troy Book describes the fighting before Troy as the greatest battle before Doomsday, fought by the best warriors ever assembled. (Lines 35-42, cited Benson 1980 Part 2 ch.IV, p.77) Tolkien describes in BOLT the hosts of Melko in a similar fashion:
'Then on a time Melko assembled all his most cunning smiths and sorcerors, and of iron and flame they wrought a host of monsters such as have only at that time been seen and shall not again be till the Great End.' (BOLT vol. II, ch. 3, p.170)

XI; Overall Conclusions

J.R.R. Tolkien's story of *The Fall of Gondolin* centres on a much altered yet still recognisable version of the medieval Tale of Troy, in which the besieged Trojans are the heroes. His use of this material when writing the first known version of the story of Gondolin in 1916-17 need involve only reasonable memory of one text - one version of the medieval Tale of Troy. We can be certain that Tolkien had considerable knowledge of more than one such piece, as explained in chapter one. A context therefore exists in which Tolkien would have known about this material before writing his story of Gondolin. Like the other *Book of Lost Tales* stories, *The Fall of Gondolin* was revised (once heavily, once more sporadically) while this particular project was still Tolkien's chosen framework. Both revisions probably happened in 1919, and therefore at a point when Tolkien was back in Oxford, working for the Oxford English Dictionary, and so would have been able to consult books to refresh his memory or to suggest ideas which could be applied to the new circumstances of his own story, if he wished to do so. As for the properly Classical material, which though a much less important source - and one not certainly incorporated until after the War - is nonetheless present, a onetime grammar-school student who went to Oxford to read Classics must have virtually known by heart both the *Iliad* and the *Aeneid*. We should remember that as an undergraduate, Tolkien would almost certainly not have been thinking about trying to turn either the classical or the medieval Troy-story into a new piece of his own. That most probably only happened when Tolkien began to write in 1916 or thereabouts, under very different circumstances. In the story of *The Fall of Gondolin*, another major element, the Eärendel story (which is discussed in the following chapter) is linked with this Trojan material through the long-standing 'untied thread' of the survivors of Troy.

Of the medieval sources involved which we have been able to examine, the most important appear to be the alliterative *Destruction* and the Latin prose *History of the Destruction of Troy* by the Sicilian judge and writer, Guido delle Colonne. The former was published by the Early English Text Society in 1869-74 and appears likely to be the largest influence of the BOLT *Fall of Gondolin* ; the latter did not appear in a modern edition until 1936, but this is still early enough for it to have influenced both the later versions of the Tale of Gondolin in the 1937 Silmarillion and 1950's 'Tuor', and *The Lord of the Rings* (of which more later). Tolkien could also have known Guido's work at an earlier date through the older editions and translations, most notably Caxton's *Recuyell of the History of Troy*, an English translation of a French translation of delle Colonne which was several times republished in the late 19th and early 20th centuries. It is worth noting that all the passages in Guido delle Colonne's book which bear striking resemblances to Tolkien's writing appear in the first half of the work. References to the alliterative *Destruction* are more widely spread through that poem, but they are still biassed in favour of the earlier parts. Firstly, by the time Tolkien reached the later stages of his own story he may have become more confident in developing new ideas out of the situation he had already created. Secondly, there may be a source which we have either not been able to track down or not been able to obtain and read. Caxton's *Recuyell of the History of Troy*, for instance, is currently unavailable though the British Library lending system. There is also a version of 'Dares and Dictys' (the Trojan historical forgers) in the great Welsh medieval manuscript now in Oxford, the *Red Book of Hergest*, and an edition of this was published before the First World War. Welsh 'translations' are often very free with their original, so this version may contain important motifs which are missing from the sources we have looked at. Tolkien's command of Welsh in general and Old Welsh in particular was far better than we usually think (Letters, no.2; and discussed in detail in our next book), so he could have made use of this.

Compared to the Tale of Troy, Tolkien polarises the political situation around Gondolin, reducing the enemy to a faceless horde with a very few named members - e.g. Gothmog the balrog and orc champions such as Orcobal. None of these characters ever speak, apart from Morgoth - and that very briefly. Tolkien does this to increase the dramatic tension by polarising the two sides and creating more risk and more empathy for the folk of Gondolin. In the Classical story, there is little or nothing to choose between Greeks and Trojans; they have the same kinds of names, they appear to speak the same language, and they worship the same gods in the same way. Greeks and Trojans are related by blood as well as knowing each other by reputation. So Troy may be at risk, but this is no major fight between the forces of good and evil, there is no great clash of ideologies. We hear the tale from both sides, see characters both Trojan and Greek wrestling with their legitimate problems. Not so in Tolkien - we only know anything about the people of Gondolin. Morgoth and his supporters are all classed as thoroughly evil and bent on destruction and enslavement.

Similarly on a higher level, the Trojan legends have the Olympiad split in their loyalties between Troy and Mycenae - there are no 'good' or 'bad' Gods. The end is foretold, but for instance Thetis and Athena are rooting for the Greeks, and Venus and Hera are supporting the Trojans. In contrast, Tolkien has the Valar on the one side who are all good/indifferent and one bad Vala, i.e. Melko/Morgoth who is responsible for all the ill that happens. By altering the balance of good versus evil and polarising it in this way, Tolkien creates a far tenser storyline. A more 'modern' story, one might suggest.

Hereunder we give the original Middle English text of the poems:

Note 1:

'All merknet the mountens & mores about'

(Panton & Donaldson 1968, bk.XVII, line 7350)

Note 2:

'Your seluyn sothely asayet haue before
I told you neuer tale in tyme that is past
But ye faithfully haue found it fore as I said.
Therefore putte of this purpos; let Paris not go
On no wise in this world, for woo that may happyn
I say you for certen, and it so worthe,
That Paris be put furthe his purpose to hold,
Gird vp into Grese, & any grem wirke;
This Cite full solempne sesit be then
With the Grekes to ground gird under fote
And we exiled for euer; this Aunter shall falle.'

(Panton & Donaldson 1968 bk.VI lines 2489-99)

Note 3:

'A! nobyll men of nome, what noyes your hertes?
Why are ye troublit this time, and your tung lost?
And meuyt so mykell, for a mad priste
That neuer colde of no knighthood, but in a kirk chyde?'

(Panton & Donaldson 1968 bk.VI lines 2526-9)

Note 4:

'But I may say sothely, & for sure holde, -
Hade the counsell ben kept of the knight Ector
and the Ernest speche eftward of Elinus the bysshop,
Cassandras care considret with all
With the prophesy of Protheus put into hertys
Troy with thi toures had bene a toune noble
And wond in his weile to the worldes ende.'

(Panton & Donaldson 1968 bk.VI lines 2711-5)

Note 5:

'Yet meruelt hom more ymyddes the halle
Was a tre, that was triet, al of tru gold
Meruelous and mekyll men to be-hold.
The bole was of bright gold, bret to the myddes,
Largior then a lawriall and lengur with all
(XIJ cubettes by course all of clene heght)
That fourmyt was full faire to the fre boghes.
The brede of his boghes borly to se,
Large and longe (light as the sun)
Ffro the dese to the dore doblit on brede
And the sydys by a sercle of the same halle.
The braunches were borly, sum of bright gold,
Sum siluer for sothe, senlist of hue
With leuys full luffly, light of the same;
With burians aboue bright to be holde;
And frut on it formyt fairest of shap,
Of mony kynd that was kuyt, knagged aboue,
That shemert as shire as ony shere stonys.'

(Panton & Donaldson 1968, book XII lines 4958-74).

Note 6:

'Before the dore was set a tre
That fair and semely was to se:
The tre was al of riche gold
Fro the ground vnto the mold,
And all the bowes of that erberye
Were siluer & gold with-outen lye;

For euere was on of siluer bry3t
A-nother of gold that was so ly3t.
Ther was neuer fruyt that euere grewe
That thei ne hongen ther in here hewe,
But al was siluer and gold with-Inne
This werk was mad with quaynte ginne.'

(Laud Troy Book, lines 9529-40)

Note 7:

'Polidarius was pluccid as a porke fat
ffull grete in the grippe, all of grese hoge.
So bolnet was his body, that burthen hade ynoghe
The fete of that freke to ferke hym aboute,
Or stond vppo streght for his strong charge. (3837-41)'

(Cited Benson 1980 Part 2 ch.III, p.51)

Note 8:

'THE DETHE OF AIAX BY PARIS SLAYNE.'
'Paris (with) pyne was pricket at his hert
To se his men so be-mard & murtherit to dethe,
With the birr of his bowe & a big arow
That put was in poison, he pairet his armur
Rut thurgh his rybbes, rent him with in
That all backonet his blode, and his ble chaungit
Than feld wele the freike that he fey was
And ded of the dynt or the day past.'
'THE DETHE OF PARIS BY AIAX SLAYNE.'
'He presit vnto Paris in his pale angur
And as he faght in the feld, to the freike said
"Paris, thou prestly hath put me to dethe
And shent me with shot of thy sharp geire
But I degh of thy dint, and damp into helle
Thou shall first go before and fraite of our way
Hit is reason and right for thi ranke loue
that thou part now with pyne fro thi prise elan
that is cause of this care, and this cold angur
And mony doghty ben dede of Dukes and Knightes."
Then he bere to the buerne with a bigge sworde
Hurlyt thurgh the helme and the hard chekys
And he girt to the ground & the gost yalde;
Euyn ded of the dynt, deiret no mo.
Than Aiax also, angardly swithe
Ffel of his fole, flat to the erthe
Ffor payne of his pale wound passit o lyue
Euyn ded of the dynt, & to dole went.'

(Panton & Donaldson 1968, book XXVI, lines 10700 - 10726)

Note 9:

'Priamus, for pite of his pure sons
Hade no wille for to weire, ne the wallis pas.
Two monethis with might, ere he meue wold
The yates to yeme he yepely comaundit.
The troiens in the tyme, as the text sais
with myche sorow in the Cite, sobbyng unfaire
Hade no hope of there hele; than there hert failet
And thai drepit with dole, as thei degh shuld
Agamemnon, by graith men, to the gret send
Oft-sythes, for sothe, in the same tyme
Bade him send forth his soudiouris, assemble to feld
And buske unto batell, or his burgh yelde.
The noble hym denyet for noy that might happon
He drede him full depely for desteny feble
Lest his folke in the feld were fynally destroyet;
And for hope that he hade of a help sone.
Of Amysones auntrus atlet the qwene
that was born to the burghe in the bare tyme
Honerable Ector in armes to helpe.'

(Panton & Donaldson 1968, bk.XXVII, lines 10788-10806)

Note 10:

'For suche a kyng schulde euere dispice,
For that was token of cowardise;
And ligge not ther as an hog In sty,
For that was to him a vilony.'

(Laud lines 15919-22, cited Benson 1980 Part 2 ch.IV, p.79)

Note 11:

'Closit with a clene wall crustrit [properly clustrit] with towres
Euyn round as a ryng richely wroght -
ffyue hundrith fete fully the heght; -'

(Panton & Donaldson 1968, bk.V, lines 1634-6)

Chapter Three:

Lost Tales, Found Manuscripts.

I; Introduction

There is one major question still outstanding with the writings which are bound up with the medieval tradition which is best dealt with here. What on earth was a Second Lieutenant of Signals doing, writing this sort of thing in 1916? A story about Elves in a legendary place involved in mythical battles seems Quixotic to say the least. Was Tolkien just a romantic dreamer who somehow contrived to sleepwalk through the Somme without noticing what was going on around him, coming out so untouched from World War One that he could still write about fairies and heroes? Or is there a possible reason within the context of the Great War why he might have written as he did? The relationship of *The Book of Lost Tales* to the literature of its time is a subject which deserves exploration in depth some day, but we will here attempt to summarise the state of the matter as it refers specifically to *The Fall of Gondolin* and as it appears to us right now. For with the connections to the medieval tradition and the Matter of Troy as we have shown in the preceding chapters, the whole idea of what Tolkien was doing deserves to be revisited. It throws a completely different light upon the man and the driving forces behind his early works.

Right at the start of his biographical study of Tolkien during the First World War, John Garth begins by asking a simple question:

'This biographical study arose from a single observation: how strange it is that J.R.R. Tolkien should have embarked upon his monumental mythology in the midst of the First World War, the crisis of disenchantment that shaped the modern era.' (Garth 2003, Great War, Preface, p. xiii)

This chapter will attempt to lay bare some of the connections and the reasoning behind Tolkien's choice of subject area and begin to help open up Garth's valid question in some very intriguing and unusual ways.

II; Beginnings

To begin to try and answer the question of why Tolkien wrote what he did in 1916, we need to forget everything we think we know about Tolkien's writings and approach the area with an open mind. The *Tale of Tuor and the Exiles of Gondolin (which leadeth into the great tale of Eärendel)*, better known to us as *The Fall of Gondolin*, was the very first of the 'Lost Tales' to be written. According to Christopher Tolkien in his introduction to the story in BOLT vol.II (ch. 3, pp.146-7), the original text dated to 1916-17 and was written in pencil in two 'school exercise-books'. This was then revised in ink, the more so the further into the tale Tolkien went. It appears that this revision 'was by no means a complete recasting (still less a reimagining)' but understandably (since the pencil text was largely destroyed by the re-writing) no detailed comparison isundertaken, and no clear idea can now be formed of exactly what J.R.R. Tolkien was doing in this revision. From the ink text, a fair copy was made and on this in turn a certain amount of revision was done, which definitely relates to Tolkien's reading of the story to the Exeter College Essay Club early in 1920. Although neither the ink revision nor the fair copy are themselves dated, the association with the Exeter College reading, and the introduction of concepts certainly dating to Tolkien's immediate post-war period when he was working for the Oxford English Dictionary, would suggest that both the revision on the original text and the copy made from it date to 1919.

Given all this we can confidently say that the initial creation of the tale of Gondolin lies right outside not only 'Middle-earth' (a concept probably not properly in place until the end of the 1940's if not the early 50's; see Lewis & Currie 2002, Realms of Inspiration, pp.81-180) but also the 'Beleriandic' scenario of the pre-*Lord of the Rings* 'Silmarillion'-tradition. None of that existed when Tolkien first wrote his tale of the hidden city with seven names. There was no landscape, no map, no story, no peoples, and while there were languages, they did not have anything like the context that Quenya and Sindarin were to find forty-odd years later in the far better known texts surrounding *The Lord of the Rings*. There may be direct links, there may be identical words, but the meanings of words let alone the significance of the languages cannot be assumed to be the same any more than major characters first introduced in drafts of *The Lord of the Rings* are the same as the published versions. Merely by examining the twelve volumes of 'The History of Middle earth' that much becomes clear at once. The revision of *The Fall of Gondolin* undertaken in about 1919 undoubtedly introduced names and concepts developed in the course of writing the other 'Lost Tales' and strengthened or created links between them. However, Christopher Tolkien's account of the work makes it clear that the main run of the story was in place, so far as can be told, from the beginning: 'the narrative itself underwent very little change of note in the course of this history'. In turn, that strongly suggests that, whatever later elaboration was added, *The Fall of Gondolin* was still rooted where it all began; the concepts evolved in it were the ones that helped set the mould for the whole *Book of Lost Tales* project. No later idea or concept - especially no idea dating to after the 'Lost Tales' - should be imposed on this piece without very good reason.

Moreover, we would do well to remember that *The Fall of Gondolin* was composed under extreme circumstances. The First World War was in progress; the War Office's demands for men and materials were insatiable. Tolkien was on sick-leave, invalided home thanks to 'trench fever'; at any time he could have been declared well enough to be sent back into action. He had already lost most of his closest friends in the old 'TCBS' group, and while his chances as a signals officer were somewhat better than those of someone with a line command, the life expectancy of anyone with Tolkien's rank was not good. While (contrary to White's unauthorised biography) he was not supposed to be directly involved in the fighting, Tolkien must have known all too well that on the Western Front, no-

one was safe. Long-range shelling by the Germans and short-range mistakes by the British, not to mention newfangled aircraft with bombs and guns, made the whole area near and behind the front exceedingly dangerous.
Tolkien's close friend G.B. Smith had after all been killed in December 1916 by shrapnel that struck him while he was walking down a road in a village behind the lines (Carpenter 1977, Part II, ch.8, p.93). We may have no direct evidence, but there is every likelihood that Tolkien would have felt he had scant chance of surviving a second stint at the Front. In turn, this means that there can be little doubt that *The Fall of Gondolin* was written by a man who felt as if the sword of Damocles was hanging over him; and very probably written, therefore, at speed, with little if any reference to books. Later revision could change much, but the whole course of the story must have been set in the earliest stages of writing.

III; Great Wars compared

So why Troy? Why, in the middle of the First World War, after one of its grisliest battles, would Tolkien turn to a medieval version of a Classical legend and turn it into a fairy story?

a; An Untraditional War?

Firstly, there is a general misconception which we have to get out of the way. This is the idea that it is simply impossible to understand or represent the First World War in any traditional literary or artistic form. That idea runs like a thread through every account of the impact of the Great War on English culture which we have examined. It is the primary thesis of the two most important such works, P. Fussell's 'The Great War and Modern Memory (1975) and S. Hymes's 'A War Imagined; the First World War and English Culture (1990). J. Stallworthy in 'Anthem for Doomed Youth' (2002) is far more alive to the foreshadowings of the First World War in earlier conflicts (especially the Boer War) and their associated literature, but he still barely recognises the idea of 'no tradition can work' as a thesis which can or even should be re-examined. The trouble with all this is that it is very obvious from these same writers' works that to say 'tradition cannot cope with the First World War' is to distort that tradition for a reason. The people who first came up with this saying were setting up a straw bear which Modernism (in the broadest sense) could easily defeat, without ever going near the all-too-real rough, surly creature called tradition that was snoring in its cave. 'Traditional forms' can cope with almost anything in the recorded history of mankind - *if* they are allowed to, *if* applicability and imagination are allowed to work with them. The writers who declared that the 'tradition' could not cope with the situation were people who had already moved away in new directions; they did not *want* to use any sort of 'traditional form', and it was an easy way out to say that such forms *could not* be used in the new, modern context. It also offered a powerful weapon against anyone who tried, since 'could not' can all too easily be transformed into 'should not'. Tradition was, as far as the modernists were concerned, dead and buried. In a sense, this was a parallel to Nietzsche's declaration that 'God is dead' (specifically: 'God is dead: but considering the state of the species Man is in, there will perhaps be caves, for ages yet, in which his shadow will be shown' - Die fröliche Wissenschaft (1882) Book 3, section 130). This in a deep sense underpins the whole Modernist movement in the twentieth century. For a long time Tolkien has been considered a 'shadow' or remnant of the old 'traditional approach' by critics over-influenced by 'modernism', and therefore instantly dismissed.

If we look specifically at the *Iliad* , poems invoking Homer in the context of Gallipoli or the Western Front can be 'naive' or silly only if we assume that the *Iliad* has one single meaning - that it is aristocratic, 'heroic', and glorifies war, *and does nothing else.* The moment anyone takes a wider view, the instant they read the last few books of the *Iliad* and consider the range of meanings which can be ascribed to the conduct of Achilles and Priam over Hector's dead body, that 'single interpretation' hypothesis becomes untenable - and if it is not true, then neither is the idea that the *Iliad* cannot possibly have any relevance to the First World War. Homer *does* look at the pity, horror and folly of war, as well as its splendour, glory and spoils. This is the truth of the matter. His world is one which can and does question the rights and wrongs of its own ideology; his heroes are not mindless bronze-clad monsters, but men with all humanity's potential and all its foolishness. Therefore, it is possible to select from the rich tapestry of the *Iliad* the threads which match the darker colours of the Great War. It is something which we believe had a deep impact upon Tolkien's writings.

If we move from simple critical reading of the *Iliad* to the wider realms of applicability and imagination, the situation becomes even less tenable for the anti-traditionalists. Is the Trojan War the story of a few heroic and fast-moving battles, quickly followed by the sack of a city - the pattern most 'Homer doesn't fit the First World War' theorists seem to assume? Or is it the tale of a seemingly endless conflict, with most of the Greek army locked in static warfare across a stretch of disputed terrain between their defences and those of Troy in which the number of lives lost on both sides is very high indeed, while the rest of the Greeks steadily reduce the surrounding countryside to a wasteland of sacked towns and burnt-out farms, and their High Command looks ever more foolish as it ties itself in knots with petty arguments (and more serious ones - such as the challenge of the leadership of Agamemnon) - where established patterns of combat fail to bring success, until technical innovation and underhanded behaviour finally create a breakthrough? That is applicability in action, interpreting the *Iliad* in a way that does make it relevant to the Great War; but to make such an interpretation requires imagination and a willingness to work within the tradition. 'Modernist' writers and critics did not (and do not) *want* to work in such a way within the tradition of English literature. This is of course their right; but they should not restrict the equal right of others to choose different options, as has too often been the case. They especially should not do so when it blunts and limits our appreciation of the driving forces behind such an important literary figure as Tolkien. Basically, 'modernism' is one possibility, not all things to all art, and 'traditionalism' as championed by Tolkien is still valid.

Secondly, Tolkien had a grammar-school education and initially went to Oxford University to study Classics - Greek and Latin language and literature. It was not until virtually the end of his second year that Tolkien gave up Classics to concentrate upon philology: '... he had achieved a 'pure alpha', a practically faultless paper, in his special subject, Comparative Philology.... and Exeter College took note... At the beginning of the summer term of 1913 he abandoned Classics and began to read English.' (Carpenter, 1977, Part 2, ch.6, pps.70-1)
In consequence Tolkien must both have known his Homer extremely well, and shared in the attitudes which put the Greeks in general and Homer's poetry in particular very close to the centre of contemporary British culture. It is important to understand that because of the existence of the medieval Trojan material, much of Tolkien's interest in the Trojan *story* could have survived his increasing interest in the Medieval and northern rather than the Classical and southern, which was reflected in his switch from Classics to English whilst he was an undergraduate at Oxford University. John Garth says that;
'It is possible that his [Tolkien's] unconventional tastes in Germanic literature gave him a different view of war from that of most contemporaries. Embracing the culture of the ancient European North, Tolkien turned his back enthusiastically on the Classics that had nurtured his generation at school. They had become romantically entangled with Victorian triumphalism; in the words of one commentator, 'As the long, prosperous years of the Pax Britannica succeeded one another, the truth about war was forgotten, and in 1914 young officers went into battle with the *Iliad* in their backpacks and the names of Achilles and Patroclus engraved upon their hearts.' But the names on Tolkien's heart now were Beowulf and Beorhtnoth... He [Tolkien] had become more entrenched, if anything, in his boyhood view that 'though as a whole the Northern epic has not the charm and delight of the Southern, yet in a certain bare veracity it excels it'. Homer's *Iliad* is in part a catalogue of violent deaths, but it is set in a warm world where seas are sunlit, heroes become demigods , and the rule of the Olympians is unending. The Germanic world was chillier and greyer. It carried a burden of pessimism, and final annihilation awaited *Middangeard* (Middle-earth) and its gods.'
(Garth 2003, Great War, ch.2, p.42-3)

Every point that John Garth makes here about the differences between the Germanic and the Classical myths is covered by the medieval version of the Trojan legend. Unconcerned with accuracy, medieval authors move their scene so that Troy is surrounded with northern European 'mountains and moors'; storms at sea are visualised in terms befitting the North Sea or the Atlantic (though in truth the Aegean can be as bad as either). Christians themselves, the medieval authors make it clear that the Trojans and Greeks are both pagans worshipping false gods whose time will pass; they put the blame for Troy's fall on Hector's overmastering pride just as the author of the *Battle of Maldon* blames Beorhtnoth and his *ofermod* for the Viking victory. Shippey assumes that *ofermod* is a uniquely Northern quality or sentiment (Shippey, 2000, ch.VI, p.294-5) but in actual fact it is operating in the same way between Hector and Ajax Telamonius as we have previously shown. Guido delle Colonne, and to a lesser extent his Middle English translators, take a pessimistic view of humanity in general and war in particular. The medieval Trojan legend, then, creates a clear, strong and absolutely vital bridge between the Classical poetry that Tolkien clearly loved - the 'charm and delight' he ascribes to the 'Southern' epic makes that certain - yet which he was moving away from, and the Germanic, Northern European legends which Tolkien was increasingly interested in. John Garth's point is valid if we assume Tolkien only knew Homer, like most of his contemporaries. Once the medieval Trojan legend enters the picture, however, the situation is totally different.

b; Troy and the Great War

Tolkien would not, moreover, have been alone in applying those attitudes to the First World War. The Gallipoli campaign, with its battlefield opposite the site of Troy, produced the largest crop of such works both from those commentating on the campaign and, with far more force, from those who actually fought there, such as the British writer P. Shaw-Stewart or the Frenchman J. Girardoux.
'Why against us?' says Hector
'Troy is famous for her arts, her justice, her humanity.' (Wood, 1985, ch.1 p.35)
A better-known 'war poet', Rupert Brooke, died on his way east before the fighting began, but his last fragmentary works circle around the Homeric associations of the site of the battle to come. Some of these unfinished works seem to hint at a dawning realisation that just as the *Iliad* is not all sunlight and flashing bronze, so Brooke's youthful enthusiasm for soldiering was a leaf balanced above an abyss. Nor were Homeric allusions missing from the Western Front; and again, it is not only the armchair war-poets, such as Masefield, but the men in the trenches who invoke such associations in their works. Charles Sorley's long, technically untitled poem *I have not brought my Odyssey* used a sustained Homeric metaphor for life, war and after-life, while his last sonnet ends with a reworked line of Homer. Firstly the poem:

'Of clash of arms, of council's brawl,
Of beauty that must early fall,
Of battle hate and battle joy
By the old windy walls of Troy...

And now the fight begins again,
The old war-joy, the old war-pain.
Sons of one school across the sea
We have no fear to fight, for we
Have echo of our deeds in you
We have our αοιδος too....' [Note 1]

In November 1914, writing to the Master of Marlborough, Sorley had quoted a line from the *Iliad*, spoken by Achilles - 'Died Patroclus too who was a far better man than thou' - adding 'no saner and splendider comment on death has been made.' As his last sonnet enters its sestet, he echoes that Homeric line with another instruction to his reader:

Say only this, 'They are dead.' Then add thereto,
'Yet many a better one has died before.' (Stallworthy, 2002, pps.37, 43)

Recovering from wounds serious enough that he had been reported dead, Robert Graves used the imagery of Greek myth - Cerberus and Lethe - to describe the experience in a poem (Stallworthy 2002; Wood 1985 ch.1, pp.34-5). There are likely to be many more examples lying unnoticed, disregarded by critics uncomfortable with such echoes. Nor was this confined to poetry, for the general pattern of the Trojan War provided a series of clear, widely understood and useful reference-points against which the Great War could be compared. Ideas like this appear within Tolkien's own circle. Of his close 'TCBS' friends, Rob Gilson took a Greek *Odyssey* with him to war, and G.B. Smith sent for one from France (Garth 2003, Great War, ch.6, p.116 & p.135). In 1915 his close friend Rob Gilson wrote: 'If anyone with a gift of prophecy were to tell me that the war would last ten years, I shouldn't feel the least surprise.' (ibid, ch.3, p. 63)

The reference is to Homer, and the foretelling the seer Calchas gave the Greeks;

'Seeing this portent of the gods had visited
our sacrifices, Calchas told the meaning
before us all, at once. He said:
"...Nine are the years that we shall wage this war
and in the tenth we'll take the spacious town." '
(Homer/Fitzgerald 1984, 'Iliad', bk.II, p.27)

Landscape too might rouse similar feelings, 'unHomeric' as the Western Front might appear. John Garth cites a passage from Edmund Blunden's 1928 reminiscence, *Undertones of War* :

'On the Western Front the present, for all its urgent terror, could not obscure the lamentable wreckage of the past all around, and even the recent past might seem bizarrely ancient. 'The Old British Line,' Edmund Blunden observed, 'was already venerable. It shared the past with the defences of Troy. The skulls which spades disturbed about it were in a manner coeval with those of the most distant wars; there is an obstinate remoteness about a skull.'

Tolkien never merely observed the past. He recreated it in his own wayward imagination, focussing not on Troy but on Kortirion and, by now perhaps, on the great city of Gondolin too.' (Garth 2003, Great War, ch.10, p.187)

This is half right, but as often wrong. As this chapter shows, Tolkien's imagination was anything but 'wayward'; he *was* following up a central line in the thought of the day, albeit in his own singularly widely read fashion. And the centre of that creative thread in Tolkien's thinking was *both* Troy and Gondolin, linked - as we have seen - by a forgotten episode in the medieval literature Tolkien loved so much. 'Kortirion among the trees' was to prove a passing phase, if not a red herring; but Gondolin would remain important to Tolkien into the 1950's and beyond.

Even in the Second World War, such ideas were not forgotten. As late as 1941, the British historian and biographer Philip Guedalla could rely on immediate identification and reaction when the described the evacuation fleet at Dunkirk as:

'The little ships, the unforgotten Homeric catalogue of *Mary Jane* and *Peggy IV*, of*Folkestone Belle*, *Boy Billy*, and *Ethel Maud*, of *Lady Haig* and *Skylark*... the little ships of England brought the Army home.' (Oxford Dictionary of Quotations, ed. A Partington, 1996 revised 4th edn, Oxford University Press, s.v Guedalla p.319)

The range of response to Homer and ability to apply his name and work, was and remained wider than the propagandists of the Modernist movement and their critical successors have allowed for. This is particularly obvious during the First World War, at a time central to our interpretation of Tolkien's tale of Gondolin.

Furthermore, some of the medieval versions of the Trojan story, with their emphasis on the futility of war, are even more applicable to the situation between 1914 and 1918 than is the *Iliad* itself. Guido delle Colonne, the originator of the 'historical' strand of Trojan tales, was a pessimist whose grim attitude to humanity in general, the futility of war in particular and the idiocy of would-be heroes in specific would look only too plausible if viewed from a dugout behind the Western Front (Benson 1980, Part 1, ch.I, p.23-31).

Besides all these reasons for using the medieval Trojan legend, we can also look at Tolkien's languages. John Garth points out that there was a very interesting association in early Quenya which is wildly at variance with our usual picture of Tolkien as someone in love with 'Germanic' myth and legend:

'Particularly striking is how Quenya at this stage equates Germans with barbarity. *Kalimban* is ' "Barbary", Germany'; *kalimbariё* is 'barbarity, *kalimbo* is 'a savage, uncivilised man, barbarian. - giant, monster, troll' and *kalimbardi* is glossed 'the Germans'. There is a strong sense of disillusionment in these definitions, so devoid of the attraction Tolkien had felt towards 'the "Germanic" ideal' as an undergraduate. He lived in a country wracked with fear, grief and hatred, and by now people he knew had been killed by Germans.' (Garth 2003, ch.6, p.128)

Later, Tolkien would drop such ideas; but here is good evidence to suggest that on a very personal level, Tolkien had reason to turn back to the Classics - and their medieval derivatives - for creative inspiration, since the 'Northern' legends were temporarily unpalatable to him.

A good context exists, therefore, for Tolkien using the legends of Troy, and especially their medieval variant, as the skeleton for his first attempt at a long-ish story told in straightforward prose, written in 1916. The context would be personal, relevant and quite possibly auto-biographical.

IV; Telling Tales; Names, Words and Stories

a; A Lost Tale

We believe that this first attempt at story-telling by Tolkien was almost

certainly not 'The Tale of Gondolin' as we have it. It is very likely that behind this 'Lost Tale' lies something simpler and unambiguous, a direct use of the medieval Troy-legend as a commentary on the Great War in general and the Somme in particular. The deaths of his friends certainly left Tolkien with a deep uncertainty about his creativity: 'Rob Gilson had died at La Boiselle, leading his men into action on the first day of the battle, 1 July. Tolkien wrote to Smith: 'I do not feel a member of a complete body now. I honestly feel that the TCBS has ended.' (Carpenter, 1977, Part 2, ch.8, p.92).
John Garth expands usefully on this:
'Furthermore, the letter undergoes a dramatic volte-face. Immediately after declaring 'I honestly feel that the TCBS has ended', Tolkien had added a caveat: 'but I am not at all sure that it is not an unreliable feeling that will vanish - like magic perhaps when we come together again...' Furthermore, he had conceded, 'the TCBS may have been all we dreamt - and its work in the end be done by three or two or one survivor... To this I now pin my hopes'. The indications are that what Tolkien wanted, in his isolation and grief and doubt, was not agreement that the TCBS had ended, but reassurance that it still lived.'
(Garth 2003, Great War, ch.10, pp.180-1)
And, we might add, reassurance that his creativity, which had so far always been so tied up with the TCBS, was worthwhile and would continue - come what might. Indeed, one might read the concluding line more as an affirmation of this. From the blithe hope of having an impact on the world that is actually not uncommon among groups of youngsters whose shared creativity leads them think that they have something to say and a way to say it, Tolkien had come down to earth with a bump. He was having to ask himself some very hard questions, at a time and in a place when opportunities for philosophical reflection were, to put it mildly, thin on the ground. There is a strong chance that a born storyteller and writer like Tolkien would have tried to write his way through the situation - to express his feelings and in doing so to both comprehend and (potentially) communicate them.

b; Beside the Plain of Troy...

Beside the reasons we have already given for turning to the Tale of Troy, there were two ways in which Tolkien could have met people who had been personally involved in the Gallipoli campaign, fought on the other side of the Hellespont to 'the plain of Troy' and so even more often compared to the Trojan War than the rest of World War I, or have heard their firsthand accounts. Firstly, Tolkien's regiment, the Lancashire Fusiliers, had sent men there, although his own battalion was not involved. In the general mobility of officers between units at that time, Tolkien might easily have served near or even with someone with that background.

The chance of Tolkien hearing about the events at Gallipoli is greatly increased because Lancashire Fusiliers had covered themselves in glory as well as blood at the landing there, as John Garth makes clear:

'When G.B. Smith joined the 19th Battalion, the regiment had just etched its name bloodily and tragically in the history books again. As the Oxford term began, on Sunday 25 April 1915, the British-Anzac assault was launched at Gallipoli against the Turkish allies of Germany and Austria-Hungary. The day was a foretaste of thirty-seven weeks to come; a disastrously unequal fight, with British and Anzac troops wading ashore under cruel cliffs surmounted by wire and machine-gun posts. Nevertheless, the worn word 'hero' was being reforged in galvanising fires. In the forefront of the assault, the Lancashire Fusiliers rowed into a hail of bullets at 'W Beach' on Cape Helles. As they leapt from their boats, seventy pounds of equipment dragged many of the injured to death by drowning. On reaching the shore, others foundered on the barbed wire, which a preceding naval bombardment had failed to break. The beach was secured that day but 260 of the 950 attacking Fusiliers were killed and 283 wounded. In the eyes of many at home, however, the regiment covered itself in glory, and eventually it reaped a historic six Victoria Crosses [Britain's highest award for military valour] for that morning on the beach.' (Garth 2003, Great War, ch.3, p.69)

To put this into perspective, at the battle of Rourke's Drift in South Africa in 1879 where 120 men faced off 4000 Zulus and was the basis of the 1960's movie 'Zulu', eleven Victoria Crosses were won.

It must be certain that Tolkien would have been told about these events at Gallipoli when he joined the Lancashire Fusiliers, and it is very likely that Homeric comparisons would have been used by both the Lancashires themselves and by those writing about them at home, since Gallipoli was so close to Troy. In fact, Homer does not describe the landing of the Greeks in detail, only mentioning in passing:

' ...all these
were under Protesilaus' command
when that intrepid fighter lived -
but black earth held him under now, and grieving
at Phylace with lacerated cheeks
his bride was left, his house unfinished there.
Plunging ahead from his long ship to be
the first man ashore at Troy of all Achaeans,
he had been brought down by a Dardan spear.'
(Homer/Fitzgerald 1984, Iliad, bk.II, p.37, lines 693-700)

Indeed, given the habit of writing verse at the time, in some forgotten regimental magazine or set of papers, there may well be poetry making such a comparison.

Had Tolkien wished, he might have retorted with the alliterative *Destruction*'s almost prescient description, occupying virtually all of Book XIV, of a grim day-long struggle in which wave after wave of Greeks storm ashore, only to be cut down in a rain of arrows and cross-bow bolts loosed by the defending Trojans from a high bank above the beach. The Greek commanders are driven to despair or battle madness while the sea runs red with blood, and though the beachhead is eventually won, it is at terrible cost:

'The waters grew red with the hot blood
[Of those] that were killed in the wet, and in soft sand alighted
There together were seen true sorrow and pain
And how deadly and bitter the shore was to win.
How the Greeks were thrown down into terrible death
Was never told in any romance by any man yet
[Nor] that any men in the world, that to war went
With such trouble won [their way] from the boat onto the shore
As it happened here with so fierce a fight..'

(Panton & Donaldson 1968, bk.XIV, lines 5709-17). [Note 2]

The Lancashires' Gallipoli involvement was famous enough for even the Germans to know about it. Garth notes that:

' 'A good friend of mine has been wounded on patrol and captured by the Germans. God knows if he is still living,' Smith wrote as he prepared to set out into No Man's Land that night... Smith returned safely with all three of his men that night, having seen and heard nothing of the enemy, and lived to lead further patrols. Later, a Turkish flag was hoisted above the enemy trench; clearly the Germans had learned from their captive that they faced the Lancashire Fusiliers and aimed to discomfort them with a reminder of their fruitless losses at Gallipoli.' (Garth 2003, Great War, ch.6, p.118-9)

Secondly, ANZAC units recently transferred from Gallipoli were present at the Battle of the Somme. Even if Tolkien had never met anyone who had been through that truly pointless disaster (though his later strong dislike of Winston Churchill, the author of the fiasco that was the Gallipoli campaign, might suggest that he did) their presence on the Somme must have lent a particular tinge to Army gossip in general and regimental talk in particular, given the Lancashires' previous involvement in the Gallipoli front.

c; Found Manuscripts, Forgotten Names

There is in fact evidence within the *Book of Lost Tales* to back up the idea of a simpler, clearly Trojan story at the root of the whole process. The Lost Tales are meant to survive because Eriol/Aelfwine comes to Tol Eressëa *and writes them down*. Everything else may be lost, but the book with its tale survives to be rediscovered. Now, both of the works which underlie the medieval Trojan legends, Dares Phyrgius and Dictys Cretensis, employ exactly this strategy to 'prove' their authenticity. According to the preface to 'Dictys':

'After many centuries the tomb of Dictys at Cnossos (formerly the seat of the Cretan king) collapsed with age. Then shepherds, wandering near the ruins, stumbled upon a little box skilfully enclosed in tin. Thinking it was treasure, they soon broke it open, but brought to light, instead of gold or some other kind of wealth, books written on limewood tablets. Their hopes thus frustrated, they took their find to Eupraxides, the owner of that place. Eupraxides had the books transliterated into the Attic alphabet (the language was Greek [and they were written in the Phoenician alphabet]) and presented them to the Roman Emperor

Nero. Nero rewarded him richly.'
(Fraser 1966, Dictys, p.19)

Moreover, the idea of lost manuscripts of this type being rediscovered was given a considerable boost not long before Tolkien was writing. In the winter of 1899-1900 a papyrus fragment was found which had part of the previously lost Greek original of Dictys Cretensis' work written on it. Until this discovery was made, the prevailing scholarly opinion was that no such Greek text ever existed, that both works had been written in Latin and the idea of translation was just one more fiction created by the anonymous author to make their forgery seem plausible (an idea that Tolkien would pick up on and use almost fifty years later in *The Lord of the Rings*, especially in Appendix F). The scrap of papyrus - one side has income tax returns of all things, and the other side the copy of Dictys - overturned scholarly opinion at a stroke. Just as Schleimann's discoveries at Troy and Mycenae showed that Homer was drawing on a background of stories about people and places that had once existed and were real, however changed the stories became by the time a genius immortalised them, so also the discovery of the Greek Dictys proved that what had been taken as a myth (read, outright lie) was actually a *legend*, partly true and historically accurate (Frazer 1966 Introduction). So 'found manuscripts' to do with Troy and the Trojan War were more possible in 1916 than they had been before 1900, and the reasons for this chimed exactly with Tolkien's known belief in the truth of myth and legend.

By itself, this proves nothing conclusively about the book of Lost Tales; but let us look closer at the names of the place where the not-so-lost stories are recorded. In Tolkien names matter - they always have. 'Tol Eressëa' or 'the Lonely Island' is so named from the very beginning of Tolkien's work. The names appear in 'The Cottage of Lost Play', written and fair-copied in the winter of 1916-17. 'Tol Eressëa' is mentioned in the name-list accompanying vol.I, which draws on word-books going back to 1915 (and thus before the Lost Tales proper) for Quenya, and 1917 for 'Gnomish'/Sindarin. By what is said about these lists, 'Eressëa' could well predate the writing of *The Fall of Gondolin* in 1916, and 'Tol' possibly does so as well. Conventionally, 'eressëa' is meaningless except for Tolkien's decision to assign meaning. John Garth says:

'Derivation aside, only taste dictated that fumelot means 'poppy', eressëa means 'lonely', or morwen, 'daughter of the dark', signifies the glimmering planet Jupiter.'
(Garth 2003, Great War, ch.3, p.62)

'Derivation' here means the development of a word within Tolkien's own languages, not its connection to others. However, we believe that there is a very plausible set of developments that would tie this seemingly impeccably Elvish name back to the whole complex body of Trojan legends. A linguistic tie that makes far more sense when we are considering a writer such as Tolkien.

The remarks on 'Tol Eressëa' in the name-list to BOLT make it look very much as if 'eressëa' is the original word from which the others derive - that this word and concept came first, and the linguistics which associated it with a 'root ERE' and a set of other words came later. Now, across the whole area of the

Western Aegean, there is a body of non-Greek (indeed non-Indo-European) placenames, which end in '-ss' or '-nth', with or without '-os'. Corinth (in mainland Greece) and Knossos (on Crete) are good examples of the type. If these two are interchangeable (as with Thalassa/Thalatta in Classical Greek), then:

Eressëa/Eirissia = Eirinthia

This can easily be corrupted to be Eirini Thira

Which gives us, quite easily: Eirene Thera

Santorini < Santa Eirene *or* Thera

Which are the two names of an Aegean island. An Aegean island with a great deal of resonance for Tolkien's own mythologies.

Finally, *eirene* means 'peace', but *eireme* means 'loneliness, desolation'.

So the hypothetical ancestral parallel form of Eressëa is within one letter of the meaning of the name. That has to be more than coincidence. Peace, after all, can be said to be one side of the coin to which the obverse is loneliness.

Like 'Eressëa', 'Tol' is a word with more to it than meets the eye. The BOLT vol.I name-list says:

'Under root TOLO, QL [the Quenya Lexicon] has derivatives *tol* 'island, any rise standing alone in water, plain of green, etc.', *tolmen* 'boss (of shield), isolated round hill, etc.',*tolos* 'knob, lump', *tólë* 'centre', and other such words. GL [the 'Gnomish' Lexicon] gives *tol* 'an isle with high steep coasts.' (BOLT vol.I, Appendix, p.269)

Seven out of the eight suggested meanings for five words centre on the idea of a high, rounded shape. Now, the ancient Greek word *tholos*, literally a round building, has been thoroughly confused with 'beehive' in archaeological writing ever since the mid-1800's, because the two words are used as alternative descriptions of Mycenean chamber-tombs which have a distinctive pointed-arch shape (the outline of old-fashioned straw 'skep' beehives right across Europe). *Tholos* is so close to *tolos*, and the shape implied in its use for the 'beehive' chambered tombs is so appropriate for the other meanings, as to make it all but certain that Tolkien has taken over and reworked the Greek word. This would actually not be unusual for Tolkien in the *Book of Lost Tales* phase of his writing, though it became very uncommon later, as John Garth points out in the middle of a lengthy disquisition on languages:

'Many years later, when *The Lord of the Rings* had made him famous, Tolkien expressed his puzzlement and irritation at the many 'guesses at the "sources" of the nomenclature, and theories or fancies concerning hidden meanings' proffered by enthusiasts... The true sources of his names, he wished to emphasize, are his own invented languages, the on-going products of decades of painstaking craft. His statements were undoubtedly true in 1967, and reflected his creative practice over the previous two, three or four decades... *But evidence suggests that in 1915, at least, Tolkien did create a small but significant proportion of his Quenya words specifically to show kinship with ancient recorded or reconstructed words* .'

(Garth 2003, Great War, ch.5, p.96-7; emphasis ours)

So it is entirely possible that both 'eressëa' and 'tol' might have real-world antecedents, from which they were changed deliberately and carefully by Tolkien.

This word *tol/tholos* then takes us by two possible routes back to Santorini/

Thera. First, for the whole of Tolkien's lifetime, geological opinion was that the island began as a single landmass with either a high central peak (1600m/feet is a figure often quoted) or numerous low hilltops (Friedrich/McBirney 2000 ch.10 p.119). This latter idea is distinctly close to the little bit of description of Tol Eressëa in 'The Cottage of Lost Play' where there is a hill in the centre of the island with a tower upon it. It was believed that it was the Minoan eruption which turned this high island into the broken ring of three islands we see today at Santorini, set around the rim of a deep caldera where two new volcanic islets have arisen. This belief was based partly on the 1883 eruption of Krakatoa, in which two-thirds of that island totally disappeared and the remaining peak was split in half, creating a spectacular cliff very much like the walls of Santorini. The idea was seemingly backed up by the ancient use of Stronghyle, 'round', to describe the group - though actually, the name belonged to a volcanic island close to Italy (Friedrich/McBirney 2000 ch.1 p.7). So, as a high single island with steep coasts, pre-eruption Santorini/ Thera fits the meaning of *tol /tholos* .

Secondly, there is the figurative meaning, 'chambered tomb'. Dictys' manuscript was supposedly found in the ruins of a collapsed tomb near Knossos on Crete, which strongly implies a built structure - such as a *tholos* - rather than a rock-cut one. Sir Arthur Evans did indeed find *tholos* tombs on Crete, just down the valley from his main site of Minoan Knossos (Cottrell 1955 chs. XII, XIII). Hellenistic tombs are found on Thera proper and small Bronze Age tombs made of slabs of limestone were found underneath the Minoan pumice towards the end of the 19th century. Something more imposing, such as a *tholos*, would be a logical accompaniment to the impressive Bronze Age houses with their brilliantly coloured and finely painted frescoes found on Thera from 1866 onwards (Freidrich/ McBirney 2000, ch.8 & ch.10, also described and indeed heavily emphasised by Tsountas and Manatt 1897, ch.IX, pp.236-8 and ch.X).

This in turn tells us what Santorini has to do with lost manuscripts and Troy. To survive, a 'lost book' needs a refuge, a place where fragile information can be physically preserved, like Dictys' tomb or, probably, Tolkien's *tholos* . This again takes us along two paths to the same place. Santorini had been hailed as the Pompeii of the Aegean as far back as the 1870's. Major archaeological work had been carried out, and significant finds made. At Pompeii in Italy, salvageable scrolls were found in excavations at one of the outlying mansions, the Villa Dei Papyri. There were no scrolls on Santorini - but in the island's cultural twin Crete from 1900 onwards there *were* finds of baked clay tablets covered in mysterious, indecipherable writing, all of which were then firmly believed to represent a non-Greek language. Sir Arthur Evans' excavations at Knossos not only christened the Minoan culture, they were intended to search for writings - Evans was set on the track by the discovery of inscribed 'seal stones' - and they found them. This was well-known from the very start of Sir Arthur Evans' excavations - already in 1900 the *Times* newspaper carried accounts of the amazing finds of his first season, and by 1909 there was a book - *Crete; the Forerunner of Greece* by B.M. & H.W. Hawes - which revealed still more of the discoveries of Evans and the other archaeologists working on Crete to an astonished and intrigued world. There is actually a hint that Tolkien was interested in the Myceneans and Minoans - he mentioned in a letter that his favourites among the novels of Mary Renault were *The King Must Die* and *The Bull from the Sea,* which retell the story of Theseus of Athens and King Minos of Crete (Letters no.294, 1967, note on books read).

Nowadays Santorini/Thera barely figures in books on Aegean archaeology, but in the 1897 book *The Mycenean Age*, by the Greek archaeologist C.Tsountas and the American historian J.I. Manatt, Thera takes on an extraordinary importance. In their view, it is Asia Minor in general and Troy in particular which is the first origin of Aegean civilisation. The Greek Islands then take up the torch, and among them Thera is by far the richest and most important. Finally, the Greek Mainland is the third runner in the relay, developing the glories of Mycenean civilisation that came down to later days in Homer's immortal verse. (Tsountas and Manatt 1897, 'Mycenean Age', ch.X, p.266-7). The astonishing discoveries of Sir Arthur Evans in Crete totally swamped this earlier view. Yet, the older story's likely dates allowed for the mainland to develop independently of Crete - influenced, but not overwhelmed. There was certainly a major academic dispute as to whether Crete really was, as Arthur Evans claimed, not only the fount of all civilisation in the era of the Trojan War, but also the political master of the mainland, or whether the Mycenean Greeks could be credited with a moving spirit all their own, an independence in both political and cultural terms. When that dispute surfaces around the time of the Second World War, the leader of the opposition to Evans was the professor of Comparative Philology at Oxford (L. Cotterell 1963, 'Lion Gate', ch.19, p.218). It is not unreasonable to suggest that this pattern - of Evans the archaeologist against his linguistic colleagues at Oxford - goes right back to before the First World War, and that as an undergraduate (and probably again after his return to Oxford as a professor), Tolkien would have picked up the 'philological' side of the debate with its emphasis on Thera as a central point in the history, culture and geography of the Aegean Sea to set against the archaeological emphasis on Crete.

The tablets found at Knossos proved that writing was in use within the same culture as that of Santorini, but their small slabs of clay were utterly unsuited to any long text. Some other material would be needed for a long narrative, and without the great good luck which led 'Dictys' heirs to seal up the wooden tablets of his tale in an airtight box, special conditions not found on Crete would be required to preserve it. This brings us back to the 'Aegean Pompeii' and the idea of a tomb. A sealed tomb is a very good place to hide something, as the anonymous writer behind 'Dictys Cretensis' and his *Diary of the Trojan War* already knew in the 1st century AD. With the coming of modern archaeology, it becomes even better, for in a proper excavation, even as such things were reckoned in 1916, fragile things like wooden tablets would have far more chance of survival than in an accidental discovery. All in all, anyone (such as Tolkien, for instance) looking for a plausible home for a 'found manuscript' about the Trojan War in 1916 could hardly have done better than a tholos tomb on Santorini. So we have a collection of linguistic links between Eressëa and Santorini which go much too far for coincidence to be a plausible explanation, and there is good writerly reason for those links to exist - *but only within a purely Trojan scenario* .

d; Elves, Men and Orcs

Further evidence for the existence of an underlying 'realistic' or at least historical Trojan version comes from Tolkien's wholly uncharacteristic use of 'men' to mean 'adult male of any species' in *The Fall of Gondolin*. Christopher Tolkien points this out in the notes to the story:
'20 'folk': original reading 'men'. This is the only place where 'men' in reference to Elves is changed. The use is constant in *The Fall of Gondolin*, and even occurs once in an odd-sounding reference to the hosts of Melko: 'but now the men of Melko have assembled their forces' (p.183)' (BOLT vol.II, ch.3, note 20, p.198-9)
This makes sense only if it represents an unrevised hangover from a version of the story in which all the people involved are men - as would be the case in a 'Trojan version'. It may also account for the radical change in Tolkien's conception of 'elves' or 'gnomes', from the very Edwardian little filmy creatures of his prewar poetry to the tall, majestic folk of *The Book of Lost Tales*. Not only do Tolkien's 'elves' have to carry a far greater weight of story in the works written during or after the Great War, they may well also have inherited the stature of the Greek and Trojan heroes.

All of this is buried within *The Book of Lost Tales*, like a carved block reused in a later wall. As has been pointed out by us (Uncharted Realms of Tolkien), stories tend to betray their origins in many subtle ways, even when an author has attempted to alter them over a passage of time.

e; Survivors and the Sea

In his epoch-making article *Beowulf; The Monsters and the Critics*, Tolkien complained with good reason about those critics who pushed over the tower of the poem to study the stones of its makeup, forgetting that from the top of the tower the poet could see the sea. But there may be more than one sea, and more than one view worth having. It does not diminish the astonishing achievement of the *Lost Tales* to glimpse behind them a story which was strange and rich in itself. In a sense, one might say that if a tower had been built on the site of the great hall Heorot, perhaps no sea might have been glimpsed, but had those same stones come from Troy, then a tower there *would* have been within view of the sea.

Indeed, it is actually possible to guess who it was who sailed from Troy and left this record behind after calling, perhaps only briefly, at Santorini. In *The Fall of Gondolin*, it is Tuor, who has carried a warning from the Gods to King Turgon only to be ignored, and later married the King's daughter and effectively became his heir, who leads the escape from the city. This parallels the medieval story of Helenus son of Priam, a priest inspired by the Gods who warns the King against war with Greece and is ignored, just as Tuor carries the message of Ulmo to

Gondolin, asking Turgon to take action against Melko, and is ignored. The base idea is the same, the messages are reversed; and in the 1930 Quenta Noldorinwa, the story would shift back to the Trojan pattern of warning Turgon not to fight, not to trust in walls and swords. So the influence of the Tale of Troy on the Tale of Gondolin was no passing thing, but a longlived one - something we have seen several times already. In the *Aeneid*, Aeneas finds Helenus established as lord of his own small kingdom on the west coast of Greece, a land he carved out of the realm of Thessaly after its king Pyrrhus/Neoptolemus, son of Achilles, was killed; Helenus is married to Andromache, the widow of his brother Hector and former concubine of Pyrrhus; later they were said to have sailed to Asia Minor and founded the great city of Pergamum. So Helenus is a very plausible 'sailing survivor' who in his passages through the Greek isles could well have landed on Santorini/Thera at some time and deposited some record of his experience there.

The similarity of the names of Tuor/Tûr and Turgon could well hint at a time when they were father and son, before the incoming Eärendel legend moved Tuor into a different position as the outsider who marries the princess (as we will shortly see). Tuor's axe Dramborleg also points in the same direction. In so far as anyone has thought about this unique instance in Tolkien's work of a hero carrying a named weapon which is an axe (even Gimli does not give his axe a name in *The Lord of the Rings* while in *The Hobbit*, Thorin Oakenshield, the most important of the dwarves, prefers a sword to an axe), it has been vaguely assumed that Tuor has some kind of Viking antecedents. However, one of the most important religious symbols in the Minoan (and, to a lesser extent, the Mycenean) culture was the double-bladed axe; as a priest, Helenus son of Priam might well be associated with such an item, both weapon and sacred object. It was only after making this guess that we found C.Tsountas and J.I. Manatt in 1897 describing an archaeological discovery of almost exactly similar implications:

'We may therefore take this [the double-bladed axe] to be the typical Mycenean battle-axe [six similar specimens also being found at Troy]; but the Vaphio tomb has given us one of a very different type. It is crescent-shaped, with two large holes (possibly to lighten the blade), while the back is cut out in three teeth. Through these is the hole for the helve [shaft] which was guarded by a sort of annular cap distinct from the axe head. With this unique specimen before us, we can at last understand the feat of Odysseus in sending an arrow through the rings of twelve axes set up in a row. From the same tomb we have a gem on which is represented in intaglio *a man in very peculiar costume, (possibly a priest), bearing on his shoulder an axe of this very type.*'

(Tsountas and Manatt 1897, 'Mycenean Age', ch.VIII, p.207-8, emphasis ours).

This priestly, axe-bearing figure exactly matches the idea of Helenus/Tuor as axe-bearer and wielder.

More axe-connections run through Tolkien's names and linguistics. The name of Tuor's father, 'Peleg', is simply the Gnomish/Sindarin word for 'axe' (BOLT vol.II, Appendix on Names s.v.Peleg). This word is the 'twin' of Quenya 'pelekko', which, as John Garth points out, is if not quite a real word, very close: 'Philologists have derived the Greek and Sanskrit words for 'axe', *pelekus* and

parasu, from a lost non-Indo-European source; but Tolkien 'rediscovered' that source in the Quenya word *pelekko*.' (Garth 2003, Great War, ch.5, p.98)
In this context it is well worth noting another non-Indo-European loanword into Greek, *labyrinth*, which from an uncertain date early in the 20th century was taken as a placename (for Knossos in Crete) adapted to describe a thing (the intricate ruins of the Minoan palace, which in the legend of Theseus became the original maze). 'Labyrinth' was broken down by philologists into two halves; *labrys*, meaning 'double axe', and the -nthos placename ending we have already spoken of above, in connection with 'eressëa'. This reinforces the likelihood that Tuor inherited his great axe not from any Old Norse source, but from the historical world of the Aegean where the Trojan legends began. Furthermore, one of the most impressive finds made in the early excavations on Santorini was a bronze dagger-blade, inlaid with gold in the exact same technique as the far more famous weapons found in the Shaft Graves at Mycenae by Heinrich Schliemann. Now in the Copenhagen museum, this blade is decorated with nothing less than a line of single-bladed axes. Exactly this piece appears in an illustration in the 1897 book *The Mycenean Age* by C.Tsountas and J.I. Manatt, where it is discussed in considerable detail (Tsountas and Manatt 1897, ch.IX, p.235, Fig.118). It is therefore entirely possible that Tolkien could have known of this particular inlaid blade - and indeed of all the other material we have been citing from Tsountas and Manatt's book - especially if we consider that Tolkien's Classics tutor, Lewis Farnell, was very interested in the discoveries at Troy and Knossos, and in the undeciphered script that Sir Arthur Evans had discovered (Garth 2003, Great War, ch.1, pp.29-30). So Tuor's axe also fits extremely well with a Trojan context drawing on the history that archaeology was revealing, and a story linked to the southern Aegean and Santorini/Thera.

Perhaps Tolkien was thinking of a Helenus who called at Santorini and was welcomed there, just as Aeneas calls at Delos in Virgil's poem and his prayers are answered by the omen of a mighty earthquake and a bull-like bellowing - far more fitting for volcanic Santorini and Poseidon the Earth-Shaker, than the peaceful if haunted isle of Apollo. Aeneas then sails for Crete, mistakenly believing the Gods mean him to settle there, which again takes us into the Minoan sphere and past Santorini/Thera. On Santorini, Helenus probably buried one of his company with honour - maybe his wife if he comes there on his way to Greece, since Tuor and Idril are separated in many of the outlines for the Tale of Eärendel, or perhaps a son if he was sailing for Asia Minor with Andromache, since Elwing and Eärendel are afraid their son Elrond will die when the Havens are overrun by the Fëanorians. Left behind with whoever it was laid to rest in the tomb was something more valuable than any golden treasure, a record of the 'true' story of Troy and the Trojan wars. The tale would then have survived by hairsbreadth chance when the wrath of the Gods fell upon the Mycenean Greeks and overcame them, in the double shape of the Dorian invasion and the Santorini eruption. The date of that eruption was then unclear, and such a major volcanic outburst can in any case be far more plausibly associated with the 1200-1100 BC era after the Fall of Troy, when the whole fabric of Aegean civilisation crumbled and much of the Near

East went up in flames too, than with the date Sir Arthur Evans favoured of around 1450 BC when nothing much else can be said to have happened. Unimaginable years later, Helenus' book would be found and then deciphered - perhaps by an Oxford scholar serving in the British Army, who found himself by chance on Santorini on the way to or from the Gallipoli campaign.

Might any of this - or any other story on a similar theme - have been written down by Tolkien? There are practical problems with that idea; writing whilst actually 'in the trenches' was impossible and writing whilst on 'rest' behind the lines was fraught with risk of losing manuscripts. Then, too, Tolkien might have been composing in his head - let alone the achievements of fundamentally oral poets such as Homer and the *Beowulf* -poet, one of the authors can attest how even a memory much less well-trained than Tolkien's must have been (since in his day education was based on memorising almost everything from multiplication tables to Classical Greek verse), can retain the incidents of a developing and quite complex tale over a span of many years. Still, there is a reasonable probability that Tolkien would have tried to write *something* down, and there is a faint chance that evidence of some sort for or against the proposition may still survive in Tolkien's papers. It is worth noting that in the original BOLT versions, Eärendil fails as a messenger even though he becomes the morning star, and it is only later (in the 1930's) that he succeeds and the sentence ending is changed to: 'the greatest mariner that ever lived'.

All this linguistic and archaeological evidence can seem very 'dry'. Yet Tolkien created a powerful *story* out of all this material. So it is worth spending a moment looking beyond the words, at a vision which could indeed carry the creative power to generate such a tale. The ancient Aegean may have come down to us in words whispering on parchment, and mute fragments of pottery in the earth: but there is also the gleam of gold, the glitter of sunlight on that changeful sea which Homer called 'wine-dark' - the beat of hooves and the rush of a ship through the waves, the shouts of men in battle and the quiet words of husband and wife reunited at last after twenty years apart - the scent of thyme and wild olive on the breeze - and over it all that famously magical light of Greece, the light that Tolkien unexpectedly evokes when, in his famous letter to Milton Waldman, he says that:

'It should possess the tone and quality that I desired, *somewhat cool and clear...*'
(Letters no.131, p.144) (emphasis ours)

This cool, clear air could not be more different to the watery twilight which was already associated with all things Celtic when Tolkien wrote those words, or the smoky, 'barbaric gloom' often associated with the Anglo-Saxons. It is distinctively Greek, a sneaking hint of something Tolkien probably wanted to integrate rather than forget in his writing, just as the Tale of Troy had been woven into the medieval European legends. He might have come out strongly in the same sentence against writing specifically about 'Italy or the Aegean', but all the evidence goes to show that Tolkien did not want to lose touch with the longer roots of medieval Northern European civilisation either.

For the ancient Aegean does not stand wholly apart from the North of Europe, though modern commentators entirely ignore the point; it is not hermetically sealed away from the 'pathless Mirkwood' of later legend and the speakers of Germanic language and legend. C.Tsountas may have been a Greek archaeologist and his collaborator J.I. Manatt an American historian, but they repeatedly associate the Mycenean Greeks, Homer's Achaeans, with the wider Indo-European peoples and in particular with the lands of the Alps and the Danube Valley (for example Tsountas and Manatt 1897, ch.IX, pp.246-52). Through their words the attentive reader can catch a glimpse of a lost world, of history and of story as wide-ranging and as interconnected across Europe as the legends of the Goths or the lists of kings and heroes in the Old English poem *Widsith* which Tom Shippey evoked in *The Road to Middle-earth* (2nd edn. 1992, ch.1, p.19). The long journey between the Shire and Gondor via Lothlórien and Rohan finds its real match here, twice over, on the road from Oxford to Troy and Constantinople, in both the sixth century AD and the 13th century BC.

V; Star above the Somme

If we turn from the selection of a model to the progress of the tale, it is by no means impossible that Tolkien was shaken out of the state of mind he was in after the deaths of his friends (as described first by H. Carpenter (Biography, Part 2, ch.8, p.92) and then by J. Garth (Garth 2003, Great War, ch., pp. 180-1)) by a 'star over Mordor' experience of some sort. Tolkien would not have been the only one to find sanity in an unexpected natural event on the Western Front. The poet Edmund Blunden was saved from madness after seeing friends blown to smithereens by field-mice, the smallest, most timid creatures which nonetheless survived where all else failed:

'And while I squeak and gibber over you,
Look from the wreck a score of field-mice nimble,
And tame and curious look about them; (these
Calmed me, on these depended my salvation).'
(Blunden/Taylor 1996, ch.4, 'Third Ypres', p.112)

Similarly, Tolkien in later years recalled one moment shortly after the death of his close friend Rob Gilson when:

'his hand was on the receiver of a trench telephone when a field-mouse emerged from hiding and ran across his fingers.' (Carpenter, 1977, Part 2, ch.8, p.92).

It is an odd coincidence that Blunden is saved from madness and Tolkien perhaps pulled back from despair at the loss of his close friend by something as 'insignificant' as a field-mouse. One might say that in a strange sense these field-mice are as indomitable and as close to the earth and nature as Hobbits.

Something of the 'Star over Mordor' sort is necessary to account for the fact that unlike most of the well-known Western Front authors, Tolkien writes like a man who has not only been in the tunnel, but has seen the light at the end of it. This, too, fits with the use of medieval Trojan stories as models; for their ultimate characteristic is that *people survive*. Troy may be destroyed, it may have been a futile war for nothing - but there are Trojan survivors who, in exile, carry their knowledge and their stories with them. What follows is not what might have been, but Troy's fall leads to new and unforeseen developments. Troy is the flower that has to wither in the flames to scatter its seeds and create new life. Even Guido delle Colonne in the late 13th century could say that 'unless perhaps it might be said in justification that the amount of evil which took place was the basis for good to come, since so much good has proceeded from those evils connected with the fall of Troy.' (Colonne/Meek 1974 bk.2, ll21-3, p.9) He points out that, once destroyed, Troy rose again, and its second destruction led to the rise of Rome and the establishment of civilised peoples in Britain, France and Italy. Viewed from this angle, *within the very same set of stories* it is possible to move beyond unrelieved pessimism and arrive at something close to Tolkien's theory of 'eucatastrophe', the unexpected event that undoes apparently inescapable defeat - that recognises and gives full weight to tragedy even as it leads into unlooked-for triumph (On Fairy-Stories, p.62-3 of 1988 'Tree and Leaf'). The story of Tuor and the refugees of Gondolin is a quintessential example of this.

There is another factor in this, for since the Great War, the aftermath of such trauma has become much better understood - and mostly in the years since the Vietnam War in the 1970's. 'Survivor guilt', the feeling that you should have died with the others since there seems no point to your life in particular being spared, is a real problem for veterans. It is not unrealistic to suggest that Tolkien *needed* hope, *needed* to believe that endurance and survival had a point, that his singular and specific life and creativity *were* worthwhile. The alternative was the bitter silence and mental illness that overtook an unknown - but certainly very large - number of men during and after the First World War. Cynicism and irony are all very well, but they do not provide the long-term resources to recover from damage and get on with life: and especially not, we may venture, for someone who is creative - a mindset totally ignored by most if not all psychological theories. Stallworthy's account of the 'canonical' war-poets may focus on their war and their poetry, but still makes it clear that most who survived suffered some sort of mental problem after the war. Sassoon wrote nothing between 1918 and 1926, and then became an obsessive autobiographist; Robert Graves suffered 'neurasthenia'; Ivor Gurney died in 1937 in a mental asylum; and Edmund Blunden in 1921 could write of isolation, silence, and unappeasable loss in terms not far different from Tolkien's poem 'The Sea-Bell, or, Frodo's Dreme':

' **1916 Seen from 1921**

Tired with dull grief, grown old before my day,
I sit in solitude and only hear
Long silent laughters, murmurings of dismay,
The lost intensities of hope and fear;
In those old marshes yet the rifles lie,
On the thin breastwork flutter the grey rags,
The very books I read are there - and I
Dead as the men I loved, while life drags

Its wounded length from those sad streets of war
Into green places here, that were my own;
But now what once was mine is mine no more,
I seek such neighbours here and I find none.
With such strong gentleness and tireless will
Those ruined houses seared themselves in me,
Passionate I look for their dumb story still,
And the charred stub outspeaks the living tree.

I rise up at the singing of a bird
And scarcely knowing slink along the lane,
I dare not give a soul a look or word
Where all have homes and none's at home in vain...'
(Blunden/Taylor 1996, 'Overtones of War' ch.3, '1916 seen from 1921', p.77)

It is not a coincidence that some of the poets who had actually served in the First World War and survived it later turned Catholic (Sassoon and David Jones, for example - see Stallworthy 2002). It might well be guessed that in an age without psychological counselling, their new faith ultimately gave them a support they could not find elsewhere. Tolkien did go through very bleak spells in later life, as Carpenter's 'Biography' points out ('But from now onwards there was to be a second side, more private but predominant in his diaries and letters. This side of him was capable of bouts of profound despair. More precisely, and more closely related to his mother's death, when he was in this mood he had a deep sense of impending loss. Nothing was safe. Nothing would last. No battle would be won for ever.' p.39, ch.3), but there can be little doubt either that his theory of hope was worked out and continued to be important to him for reasons that had solid experience and psychological practicality behind them rather than the groundless romanticism or maudlin emotionalism that critics unwilling to consider context might assume.

VI; Defence of the Realm?

Alongside any such change of mind we need to set the very practical point that Tolkien could have gotten into real trouble for writing an anti-war story based on a pro-Trojan version of the Tale of Troy. Again, there is an historical misapprehension to clear out of the way here. One of the many things about the Great War that has been generally forgotten is the extent of censorship and Government interference in the arts, in journalism and in political life. Britain's reputation in the Second World War as the defender of Civilisation and Freedom has conclusively obscured the willingness of British governments in both World Wars to control their Press and people in decidedly unlibertarian fashion. The Defence of the Realm Act (1914, and subsequent amendments) sounds reasonable enough; intended 'for securing the public safety and the defence of the realm' it authorised the prosecution:

'of persons contravening any of the provisions of such regulations designed
(a) to prevent persons communicating with the enemy or obtaining information with that purpose or any purpose calculated to jeopardise the success of the operations of any of His Majesty's forces or to assist the enemy; or
(b) to secure the safety of any means of communication, or of railways, docks and harbours; in like manner as if such persons were subject to military law and had on active service committed an offence under section five of the army Act.'
It sounds like a perfectly reasonable national-security measure; but in short order an amendment was made to (a) stating that the Act was also intended:
'to prevent the spread of reports likely to cause disaffection or alarm.'
And anyone doing so would be liable to prosecution and punishment as per the rest of the Act (Quoted from S. Hymes, 1990, 'A War Imagined; The First World War and English Culture').

That one additional sentence allowed the Government of the day to control the Press, the publishing industry and the infant cinema, as well as the theatre and any form of public communication. Speaking to assemblies, pamphleteering, bill-posting, sending letters or printed material abroad were all considered by the Government - and theirs was the opinion that counted - to be covered by the Act that was promptly acronymised as DORA. No amount of amusement at a name that seems better suited to a little old lady in an Edwardian farce, though, can disguise the real teeth of this law, or the impact it had. Books and other printed matter could be and were seized and destroyed; people could be and were fined or imprisoned. The Act could be and was stretched to cover almost anything that someone in authority disapproved of: Hymes's book contains numerous examples of its use, particularly against pacifism, but extending into journalism, literature and the arts.

In such an atmosphere, Tolkien could not have gone far without realising that writing something overtly critical of the war was a Bad Idea to put it politely. Writing something pro-Trojan at a time when British officers would have been steeped in Homer's version could easily look like overt support for the Germans. Anti-war sentiments by themselves could readily be construed as undesirable pacifism. As a man with a German-seeming surname at a time when most such people in Britain anglicised theirs, who was also a serving Army officer, and in the Corps of Signals of all places, Tolkien would have been a sitting duck for official disapproval. If he did not realise it himself, anyone with any idea what he might have been up to would have corrected him in short order. This is not just supposition; in the middle of 1917, Siegfried Sassoon protested publicly against the War, and it looks very much as if only extensive string-pulling on the part of his family and associates sent him in front of a Medical Board (where his friends could and did put forward a believable story that he was suffering from shell-shock) rather than a far more serious Court-Martial. Sassoon and his psychologist, W.H.R. Rivers, were well aware that he had been in real danger; he was a little too prominent to be stood up against a wall and shot, but he could easily have ended up in prison and have wrecked his chances of any sort of career, practical or literary. Rivers helped Sassoon go through his poems with an eye to the political situation, and some were considered 'too dangerous' for publication (Hymes' account of this affair (Part III, ch.8) is extensive but ingenuous; P. Fussel 1975 and J. Stallworthy 2002 are much more aware of the legal and political undercurrents).

John Garth points out an odd contradiction in the dating of *The Fall of Gondolin* between Tolkien's own statements and the evidence of other writings around this time:

'JRRT recalled that 'The Fall of Gondolin' was 'written in hospital and on leave after surviving the Battle of the Somme in 1916' (*Letters* 221; cf 336)... He also said the tale emerged 'during sick-leave at the end of 1916' (215; cf 345). Other letters (345, 386) indicate that composition continued into 1917. Feasibly the tale was written after 'The Cottage of Lost Play' (see Chapter 12) and the hospital in question might have been in Harrogate, where he spent most of March 1917.'

This last decision is reached by Garth because:

'' 'The Cottage of Lost Play'; name changes in or between the first, undated text and a fair copy begun by Edith Tolkien on 12 February 1917 match those in the early chart of names in 'The Poetic and Mythological words of Eldarissa'. which clearly predated 'The Fall of Gondolin'. The elf-king's name *Ing* in 'The Cottage of Lost Play' was emended to *Inwë* , his name in 'The Fall of Gondolin'. The sun-tree of Valinor was at first *Glingol,* a name given in the latter to the tree's seedling in Gondolin itself.'

(Garth 2003, Great War, Notes, p.353 & 355)

This seeming contradiction between Tolkien's assertion that he began work on *The Fall of Gondolin* in 1916 and the evidence of the names in that and other stories could easily be explained if we take it that the work of 1916 was the 'Trojan version', whose existence we have here shown is probable, and if we then assume that the switch to *The Fall of Gondolin* as we know it did not take place until 1917. This change might have taken place as late as the early autumn of that year, after Sassoon's opinions caused such trouble. In our view it is far more likely, however, that around the end of 1916 Tolkien had already been advised that carrying on writing the way he was going would create problems. In that case *The Cottage of Lost Play* (which at a bare 5 pages is the shortest piece in the whole *Book of Lost Tales*) would have been written in January 1917 as a 'reworking' of the (actual or projected) introduction to the 'Trojan story', with the discovery of the book on Santorini, and Tolkien would already have intended to follow through with a rewriting of the whole tale as *The Fall of Gondolin* , an intent fulfilled between then and mid-1917. That in turn would leave space for *The Tale of Tinúviel* , which was also written in 1917 according to C.J.R. Tolkien's Introduction to the piece in *The Book of Lost Tales*, volume two.

There are two good reasons, then, why Tolkien would have been pushed in the direction of fantasy in order to write inexplicitly about war; firstly to express a vision that did reach beyond waste and futility into the hope that is the only thing that makes survival bearable, and secondly to avoid the perils of realism and obvious allegory under censorship.

VII; The Mariner's Tale

In addition to this, there was a story already developing in Tolkien's mind which could be added to any existing Trojan material with the greatest of ease to create something which fulfilled all the requirements. This was the 'Eärendel' story which can first be seen developing in verse dating to before the writing of *The Fall of Gondolin*. The link is unstated, but clear nonetheless. If as we believe, Tolkien had decided that the Trojan story survived because it was preserved on an island, that preservation necessarily involved a sea-voyage both for the tale to reach the island, and for its finder (and perhaps its decipherer) to reach the place where the discovery would be made. Eärendel was already established as the Mariner in poems dating to before the writing of *The Fall of Gondolin*, so Tolkien could easily make him into the person who carries the story *to* the island. In *The Book of Lost Tales* proper, although Eärendel is not yet the messenger who causes the War of Wrath and the rescue of the Elves, his voyage is nonetheless deeply intertwined with those events. He is also said to have been in contact with the Elves of the island, at least for a time. Furthermore, there are faint but definite traces of stellar legends being associated with the Fall of Troy, as we will see in more detail later, and that too would draw in Eärendel, the Sailor who becomes a Star. Much later, Eriol/Aelfwine comes to Tol Eressëa; as, probably, a character like a philologist or archaeologist serving in the British Army had come to Santorini, a *persona*for Tolkien himself as decipherer of 'found manuscripts'. Much later in *Out of the Silent Planet* , C.S. Lewis would christen a Tolkien-style character 'Elwyn Ransom' - and Priam of Troy's name means 'the ransomed one' (in the classical versions he was let go free after the first sack of Troy by the Greeks, rather than not being there as in medieval versions). Then the motif is doubled; the decipherer, the learner of Elvish, has himself to write down what he has learned and preserve it through another turn of war and destruction, sending it on to a third, nameless and unidentified pair of hands belonging to someone who knows Old English and can read Eriol/Aelfwine's record. Thus the structure not only of *The Fall of Gondolin* but also of the Lost Tales emerges from the plot imperatives set up by the meeting of Eärendel with a Trojan survivor, and perhaps also a foretaste of the Lost Road and the Notion Club Papers that came later still.

VIII; Folklore and Fantasy at the Front

Finally, Tolkien's choice of fantasy as a vehicle for a war story with an ultimately hopeful ending may well have been influenced by the number of fantastic stories, openly fiction or supposedly true, which were set on the Western Front and were circulating at the time. Arthur Machen's famous piece 'The Bowmen', with its tale of ghostly archers aiding the beleaguered British forces at the battle of Mons, was the tip of an iceberg of 'war folklore' and fantastic fiction: 'And as the soldier heard these voices he saw before him, beyond the trench, a long line of shapes, with a shining about them. They were like men who drew

the bow, and with another shout, their cloud of arrows flew singing and tingling through the air towards the German hosts.
The other men in the trench were firing all the while. They had no hope; but they aimed just as if they had been shooting at Bisley.
Suddenly one of them lifted up his voice in the plainest English.
"Gawd help us!" he bellowed to the man next to him, "but we're bloomin' marvels! Look at those grey... gentlemen, look at them! D'ye see them? They're not going down in dozens, nor in 'undreds; it's thousands, it is. Look! Look! there's a regiment gone while I'm talking to ye."
(First World War.com - Encyclopedia - The Bowmen)

As a supposedly true counterbalance to the above, we have the account of William Kirk, a second sighted Scot serving with the Seaforth Highlanders. He gave the following account of a time when he tried to rest during a lull in the fighting when a storm forced him to seek shelter:
'In spite of his need for shelter from the hissing rain, Kirk could sense the eeriness and an air of menace all round him. The main door of the farmhouse and all the windows were bolted and barred, but one side door remained unsealed. It yielded to his elbow and led to a carpenter's bothy, full of rusted tools and dusty benches, but dry. With the storm still raging outside, Kirk fell asleep to dream of gunfire, warfare and destruction.
Suddenly he woke. Shouts, screams of women, and the whinny of tortured horses clamoured around him. He opened the door. Outside the sounds of riot raged, and above the midden he could see the red glow of a fire, 'as if some gigantic opening in the heavens threw down some malignance on the earth and here in centred.' Even the lightning paled against the flare. Yet there was not a living soul in sight.' (Sutherland 1985 Ravens and Black Rain, Part 2, ch.9, p.276)
Kirk had 'seen' events fifty years earlier. And this was confirmed by a French officer he met afterwards.
Not regarded as 'literature', and particularly despised by exactly those self-consciously literary circles that would produce the influential post-war critics and writers, this material has been largely forgotten. It was however part of the context against which Tolkien was writing 'The Tale of Gondolin' and it needs to be taken into account if we wish to think about why Tolkien chose to write what he did, when he did.

IX; Conclusions

We believe that J.R.R. Tolkien was not succumbing to romanticism or making a wild-eyed escape from reality into faery when he began writing fantastic fiction during the First World War. Contrary to what is generally said, it was possible to look at that war within the European tradition of literature if a writer was willing to use the resources of that tradition, changing them with imagination and seeing the applicability of older works, instead of rejecting the tradition wholesale. *The Fall of Gondolin* almost certainly began as a straightforward version of the pro-Trojan medieval Troy-legend, intended as comment on the futility and wastefulness of the war. This was possible because the classical 'historical forgers' and the later medieval writers took such a stance. There is evidence for it in the structure and plot and most important names of the *Lost Tales*. Tolkien subsequently changed his plans radically, for two main reasons. Firstly, he had to find a way avoid the perils of realism and obvious allegory under strict censorship. That Tolkien turned his hand to 'realistic' writing can be seen in the examples of *The Lost Road* and *The Notion Club Papers*. Secondly, he needed to express a vision that did reach beyond waste and futility into the hope that makes survival bearable. Both these points pushed strongly in the direction of fantasy instead of historical fiction. There were also good models available at the time for the use of fantasy in connection with the War itself, though they are little-known nowadays. Furthermore, Tolkien had to hand another story - as yet expressed only in poetry - which would fit in with what had already been written through the motifs of sea-voyage and island of discovery, and perhaps of change in the skies, the appearance or disappearance of stars. This was the story of Eärendel the Mariner. Combining the Trojan tale and the verse featuring the Anglo-saxon angel created *The Fall of Gondolin*.

Whatever its exact causes and antecedents, *The Fall of Gondolin* tells a story that was to remain substantially unchanged for the rest of Tolkien's life. Clearly, it meant something to him; equally clearly, it gave him even more problems than the rest of what was to prove the impossible-to-finish 'Silmarillion'. The late series of annalistic accounts of the stories set in Beleriand, dating to some time after the publication of 'The Lord of the Rings', do not go further than the death of Túrin Túrambar and so never reach Gondolin let alone Eärendil, even though this pair of stories were by all accounts the kernel of the whole business. There is something of major significance going on here, but the evidence is very scanty and hard to interpret. What we can say is that there are deep and important links between 'The Book of Lost Tales' and life and literature in the Great War. This however is a long and complex story that deserves a book to itself - and will hopefully receive one some day.

Note 1: αοιδος - given as the noun 'singer, minstrel, bard', or the adjective tuneful or musical.

Herewith we give the original Middle English text for the poems.
Note 2:

'The rynels wex red of the ronke blode,
That were slayne in the slicche, & in slym lightyn.
There sothely was sene what sorow & pyne,
And how balfull & bittur the banke was to wyn.
How the grekes were gird vnto grym dethe,
Neuer red was in any Romanse with no renke yet,
That any weghes in the world, that to werre yode,
With soche baret, fro the bote vnto bank wan
As hit happit here with so hard fight.'

(Panton & Donaldson 1968, bk.XIV, lines 5709-17).

Chapter Four:

The Tale of Tuor & Eärendil.

It is time now to look at the other major element in the story of Gondolin, the complex of ideas and stories centering on the word 'earendel', which Tolkien had certainly been working on at an even earlier date than the beginnings of *The Fall of Gondolin*. Most of the evidence for this can be found in the last section of volume II of *The Book of Lost Tales*, as well as in Humphrey Carpenter's Biography and J.R.R. Tolkien's *Letters*. Eärendel was supposed to have been the starting point for Tolkien's imaginative excursions according to Carpenter:
'Among these was the Crist of Cynewulf, a group of Anglo-Saxon religious poems. Two lines from it struck him forcibly:

Eala Earendel engla beorhtast
ofer middangeard monnum sended.

'Hail Earendel, brightest of angels/ above the middle-earth sent unto men.' ' (Carpenter, 1977, Part 2, ch.6, p.72)

I:Philological Cousins; Eärendel, Orendel and Eärendil

a; Evidence

As we have seen in the previous chapter, as soon as J.R.R. Tolkien began to look more closely at the line of Old English verse about 'earendel' which so enchanted him, he would have found himself in a tangle of legend, story and language with few equals even in the 'pathless Mirkwood' of early Northern European literature. The only substantial piece of work on any character with a name amongst the 'philological cousins' of 'earendel' is the German romance Orendel, probably composed around 1200 but surviving only in considerably later versions. It is reasonable to assume that, enchanted by the famous Eala Earendel line of poetry (as given above), Tolkien had read everything he could get his hands on about the whole matter (he might even, given Oxford's system of teaching, have been able to do so as coursework during his undergraduate years), and the Orendel-romance had been published in 1880 (Bonn, edited by A.E. Berger - ref. from Gillespie 1973, Bibliography).
In the early poem the Happy Mariners written in July 1915, and revised circa 1940, we can see that link in the final verse:
'O happy mariners upon a journey far,
beyond the grey isles and past Gondobar,
To those great portals on the final shores
where far away constellate fountains leap,
and dashed against Night's dragon-headed doors
in foam of stars fall sparkling in the deep!...

Ye follow Eärendel without rest,
the shining mariner, beyond the West,
who passed the mouth of night and launched his bark
upon the outer seas of everlasting dark.
Here only comes at whiles a wind to blow
returning darkly down the way ye go,
with perfume laden of unearthly trees.
Here only long afar through window-pane
I glimpse the flicker of the golden rain
that falls for ever on the outer seas.'
(BOLT vol.II, ch.5, p. 275-6)

In a note following this poem, C.J.R. Tolkien says:
'I cannot explain the reference 'in the revised version only, line 24' to the journey of the mariners 'beyond the grey islands and past Gondobar'. *Gondobar* ('City of Stone') was one of the seven names of Gondolin (p.158).'
Perhaps Tolkien was even in 1940 revisiting the Trojan material - perhaps in order to obtain information to use in his Minas Tirith section - and in that frame of mind rewrote the Happy Mariners to include Eärendel sailing past Gondolin and/ or Troy. This would chime in with the journey undertaken by Jason and the Argonauts through the Bosporus and into the Black Sea (M. Wood 'In Search of Myths and Heroes' 2005). In one version of Jason's story, he returns to Greece by sailing across the Black Sea, then up the Danube and down into the Adriatic. This is a geographical impossibility, but one which finds a more realistic echo in one of Tolkien's early outlines for the voyages of Eärendel:
'Mediterranean (loses his boat (travels afoot through wilds of Europe?)) or Atlantic.' (BOLT vol.II, ch.5, p.261.)

An interesting connection to this character comes in early in the writing of LotR according to C.J.R. Tolkien:
'The name of the King of Men was first written *Valandil*; above this my father wrote *E* and *Orendil*. The next part of Gandalf's story was constantly changed in the act of composition, and at subsequent occurrences the name of the King varies between *Valandil > Orendil/Elendil, Elendil > Orendil*, and then *Orendil* unchanged; I read *Orendil* throughout.' (*Return of the Shadow* , HOME vol.VI, The Second Phase, ch. 15, Note 26, p. 270-271)
Thus Orendil was a King of Men, one interchangeable with Elendil who of course is intimately connected with Eärendel throughout Tolkien's writings. The change in ending from Orendel to Orendil is an exact match for the change from Eärendel to Eärendil.

Orendel has never been translated into English, and we are deeply indebted to Miss Susanne Stopfel, without whose research and translation we would have very little idea of what this romance contains or is like. In view of this general lack of material about a potentially important source, we make no apologies for providing an extensive summary based on Miss Stopfel's work, with our own notes and some material from other sources (primarily G.T. Gillespie 1973 and

Gerritsen and van Melle 1998). Italicised passages below are our comments; plain text is the account of the original story.

The story starts with a description of how the Coat of Christ ends up being swallowed by a whale. After this, the tale then turns to Orendel, youngest son of King Ougel of Trier [*according to G.T. Gillespie the nearest equivalent of this name belongs to a dwarf, Eugel, which offers room for the interpretation that one of the major characters is of partly or wholly supernatural descent*]. Orendel sets out with seventy-two ships, intending to win the hand of Bride, Queen of Jerusalem. All the ships are wrecked and Orendel is the only survivor [*as Voronwë is of* his *fleet in the 1950's version of The Fall of Gondolin*]. The prince then tries to take service with a rich fisherman [*who sounds suspiciously like the Grail King, often known by that title*], who demands proof that he knows something about fishing [*an episode reminiscent of the BOLT 'Tale of Tinúviel's account of Beren's interview with the cat-demon Tevildo, who wants proof of Beren's prowess as a huntsman*]. Since Orendel knows nothing at all about fishing, he prays to God and St Peter for help, and is rewarded with a huge catch of fish, amongst which is the whale that had eaten the Grey Coat of Christ [*as mentioned by T.A. Shippey 1992, ch.7, p.219*]. The Archangel Gabriel now appears, telling Orendel to buy the mysterious grey mantle from the fisherman, and even giving him the thirty gold pennies he needs to do so [*similar to Tuor's gift of a grey cloak from the Vala Ulmo, Lord of Waters, in the 1950's version*].

Next, Orendel sets out for Jerusalem, where everyone calls him 'Greycoat' after the mantle he wears. He borrows a horse and armour from two heathen brothers who are knights, in order to be able to join in the jousting that is going on, and, hopefully, impress Queen Bride. Orendel defeats everyone else (among others he kills one of the two brothers who lent him his horse and gear, a giant riding an elephant, and a complete Syrian army). The queen is duly impressed and lends Orendel her father David's sword, which he uses to defeat yet another army (always wearing his grey coat, which protects him from harm). Bride and Orendel are wedded, but an angel appears and tells Orendel not to consummate the marriage for at least a year. More armies appear and challenge Orendel, and on one occasion Bride herself dons armour and rides out to help her husband [*an episode resembling Idril's martial conduct and clothing in the BOLT account of the sack of Gondolin*]. Orendel's onetime employer Master Ise the fisherman joins them and is made a duke. On a campaign ordered by Master Ise, Orendel is taken captive and imprisoned in an enemy's castle. Bride lays siege to the castle [*looking at this point somewhat like Lúthien outside Tol-in Gaurhoth*], and one day is visited by a dwarf named Alban who promises that he will take her to see her husband. Once inside the castle the dwarf tries to rape Bride but is beaten up by her, though he finally imprisons her alongside Orendel. They are rescued by an angel who leads them out through an under-ground passage [*much as Tuor, Idril and the others escape from Gondolin*]. Alban submits and serves Orendel and Bride after this [*In note 1 to s.v Alberich, G.T. Gillespie compares Alban's actions to those of Alberich in the* Nibelungenlied *(where the dwarf is a reluctant but faithful servant of Siegfried) and in* Ortnit *(where Alberich is the helpful father of a hero seeking a heathen bride in the Holy Land) which rather reinforces the possibility of supernatural parentage suggested by the name of Orendel's father Eugel*].

Orendel now learns that his home town of Trier is besieged by a huge army [*paralleling Gondolin and Troy*], and leads a fleet there to help, accompanied by Bride and Master Ise. Orendel does not have to fight to save Trier; when he arrives, the heathen army besieging the city surrenders at once and pleads for baptism. No sooner is Trier safe, though, than news comes that Jerusalem has been conquered by a heathen king and his army. Orendel, Bride and Master Ise set off once more to Jerusalem; but before they leave, yet another angel appears to Orendel and tells him to leave his grey mantle behind at Trier. On the way back to Jerusalem Bride is imprisoned by the king of Babylon who tries to make her marry him [*reminiscent both of Maeglin's designs on Idril in BOLT and Lúthien's treatment at the hands of the Sons of Fëanor in Nargothrond in the Lay and later versions*]. Orendel and Master Ise attempt to rescue her and end up in prison as well. The Virgin Mary writes a letter to Orendel's army, which then lays siege to the castle of the King of Babylon, but Bride, Master Ise and Orendel manage to free themselves. Bride then goes to Jerusalem in disguise and enlists the help of an old ally to kill the heathen king and open the gates to Orendel and his army [*suggesting the actions of Lúthien at Angband and Tol-in-Gaurhoth respectively*]. That evening Orendel is visited by an angel who tells him not to consummate his marriage with Bride at all. The angel also tells Orendel that he and Bride will both die in half a year and two days. They spend the remainder of their lives in a monastery, and die on the expected date. At one point in the story a knight named Wolfhart attempts to carry off Bride, but she is rescued by the good heathen Dûrîân, who beheads the would-be abductor [*an episode resembling Idril's problems with Maeglin in the BOLT account of the sack of Gondolin*].

The edition used was W.J. Schröder (ed. and trans.) 1976, 'Spielmannsepen, Vol II; Sankt Oswald, Orendel, Salman und Morolf', published at Darmstadt.

b; Discussion

1;What sort of Poem?

Orendel is a poem of a sort not normally given much attention for either its literary quality (every source we have is dismissive of it, and Miss Stopfel describes it as episodic and repetitive) or its value as a source for legend and character (G.T. Gillespie does refer to it in his *Catalogue of Persons Named in German Heroic Literature*, but it never appears as the source of the first entry in a listing and is often only mentioned in footnotes). In German academic terms *Orendel* is classed as a *Spielmannsepos*, literally a 'minstrel epic', which can be very loosely defined as a later medieval, popular work with a strong tendency towards the Christianized fantastic, a habit of throwing material from all sorts of sources into a very loosely organised plot, and a near-total unlikeness in style and subject to the *Heldensage* or 'heroic sagas', the pieces which are certainly courtly epics. *Orendel* has no obvious predecessors in previous European medieval literature and very little posterity in later works either. As Gerritsen and Van Melle put it:

'This last fact [the bringing of the Mantle to Trier at the end of the poem] probably tells us something about the time when the legend originated, for on 1 May 1196 the Mantle, together with other relics, was solemnly transferred to the new altar of St Peter's in Trier.The appendix to the Strassburg Heldenbuch (15th century) names King 'Erentheil' of Trier as the earliest of the heroes. Saxo Grammaticus in his *Gesta Danorum* (c.1200) mentions one 'Horwendillus' as the father of 'Amlethus' (=Hamlet). The name is also found as a personal name among the Lombards ('Auriwandalo') and in Old High German ('Orentil'). Partly because of this, it has been thought that there must have existed an older epic about a hero called Orendel. The King's name has been linked to the Old English word 'earendel' (daybreak, morning star, beam of light) and with the Old Norse 'Aurvandill', the name of a semi-mythical figure. This, however, is extremely problematic. It is even questionable whether a heroic lay about Orendel - that is, without the Holy Mantle legend - ever existed. It seems more likely that the legend of the Holy Mantle was expanded using motifs current at the time (> Oswald and > Rother).' (A. Quak in Gerritsen and van Melle 1998, s.v. Orendel)

2; Places and Names; Trier as New Troy

Trier's name may be very close to the Classical form Troia - but is there any evidence that Tolkien could have used to link these two cities and so connect the story of Eärendil/Orendel with the Tale of Troy? We think there is.

The story starts with the geography of *Orendel*, which is not far off being nonsense. Trier may be on the river Mosel (also known as the Moselle), but even nowadays with all the 19th-century improvements to navigation it would be difficult to bring a medieval oceangoing ship (let alone a fleet of 72 sail) from Trier down the Mosel to the Rhine. After that the story demands a voyage along the Rhine to its mouth, through the English Channel, across the Bay of Biscay, through the Straits of Gibraltar and right along the Mediterranean to the Near East and the coast nearest Jerusalem. However, the appearance of the Holy Mantle of Christ as a relic at Trier Cathedral provides a clear occasion on which an *Orendel* -like story could have been moved to Trier from somewhere that *did* make geographical sense.

Trier's history, too, offered parallels to the legend which would help anyone who wanted to reset *Orendel* at that place. Whilst there never was a 'kingdom of Trier', the city had been the capital of Late Roman Gaul; one of the authors has been there and can attest that it has the only surviving Late Roman palace hall in Western Europe, two impressive sets of ruined Roman baths, a onetime city gate turned into a church in medieval times (the *Porta Nigra*) and a cathedral built over and incorporating half of the original Roman structure, amongst other Classical remains. Trier had also been captured four times by the pagan Rhineland Franks, most memorably in 440 AD (or thereabouts), when the sack of the city was so bad that it drove churchmen to flee as far as the Mediterranean coast in search of safety. Lastly, an enclave of Romance speech survived around Trier until the 10th or 11th century, creating an environment in which copies of the relevant chronicles and histories could survive long enough to be remembered (James 1988 ch.1 section 4 p.54, 56; ch.3 p.119 p/b). The vague outlines of the real history of Trier would therefore provide ample excuse for importing the story of Orendel.

The *Orendel* story is closely related to two much more respectable medieval German legends, the tales of *Ortnit* and *Wolfdietrich*, Both of these tales are set in the 'north Italian' region on the shores of the Mediterranean, a far better geographical possibility for a story involving Mediterranean voyages. In two versions of *Wolfdietrich*, a set of events paralleling Orendel's finding the grey robe of Christ is associated with a place which is called ' diu alte **Troye**' (Gillespie 1973 s.v. Else f., p.36). It would take no great leap of imagination for Tolkien to suggest that the *Orendel* story, like its relatives, might originally have been set in Northern Italy, where not only does *Wolfdietrich* have the Troy-name but there is also the city of Trieste, whose name could, medieval-style, be taken as 'Troia oueste', western Troy - and if anyone knew just how bad medieval mishandling of names could be, it was Tolkien. So there is an attractive run of similar names from Trier in Germany via Trieste in north Italy to Troia/Troy, which, whatever their actual origins, dates and meanings, are well within the range of medieval misspelling let alone imaginative association.

A close parallel to such mixups of names and history can be found in the medieval belief that the city of Troyes in France had a Trojan link; the German-speaking medieval historian Otto of Freising recorded in his history of the world, *The Two Cities*, the two competing theories that either, firstly, France and 'Troy' had been founded by the Trojan leader Franco, or secondly that the 'French Troy' had been founded by Ulysses (Colonne/Meek 1974, Introduction p.xvii). In actual fact Troyes derives its name from the Gaulish tribe of the Tricasses via a Roman version, just as Trier was originally *Augusta Treverorum*, from the tribe of the Treveri. The confusion was probably helped on by an early martyr buried in the town who had the name of Patroclus, the Greek hero who was Achilles' best friend and was killed by Hector before the walls of Troy. What all these medieval mistakes do is to create a situation where the *Orendel* -story certainly could have migrated from a North Italian setting to Trier. This kind of story-movement across national borders and cultures was attractive to Tolkien, as his specialisation in Beowulf shows.

It is also possible to imagine that the real place-name underlying that of Trier was Troy itself, which fits the criteria of geographical plausibility better even than North Italy. Furthermore, the pre-Trier story of *Orendel* would then be a reversal of that of Helen of Troy, with a Trojan prince winning a legitimate bride and saving his city, rather than taking a woman he has no right to and destroying it. By looking at the story in this way it is possible to see it as a very close match for Tolkien's Tale of Gondolin, in which a man who wins a rightful bride, in opposition to an unrightful suitor, is the hero who leads the only survivors of the destruction out of the city. Reversal of old motifs to create new ones is a strategy which Tolkien very often used.

Given that J.R.R. Tolkien was fascinated with the word-concept *earendel*, and that he was prone to think that medieval authors knew what they were talking about, we can guess that regardless of the difficulties and late nature of the sources, Tolkien would have preferred to believe that *Orendel* was, at however long a range and however badly misunderstood, a reflection of an older story. This would not be unreasonable in the context of medieval storytelling, where we are continually hampered by loss of material and the late appearance of stories which certainly do have early roots. An example of just such an occurrence is the story of Theodoric the Great's adventures in the Otherworld and his rescue from captivity at the hands of supernatural creatures by faithful friends. The only real version of this story which survives is in the German romance *Virginal*, written c. 1300 and preserved in three different later versions; but a reference to the story occurs in a much older source, the Old English poem *Waldere*, written between the 8th and 10th centuries, with the surviving fragments probably coming from a manuscript copied c.1000 (G.T. Gillespie 1973, Bibliography & s.v Dietrich, Virginal, Walther; Shippey 1992, ch.1, p.20-21). Within what was then an ongoing debate about *Orendel* (Gerritsen and van Melle cite M. Curschmann's 1968 book, *Spielmannsepik; Wege and Ergebnisse der Forschung von 1907 bis 1965*, or 'Minstrel Epics; from 1907 to 1965'), in which the modern consensus about the poem's date and origin had not yet emerged, Tolkien could have justified his use of this work as a source even in academic terms, let alone for imaginative writing. Combining the two (story and academic research) is the hallmark of Tolkien's approach in so many instances across his career (the most famous example would perhaps be his Beowulf, the Monsters and the Critics).

Trieste is of some extra interest in the context of cities with 'New Troy' place-names and Tolkien's writing as it was the nearest good-sized nameable town to the Isonzo valley, where by 1917 the Italians and the Austrians had fought no less than twelve battles (J. Keegan 1998 ch.7 pp.245-8, ch.9, pp.370-6), a frequent number in medieval literature but also one associated with the major battles before Troy. Given its modern misfortunes, Tolkien is quite likely to have heard of or read about Trieste. Furthermore, Trieste was the last home of Richard Burton, explorer, writer and translator extraordinary, who is likely to have been known to Tolkien not just on general principles (it is unlikely anyone of Tolkien's age and class had *not* heard of Burton and his adventures in exploration) but also because Burton's wife Isabella was a Roman Catholic. Isabella was devoted to her husband, but she was a disaster precisely because she was a good, pious and inflexible woman; her missionary activity led to Burton being expelled from Syria when he was British Consul in Damascus, and she burned all his papers after his death in a misguided attempt to protect his reputation, an act that has earned her the permanent hatred of historians, biographers and anthropologists.

Incidentally, the medieval historian Otto of Freising also says of Aeneas that he is 'according to others a betrayer of his country and a necromancer, inasmuch as he even sacrificed his own wife to his gods.' (Colonne/Meek 1974 p.xvii, citing Otto of Freising, *The Two Cities*, trans C.C. Mierow 1928, p.143). This offers an interesting parallel to Tolkien's Isildur as follows: Aeneas in Virgil's version is the man who escapes from Troy with his father and son, gathers together the survivors and sets off in search of a new home, eventually founding in Italy a city and a family ancestral to Rome and its first dynasty of emperors. Isildur is the hero who saves the fruit of the White Tree of Númenor, one of the leaders of the surviving Faithful and the co-founder of Gondor - but he is also the man whose curse is powerful enough to condemn the Dead Men of Dunharrow to their ghostly afterlife trapped in Middle-earth. This is a close parallel to the accusation of necromancy against Aeneas by Otto of Freising.

3; Orendel, Troy and the Elves

The *Orendel* - legend has a number of links to German romances which are much more 'respectable' in terms of their literary quality and legendary status. These romances contain a series of references to supernatural creatures and Troy. Individually, these references are slight affairs; but when set together, they create an interesting picture. Firstly, they offer support for Tolkien's strategy of using the Tale of Troy as the central plot thread for a story about city inhabited by elves. Secondly, they act as links between the Trojan legends and the Germanic legends, performing part of that 'weaving together' of seemingly disparate stories which as we have already said is a very important part of the medieval Trojan legend, and one which might well appeal to Tolkien.

In one of the medieval German romances, Troy becomes virtually a cipher for the otherworld:

'In **Wd(B)** 'diu rûhe Else von alter Troyen' comes from the forest on all fours; she bewitches Wolfdietrich so that he wanders mad in the forest; finally he agrees to marry her; she shares her kingdom 'diu alte Troye' with him and is baptised 'Sigeminne', being transformed into a beautiful woman; she then gives Wolfdietrich a protective shirt. Later she is abducted by Drasîân but is rescued by Wolfdietrich. **AHb** follows the account of **Wd(B)**.'

(Gillespie 1973 s.v. Else f., p.36)

'Wd(B)' is the c.1250-1300 variant of the German story of Wolfdietrich, a romance in which the hero is mostly trying to regain his own kingdom and punish the treacherous brothers who threw him out and imprisoned his faithful men, but has any number of adventures along the way; it was published in 1871 as part of the *Deutsches Heldenbuch* series (eds. A. Amelung, O. Jänicke, E. Martin, K. Müllenhof, J. Zupitza, 1866-73 repr. 1963-8, Berlin, 5 vols; vol.III, pp.167-301). 'AHb' is the probably 15th century foreword to the 'Strassburger Heldenbuch' compilation, which includes a version of the *Wolfdietrich* story as well as a variant one in the supposed summaries in its prologue; it appeared in 1867 in A. von Keller's 'Das Heldenbuch' (Stuttgart). The appearance of the lady 'on all fours' makes one wonder if she is not a shapechanger as well as someone of varying looks. Gillespie also notes that 'Else' appears as a water-spirit who goes through the same transformation of ugly to beautiful in the pre-1250 variant of *Wolfdietrich*, where she gives the hero a strength-bringing herb and marries one of Wolfdietrich's numerous brothers (the episode with the herb is like the passage where Lúthien treats Beren's wound after they are ridden down by Celegorm and Curufin, and Beren throws himself in front of an arrow meant for Lúthien. Remember also that Lúthien is able to transform herself into a large bat and has uncanny abilities such as growing her hair quickly and using it to put her guards to sleep). We have here therefore a case of Troy being regarded apparently as a remote or hidden realm, which is ruled by a princess of partly or wholly supernatural origins, who nonetheless marries a mortal man; and this story is found in works which were definitely published before Tolkien was thinking about 'The Book of Lost Tales', volumes which someone with his personal and professional interest in Germanic language and story might well have read.

The *Wolfdietrich* stories contain two more sidelong references of interest. Firstly, Wolfdietrich himself adopts the name of his wife Else's realm as part of an alias, calling himself 'Pilgerîn van Troyen' whilst resisting the blandishments of yet another heathen princess and defeating her father in a knife-fight (Gillespie 1973 sv Pilgerîn (2), Wolfdietrich). Secondly, in another of Wolfdietrich's many adventures there is a reference to another place with an interesting name :

'BELMUNT

A heathen giant, brother of Olfân (1) and ruler of *Troimunt*. Wolfdietrich kills him and wins from him the 'sant Jörgen hemt' (shirt of St George) which thenceforth preserves the hero's life

ref: **Wd(D)**, IV 6, 3; **Wd (Gr)** 396, 3.'

(Gillespie 1973 s.v. Belmunt; emphasis ours)

'Wd (Gr)' is *Der Grosse Wolfdietrich* A Holtzmann 1865, Heidelberg, and according to Gillespie this is the only comprehensive edition of the early-14th century version of this story, which is the one included in the same Strassburger Heldenbuch that includes a reference to King Erentheil/Earendel of Trier as the earliest of the heroes. 'Wd(D)' is an 1873 edition giving parts of this version and of one from about fifty years earlier.

This episode is the more important because it parallels the section in *Orendel* (whose eponymous hero is one of Eärendel's philological cousins) where the hero finds the seamless robe of Christ that thereafter protects him from peril (just as Ulmo's cloak protects Tuor in the 1950's work, *Of Tuor and his Coming to Gondolin*). As a result of this likeness, Wolfdietrich's adventure is likely to have been cited in any discussion of the episode in *Orendel*, and therefore is actually quite likely to have been known to Tolkien. It associates a place with a near-Trojan name (*Troimunt*, the hill of Troy?) firstly with supernatural creatures, secondly with the Orendel/Eärendil group of stories in specific, and thirdly it might also offer (though this is much more speculative) a reason for why Gondolin's king, Turgon, comes to be called 'the tallest of all the Children of Iluvatar' in notes associated with the 1950's *Tuor* , and therefore is a giant by any other name. This episode also naturally draws in the alternative version cited above, where it is Else van Troyen who gives Wolfdietrich the magical shirt. Guido delle Colonne also says that Priam 'was tall in stature, slender and attractive...', a detail not actually in Dares, whom Guido cites as his source (Colonne/Meek 1974 bk.8, l.205, p.84). This magical shirt may well reappear in another guise in the Hobbit, where Thorin Oakenshield gives Bilbo Baggins a mithril shirt (TH, ch.13, p.201) which thereafter preserves another hero's life - that of Frodo in LotR (Book II, ch.5, p.341-2 and ch.6, p.350). Indeed, reading the relevant passage in *The Hobbit*, one is drawn to wonder whether the mithril shirt that Thorin Oakenshield gave to Bilbo Baggins might not have derived from the mail shirt/ small coat which young Eärendel was wearing in Gondolin at the height of the assault, which turned the knife of Meglin (BOLT vol.II, ch.3, pps.174, 178).

Another instance where Troy and supernatural creatures appear in some relationship in German epic and romance is worth citing at length, because it connects two very important bodies of legend; the Tale of Troy and the Volsung stories. Hagen (a close relation of the Burgundian princes in the Nibelungen / Volsung complex) has an epithet which varies from 'von Tronege' to 'von Troy'. G.T. Gillespie explains that:

'Hagen's seat has been localised most plausibly at Kirch-heim in Alsace, formerly Nova Troja (see Hempel, Nibelungenstudien, 21f.); other localisations suggested are Xanten(...), Tournay(...), Troneck in the Hunsrück (...), and Tongres in Belgium(...). In **W**, Hagano is referred to as of Trojan origin, 'veniens de germine Troia' (28) which tallies with the fictitious Trojan origin of the Franks; 'Högni af Troia' of **ThS** II.322, 10, may well depend on **W**; in **AHb**, too, he is termed 'Hagen von Troy' (p.2, 35), and in a 15th-cent. document of the bishop's court at Xanten 'Haegen van Troien' (...)'

(Gillespie 1973, s.v. Hagen(E)von Tronege, & note 4, p. 57; ThS=Thidreks saga af Bern, c.1250: W=the Latin poem Waltharius, c.900) Gillespie also notes that:

'In **ThS**, Högni (I.321, 2) is the son of Oda, wife of Aldrian, by a demon who has ravished her while she was asleep in a garden; he is, therefore, the half-brother of Gunnarr, Gisler, Gernoz and Grimilldr [the princely family associated with Sigurd/ Siegfried]...'

Or as Thidrek's Saga puts it:

'There was a king named Aldrian who ruled over Niflungaland. He was a powerful man and his wife was the daughter of a powerful king. It happened one time, when she was drunk with wine and when the king was not at home in his kingdom, that she fell asleep in a garden outdoors and there came a man and lay with her. When she awakened she thought she recognised King Aldrian, but before she was completely awake the man disappeared. When some time had passed, the queen was pregnant. Before she gave birth, it happened that she was standing alone and the same man came to her and told her what had happened the first time they had met. He told that she was pregnant and the child was his with her.

He said that he was an elf. "If that child should grow up, tell him about his paternity but keep it secret from everyone else. It will be a boy, as I can already tell, and he will be a great man. He will often be in great danger and whenever he stands in such danger and cannot help himself, he should call on his father, and I will be there when I am needed." The elf then disappeared like a shadow.'

(E.R. Haymes 1988, The Saga of Thidrek of Bern; section 169, p.110)
Strictly speaking the king should be named Gjuki/Gibicho and the elf should be Aldrian, as in the *Nibelungenlied* (and in *Der Rosengarten*, which links the Nibelung and Dietrich legends). In both works Hagen's father is known as Aldrian, a name that is certainly better suited to an elf than a mortal king, as the '-ian' ending (derived from Latin and thus classical literature) was routinely used for dwarfs, giants and the like in German medieval tales - an interesting idea in itself, since such supernatural creatures are often regarded as peculiarly Northern European (Gillespie 1973 s.v. Drasîân). Evidently, medieval German writers did not necessarily agree with this idea. Since *Thidrek's Saga* elsewhere calls Högni/Hagen 'af Troia', it does give us someone of half-elven blood associated with Troy. So, overall, Hagen connects the Trojan and the Volsung legends, and he brings a strong supernatural and specifically elvish element into the story. No surviving medieval version makes much of this, but the potential is there.

Lastly, M. Scherer quotes a medieval version of the Judgement of Paris from 'the fourteenth-century English minstrel's romance, *The Siege and Battle of Troy* ' (a stanzaic rather than alliterative piece to judge by her terminology for other works) as having Paris be enveloped in a sudden mist whilst hunting, then lie down and fall asleep beneath a tree (very much in the vein of King Orfeo or Tam Lane), where he dreams a dream. The poet goes on to say;

'Four ladies of Elfin land,
Of them I then knew not at all
But soon thereafter I knew them well.
And then the ladies began to play;
They had found a ball of gold by the way
It was a full rich ball
Of burnished gold was it all.
And thereon was lettering
Of silver, in fair writing,
So that anyone could read it,
Who had ever been at any school.
The letters said 'The fairest woman of all
Shall have and hold this costly ball.' '
(Scherer 1963, ch.1 Before the Iliad, p.16)

The transformation of Classical goddesses into medieval elf-queens in this version of the 'Judgement of Paris' is certainly interesting in view of the transformation of Troy into the elvish city of Gondolin which Tolkien undertook.

We have seen that the *Orendel* romance's connections with other medieval German tales bring out a specific association of Troy and the supernatural. A similar connection in the person of Hagen/Högni 'von/af Troia' links the Trojan legend, the Volsung tales, and, specifically, elves. Medieval writers could also assimilate the Classical supernatural to their own brand of this material, as when a Middle English writer referred to Classical goddesses as elf-queens. All of these are ideas which find very strong echoes in J.R.R. Tolkien's tale of *The Fall of Gondolin*. As we have seen, Gondolin is very clearly based upon Troy, in the medieval version of the story of that city. Gondolin is inhabited by elves rather than mortal men - which is exactly the line that the romances associated with *Orendel* take. Lastly, in *The Book of Lost Tales* Tolkien brought together stories which inspired by material usually put into quite different classes - Norse/ Germanic, Classical and Celtic. This sort of wide-ranging linkage is exactly what we find embodied in Hagen von Troia, vassal and kinsman of the Burgundian kings, deeply involved with the fate of Siegfried and Brunhilt. In later versions of the tale, the story of Gondolin becomes intertwined with the story of Túrin, which is clearly connected to the Volsung/Nibelung legends, again echoing the link that Hagen symbolises.

4; Conclusions to Pt I - Philological Cousins

We are looking with Orendel at the 'first mortal hero'; which is a cusp of story. He represents a boundary between the demi-God heroes of mythology that came before, and a truly human named hero in a real place (if fictionalised and drawn from the Trojan material in actual fact). Eärendel was a mariner - and may be considered entirely mortal if he is a straight follow-on from Aelfwine, if touched by a wanderlust, but Eärendil is half elf, half man. The entire Silmarillion can be said to represent the transition between heroes that do great deeds that are firstly the Vala, then the Eldar, and finally mortal Men. It is hardly surprising then, right at the end of QS (p.367) in 'Of the Rings of power and the Third Age' that the final phrase of the final line of the book reads: '... and an end was come for the Eldar of story and of song'; now it was the time for 'recorded history'. With Troy, too, one might say that Tolkien could have considered the fall of that city to represent the first cusp point that linked the legendary falls of cities (such Thebes in Grecian legend) with ones that were real and historical. Snorri Sturluson would have considered Troy as a real place, as would other medieval writers, but by the nineteenth century, it was considered to be fictive - and then came Schliemann and his excavations and he overturned all of that. These cusp-points, moments of real change are important to Tolkien. With the Beowulf poet, it is the cusp between paganism and Christianity, as Tom Shippey points out. With Tolkien's short story Leaf by Niggle, it is the cusp of life and what lies beyond the Journey. With his late short story Smith of Wootton Major, it is owning the Star, and passing it on to a new recipient.

c; Orendel and the Tale of Gondolin

Such an explicitly Christian tale as *Orendel* might seem certain to have been disliked by Tolkien, since Humphrey Carpenter tells us in his *Biography* that one of Tolkien's complaints against the Arthurian legends was their open use of Christian motifs. However, Tolkien was willing to use Christian references when he thought the narrative situation required it, as is shown by the appearance of exactly such material in his poem *Aotrou and Itroun*. The two characters Aotrou and Itroun are a medieval Breton lord and his wife; as the historical situation demands, they are Christian; and Tolkien as narrator adds Christian references in his comments on their plight. Furthermore, the correspondences between the story of *Orendel* and the tale of Gondolin are such as to suggest that as so often happened, disliking something - especially something which appeared to be a late and badly misunderstood version of a story - was enough to make Tolkien think that he could do much better with the available material. There are in fact several pieces of evidence which strongly suggest to us that influence from the Orendel-romance or material relating to it was acting on the Tale of Gondolin as early as the *Book of Lost Tales* version.

1: Names

Firstly, there is the name of the hero, Tuor or Tûr himself (BOLT vol.II, ch.3, p.202). As G.T. Gillespie (1973) points out:
'TÛRîÂN (1) Isterrich(Istria)
Brother of Mimunc and companion of Dietwart [Ancestor of Dietrich von Bern/ Theodoric the Great]
ref: **DF** {'Dietrichs Flucht'} 433
In *Orendel* (12th cent.), the heathen Dûrîân (2384) beheads the abductor of Bride, Wolfhart. In Wolfram von Eschenback's *Parzival*, a certain Taurîân is the brother of Dodines (271, 12)
TÛRîÂN (2) von Spôlít(Spoleto)
Ermenrich's man
ref: **DF** {'Dietrichs Flucht'} 6524'

Gillespie's conspectus of German heroic names makes it clear that the '-îân' ending is not Germanic but derives from Latin/Romance 'ianus', and that it was mostly used in names of giants, dwarfs and heathens (Gillespie 1973 s.v.Drasîân). It would therefore be reasonable for Tolkien to shorten the name to its first element for re-use. The spelling of 'Tuor' fits with a number of names from German heroic literature; there are eight men and six women with names involving an -uo- spelling in Gillespie's catalogue. In short, it looks very much as if 'Tuor/Tûr' is a name altered from memory, which has been recalled by Tolkien as being associated with Orendel and the rescue of a woman, and applied to the hero of his new tale.

2: The Princess and the Miner; Idril & M(a)eglin

There is one particular episode involving Idril which almost certainly draws on the *Orendel* story. During the sack of Gondolin:
'...Voronwë told him [Tuor] of how he and she had waited before the doors of the house while the noise of those battles grew and shook their hearts; and Idril wept for lack of tidings from Tuor. At length she had sped the most part of her guard down the secret way with Eärendel, constraining them to depart with imperious

words, yet was her grief great at that sundering. she herself would bide, said she, nor seek to live after her lord; and then she fared about gathering womenfolk and wanderers and speeding them down the tunnel, and smiting marauders with her small band; nor might they dissuade her from bearing a sword.'
(BOLT vol.II, ch.3, p.187-8)
There is nothing like this in the Trojan legends. The women of Troy are passive in their disaster; they may run to temples in the vain hope of sanctuary (like Cassandra) or huddle together as Virgil depicted Hecuba and her daughters and daughters-in-law gathered in the inner halls of Priam's palace. In no version we have seen do any of them take an active part in events, as Idril does by gathering 'womenfolk and wanderers' and sending them to the tunnel that is the only hope of escape. Nor does any Trojan woman bear arms. These motifs do feature prominently in *Orendel*. In the summary provided by Miss Stopfel, at one point: 'More armies appear and challenge Orendel, and on one occasion Bride herself dons armour and rides out to help her husband.'
While G.T. Gillespie notes that:
'In the 12th-century 'Spielmannsepik' *Orendel*, a dwarf named Alban (2414) attempts to ravish the Amazonian heroine Bride, who tramples on him, after which he submits and aids her and the hero, Orendel; thus he plays the roles of Alberîch in **N** and **O.**' (Gillespie 1973, s.v. Alban & note 1 on p.4)
Miss Stopfel also says that this episode is associated with an escape by underground tunnel, like the escape of the fugitives from Gondolin.

The presence of the dwarf in this section of *Orendel* , and the nature of his actions, may well account for Meglin's attitude to Idril and his occupation, that of miner, in Tolkien's story of Gondolin. Firstly, Meglin/Maeglin wants to marry Idril, and in the BOLT version he is willing to use force to make Idril accompany him. When faced with the reality of siege and sack Meglin thinks matters over and decides that 'seizing Idril he would constrain her to guide him to the secrets of the passage, that he might win out of this terror of fire and slaughter and drag her along with him to the lands of Melko.' Then he puts his decision into action; 'Now then Meglin had Idril by the hair and sought to drag her to the battlements out of cruelty of heart, that she might see the fall of Eärendel to the flames; but he was cumbered by that child, and she fought, alone as she was, like a tigress for all her beauty and slenderness.' (BOLT vol.II, ch.3, pp.177-8). This fits with Alban's attempted rape of Bride and her resistance.

Secondly, Meglin is a miner. No profession other than that of 'lord' is given for any Trojan or Greek hero in any version of the Trojan legends. Dwarves in Northern European legend are however characteristically miners and metalworkers. So, if Meglin is a miner he is acting like a dwarf. This would only be reinforced if any commentary on *Orendel* that Tolkien read made the link between Alban and Alberich as G.T. Gillespie does in the quote given above. In Ortnit, Gillespie's second reference, Alberich has succeeded in having his way with a princess; their son is the hero Ortnit, who is helped for a while by Alberich. After Ortnit is killed by his father-in-law, Wolfdietrich marries Ortnit's widow - and as we have seen, the Wolfdietrich stories contain parallels to Orendel as well as instances of the name of Troy being linked to elves (section a.3 above), closing the circle of connections.

So, it is very probable that Tolkien took two specific motifs from the *Orendel* story to use in *The Fall of Gondolin*. The first is that of the active princess, willing and able to fight as Idril does in the sack of Gondolin. The second is that of the dwarf or supernatural miner with improper desires on princesses; thus, M(a)eglin is a miner and leader of miners, who wants to marry Idril, is rejected as a 'wrong' suitor and is willing to use force against Idril.

3: Greycloak

In the medieval German story, Orendel is called 'Der Graurockë', which can be translated as Greycoat, or the Grey-Coated Man. This epithet or its near relations crop up in several places in Tolkien's writings. Firstly there is Thingol of Doriath, who in the 'Silmarillion' as published in 1977 is explicitly given this epithet:

'*Elwë* Surnamed *Singollo* 'Greymantle'... Called (*Elu*) *Thingol* in Sindarin.'
(QS, Index p.394)

This however is a fairly late decision on Tolkien's part, made after *The Lord of the Rings* was written. Although the actual name of Thingol goes back to *The Book of Lost Tales*, (albeit only in the very last phase, the typed version of the *Tale of Tinúviel*, dating to 1920 or shortly after), the double name and the meaning *Greymantle* are not given until 1950/51, in the *Annals of Aman* and the *Later Silmarillion* (*Morgoth's Ring*, HOME vol.X, Part 2, p.82 & 86; Part 3 section I, ch.IV, p.172-3). An intermediate form appears in the 1937 Silmarillion:

'...that Elf who first was named Sindo, the Grey, brother of Elwë, but is called now Thingol in the language of Doriath.'
(*The Lost Road*, HOME vol.V, Part 2, ch.VI, p.215)

The original meaning of *Thingol* (if indeed the name *had* a meaning) is nowhere recorded in Tolkien's published works, and nor is the reason for the change to 'Greymantle'. Intriguing variants appear at several stages, but explanations are lacking. At present the name *Thingol* seems to be one of those which Tolkien invented first and only later explained in terms of Elvish languages. So we cannot be sure if there is actually any connection between 'King Greymantle' of Doriath in Tolkien's writings and Orendel Greycoat in medieval story.

Secondly there is Gandalf, who is called Greyhame by the men of Rohan. In 'The Two Towers', both Éomer and Théoden use this epithet for the wizard:

' "Gandalf!" Éomer exclaimed. "Gandalf Greyhame is known in the Mark; but his name, I warn you, is no longer a password to the king's favour.'

And:

' "The gift seems already to be given," said Théoden. "But hearken all! Here now I name my guest, Gandalf Greyhame, wisest of counsellors...'
(TT, Book III, ch.2, p.37 & ch.6, p.129)

'Hame' is a good Old English word, which in combinations such as 'Greyhame' means 'covering or garment' (OED sv Hame 1), so Gandalf is another 'greycoat' or 'greycloak' character. In his case there is a simple explanation given within the story; as part of an Order of Wizards whose members are distinguished by their emblematic colours, he habitually wears grey robes and cloak. What is not clear is when Tolkien attached the nickname to Gandalf. As a messenger from the West who brings hope, Gandalf in *The Lord of the Rings* certainly echoes some of the ideas associated with Eärendil, so the epithet could well be meaningful. If we knew how these connections arose, we would almost certainly have a better idea of how Tolkien developed the character of Gandalf from the little old man with a long wagging beard of the First Edition *Hobbit* to the mighty wizard of *The Lord of the Rings*.

Returning to *The Fall of Gondolin* , there is no clear mention of any grey cloak in the BOLT version of the story. However, among the notes cited under *The Tale of Eärendel* there is one possible reference, in the mention of how:
'(ii) 'The Oarni give to Eärendel a wonderful shining silver coat that wets not.' (BOLT vol.II, ch.5, p.263).
A far more definite use of the same object appears in the 1950's version of *The Fall of Gondolin*, where:
' "What then is my goal, Lord?" said Tuor.
"That which thy heart hath ever sought," answered Ulmo: "to find Turgon, and look upon the hidden city. For thou art arrayed thus to be my messenger, even in the arms which long ago I decreed for thee. Yet now thou must under shadow pass through peril. Wrap thyself therefore in this cloak, and cast it never aside, until thou come to thy journey's end."
Then it seemed to Tuor that Ulmo parted his grey mantle, and cast to him a lappet, and as it fell about him it was for him a great cloak wherein he might wrap himself over all, from head to foot.
"Thus thou shalt walk under my shadow," said Ulmo. "But tarry no more, for in the lands of Anar and in the fires of Melkor it will not endure..." '
(UT Part One, ch.1, p.28-9)
And again:
' "Death is all about us," said Tuor. "But I have strength left only for the shortest road. Here I must cross, or perish. I will trust to the mantle of Ulmo, and you also it shall cover. Now I will lead!"
So saying he stole to the border of the road. Then clasping Voronwë close he cast about them both the folds of the grey cloak of the Lord of Waters, and stepped forth.' (UT Part One, ch.1, p.39-40)

Just as the grey robe of Christ protects Orendel from harm, so too Ulmo's cloak protects Tuor and Voronwë. Like Orendel, Tuor goes on through perils to carry a warning to a very special city. Unlike Orendel, who is able to save both Trier and Jerusalem, Tuor's warning is ignored. This follows a pattern derived from the medieval Trojan legend which was already set in the *Lost Tales*, where Tuor plays the part of Helenus son of Priam, who warns against war with the Greeks, is ignored, and turns out to be right but himself escapes the ensuing disaster. The grey cloak of Ulmo in the 1950's 'Tuor' seems to be a massive development of an idea from *Orendel* which is only marginally present in the

Book of Lost Tales version. Just as the change to Voronwë's story, from inland thrall of Melko to sailor and last survivor of Turgon's messenger fleet, appears to represent a continuation of the Trojan links in the tale, so the addition of the 'grey cloak' motif seems to be a continuation of the Orendel/Earendel links. Furthermore, just as in the *Lost Tales*, Tuor inherits a motif rightfully associated with Eärendil. So we can say that the same sources which lie at the root of the *Book of Lost Tales* version of *The Fall of Gondolin* are still active and still fruitful in Tolkien's imagination in the 1950's, almost thirty years later, and some of the same patterns of adaptation - such as Tuor playing Orendel's role - are still working as well.

II; Sailing to the Promised Land

At some point early in the development of his 'Eärendel'-legend, Tolkien evidently decided that his hero should become a star by way of being a sailor. In BOLT vol.I, 'You and me and the Cottage of Lost Play' was written in April 1915 when Tolkien was still an undergraduate has no connection with the Eärendel material, being about where children went to play when they were asleep, though the sea is a strong motif even here:

'We wandered shyly hand in hand,
small footprints in the golden sand,
and gathered pearls and shells in pails,
while all about the nightingales
were singing in the trees.' (BOLT vol.I, ch.1, p.30)

Kortirion among the Trees in its first November 1915 version has an indication of the idea of sailing across the sea:

'Still bearing downward over numerous falls
One year and then another to the sea;
and slowly thither have a many gone
Since first the fairies built Kortirion.'

and, when speaking of a grove of trees, the image of ships sailing is invoked:

'Sing then of elms, belov'd Kortirion,
How summer crowds their full sails on,
Like clothéd masts of verdurous ships,
A fleet of galleons that proudly slips
Across long sunlit seas.'

and;

'Now are thy trees, old, old Kortirion,
Seen rising up through pallid mists and wan,
Like vessels floating vague and long afar
Down opal seas beyond the shadowy bar
Of cloudy ports forlorn:' (ibid, pps. 33-35)

By the 1937 rewriting of this poem, the passage of Elves across the sea is a far more definite motif:

Oh holy Elves and fair immortal Folk.
You sing then ancient songs that once awoke
Under primeval stars before the Dawn;
You whirl them dancing with the eddying wind,
As once you danced upon the shimmering lawn
In Elvenhome, before we were, before
You crossed wide seas unto this mortal shore.' (ibid, p.38)

Of far more relevance to us is Tolkien's poem 'The Happy Mariners' written in July 1915 which according to Christopher Tolkien has six preceding versions to the one given:

'Ye follow Earendel through the West,
The shining mariner, to Islands blest;
While only from that sombre rim
A wind returns to stir these crystal panes
And murmur magically of golden rains
That fall for ever in those spaces dim.' (BOLT vol.II, ch.5, p.274)

This idea of a sailor-hero in turn appears to us to have drawn in the legend of St Brendan the Navigator, the Irish abbot who voyaged west-over-sea to the Earthly Paradise. Tolkien is likely to have encountered the St Brendan legend in his childhood, in print or by word of mouth at the Birmingham Oratory. Its founder, Cardinal J.H. Newman, had been deeply involved in the setting up of Dublin's Trinity College in Ireland, the first university established there and a large part of Birmingham's Catholic population consisted of recent Irish immigrants, so there is an excellent chance that the Oratorians not only knew of St Brendan, but had one or more books detailing his colourful life and legend. One good possibility would be Denis O'Donoghue's 'St Brendan the Voyager in Story and Legend' of 1893 (Browne and Nolan, Dublin; republished as 'Lives and Legends of St Brendan the Voyager' by Llanerch in 1994), which includes both the Life and the Voyages in an assortment of English and Latin versions. This book has the original *Navigatio* and also the Middle English 'South English Legendary' version of the voyages of Saint Brendan.

The very early 'Eärendel' poems given in BOLT vol.II, chapter 5, show no sign of Brendan-motifs. We cannot be sure if the very first, pencilled version of *The Fall of Gondolin* included such ideas, but as matters stand, they first appear in the large block of 'cosmological' stories running from 'The Music of the Ainur' to 'The Hiding of Valinor', probably written from the 2nd half of 1918 to the middle of 1919. Towards the end of this time (probably), this new and fruitful source of ideas was brought to bear on the revision of 'The Fall of Gondolin', which is most extensive in the later section, just where these ideas turn up.

There is a definite if slight connection between St Brendan and the Trojan story which we have shown is the other half of the story of Gondolin, through the grandfather of medieval 'historical Troy' writing, Guido delle Colonne. The late-13th-century Sicilian writer actually cites Saint Brendan at one point in his work: 'He is also called Leviathan, according to Isidore, a water serpent. For this reason it is read in the *Apographia* of Saint Brendan that while he was voyaging through the ocean, this saint saw that this beast was of amazing length and huge size, and that he was cast down in the depths of the sea and confined there at the command of God until the Day of Judgement.' (Colonne/Meek 1974 bk.10, ll.210-16, p.93) Isidore, incidentally, is the very popular medieval encyclopedist Isidore of Seville, in his *Etymologies* (a modern edition was ed. W.M. Lindsay, 1911, Clarendon Press Oxford), and Guido delle Colonne is almost certainly writing about a version of the *Navigatio Sancti Brendani*, the 'Voyages of St.Brendan. The same information, with the source, also occurs in the alliterative 'Destruction of Troy', in book 10, lines 4438-41. This is of no real interest in itself in relation to J.R.R. Tolkien's published works (though we might perhaps look for sea-serpents and the Great Whale Uin to play a part if there is any unpublished material on Eärendil). It does create an interesting link between Brendan and the Trojan story.

One obvious link between Orendel and Brendan is that both are looking for the Promised Land - the Holy Land and Jerusalem in the *Orendel* story, the *terra repromissis sanctum* or Promised Land of the Saints in the Latin *Navigatio* of Saint Brendan (Barron & Burgess 2002 ch.1 p.19). Another connection lies in the names of their womenfolk, and this also becomes a link between both characters and Tolkien's Eärendil. Orendel's princess was Bride or Brigida, an Irish name early adopted into German-speaking usage (Gillespie 1973 s.v. Brigida); Brendan's sister was Brig and one of his important influences was St Brigid, whom he met in her old age. Another connection between Brendan and Brigid is hidden in the episode of the island abbey whose lamps are lit every evening by a fiery arrow from God. Brigid's name was explained by medieval Irish Christian commentators as *'Breo saighit*, a fiery arrow' (Baillie 2002 ch.9, p.131), so this abbey granted a fiery-arrow miracle really ought to be dedicated to St Bridget rather than its founder, St Ailbe. The connections between Brendan and Tolkien's Eärendil also revolve around names. These points are all small, but together they are significant. Firstly, the saint's 'Life' tells us that St Brendan's mother was named either Cara or Broinngheal, the former being a straight Romance 'beloved' even if it also has an Old Irish explanation, and the latter name meaning 'bright or shining breast'; when he is a year old, Brendan is fostered with the nun Saint Ita (Barron & Burgess 2002 Introduction). Eärendil's mother's name has the consistent Gnomish/ Sindarin form Idril, while in Quenya it is Irildë, later Itaril/Itarillë (the change being very late indeed, sometime after 1968 - intro. to The Shibboleth of Fëanor, *Peoples of Middle earth*, HOME vol. XII, Part 2, ch.XI, p.331). In the very early linguistic material associated with the Lost Tales *idril* is a Gnomish word meaning sweetheart, beloved, and therefore paralleling *Cara* (BOLT vol.II, Appendix on names). The early Quenya form means 'mortal maiden' (ibid) changed to 'wise' by 'The Lost Road' (Etymologies); the late Quenya form is of interest as it expands Ita's name and means 'shining, sparkling' (*Peoples of Middle-earth*, HOME vol. XII, Part 2, ch.XI, p.363 note 42), corresponding to one element in *Broinngheal*. Even at this late date, consciously or otherwise Tolkien seems to be drawing on his original sources to enrich his tale with fresh layers of imagery and meaning.

In the voyages of Brendan, the North is a place of peril. It is when he and his monks voyage north from their regular stopping-places on the Isle of Sheep,

Paradise of Birds and Isle of Monks that Brendan faces the worst dangers. These are the Isle of Smiths, the nearby High Island where one of Brendan's monks surrenders to the demons, and the Coagulated Sea. In this respect the anonymous, probably Irish, writer of the *Navigatio* anticipates what was to become standard British folk-belief of the Middle Ages and later. In the story of 'Culhwch and Olwen' in the *Mabinogion*, the Highlands of Hell are in the North. L.C. Wimberly in 'Folklore in the English and Scottish Ballads' (1928) points out that the ballads of 'Thomas the Rhymer' and 'The Demon Lover' both envisage hell as a mountain covered with frost and snow (ch.XII); but this is too late to be Tolkien's primary source for *The Book of Lost Tales*, written c.1916-20. For the concept in the Lost Tales, he must have been drawing directly on either medieval texts such as the voyages of Brendan and the *Mabinogion*, or perhaps the ballads in the great collection of F.J. Child, 1882-98. The loss of the latter part of the early pencil version of *The Fall of Gondolin* and the whole first version of *The Tale of Tinuviel* makes it impossible to be sure when the idea of evil coming from the North entered the 'Lost Tales'. Certainly by the time of the ink revision, this concept was already present in maps and in the cosmological stories. Melko is a creature of the North; his fortresses are there.

'In this dimness the Gods stalked North and South and could see little; indeed in the deepest of these regions they found great cold and solitude and the rule of Melko already fortified in strength; but Melko and his servants were delving in the North, fashioning the grim halls of Utumna for he had no thought to dwell among the others, howso he might fain peace and friendship for the time.'
(BOLT vol. I, ch.3, p.69)

By comparison, in the *Navigatio*, Brendan comes to an Island of Smiths in the north where he encounters evil creatures. In the South English Legendary (in the Laud 108 version published by the Early English Text Society in 1887, the only one Tolkien could have used until much later), the same episode is described as follows;

'Then saw they far in the north: a very dark land
that stank foully of smoke: and their ship was driven towards it
Then they heard great blowing; as of many bellows there
And great beating and such noise: as if it were thunder
Then was Brendan very troubled, and blessed himself very swiftly
Then came there out a loathly wight/creature: most hateful to see
All over black and burning: and looked about him
And turned away at once again - those monks were terrified
That loathly creature gave such a cry: as men might hear far and wide
Then came out there more such devils: thronging on every side
Many with flaming tongs and hammers
To the water's edge they quickly ran: after that ship every one
When they might not come near it: they soon began to yell
Their hammers all burning: after these men they threw
That men might neither see nor hear any thing except fire
The sea was burning all about: as if it too were ablaze

each threw his hook one after another: and some they threw on high
they threw all about that ship: but none came near to it.'

(Horstmann 1887 ch.36, lines 470-87) [Note 1]

These black and burning devils with their hook-hammers make some of the most plausible Balrogs in pre-Tolkien literature. Their great numbers fit with the 'host of Balrogs' in the BOLT *Fall of Gondolin.*

There is another possible reflection of the South English Legendary in the BOLT *Fall of Gondolin*, but this time from the material given under St Michael the Archangel. Shortly after the birth of Eärendil, Tolkien says that:

'Behold now many years have gone since Tuor was lost amid the foothills and deserted by those Noldoli; yet many years too have gone since to Melko's ears came first those strange tidings - faint were they and various in form - of a Man wandering amid the dales of the waters of Sirion. Now Melko was not much afraid of Men in those days of his great power, and for this reason did Ulmo work through one of this kindred for the better deceiving of Melko, seeing that no Valar and scarce any of the Eldar or Noldoli might stir unmarked of his vigilance.' (BOLT vol.II, ch. 3, p.165)

Describing the Devil, the South English Legendary says:

'For what time that the Fiend / our first father had won
(through that apple that he gave to him / master was he of man)
Then he had all men securely bound to him / until our Lord bought us
And since men were all his / he cared the less for them
He did not keep them carefully / as rascals never do
For plenty makes no dainty / as we see every day.
He went as does a free dog / brought up in a free-trade town
For he goes often in the sight of men / among them up and down
He neither growls nor bites at men / nor barks at them not one
But among men he goes quietly enough / that no man notices him
Just so fared the devil then / for mankind was all his
And he had of them such great numbers /he kept no count thereof, indeed

Which is just as well, because:

'Had he been such before / as he was after indeed
Scarcely was there any man / that had not been all his .'

(Horstmann 1887, St Michael Archangel, lines 261-72, 277-8) [Note 2]

Tolkien's Melko who does not bother about Men but keeps a close watch on Elves and Valar is much the same as this medieval lazy Devil who had thought Men completely won over and thus not worth bothering with.

III; Star of Troy

There is one important link still to be made, for so far we have mentioned very little that would connect Eärendel, the Mariner who becomes a Star, with Troy. There are however two probable and interesting connections here to give us the Trojan source for this character.

a; Sailing Away

Voyages are involved in any story of return from Troy (for the Greeks) or escape from Troy (for the Trojans). Aeneas the Trojan leads his fleet back and forth across the Aegean on his way towards Italy, calling at Delos, Crete and the west coast of Greece. Most famously of all, the Greek hero Odysseus takes ten years to reach his home on the island of Ithaca, off the west coast of Greece, after a voyage in which he has all sorts of adventures, including a visit to an 'earthly paradise' of sorts in the mysterious country of Phaecia. In the *Aeneid*, Helenus, the only son of Priam to escape the fall of Troy, is found in northwestern Greece ruling a kingdom carved out of the onetime realm of Achilles; he has crossed the Aegean to get there and in some versions, he later moves on, crossing back again to found Pergamum in Anatolia. Since as we have seen the story of Gondolin as a city is very closely tied to that of Troy, it is natural for the 'next part' of the other half of the story, to involve a character whom Tolkien had already established as a great voyager - Eärendel.

b; Changing Stars

From the very start, Tolkien identified Eärendel as a star. Therefore it is very important that there are faint but definite hints in Greek mythology and legend of changes in the stars being associated with the Fall of Troy. According to the 1st-century BC author Hyginus: 'But after the conquest of Troy and the annihilation of its descendants... overwhelmed by pain she separated from her sisters and settled in the circle named Arctic, and over long periods she would be seen lamenting, her hair streaming. That brought her the name of comet.' It appears that in Greek legend it was said that a minor star-goddess was sufficiently grief-stricken for Troy that she left her appointed place in the sky and changed from a permanent star into an inconstant comet. By Tolkien's favourite tactic of reversal, this Classical loss of a star becomes the rising of a star - the appearance of Eärendel, the Morning Star. It is probable that the star in question was one of the Pleiades, which are interesting in this connection: They were the daughters of Atlas who were chased so persistently by the giant Orion, son of the sea-god Poseidon, that they took refuge in the sky and became stars, according to Greek mythology. Orion continued to pursue them after he himself was transformed into a constellation. Tolkien's Eärendel is a sailor whose birth has been foretold and whose father was favoured by Ulmo, the Vala of the waters - not quite a son of Poseidon, but a close analogy within Tolkien's framework. In *The Book of Lost Tales* there are various suggestions for how Eärendel became a star. It is also said that: 'Manwë bade therefore Ilinsor, a spirit of the Súruli who loved the snows and the starlight and aided Varda in many of her works, to pilot this strange-gleaming boat... but Ilinsor is it rather who hunts the stars.' (BOLT vol.I, ch.8, p.192-3). Ilinsor hunts Eärendel across the sky, just as Orion, famed as a huntsman, pursues the Pleiades: 'The Moon mariner chases him [Eärendel] for his brightness and he dives through the Door of Night.' (BOLT vol.II, ch.5, p.255)

So there are two attributes which Tolkien gives to Eärendel in poetry preceding the writing of the *Book of Lost Tales*, which actually connect well with the story of Troy. Firstly, Eärendel is a voyager, and movement away from Troy always involves sea-voyages. Secondly, Eärendel is a star who is chased by the moon, and Greek myth associates the Fall of Troy with the disappearance of one of the Pleiades, a star-group pursued by Orion the Hunter.

IV; Tuor

When we first began to look at the story of Gondolin, it seemed possible that the once-popular romance of *Guy of Warwick* (a medieval bestseller, and story that was still available in Britain up to the Second World War, though utterly forgotten since) had played a part in the development of the story of Tuor. As our research continued, however, it became clear that much as Tolkien loved Warwick, and important as the town was in the *Book of Lost Tales* ,*Guy of Warwick* could only be a late and marginal influence to his writings, if that. Far more important was the collision of the *Orendel* story with the medieval Tale of Troy. The *Orendel* connection effectively creates the first part of the story of Gondolin, and thus the makings of a story of Tuor, because it is only here that the motif of *quest* which is such a marked factor in *Orendel* and its near relatives can easily be added, and in that motif the person undertaking the quest has to be an outsider to the people whose princess they marry.

a; In the Book of Lost Tales

1; Origins

In this first phase of the story of Gondolin, Tuor does not really have a background at all. Tolkien tells us that:
' "...Tuor was a man who dwelt in very ancient days in that land of the North called Dor Lómin or the Land of Shadows, and of the Eldar the Noldoli know it best. Now the folk whence Tuor came wandered the forests and fells and knew not and sang not of the sea; but Tuor dwelt not with them, and lived alone about that lake called Mithrim, now hunting in its woods, now making music beside its shores on his rugged harp of wood and the sinews of bears. Now many hearing of the power of his rough songs came from near and far to hearken to his harping, but Tuor left his singing and departed to lonely places. Here he learnt many strange things and got knowledge of the wandering Noldoli, who taught him much of their speech and lore; but he was not fated to dwell for ever in those woods.' (BOLT vol.II, ch.3, p.149)

Here there is absolutely nothing to compare even with the condensed account in chapter 23 of the 1977 *Silmarillion* ; indeed, it is not easy to reconcile this passage even with the rest of the *Lost Tales*. Who are these Men who seem to wander free in Dor Lómin, while the rest of the land is under the shadow of

Melko/Morgoth? Which Noldoli are independent enough to teach Tuor (and later to send him wood when he dwells for a while on the seashore) when later in the same story Tuor meets Elves who are only free of the binding spell of dread that Melko lays on his thralls when they enter Gondolin's guarded plain? How old is Tuor; who are his family, and why does he dwell alone? Tolkien tells us nothing with which we could answer such basic questions about the character.

Elsewhere we do learn a little more. When he first arrives in Gondolin, Tuor declares his name and lineage:

' "I am Tuor son of Peleg son of Indor of the house of the Swan of the sons of the Men of the North who live far hence.." ' (BOLT vol.II, ch.3, p.160)

The name of Tuor's father also appears in slightly different form when it is used as a patronymic for Tuor himself, 'Tuor Pelecthon' (BOLT vol.II, Appendix on Names s.v.*Idril* and *Peleg*). As we pointed out in Chapter 3, 'Peleg' is the simple Gnomish/Sindarin word for 'axe', derived directly from the Classical Greek word. Tuor's grandfather Indor also has a name which appears to be a simple word, 'lord, master of a house' (ibid, s.v. *Indor*). This type of name is the same as that which Tolkien used for the Kings of Rohan in LotR, most of whose names are Old English words for king or lord.

2; Swans and Knights

Tuor's association with swans seems to be a complete innovation by Tolkien, unparalleled in any of the possible sources or related works. However there is more to this than meets the eye, and the potential links run from Classical to early Germanic sources.

One possible influence on Tolkien's use of the swan motif is perhaps a reminiscence of a passage in Virgil's 'Aeneid', where Venus (in disguise) is trying to cheer up Aeneas and says:

'All this is true unless my parents have failed in their efforts to teach me to interpret the flight of birds. Look at these twelve swans flying joyfully in formation. The eagle of Jupiter was swooping down on them from the heights of heaven and scattering them over the open sky, but now look at them in their long column. Some are reaching land. Some have already reached it and are looking down on it. Just as they have come to their home and their flock has circled the sky in play, singing as they fly with whirring wings, so your ships and your warriors are either already in port or crossing the bar in full sail. Go up now, and follow where the road takes you.' (Virgil trans West 1990/2003, book I, p.14)

This is not really very close, however. Most importantly, Virgil's swans are omens of other people's fates, not the hero's own guides. Less importantly, they are twelve rather than seven in number, though sheer alliteration could account for that. As we have pointed out already, we can find very few references to the 'Aeneid' in Tolkien's work, but where they do occur they have an awkward habit of being significant.

On the other hand, given the associations of Tuor with medieval German

literature, it is not impossible that there is some faint influence from the sprawling complex of 'Swan Knight' legends acting on Tolkien's story. In 1912, R.W. Chambers cited one of the early German editors of Beowulf as follows:
'...Leo connected the stories of Sceaf, Lamissio and the Knight of the Swan...'
(Chambers 1912, 'Widsith', ch.III, p.123, note 4)
The common thread linking all of these three, and Tolkien's Tuor, is the idea of a hero who comes from the sea (or the water) in mysterious circumstances, proves to be a mighty champion who comes to the aid of a people in need, and then departs as strangely as they came. The full complexity of the possible links of Tuor to Northern European legend cannot be looked at here (that will have to wait for the book we are planning on Tolkien's use of those sources) Here we can say that Tuor, 'of the house of the Swan in the far North', seems to do two things. Firstly, in *The Fall of Gondolin* Tolkien's geography is vague, but Dor-Lomin is not 'far North' of Gondolin; therefore, this statement could draw on an earlier form of the tale with a different setting (such as one where a Northern, Germanic hero comes to Troy to help defend the city, in a more historical version of the *Orendel* story). Secondly, Tuor is repeatedly associated with bears (his harp is strung with the sinews of bears, and he wears bearskins) and this could well tie him back to Sceaf, who is best known from the poem *Beowulf* whose hero's name, 'Bee-wolf', is a transparent metaphor for 'bear'.

It is worth mentioning another 'Northern' link with Tuor here, though we cannot (yet) explain it any more than can its author, C.J.R. Tolkien, who is quoting a fragment of an unfinished 'Lay of Eärendel':
'The reading of line 7 as first written (it was not struck out, but *Tûr the earthborn was tried in battle* was added in the margins:

But Wade of the Helsings wearyhearted

is remarkable. It is taken directly from the very early Old English poem *Widsith*, where occurs the line *Wada Hælsingum*, sc. *Wada [weold] Hælsingum* , 'Wada ruled the Hælsingas'. One may well wonder why the mysterious figure of Wade should appear here in Tuor's place, and indeed I cannot explain it; but whatever the reason, the association of Wade with Tuor is not casual.'
(*Lays of Beleriand*, HOME vol. III, Part II section 2, p.143)

It is also possible that Tuor's swan-connections were a late addition to the story, brought about by links elsewhere in the *Lost Tales* to Wolfram von Eschenbach's medieval German Grail-story *Parzival*, where the hero is the father of the Swan Knight, Lohengrin. Since Eärendil came to marry Elwing and so be the next generation in a lineage associated with the Grail, swan-imagery almost had to creep in somewhere. The very unfocussed story of Tuor would be one place where it could easily be added for a bit of 'local colour' in an otherwise bare account of the hero's youth. The 'swan-prowed boat' (BOLT vol.II, ch.3, Commentary, p.204) in which Tuor travels on Lake Mithrim and the way in which he is led by swans south along the coast to the mouth of a river, which the reader eventually discovers is the famous Sirion, are distinctly like the tale of Lohengrin, with his boat drawn by a swan.

<u>3; Prophets and Princesses</u>

If the story of *Orendel* is to be linked to the medieval Trojan legend, someone has to become an incomer to the hidden city, and in all probability the husband of a local princess, following the pattern of Orendel's arrival in Jerusalem as a suitor for Bride's hand. Yet from the very start there is a dislocation, for Tuor does not set out from home to find a bride, unlike Orendel, Oswald or Rother. His journey in the BOLT version is motiveless, mere wandering, until he meets Ulmo in the Land of Willows. After that Tuor has a purpose, to find Gondolin and give Ulmo's message, but it is not a motif to be found in either of the source-stories, and may well have been invented by Tolkien to get round the lack of any possible meeting-point between them as they stood. In the Trojan legends there is no reason why anyone should arrive from outside and marry a princess, yet this is the one thing which is almost inevitable in any tale drawing on *Orendel*. So something new is required, and the Trojan legend provides the solution; the gods' warning against war has to come from outside the city, not inside it. Since the most prominent warnings come from Priam's children, and in the medieval version Priam's son Helenus is the first and most important warner, moving the source of the warning outside the city almost automatically removes the idea that the person making the prophecy is the king's son. It thus moves the story towards the *Orendel* position, where the king has no sons and the princess whom the stranger marries is the sole child and heir of the resident king. The Tuor of the *Book of Lost Tales* seems to start therefore as a character 'outside' Gondolin and stray into the story. It is possible that several ideas collided together and out of their fusion came the story as we know it. It may be that the 'Eärendel-figure' fulfilled all the roles within the original story and that as is often the case with the way Tolkien's expands a tale, a generation was 'added' and Tuor brought in from wherever he was 'wandering'.

In the *Book of Lost Tales* version, we have in 'early Tuor' what seems a 'story in miniature' before the main story itself really takes off. Geographically and in terms of the needs of that part of the story it seems to be a very long way up the river. There are three stretches of 'many days' march, one stretch before the Land of Willows, where Ulmo appears from the river and does not give Tuor a cloak; one stretch afterwards with the help of the 'gnomes' all of whom desert Tuor out of fear except Voronwë; and the third stretch between the meeting with Voronwë and the finding of the mouth of the tunnel that leads to Gondolin.

<u>4; Rough Carpentry; Junction-Points in 'The Fall of Gondolin'</u>

There are two clearly visible points in the story of Tuor and the Exiles of Gondolin where otherwise independent stories have been joined together in a way that is never quite resolved or fully smoothed over. The first and most obvious is the point where the *Orendel* material is joined onto the Trojan story, which can clearly be seen when Tuor does not actually have to do anything to win the hand of the princess Idril. Once Tuor reaches Gondolin, he learns about many things, but there is no suggestion that anyone requires this of him. It helps him, and:

'Now for his skill and his great mastery over all lore and craft whatsoever, did Tuor become a comfort and stay to the king who had no son; and he was beloved by the folk of Gondolin.'

which in turn leads to:

'Now came days when Tuor had dwelt among the Gondothlim many years. Long had he known and cherished a love for the king's daughter, and now was his heart full of that love. Great love too had Idril for Tuor, and the strands of her fate were woven with his even from that day when first she gazed upon him from a high window as he stood a way-worn suppliant before the palace of the king. Little cause had Turgon to withstand their love, for he saw in Tuor a kinsman of comfort and great hope. Thus was first wed a child of Men with a daughter of Elfinesse, nor was Tuor the last.' (BOLT vol.II, ch. 3, p.164)

What is singularly missing in all this is the medieval motif which is the core of *Orendel*, the idea of a hero having to win his bride by performing some deed or deeds. Missing too is any suggestion of why Idril is the heir, why Turgon has no son, who Turgon's wife is and why she is nowhere to be seen. Meglin (Maeglin) does appear as someone who is unhappy about the marriage, but in this version although he is the King's nephew, he has actually asked Turgon for Idril's hand, and has been refused not on grounds of too close a relationship, but of Idril's reluctance and Turgon's feeling that Meglin is interested in power rather than truly loving Idril. There is thus a slightly but definitely awkward meeting between the Trojan story, where the heroes are lords or princes born to that city, and their status needs no explanation, and the *Orendel* story, where the hero who marries the princess is an outsider who wins his place by prowess. Although many of the problems would be resolved or smoothed over in later versions, this central 'rough spot' would remain. Thus Tuor seems to be rewarded with a high status bride for no obvious reason - he has not as yet done anything heroic to prove his worth to Turgon and has not the lineage (in elvish eyes) to rightfully claim a princess as his bride (c.f. Thingol and Beren). The heroic deeds of Tuor that follow during the sack of the city are to a great extent a way to 'prove' his heroic credentials.

As husband of Idril and father of her son, as the effective heir to the crown of Gondolin, and as the leader of refugees to safety after the fall of the city, Tuor has now taken on a role combining aspects of Hector (heir to the throne of Troy, husband of Andromache and father of Laomedon the Little, who in the medieval version both live on past the destruction of Troy) and Aeneas (who himself survives the fall of Troy in all the versions, and leads Trojan refugees to a new home in company with his son Iulus and father Anchises). In Tolkien's story it is a complete family, husband, wife and son, which escapes, not the broken families of the parallels; and the son is destined for greater things than his parents, for he is Eärendel.

The second awkward junction of related stories occurs after the end of the tale of Gondolin proper. Having been invented first of all the heroes in BOLT, Tuor's story now founders on the incompleteness of the last part of the story sequence. All the notes and outlines given under *The Tale of Eärendel* in BOLT vol.II suggest that Tuor finally sails westward, moved by both age and sea-longing. This is in fact another clear junction-point between stories whose relationship has not really been resolved as yet. Tuor and Idril sail west, but it is Eärendel who actually gets there first. Quite how this happens, the latest BOLT versions do not resolve; but an earlier one clearly has Tuor and Idril succumb to the perils of the Shadowy Isles, since Idril is the Sleeper in the Tower of Pearl (BOLT vol.II, ch.5, p.256). Since in the *Book of Lost Tales* Eärendel sets out in search of his father, not to carry messages to Valinor, it looks as if Tuor has been set back a generation to fit in the Trojan motif of the survivor's son being important (as with Laomedon the Less, son of Hector and Andromache, who comes to rule the Greek kingdom of Thessaly in the medieval Trojan legend, or for that matter Iulus/Ascanius son of Aeneas in Virgil's *Aeneid*, who founds the Julian house that Virgil's patron Augustus was descended from). We know that Tuor does eventually reach Valinor, where in later versions he is counted among the Elves, an extraordinary departure from Tolkien's usual insistence on the mortality of Men.

b; In the 1950's Version

With 'Tuor and his Coming to Gondolin', we are at once in a world of the mature Tolkien writing at the height of his powers in the time just after the completion of LotR. Tolkien knew that there was a major problem in presenting the material in QS - no mediators such as Hobbits, no 'Everyman' to link the readers with the high-flown world of the past. As Tom Shippey suggested lack of mediation is a 'fault' of the Silmarillion as it was published:

'Aridness is, however, a vice of which *The Silmarillion* stands accused: partly, no doubt, from a (mistaken) disappointment in those who wanted a second *Lord of the Rings*, but largely, as was said at the start of this chapter, because of the absence from it of 'mediators' like the hobbits and a generally novelistic mode of presentation.' (Shippey, 1992, Road to Middle-earth, 2nd Ed., ch.7, p.220)

It is only through knowing the History of Middle earth volumes that we can now understand that Tolkien faced an unenviable choice of variants. But that is not to suggest that the matter of bridging the gap between modern readers and the heroic had completely baffled him. It can be asserted, we believe that Tolkien had indeed worked towards a potentially good solution to his problem, at least for the body of the *Silmarillion*, if not for the early sections. For in the 1950's unfinished version of the Gondolin story Tuor is potentially a *mediator* between the reader and the world of the elves, just like hobbits. He is a (relatively) ordinary character, through whose eyes we see the story unfold, who should be our guide to the marvellous elvish realm of Gondolin, and whose transformation from a lone wolf into a leader of peoples we should witness, given the story-pattern set up by the earlier BOLT version. Compare this with Bilbo first arriving at the marvellous Elvish house of Rivendell in *The Hobbit*, or his transformation from a timid hobbit to a hero who may not kill dragons, but certainly argues with a live one! Bilbo ultimately leaves Middle-earth, at the end of *The Lord of the Rings*, though he only goes to Tol Eresseä, just east of the true Undying Land of Valinor. In *Letters* no.246,

Tolkien says that this is both a reward, an opportunity for Bilbo to experience a pure elvishness unmatched even in Rivendell, and a chance for him to get rid of the last trace of the Ring's influence, visible in the lingering wish to see it again that he expressed to Frodo when they met in Rivendell after the end of the War of the Ring (LotR/RotK, bk.6, ch.6).
A similar departure - but a far more dramatic transformation - awaits Tuor at the end of his story:
'In those days Tuor felt old age creep upon him, and ever a longing for the deeps of the Sea grew stronger in his heart. Therefore he built a great ship, and he named it Earrámë, which is Sea-Wing; and with Idril Celebrindal he set sail into the West, and came no more into any tale or song. But in after days it was sung that Tuor alone of mortal Men was numbered among the elder race, and was joined with the Noldor, whom he loved; and his fate is sundered from the fate of Men.' (QS, ch.23, p.295)

So, like Bilbo, Tuor is in potential a character who can carry us all the way from ordinary beginnings, through ever more marvellous experiences, to the mysterious realms of the West. It is not impossible that after the experience of writing *The Lord of the Rings*, with the beginnings of reader response to that book and with publication of *The Silmarillion* in some form a real probability, Tolkien was sketching this pattern deliberately. He knew that it worked well in both TH and LotR, and that it could offer one sort of answer to the huge problems of presenting *The Silmarillion* to an audience. Tolkien was certainly aware that such problems existed, for in *Letters* No.227 (January 1961) he says:
'I am now under contract engaged (among alas! other less congenial tasks) in putting into order for publication the mythology and stories of the First and Second Ages - written long ago, but judged hardly publishable, until (so it seems) the surprising success of *The Lord of the Rings*, which comes at the end, has provided a probable demand for the beginnings. But there are, I fear, no *hobbits* in *The Silmarillion* (or history of the Three Jewels), little fun or earthiness but mostly grief and disaster. Those critics who scoffed at *The Lord* because 'all the good boys came home safe and everyone was happy ever after' (quite untrue) ought to be satisfied. They will not be, of course - even if they deign to notice the book!'
So Tolkien might well have realised that by happy accident he had created a role for characters who lead readers into a story, and have tried to adapt the existing figure of Tuor to fit the purpose.

Tuor's potential as a mediator is however left unfulfilled, and there are two reasons for this. The first is the simple incompleteness of the 1950's *Fall of Gondolin*, and the second is a series of awkwardnesses in its early section which deals with the youth and early adventures of Tuor. If anything, the front end of the 1950's *Gondolin* is overloaded with plot motifs whose logical consequences cannot be worked through in the scenario which Tolkien has to hand. Most of what happens to Tuor before his coming to Gondolin is a commonplace of medieval story. The closest parallel is with the life and adventures of Reynbrun, son of Guy of Warwick. Guy himself was still prominent as a medieval hero in children's books up until the Second World War, including a version in a schoolbook that Tolkien might well have encountered. Warwick as a place was dear to Tolkien's heart and prominent in his imagination during the *Book of Lost Tales* phase of his writing, and the medieval romances which included the extension beyond Guy to his son would have been available for Tolkien to read in recently edited editions produced between the wars. There are reasons, then, why material associated with Warwick could be reworked by Tolkien with the aim of improving the difficult early section of *The Fall of Gondolin* which deals with Tuor and his adventures.

Turning to the story itself, Reynbrun is entrusted to foster-parents as a very young child because his father Guy of Warwick has disappeared on pilgrimage to Jerusalem and his mother is staving off sorrow by keeping herself busy with charity and running the family fief. The boy shows early valour and martial skill, thanks to good training; but he is stolen and sold into slavery; his guardians search unsuccessfully for him; meanwhile he wins his freedom by his own efforts; after which he undertakes an adventure, fighting a 'fairy knight' to rescue an old companion of his father, one Amis of the Mountain, from captivity. Compare this to Tolkien's character: the young Tuor is brought up by foster-parents because his father has died in battle and his mother has died of grief; he shows early valour and skill with weapons; but when his foster-parents are attempting to escape oppressors he is taken captive and made into a serf; he eventually escapes and, after a period as an outlaw, goes in search of an elven-king associated with his father.

Abandonment at birth, fostering by strangers, enslavement and escape, outlawry, going on a quest - all these are familiar events in the life-histories of medieval heroes. Using them in the combination he does, however, sets up potential problems for Tolkien. Tuor's mother Rian wanders off for no visible reason other than being distraught; although her husband is the brother of the chief of the main surviving house of the Edain, Rian seems to have no one who would even try to keep her out of trouble or upon whom she can rely. Medieval heroines - even those imprisoned by jealous fathers - usually have at least one confidant somewhere who helps them. She also does a most un-motherly thing in abandoning her baby. Reynbrun of Warwick's mother is a noble lady with a whole household at her beck and call, including her husband's old foster-father, to whom in turn she entrusts her son when he is of an age for fostering. This man plays a major part later on as a source of knowledge of Reynbrun's past and of help for him; Tuor has no equivalent figure to turn to in order to learn of his past and this is a tangible weakness, as his sudden interest in Gondolin has no plausible source (other than a nebulous awakening within him by Ulmo). Again, the elves who take Rian in have no reason for doing so apart from plain kindness - feasible for Tolkien's elves, but not within the medieval story-patterns where genuinely helpful supernatural fosterers are likely to be the real parents of the hero. A tension is therefore created within the 'fosterchild' motif as well as undermining Tuor's potential everyman/ mediator status. People brought up by elves rather than mortal Men are not people whom we can readily associate with. Tolkien has to turn this 'wild man who lives alone', a fugitive with a price upon his head into a normal everyday person embarking upon an adventure.

Furthermore Tolkien has created a major problem for himself by making the takeover of Hithlum by the Easterlings too overwhelming, too much an Anglo-Saxon Migration rather than a Norman Conquest. There is no plausible niche left for Tuor to be brought up as a free man by mortal Men of his own kin. This is in contrast to medieval story-patterns - there are numerous examples in *Thidhreks Saga af Bern* - where conquered peoples pretty much carry on with their lives, and it is only the people to whom they pay their taxes that have changed. The new overlords may be oppressors, but they do not enslave or wipe out the current occupants of the land in such drastic fashion as Tolkien's Easterlings. Even within the overall story that Tolkien is by this point in time telling, this is overkill, for there have to be enough Edain left somewhere to provide a population for Númenor, and Tolkien is in real danger of not having enough people to carry forward his tale in reasonable terms. Reynbrun of Warwick's anonymous author handled the whole matter with far more ease by having slavery preceded by kidnapping to a distant country. For some reason Tolkien does not take this approach, and we do not know why.

Moving on, Tuor's escape and outlawry again set up tensions between logical consequences if we follow through the associated story-patterns, and the tale that Tolkien is actually telling. If we follow medieval precedent, Tuor ought to be able to gather at least a few followers (as Turin does), and either retake his ancestral lands or set off with his companions, knowing that he can rely on their help in whatever quest they have decided to undertake. Reynbrun of Warwick meets his foster-brother and foster-father after he has gained his freedom; they work together to achieve Reynbrun's quest and then to return home where Reynbrun can reclaim his place and lands. In Tolkien's story Tuor has to do everything by himself, and valuable as this is in some ways, it is also a weakness in others. We have seen too little of Tuor at this stage for his ability to survive so long alone to be really plausible; again, the mediatory function is undermined. More, the lack of anyone to provide information or take part in decision-making causes Tolkien to rely on a marvel - the overflowing spring that runs west - in a way quite uncharacteristic of him. It is not necessary as a preparation for the appearance of Ulmo in the tale - the Lord of Waters turns up quite satisfactorily in the earlier version with no such herald. In the 1950's version, Tuor has a fascination with Gondolin which is inexplicable, because there is no-one to tell him of the family association with the place. Again, Tolkien is usually more realistic than this. Until he meets Ulmo, Tuor's quest is almost as aimless in the later version as in the earlier one. He travels, and he hopes his travels may lead him to Gondolin, but he has no particular reason for wishing for this - there is no positive draw, only the negative desire to leave Hithlum where he is alone. Tuor is not seeking either a bride or, in the other pattern that medieval parallels would lead us to expect, an old ally of his family who can help Tuor retake his ancestors' lands and free his people.

At Vinyamar, this non-quest acquires an aim and Tuor finds a companion in the shape of the elf Voronwë. The pattern of the story is improved at once, but in ways that do not sit well next to what has gone before. Voronwë's arrival out of the storm probably represents a double borrowing from both the major existing strands in the story of Gondolin. On the one hand, in the *Orendel* romance, Orendel sails with seventy-two ships but meets with a storm and catastrophic shipwreck, from which he alone survives. Likewise, Voronwë is the only survivor of the crew of his ship, which itself was the last survivor of a number of ships. On the other hand there is a similar episode in the medieval Troy story. After rebuilding the city, Priam of Troy has decided that he is willing to be at peace with the Greeks if they will only return his sister Hesione, carried off as a slave in the first Sack of Troy when Priam's father was killed. As a messenger, Priam sends his most trusted lord, Antenor; but the Greek kings react with such arrogance and so many threats of violence that Antenor and his men have to flee for their lives, into a storm which their ships escape only by the grace of the gods:

'Then a tempest fell on them, on the high-towering waves
A fog and a fierce wind rose in their sails
The mist and the darkness was marvellous to see;
With a roaring rain that was pitiful to behold,
It thundered most terribly with a heavy fall of hail;
While a flashing light like fire aglow
Flamed over the broad sea as if to set it ablaze.
The sea with a fierce rush flew up ever higher
Rose up over the rocks in rugged hills of water
So mad were the waves and the wild breakers
Everyone seemed likely to die who was not on the land.
The ship ever rushed forward on the foaming waves
Like one who climbs a cliff or a rocky hill
Then was dropped in the deeps as if they would all drown.
There was no steering by stars, nor any strong ropes
Nor any sail, that could help in harmful weather
But all the bold men in the ship, as they thought best
Prayed to saints and to many gods .'

(Panton & Donaldson 1968, book V, lines 1983-2000). [Note 3]

Compare this with the accounts of the encounter with Voronwë and his story of survival in *Unfinished Tales* :

'Now Tuor felt his feet drawn to the sea-strand, and he went down by long stairs to a wide shore upon the north side of Taras-ness; and as he went he saw that the sun was sinking low into a great black cloud that came up over the rim of the darkening sea; and it grew cold, and there was a stirring and murmur as of a storm to come... and he stood beneath the thunder of the storm, and lightning many-branched rent asunder the heavens above him. And Ulmo was gone, and the sea was in tumult, as the wild waves of Ossë rode against the walls of Nevrast.

Then Tuor fled from the fury of the sea, and with labour he won his way back to the high terraces; for the wind drove him against the cliff, and when he came out upon the top it bent him to his knees. Therefore he entered again he dark and empty hall for shelter, and sat nightlong in the stone seat of Turgon... Then he saw that the great waves in the night had ridden high upon the land, and

had cast their crests above the cliff-tops, and weed and shingle-drift were flung even upon the terraces before the doors. And Tuor looked down from the lowest terrace and saw, leaning against a wall among the stones and the sea-wrack, an Elf, clad in a grey cloak sodden with the sea. Silent he sat, gazing beyond the ruin of the beaches out over the long ridges of the waves. All was still, and there was no sound save the roaring of the surf below.' (UT, Part One, ch. 1, p.30-31)
And again:
'For even as we descried a mountain from afar, and I cried: " Lo! There is Taras, and the land of my birth," the wind awoke, and great clouds thunder-laden came up from the West. Then the waves hunted us like living things filled with malice, and the lightnings smote us; and when we were broken down to a helpless hull the seas leaped upon us in fury. But as you see, I was spared,: for it seemed to me that there came a wave, greater and yet calmer than all the others, and it took me and lifted me from the ship, and bore me high upon its shoulders, and rolling to the land it cast me upon the turf, and then drained away, pouring back over the cliff in a great waterfall.' (ibid, p.36)

The emphasis on thunder, lightning and darkness in both the storm in the Trojan legend and *Unfinished Tales* is noticeable, as is the idea of waves like hills, high enough to wash over the cliffs and high terraces of Vinyamar (not as fantastic as it might seem; one author's father, a former ship's engineer, informs her that the top of the lighthouse rock of Muckle Flugga off Shetland is regularly overwashed by waves in winter, some two hundred feet above sea-level). What in the poem is a purely conventional ascription of personality to the waves becomes real in Tolkien's version, where there actually is an intelligent malice behind the storm - the malign power of most of the Valar, and the immediate threat of Ossë, the Maia or lesser spirit in charge of the waves on the sea, who has chosen to serve their will rather than that of his true superior, Ulmo. Neither crew can do anything physical to help themselves, but where the medieval Trojans can pray successfully, the elvish sailors are doomed. Voronwë and his companions are like Antenor and his fellows in that they had been sent out as messengers by their king - in Voronwë's case, Turgon, king of Gondolin, who was seeking to make peace with the Valar and persuade them to forgive the faults of the Noldor (in Antenor's, King Priam of Troy wishing to make peace with the Greeks). However, they cannot even reach Valinor, and are destroyed by the wrath of the Valar. Only Ulmo, Lord of Waters, dissents and aids the last ship, saving Voronwë to help Tuor to reach Gondolin and so create an unlooked-for hope. As such, Voronwë reverses Antenor's role (one of Tolkien's favourite devices for turning an old idea into a new story, as we have often seen in previous chapters) for it is Antenor who is the prime traitor in the medieval Troy-story. Voronwë we are told is one of the survivors of the sack of Gondolin, escaping with Tuor and his family and other refugees.

The situation of Vinyamar next to a mountain at the end of the range that forms the southern border of Nevrast is to some extent prepared for by the remark in the BOLT version about 'the Iron Mountains whose spurs run even to the sea' (BOLT vol. II ch. 3, p.153). There is also a faint but attractive possibility of a geographical Trojan link, in view of the Trojan connections of Voronwë and his shipwreck; the emergence of Mount Taras as a dominating landscape feature and important landmark for sailors may well have been influenced by the high peak of the island of Samothrace, the classical and Homeric Samos. This mountain is a prominent landmark to this day in the approaches to the Hellespont; its appearance from Troy, looming over the intervening island of Imbros, has been hailed as an example of Homer's accuracy by commentators who have visited the area since the 15th century; it is also the seat from which, in the *Iliad*, Poseidon watches the fighting before Troy (Wood 1985 ch.1, p.37; Homer/Fitzgerald bk.XII, p.217) .

V; Conclusion

Tuor, Eärendil and Orendel - three facets of a bridging hero. We have shown that the connections underlying these characters are quite clear; the first man who is a hero described Orendel, and Tuor is the first man said to reach the western sea. Eärendel is the first to reach the West and overcome the Ban of the Valar. All three sail on adventures and all are 'touched by higher powers' - Orendel by the angel who visits him, Tuor by Ulmo, and Eärendel by reaching Valinor, speaking to the Valar, and being placed in the hallowed vessel in the sky with a Silmaril bound to either the mast top or the brow of his head. It is hard to examine these three characters without colliding with the medieval Trojan legends. The fact that Tolkien knew of Orendil and used the name at one stage early in the writing of LotR for a King-hero of old and that Eärendel was the starting point for what followed in his Legendarium makes the connections we have revealed in this chapter of the utmost importance to Tolkien's mythic storytelling development over the entire course of his life. Some further points of note are made below:

The 1950's version of Tuor and his Coming to Gondolin is very close to the *Book of Lost Tales* story as pointed out by Christopher Tolkien:

'In places the later *Tuor* (the abandonment of which is one of the saddest facts in the whole history of incompletion) is so close in wording to *The Fall of Gondolin*, written more than thirty years before, as to make it almost certain that my father had it in front of him, or at least had recently reread it.'

(BOLT, vol.II, ch. 3, Commentary §I, section (i), p.203).

We can also now say that in writing this later version, J.R.R. Tolkien drew on the same sources for new material as he had when writing the original. Some of this was direct, as in the case of Voronwë's shipwreck or the grey cloak that Ulmo gives to Tuor. In other places there are signs that ultimately Trojan ideas had arrived in the tale of Gondolin through their use in *The Lord of the Rings* - a situation we will be exploring in a later chapter in this section. For now it is enough to mention that the Seven Gates of Gondolin, and the dialogue of Voronwë and Tuor with their first guardian Elemmakil appear to relate closely to the idea of a sevenfold city derived from Troy and explored in Minas Tirith, and also the dialogue of Gandalf with the men at the Rammas Echor upon his arrival with Pippin upon Shadowfax.

A point worth making is that compared to its likely sources, the element of personal adventure is much reduced in *The Fall of Gondolin.* The bride-quests present in Tolkien's sources typically involve their hero in far more difficulty than Tuor faces - 'Beren and Lúthien' is a good example of a more 'traditional' story of this type within Tolkien's own work, as is 'Aragorn and Arwen'. This reduction in personal adventure in the Tale of Gondolin is due to the collision of the bride-quest motif which is at the centre of *Orendel*, with the questless Tale of Troy. Similarly, when Tolkien is describing the factual battle for Gondolin and the fall of the city, the detail, although rich by his standard, is nowhere near as full as in any of the battles in the medieval Troy stories, or for that matter in *Orendel*. Tolkien's focus is much tighter than that of his sources. He is also working on a much smaller scale, and most of the characters who appear during the sack of Gondolin have not previously been introduced to us - and we only get to meet those on the Elvish side; Melko's forces remain as a voiceless 'enemy'. But to have tried to fill out Gondolin to the same extent as the Trojan legends would have required a great deal more detail. That would probably deter even a medieval author from expanding too far, let alone Tolkien.

In this connection it is very important to understand that Tolkien's 'Fall of Gondolin' is an infinitely shorter work than any of the medieval pieces, whether in prose or poetry. Even if the 1950's version had been carried through to completion, it would still probably have been much shorter than any of the medieval Troy-tales (see below). Guido delle Colonne's Latin prose version is 265 pages long in the English translation we used; the alliterative *Destruction of Troy* occupies 459 pages, 14044 lines of verse, in the EETS reprinting of 1968. The BOLT 'Gondolin' takes up 47 pages of story, with 18 more of introduction and notes. The QS version is a mere 9 pages long (ch.23), the 1950's version as far as it gets is 35 pages long. Indeed, a 'reconstruction' of the relevant parts utilising the unfinished 1950's version called the Illustrated and Illuminated Tale of Gondolin (Lewis/Lacon 1994) comes to 170 pages in large print (equivalent to 85 pages in the same print size as above).

Such compression is only achievable by cutting out all irrelevance. Some of the shortening is authorial and part of the tightening of the plot; there is one decisive battle in 'Gondolin', compared to anything from 12 to 24 in the Troy-books. A great deal more of the reduction consists simply of not going into things in detail. The description of the fall of Gondolin in BOLT seems richly detailed by comparison to the *Quenta Silmarillion* versions. Yet we only have to look at the account of the siege of Minas Tirith and battle of the Pelennor Fields in LotR to see how much more could be done with such a story. The account of the fall of Gondolin occupies 22 pages, the battle for Minas Tirith 87 pages (4 chapters). It would not be surprising if one of the single most important obstacles to Tolkien's actually completing *The Silmarillion* was the awful realisation of just how long it was actually going to be, if each story was to be told in anything like the form that he had mastered in *The Lord of the Rings*.

Herein we give the original Middle English text of the poems:
Note 1:

'Tho i-sei3en huy feo in the north: a lond deork i-nou3,
Smoke stynkinde foule: and thuder-ward heor schip drou3.
Tho i-heorden heo gret blowynge: of manie beolies there
And gret betynge and noyse i-nou3: thondre ase thei it were.
Tho was Brendan sori i-nou3: and blessede him wel faste.
Tho cam thare out a luther wy3t: ful Atelich ate laste,
Thoru-out swart and brenninde - : ope heom is ei3ene he caste
And tornede him anon a-3en - : this Monekes weren a-gaste.
That luther wi3t 3af a cri: that Men mi3ten i-heore him wide.
Tho come thare out swuch schrewes mo: thicke on eche side,
With tongen and with hameres; brenninde mani on;
Op-on the watere heo ornen faste: After that schip ech-on.
Tho huy ne mi3ten thare-nei3 come: huy gonne to 3eolle faste,
heore hameres all brenninde: after this men huy casten,
that men ne mi3ten no-thing bote fuyr: nother iseo ne huyre;
the se was brenninde al-a-brod: as thei heo were a-fuyre.
euer-ech cast is owel op othur: and some huy threwen an hei3,
huy threwen alle a-boute that schip: ake non ne cam thare-nei3.'

(Horstmann 1887 ch.36, lines 470-87)

Note 2:

'For thulke tyme that the feond / ore furste fader i-wan
thoru3 that appel that he him 3af / mayster was he of man;
he hadde faste al to him men i-bounde / for-to ore louerd us bou3te:
And for men weren so alle his / the lasse of heom he rou3te,
Ne nothing he nas ginful / ase the schrewene nouthe beoth -
for plente nis no deinte / ase we al day i-seot.
he fierde ase doth a port-doggue / I-norishet in port-toun:
for he geth ofte in prece of Men / a-mong heom op and doun,
Ne 3eme ne nimeth he to men / to beorken on heom nou3t ene,
Ake a-mong men he goth stille I-nou3 / bote ani man him hene:
Also fierde the deuel tho / for mankun was al his,
And hadde of him so gret plente / he ne tolde nou3t that-of, i-wis.'

Which is just as well, because:

'Hadde he i-beo swuch bi-fore / as he was er i-wis
Onnethe was thare ani Man / that ne hadde i-beon al his.'

(Horstmann 1887, St Michael Archangel, lines 261-72, 277-8)

Note 3:

'Then a tempast hom toke on the torres high
A rak and a royde wind rose in hor saile
A myst and a merkness was meruell to se;
With a routond rayne ruthe to be hold,
Thonret full throly with a thicke haile;
With a leuenyng light as a low fire
Blaset all the brode see as it bren wold
The flode with a felle course flowit on hepis
Rose vppon rockes as any ranke hylles.
So wode were the waghes and the wilde ythes,
All was like to be lost that no lond hade.
The ship ay shot furth o the shire waghes,
As quo clymbe a cliffe or a clent hille,
Eft dumpe in the deep as all drowne wolde.
Was no stighlyng with sterre, ne no stithe ropes,
Ne no sayle, that might serve for vnsound wedur.
But all the buernes in the bote, as hom best liked,
Besoght vnto sainttes & to sere goddes;'

(Panton & Donaldson 1968, book V, lines 1983-2000).

Chapter Five:

A Tale of Two Cities; Troy and Minas Tirith.

We have now looked at the effect of the medieval Matter of Troy on the *Silmarillion*, and the evolution of the Tale of Gondolin. Thus, we know that Tolkien carried on using the medieval Trojan legends as a source for the Tale of Gondolin for as long as he was working on this story. The question we have to ask now is, did the Trojan material affect any of Tolkien's other stories? In particular, can we discover any trace of this same source material in *The Lord of the Rings*? Initially we thought that surely Gondolin was of itself a complete enough tale for the medieval Trojan legends to be utilised in, and that Tolkien would surely turn to other places as sources for other tales. But then we were drawn to consider that Tolkien was a great 'recycler' of stories. The whole Aragorn and Arwen story in LotR was a revisiting of the tale of Beren and Lúthien from the 'Silmarillion' tradition. It was therefore possible to ask if other 'Silmarillion' stories - and their sources - were also used in *The Lord of the Rings*. So we began to examine *The Lord of the Rings*, and immediately it was clear that we were onto something important. *The Lord of the Rings* is not borrowed wholesale from one source only, but is a patchwork of parts drawn from many earlier writings by Tolkien. Medieval Trojan legends were quite evidently at the root of some of the most significant passages in this work. We believe that Tolkien indeed revisited the same sources he had already used for the 'Silmarillion' when he was writing LotR, and that there is a complex interaction between the various versions of the Gondolin story and the Gondorian chapters in *The Lord of the Rings*.

One has to ask, perhaps, why this should be so. The answer may be quite straight forward; in writing *The Lord of the Rings*, Tolkien was very often 'writing blind' and needed to draw upon previously written material to drive the narrative onwards. This has been conclusively proven in our previous book (see Uncharted Realms of Tolkien, Lewis and Currie, 2002, Realms of Inspiration: 2). Repeatedly, Tolkien turned to his unpublished *Silmarillion* stories for characters, inspiration and useful colour to put into the new tale he was working on. Tolkien always altered what he imported, for he had soon found that borrowing too much and too directly was dangerous. That might lead to the 'Silmarillion' stories becoming so involved with LotR that he would never be able to publish them as a serious, separate work. This was still the time when *The Lord of the Rings* was in transition between being a trivial work, a New Hobbit, and becoming the lynch-pin of his Legendarium. As Tolkien slowly wrote his way forward, though, he learned to balance the need for help and the need to keep the Silmarillion' and LotR separate. Despite the changes he made in borrowing old ideas, however, their sources are still quite recognisable of we know what to look for. So we can work out what happened at a certain critical point in time, when Tolkien the writer needed a new city of men that would be besieged. Some of his principal characters were heading in that direction - a place that had been dimly foreseen from the time when Bingo Bolger-Baggins had set out from the Shire on a jolly adventure with his friends. Now, though, the tone of the book was quite different, and many of the ideas Tolkien had planned to use for 'Ond' (which we know as Gondor) had already gone into the makeup of Rohan, a kingdom virtually unforeseen before Tolkien reached the Falls of Rauros (as is described by C.J.R. Tolkien in *Return of the Shadow*, HOME vol.VI, and *Treason of Isengard*, HOME vol.VII). So once more, Tolkien turned his attention to the *Silmarillion* material and through that, to its sources. In this case, we ended up with something like and yet unlike (as Gimli said of Saruman when comparing him to Gandalf). Tolkien's Minas Tirith and Gondolin became two great cities with different fates but which were both based upon an older and enduring legend of a city that had fallen spectacularly; ancient Ilium - noble Troy.

I; Sevens

To begin to uncover the connections between Minas Tirith and the medieval Trojan legends, we need to examine the significance of numbers. This is not numerology for its own sake, which would be unscientific, it is an analysis of the physical similarities between two cities. So, for Minas Tirith we have seven circles of a city, seven walls, in each of which there is a gate - therefore seven gates. It is evident that in Minas Tirith there is a match which can associate it with the seven gates at Gondolin and beyond.

'For the fashion of Minas Tirith was such that it was built on seven levels, each delved into the hill, and about each was set a wall, and in each wall was a gate. But the gates were not set in line: the Great Gate in the City Wall was at the east point of the circuit, but the next faced half south, and the third half north, and so to and fro upwards; so that the paved way that climbed towards the Citadel turned first this way and then that across the face of the hill. And each time that it passed the line of the Great Gate it went through an arched tunnel, piercing a vast pier of rock whose huge out-thrust bulk divided in two all the circles of the City save the first. For partly in the primeval shaping of the hill, partly by the mighty craft and labour of old, there stood up from the rear of the wide court behind the Gate a towering bastion of stone, its edge sharp as a ship-keel facing east. Up it rose, even to the level of the topmost circle, and there was crowned by a battlement; so that those in the Citadel might, like mariners in a mountainous ship, look from its peak sheer down upon the Gate seven hundred feet below. The entrance to the Citadel also looked eastward, but was delved in the heart of the rock; thence a long lamp-lit slope ran up to the seventh gate. Thus men reached at last the High Court, and the Palace of the Fountain before the feet of the White Tower: tall and shapely, fifty fathoms from its base to the pinnacle, where the banner of the Stewards floated a thousand feet above the plain.'
(RotK, Book V, ch.1. pps. 23-24)

These gates are like and yet unlike those in Gondolin, for they are nested, rather than having one main wall of the city and 7 gates in a line outside (later

Tuor) or the unclear situation as exists in BOLT:
'Maeglin told them of all the fashion of that plain and city, of its walls and their height and thickness, and the valour of its gates..." (BOLT vol.II, ch.3, p.168)
'But now Gothmog lord of Balrogs, captain of the hosts of Melko, took counsel and gathered all his things of iron that could coil themselves around and above all obstacles before them. These he bade pile themselves before the northern gate; and behind, their great spires reached even to its threshold and thrust at the towers and bastions about it, and by reason of the exceeding heaviness of their bodies those gates fell, and great was the noise thereof...' (ibid, p.176)
So, is this northern gate the only one? But to call it 'northern' would be to indicate the existence of other gates. Tuor comes first to Gondolin and passes through the Great Gates.
So in QS, Gondolin has a Great Gate in the actual city wall, which is quite separate to the famous seven gates at the passage through the mountains to the Hidden Kingdom. And as to Troy? Troy sits upon a plain, but is built upon a hill - which is very reminiscent of Minas Tirith. And in one particular medieval Trojan legend source, Guido de Colonne, the height above the plain from the top of the tower is - one thousand feet:
'From its foundation to the highest point which roofed it over in the shape of a sphere, its height reached a summit five hundred feet above the tops of the towers not far from it on the ramparts, which were themselves far higher than that same height.' (Colonne/Meek 1974, bk.5, lines 170-183 & 202-211, pp.46-7)

In the real world, there are a number of Aegean sites which offer parallels with the structure of Minas Tirith. On the one hand there is Lindos on Rhodes, where a 'wedding cake' of settlements of visibly different dates surrounds a hill. Back in 1897 in the book *The Mycenean Age* , the Greek archaeologist C.Tsountas and the American historian J.I. Manatt described how:
'...the English Consul Bilotti had opened forty-two rock-hewn tombs of the same age at Ialysos in Rhodes. The furnishings of these tombs, consisting largely of rich vases, had been presented by John Ruskin to the British Museum, where they were relegated with other nondescripts to the basement. but in the new light from Mycenae [Sir] Charles Newton at once saw the relation of these several finds and thus laid the real foundation of Mycenean archaeology.'
(Tsountas and Manatt 1897, ch.1, p.5)
So, since these finds from Rhodes were exceedingly important in the development of a historical picture of the era of the Trojan War, and thus the background to Homer's poetry, it is not impossible that Tolkien (the one-time Classics student whose teacher Lewis Farnell was interested in exactly these points, even if he kept setting Tolkien essays on later material, as John Garth points out in 'Tolkien and the Great War', ch.1, p.20-30) had read about Rhodes and knew of Lindos. Rhodes was the site of the famous Colossus, one of the Seven Wonders of the World, and thus well enough known to attract the attention of a Classics undergraduate such as Tolkien.

On the other hand there is the archaeological parallel at the hill of Hissarlik, ancient Troy, where Heinrich Schliemann found seven successive cities with their walls in varying places vertically and horizontally round the hill, all with their respective gates. According to the German pioneer's more scientific successors there were nine cities on the hill, but the most important was the seventh, maintaining the association of number and place. It is also worth noting that the English Homeric scholar W. Leaf pointed out in 1912 that in the sixth city of Troy (then one of the strong contenders for 'Priam's Troy') there were three known gates within less than half the circuit of the walls; it takes no great leap of imagination to expand this to seven gates in total around the whole circuit (Leaf 1912 ch.III, p.92). Less speculatively, Leaf also described the way in which the Sixth City of Troy was built in concentric terraces; one known for certain, a second probable, and any others removed by Roman remodelling of the top of the hill to serve as foundations for a large temple-complex (Leaf 1912, ch.III, p.95-9)

It is highly improbable that Tolkien did *not* know about Schliemann's discoveries at Troy, and the work of Schliemann's successors there. We remind readers that Tolkien's original academic speciality was Classics, after all, and we know that his Greek was excellent. According to Carpenter's *Biography* :

'There was a custom at King Edward's of holding a debate entirely in Latin, but that was almost too easy for Tolkien, and in one debate when taking the role of Greek Ambassador to the Senate he spoke entirely in Greek.' (Carpenter 1977, Part 2, ch.4., p.56) Tolkien's Greek was good enough for him to score a 'pure alpha' in Greek Philology at Oxford; Carpenter describes this as 'a practically faultless paper' (ibid., p.70).

By the time Tolkien was studying the subject, any recent commentary on Homer is likely to have mentioned Schliemann and his successors in the field of Aegean archaeology - his own onetime assistant Dörpfeld, the Greek Tsountas who worked at Mycenae (and elsewhere), and the English archaeologist Sir Arthur Evans who discovered the Minoan civilisation on Crete, among many others. All of these men wrote books on their discoveries. There were also books available which dealt with the archaeology of the Aegean as it linked in with Homer's poetry, such as Andrew Lang's *The World of Homer* in 1910, or W. Leaf's *Troy; A Study in Homeric Geography* of 1912. All of this creates a situation in which it is very likely that Tolkien knew something - perhaps rather a lot - about the surviving monuments of the Aegean Bronze Age. Schliemann's books were translated into English, and W.Leaf's *Troy* provides a convenient summary about what was known of that site in 1912.

One detail might suggest that Tolkien knew Leaf's text in particular. Discussing the concentric terraces of houses which filled the city in the Sixth Stratum, Leaf points out that:

'The houses show remarkable differences in the excellence of their masonry. This is particularly noticeable in the adjacent houses marked VI.E and VI. F on the plan. The contrast between the rough work and imperfectly finished stones of VI. F and the extraordinarily fine masonry of VI. E cannot fail to strike an observer. VI. E is indeed of such excellence that in Dörpfeld's words "no archaeologist would hold such a wall, had it been found alone, to belong to the Mycenean period. The almost rectangular stones perfectly polished on the outer side, the fine and hardly visible joints, and the two carefully worked corners remind us of Greek walls of the 5th or 6th century." It appears therefore that these houses have been from time to time rebuilt, and that while VI. F dates from one of the earliest periods of the city, VI. E must belong to one of the latest. The houses thus agree with the walls in proving a continuous growth in technical knowledge and architectural execution.' (Leaf 1912, ch.III, p.97-8)

Compare this with Tolkien's description of Minas Tirith in *The Lord of the Rings*:

'Pippin gazed in growing wonder at the great stone city, vaster and more splendid than anything that he had dreamed of; greater and stronger than Isengard, and far more beautiful. Yet it was in truth falling year by year into decay; and already it lacked half the men that could have dwelt at ease there. In every street they passed some great house or court over whose doors and arched gates were carved many fair letters of strange and ancient shapes: names Pippin guessed of great men and kindreds that had once dwelt there; and yet now they were silent, and no footsteps rang on their wide pavements, nor voice was heard from their halls, nor any face looked out from door or empty window.' (RotK, Book V, ch.1, p.24)

In further descriptions of Minas Tirith, Tolkien reverses the dating of the good and bad stonework found at Troy:

''There is some good stonework here,' he [Gimli] said as he looked at the walls; 'but also some that is less good, and the streets could be better contrived. When Aragorn comes into his own, I shall offer him the services of stonewrights of the Mountain, and we will make this a town to be proud of.'

(RotK, Book V, ch.9, p.148) and also:

"If Gondor has such men still in these days of fading, great must have been its glory in the days of its rising.'

'And doubtless the good stone-work is the older and was wrought in the first building,' said Gimli. 'It is ever so with the things that Men begin: there is a frost in Spring, or a blight in Summer, and they fail of their promise.'

'Yet seldom do they fail of their seed,' said Legolas. 'And that will lie in the dust and rot to spring up again in times and places unlooked-for. The deeds of Men will outlast us, Gimli.'

'And yet come to naught in the end but might-have-beens, I guess,' said the Dwarf.

'To that the Elves know not the answer,' said Legolas. (ibid, p.149)

By doing this, Tolkien creates the idea of a city slipping into a 'Dark Age' of lessened knowledge and skills, with fewer and fewer citizens to man it. This fits well with the generally post-Roman atmosphere he has already established in the rest of LotR. It also seems to indicate that Tolkien was more than aware of the various theories of the decline and fall of cities. He subscribes here with this portrait of Minas Tirith to the 'slow death' theory, in which people either move off or die and are not replaced until a city eventually literally 'dies' because there is no one left there to live any longer, or no one wishes to live in that place and it is deserted. Other methods would involve less gradual and more cataclysmic forces; plagues, wars, earthquakes or other natural disasters, lack of water and/ or over-exploitation of surrounding land so that it can no longer support the population of that city. Tolkien seems to favour this gradual diminishment theory

with respect to Gondor in the Third Age in particular. Both Osgiliath and Minas Ithil 'fall' or perhaps it would be best to say 'fail' due to lack of diligence and manpower, rather than by any single 'moment of destruction'.
Even beyond this in Middle-earth, Tharbad is said to fall into decline before a flood forces out the last dwellers, and Arnor seems to dwindle and split and weaken and then lose its status as a working kingdom. This contrasts strongly with the *Silmarillion* where the likes of Gondolin, Nargothrond and Menegroth 'fall' in the classical 'cataclysmic' fashion. One can also extend the contrast from the First Age to the Fall of Númenor in the Second Age, as well as the siege of Barad Dur and fall of Mordor at that time. This change in emphasis will be returned to and analysed in the next volume of our series.

The passage which immediately follows the quote in Leaf's book given above is also markedly suggestive of the 'back story' which Tolkien eventually developed for Minas Tirith:
'Although the general arrangement of the citadel with its concentric terraces and radial passages leading up to the centre might seem to imply a single idea carried out once and for all, we see that this cannot have been the case; the general plan may have been laid down from the first foundation of the fortress, but the constructional detail was subject to continued modification and improvement, probably through a very long period of time.' (Leaf 1912, ch.III, p.98)
If we turn to Appendix A of RotK we find that Tolkien states:
'It was Ostoher the seventh king who rebuilt Minas Anor, where afterwards the kings dwelt in the summer rather than in Osgiliath.' (p.324),
Furthermore, in Appendix B in the Tale of Years:
'1640 King Tarondor removes the King's House to Minas Anor, and plants a seedling of the White Tree. Osgiliath begins to fall into ruin.' (ibid, p.367)
'1900 Calimehtar builds the White Tower in Minas Anor.' (ibid, p.368)
'2475 Osgiliath finally ruined, and its stone-bridge broken.' (ibid, p.368)
'2698 Ecthelion 1 rebuilds the White Tower in Minas Tirith.' (ibid, p.369)
'2852 The White Tree dies, and no seedling can be found. The Dead Tree is left standing.' (ibid, p.369)
Another quote may be relevant to the comparison of Minas Tirith with Troy. This passage comes from the chapter where W. Leaf compares the extant remains at Hissarlik to Homer's descriptions:
'As seen from the north, the natural approach for the stranger, on the steep scarp of the hill, rising to at least 100 feet above the plain at its feet, circled certainly with a double, probably a triple ring of great walls of masonry, and crowned at the top no doubt with a palace and perhaps a temple, Troy must, in this country of small heights, have formed a really imposing mass.' (Leaf 1912, ch.IV, p.150)
It is worth noting also that in the same passage from which the above quote is drawn, Leaf cites Dörpfeld's solution of Homer's calling Troy 'wide-wayed', pointing out that in the Sixth Stratum, while the houses were separated by mere lanes, the main road running round the inside of the walls was 'from 25 to over 30 feet wide'; it takes little practicality let alone imagination, faced with the idea of concentrically organised terraces, to expand this into the wide main road of Minas

Tirith threading through the Circles of the City:
'He came at last by arches streets and many fair alleys and pavements to the lowest and widest circle, and there he was directed to the Lampwright's Street, a broad way running towards the Great Gate.' (RotK, Book V, ch.1, p.41)

A similar but even more exact parallel with Minas Tirith occurs at Mycenae itself, where as the British archaeologist Alan J.B. Wace pointed out (1949 Archaeological Guide, drawing on his excavation reports published 1932 and before, as well as previous work on the site) the road leading from the famous Lion Gate to the Palace must have taken a zig-zag course up the hill, past several terraces full of buildings (Chapter XI, esp. p.68; ch. XII & relevant plans).
Overall, however, we think it is most reasonable to suggest that Minas Tirith can be taken as representing an imaginative transformation of the idea of seven cities and seven circuits of walls on one hill, into a situation where all coexist simultaneously.

Interestingly, a not dissimilar idea of history becoming simultaneity occurs in the writings of the pioneer psychologist Sigmund Freud, of all people;
'Now let us, by a flight of imagination, suppose that Rome is not a human habitation but a psychical entity with a similarly long and copious past - an entity, that is to say, in which nothing that has once come into existence will have passed away and all the earlier phases of development continue to exist alongside the latest one. This would mean that in Rome the palaces of the Caesars and the Septizonium of Septimus Severus would still be rising to their old height on the Palatine...the same piece of ground would be supporting the church of Santa Maria sopra Minerva and the ancient temple over which it was built.'
Sigmund Freud, trans J.Strachey, Civilisation and its Discontents; this edition W.W. Norton 1961 but the first British publication was in 1930. That is early enough for Freud's comments to have reached the Inklings, and we know that Tolkien and C.S. Lewis - and probably the others - were discussing time-travel and space-travel, as this was what led to the famous pact to write one book about each between Lewis and Tolkien.
'In the late nineteen-thirties... 'C.S. Lewis who (Tolkien reported) one day said: 'Tollers, there is too little of what we really like in stories. I am afraid we shall have to try and write some ourselves.' 'We agreed' (said Tolkien) ' that he should try "space-travel", and I should try "time-travel". They also decided that each story should lead to the discovery of Myth.' (Carpenter, 1977, Part 4, ch.6, p.172)
Freud's idea is an imaginatively powerful one, so much so that he declined to follow it far, saying that 'it leads to things which are unimaginable and even absurd', which makes us wonder whether it was in fact original to him, or whether Freud was borrowing from somewhere unknown. Despite the timing, it seems far more likely that Tolkien and Freud were working from a common source. Such a strong idea may have been circulating in contemporary and earlier literature in ways now impossible to track.

However, there is a possibility that, as Verlyn Flieger points out, Tolkien might have been influenced in his thinking by a popular book by J.W. Dunne, the 3rd and much expanded edition of which was issued in 1934: An Experiment with Time. Flieger suggests: 'Language and dream connect to memory, and all three connect to time past. Time, as Tolkien envisioned it, was not a simple forward progression but a complex field of experience encompassing past, present and future, a field of experience to which dream, memory, and language all gave access.' (Flieger, A Question of Time, 1997, Intro., p.5)

Flieger also quotes the famous event in 1901 known as the 'Trianon adventure': 'In 1901 two quite ordinary, and to all appearances quite unmystical, schoolteachers found themselves taking an unexpected walk into the past.... Touring Versailles [they] had what they subsequently came to believe was a psychic experience. While exploring the grounds on August 10, 1901, the two women lost their way. They entered a lane that took them trough a wood, past a kiosk or summerhouse, and across a small rustic bridge before bringing them by a circuitous route to the rear of the Petit Trianon... On the way they variously encountered or saw at a distance men in antique costume, whom they took at the time to be gardeners or grounds attendants. In addition, Miss Moberly saw, seated on the lawn below the terrace of the Petit Trianon, a lady in an old-fashioned, full-skirted summer dress. Though they both passed directly by the spot, Miss Jourdain saw no one.... Miss Moberly speculated that she and Miss Jourdain "had 'entered within an act of the Queen's [Marie Antionette's] memory,' when during her detention at the outbreak of the Revolution she 'had gone back in such vivid memory to other Augusts spent at Trianon." (ibid, p.36-7)

She then concludes: 'Of the influences on Tolkien so far examined, the least literary is that of J.W. Dunne. It is in many ways, however, the most immediate, or perhaps most practical, in its impact. There would be little doubt, even without corroborating evidence, that Tolkien and his Inkling friends had read and discussed Dunne, for it is very much the kind of thing that would have engaged their intellects.' (ibid, p.47)

One can thus see an undercurrent of possibly popular theory if not outright held pseudo-scientific belief at the time drew in Freud's ideas. Therefore a Minas Tirith constructed out of all seven temporal levels of ancient Troy co-existing would be no great leap of imagination on the part of Tolkien.

II; 'The Old Work of Giants'

It is by no means impossible that Aegean archaeology had another effect on Tolkien's depiction of Minas Tirith and related places. One of the most noticeable things about Mycenean ruins, and contemporary works in Troy and its region, is the sheer scale and visual power of the stonework. Written descriptions continually refer to it; photographs emphasise it. From Tsountas and Manatt in 1897 to Michael Wood in 1985, Mycenean and Trojan stonework is regarded as being impressive and worth devoting space to. The classical Greeks described such walls as 'Cyclopean', because it was believed that no mere man could have raised such structures, only legendary giants such as the Cyclopes.

One Mycenean site is particularly relevant - Tiryns, in Argos, whose name (*Tirynthos* in Classical Greek) echoes that of Minas Tirith. Homer calls it 'Tiryns of the Great Walls' and modern commentators often refer to the ruins as being like a ship. Leonard Cotterel in *The Bull of Minos* said of Tiryns that: 'From a distance it rides the peaceful fields like a battleship...' (Cotterell 1955, ch.VI, p.78). More recently, Michael Wood used the same metaphor; 'Rising like a ship from the plain of Argos, Tiryns lies 9 miles south of Mycenae on a low, rocky promontory now about a mile from the sea.' (Wood 1985, ch.2, p.72).

This appears to be a long-standing description of Tiryns, which matches Tolkien's description of Minas Tirith as being like a ship:

'For partly in the primeval shaping of the hill, partly by the mighty craft and labour of old, there stood up from the rear of wide court behind the Gate a towering bastion of stone, its edge sharp as a ship-keel facing east. Up it rose, even to the level of the topmost circle, and there was crowned by a battlement; so that those in the Citadel might, like mariners in a mountainous ship, look from its peak sheer down upon the Gate seven hundred feet below.'

(RotK, Book V, ch.1, p.24)

At Mycenae itself, the walls are by all accounts awe-inspiring, though hard to photograph as they tend to blend into the surrounding rocky hillsides. The famous Lion Gate is an exception to this, having been the subject of pictorial study from an early date in the development of the archaeological study of the site. 'Cyclopean' masonry tends to be made up of huge blocks, somewhat roughly squared as a rule, levelled up and wedged in place with smaller stones. In some places it can be neat, and at its peak it can be awesomely well-finished, as in some of the great tholos or 'beehive' tombs at Mycenae. An example of this is the so-called Treasury of Atreus, another favourite subject for illustrators and photographers (parts of whose surviving marble decoration are in the British Museum).

This preponderance of impressive stonework is certainly reflected in Tolkien's descriptions of Minas Tirith and associated places. There is also one specific verbal echo, for in the first description of Minas Tirith Tolkien says:

'And upon its out-thrust knee was the Guarded City, with its seven walls of stone so strong and old that *it seemed not to have been builded but carven by giants out of the bones of the earth.*' (ibid, ch.1, p.23; emphasis ours)

This is cyclopean masonry by literal description, and in *The War of the Ring*, HOME vol.VIII, we find Tolkien employing the actual word in one of the earliest outlines to cover this section of the book:

'Gandalf and Pippin reach Minas Tirith dawn. Description of Minas Tirith and its huge 'cyclopean' concentric walls - it is in fact a fort and town the size of a small mountain.' (*The War of the Ring*, HOME vol.VIII, part 3, chapter II, p 260)

There are no descriptions of impressive stonework in the Númenorean stories that Tolkien wrote before he created these passages in LotR (*The Lost Road* and *The Notion Club Papers*) so this element in the description of Gondor cannot come from Tolkien's likely sources for Númenor, the ancient Near Eastern realms of Assyria and Egypt. Therefore it is certainly worth considering the idea that descriptions or images of Mycenean ruins may have had an influence on the early development of the 'look' of Gondor, whatever other ideas Tolkien may have brought in afterwards. It is also mentioning that in 1912 the distinguished Homeric scholar W. Leaf repeated in his book *Troy; A Study in Homeric Geography* an interesting suggestion:

'Dörpfeld also calls attention to the fact that the masonry, and especially the batter [slope] of the lower part of the wall, finds its exact counterpart in Egypt in many buildings of both the old and later kingdoms. The resemblance is in some cases so striking as to lead him to suppose that there must be a distinct connexion. It is, of course, quite possible that foreign builders were imported in order to construct these great fortifications.' (Leaf 1912, ch.III, p.89)

Dörpfeld here is of course the German architect and archaeologist, Schliemann's onetime assistant, who continued his work at Troy; as Dörpfeld's book has never been translated, W. Leaf's English-language summary (with numerous photographs and a good plan) was and is important. There is therefore in the archaeological material about Troy which had been published when Tolkien was writing LotR a pre-existing suggestion of a connection between monumental Mycenean-style masonry and the ancient civilisations associated with Númenor, of exactly the sort that emerges in Tolkien's writings with the connection between Gondor and Númenor. Given the likely dates, it is not impossible that such ideas helped reinforce the developing links between Númenor and the world of *The Lord of the Rings* in Tolkien's mind.

It is also worth remembering that surviving Near Eastern works do not include roads or bridges, but exactly such things are cited in association with Mycenean Greece in general, and the site of Mycenae in particular. The famous citadel stands at the heart of a network of paved roads (at least five have been traced), all equipped with culverts to take stray drainage water in the winter rains, and large, well-built bridges across more considerable streambeds which could easily take two passing chariots or one heavy ox-wagon (Wood 1985 ch.5; Wace 1949 ch.VI; figs.38a, b). These sources post-date the writing of the Minas Tirith chapters in *The Lord of the Rings*, but C. Tsountas and J.I. Manatt's *The Mycenean Age* was published almost fifty years before Tolkien invented Gondor. They give detailed descriptions of the wider Mycenean road network in the Peloponnese in Greece, and the book includes a number of illustrations of bridges, culverts and roads as well as a map (Tsountas and Manatt 1897, ch.II, pp.12-13, 35-8). As depicted by Tolkien, one of the most obvious achievements of the Exiles of Númenor in Middle-earth is their construction of roads and bridges. The bridge of Osgiliath is repeatedly mentioned in LotR as an important point of defence or attack. Roads are mentioned in connection with the Ride of the Rohirrim, both the main road which is blocked by the armies of Mordor and the forgotten but still passable side-road which the Drúedain tell Theoden about.

In the accounts of Ithilien in LotR, roads and road-works are described: 'The road had been made in a long lost time, and for perhaps thirty miles below the Morannon it had been newly repaired, but as it went south the wild encroached upon it. The handiwork of Men of old could still be seen in its straight sure flight

and level course: now and again it cut its way through hillside slopes, or leaped over a stream upon a wide shapely arch of enduring masonry; but at last all signs of stonework faded, save for a broken pillar here and there, peering out of bushes at the side, or old paving-stones still lurking amid weeds and moss.... It dwindled at last to a country cart-road little used; but it did not wind: it held its own sure course and guided them by the swiftest way.' (TT, Book IV, ch.4, pp.257-8)
Obviously, Middle-earth's road system seems at first glance to have been inspired by Europe's Roman roads, which long survived the fall of the Western Empire both as practical trackways and in folklore. Although Roman roads are common enough in Britain, there are no standing bridges and these are a rarity even in Europe. However, roads and road-works such as bridges also appear in connection with the Mycenean Greek civilisation, and therefore with the Tale of Troy, which appears to have a stronger association with Minas Tirith and the Men of Gondor than does any post-Roman legend. It is interesting to add that there are not only roads remaining from Mycenean Greece but also bridges. This makes it more likely that the older Mycenean source of the idea is the one which influenced Tolkien in this case.

III; Watchtower

Turning to the names of both cities, Minas Tirith's name is variously interpreted as the Tower of Guard, or the Guarded City. It was originally called Minas Anor, Tower of the Sun. The seven names of Gondolin are given in full in the published material only in the BOLT version, where one is 'Gwarestin', explained in the Appendix on Names as: 'Rendered in the Tale as 'Tower of Guard', and so also in NFG ; GL glosses it as 'watchtower (especially as a name of Gondolin)'. A late entry in GL gives *estirin, estirion, estrin* 'pinnacle', beside *esc* sharp point, sharp edge'. The second element of this word is *tiri(o)n* : see I 258 (*Kortirion*). For *gwar* see *Amon Gwareth* .'
Although one might perhaps claim that in the face of an implacable enemy - in the case of Gondolin, Melko and in the case of Minas Tirith, Sauron - the most obvious name for a city would involve the adjective 'guard' or 'fortress' - and thus the correspondence could be seen as 'accidental'. However, Tolkien usually took care with names, especially when using elements - such as *tirion/tirith* - which were well established in his languages. It is highly probable that the linguistic connection between Gondolin and Minas Tirith is real and significant. This is especially so in view of all the other similarities between these two cities as discussed in this chapter.

The plain of Gondolin is described as being smoothed so as to guard against the entry of any spies: 'Now however was the guard of the hills maintained rather by custom than necessity, for the Gondothlim had long ago with unimagined toil levelled and cleared and delved all that plain about Amon Gwareth, so that scarce Gnome or bird or beast or snake could approach but was espied from many leagues off, for among the Gondothlim were many whose eyes were keener than the very hawks of Manwë Súlimo Lord of Gods and Elves who dwells upon Taniquetil;

and for this reason did they call that vale Tumladin or the valley of smoothness.' (BOLT vol.II, ch.3, p.163)

IV; Imagined Geographies

If we now consider the geographical setting of Minas Tirith it is in and of itself very interesting: 'For ten leagues or more it [the Rammas Echor] ran from the mountains' feet and so back again, enclosing in its fence the fields of Pelennor: fair and fertile
townlands on the long slopes and terraces falling to the deep levels of the Anduin... At its nearest point the wall was little more than one league from the City, and that was *south-eastward*. There Anduin, going in a wide knee about the hills of Emyn Arnen in South Ithilien, bent sharply *west*, and the out-wall rose upon its very brink; and beneath it lay the quays and landings of the Harlond for craft that came upstream from the *southern* fiefs...
To his left lay a sea of mist, rising to a bleak shadow in the *East*; but to his right great mountains reared their heads, ranging from the *West* to a steep and sudden end, as if in the making of the land the *River* had burst through a great barrier, carving out a mighty valley to be a land of battle and debate in times to come.' (RotK, Book V, ch.1, p.22-3)
The italics in the text above are ours for emphasis. It is rather interesting - when Tolkien takes such care with his texts - that in the earlier part of the description, all directions are given in lower case lettering, whereas in the latter part where Gandalf rides towards the city, barely half a page later on, all directions are given in capitals: East, West - and the watercourse is also capitalised: the River. Is this perhaps a small indication that this latter section of descriptive has been lifted out from some other place to be utilised in this particular point in LotR? If so, might this be from some Trojan version of the fall of a city which has been rendered into both Gondolin and Minas Tirith at different times? We have checked all editions of LotR from the First (1954/1955) through the Second (1966) to the Third and it is given in exactly the same way in all versions. Seeing as the Third edition was reset in 1979, it would have been a timely moment to change such discrepancies - but Tolkien and his Executor leaves them as they are.

In comparison with the Trojan material, if we substitute Scamander for Anduin, have Scaean Gate rather than Great Gate, and change Mindolluin's name to Ida - the description is then a close match for Troy as that place might be imagined from the 'Iliad'. Tolkien with his geography of Minas Tirith, the Pelennor Fields and Mount Mindolluin has collapsed the distance between Mount Ida and Troy. Even though Mount Ida is consistently referred to as a place from which the Olympian gods can watch over the fighting at Troy, it is actually some 30 miles away, though it *is* 5800 feet high, and Troy can be seen only from its summit (W. Leaf 1912 ch.I, p.10-12, and foldout map of The Troad). It is an even closer match for the Greek site of Mycenae (citadel of Agamemnon 'King of Men' in Homer, and many Mycenean Greek sites follow the same pattern of a defensible hill poised between fertile plainland and higher hills that offered grazing and forest resources

(L.Cotterel, 1963 repr 1967, The Lion Gate', Pan Books, ch.23, p 258).

The best comparison of all that we have seen so far is with Argos, south of Mycenae in the plain of the Argolid:

'Further south the impetuous Charadros, now called Xerias, rushes down its short course to join the Inachos close to Argos. At the mouth of the narrow pass where it breaks through from the hills stands an isolated acropolis-like mount which, when lighted by the sun against the darker shade of the gorge behind, might be guarding the gateway into a magic valley, a home of Pan and of the nymphs. South of the Charadros the lofty citadel, the Larisa, of Argos with the white Monastery of the Virgin on its side stands out against the higher peak behind. It is crowned by a fortress representative of every period of Greece between its two heroic ages, from the Mycenean period of Amphiaraüs and Diomede to that of the Greek Revolution when Demetrios Hypselantes valiantly defended it against the Turks in 1822. At its eastern foot can be seen the roofs and gardens of modern Argos, half concealed by the hill of Aspis, another prehistoric settlement. Southward the eye follows the romantic outline of the coast of Kynouria till mountain and sea blend together.' (A.J.B. Wace 1949, 'Mycenae; An Archaeological History and Guide', ch.1, p.4 and map 1)

According to the map, the Larisa hill itself juts from the side of a much larger (though unnamed) hill, which in turn is part of a still larger range. On the one hand this description itself contains many of the essentials of the form of Minas Tirith - a citadel located on a hill jutting from the side of a mountain at the end of a range, at a narrow pass with a river, and a larger town on the low ground nearby, with sea and mountains to the south and fair countryside nearby, 'an abode of Pan and of the nymphs' in the shape of Ithilien with its 'dishevelled dryad loveliness'. On the other hand, W. Leaf's maps of 1912 show that much of this can equally well be matched to Troy - which also stands on a hill at the end of a ridge (though both much less impressive than at Argos), at a narrowing of the plain, above the rivers Scamander/Mendere and Ximois; only Mount Ida needs to be moved closer to fit the bill, and even the sea being to the west (rather than the south) is not an insuperable obstacle, given the way in which Tolkien rearranged his geography in the early stages of constructing LotR and creating a location for the kingdom of men called 'Ond'. (see Lewis & Currie 2002, Uncharted Realms of Tolkien).

It is quite possible that, just as Gondolin's shape and the geography around it in the *Book of Lost Tales* were based on Lake Copaïs in Greece rather than Troy, Tolkien deliberately changed the geography of Minas Tirith and the surrounding area in the course of adapting the 'historical' and archaeological Trojan material to create Gondor. This would both hide a reference that at the time would be fairly obvious to any educated reader, and give Tolkien greater creative freedom. Very likely, he simply wanted to have 'Mount Ida' closer to 'Troy'; but that the Larisa/Argos site was picked up and used, perhaps first by happy accident but very probably later by deliberate choice, is shown by what happens around Minas Tirith. Let us look at C.Tsountas and J.I. Manatt again:

'The Plain of Argos... is thick sown with heroic legends and crowded with heroic

strongholds. At the eastern extremity rises the impregnable rock of Palamedes, "the Gibraltar of Greece" as Tozer calls it, guarding the rocky headland on which Nauplia is built; across the plain, on the north-west, looms its counterpart - the steep, sharp Larisa of Argos - with a city that has never ceased to exist lying at its foot. Between Argos and Nauplia, and less than three miles from the latter, lies Tiryns on a rock that hardly breaks the general level...'
(Tsountas and Manatt 1897, 'Mycenean Age', ch.II, pp.14-15)

So here we have two ancient hill-citadels rising each above its own town, with between them a larger, lower-lying and far better-known city. This is an exact match for Tolkien's description of Minas Tirith, Minas Morgul, and Osgiliath between them. Tiryns unlike Osgiliath does not lie on a river, though it is clear that there has been so much change in local watercourses that it could have done so in the era of the Trojan War. Similarly, Tiryns is now an inland site, but it was formerly close to the shore, and so was a clear parallel with Osgiliath, to which Aragorn can bring the Black Fleet he took from the Corsairs. It is worth noting further that Argos itself is a good parallel with Minas Tirith in terms of the time it has been in existence. Minas Tirith is somewhat over three thousand years old in *The Lord of the Rings*; Argos (founded in Mycenean times, still inhabited, and last defended by the Greeks against the Turks in the War of Independence in the 19th century - Wace 1949 ch.I) is some 35 centuries old.

The late 13th-century Sicilian writer Guido delle Colonne's description of Troy in his very influential *History of the Destruction of Troy* may have contributed to the picture of Minas Tirith and its neighbours (the first modern edition was in 1936, so Tolkien could have read it before writing these descriptions; Caxton's *Recuyell of the History of Troy*, a translation of the work, had also then been recently edited and would have been available). Two passages are particularly relevant and are worth quoting here. The first runs as follows:
'Through the middle of the city ran a river called Xanthus [Scamander], which, by dividing the city into two equal parts, in its unfailing course offered many conveniences to the inhabitants of that city. For since countless mills had been constructed on the bank, these mills in daily use turned coarse-ground grain into fine flour for the sustenance of the inhabitants. In addition, this river, flowing through hidden channels on account of the requisite abundant supply of water, purified the city by prearranged floods, by means of skilfully made canals and underground sluices, and by these baths the accumulated impurities were cleaned away. The Tiber at Rome was arranged like this river, and as it burst forth in the middle of Rome, it divided in two parts the city of Rome which was made in the likeness of Troy by the Trojan Aeneas.'
(Colonne/Meek 1974, bk.5, lines 170-183, p.46)
Probably under the influence of the archaeology, Tolkien deletes this central river and its accompanying drainage system from his picture of Minas Tirith. It does however appear right next door, in the city of Osgiliath which spreads on both sides of the River Anduin.
' "What can I see there?" he [Pippin] asked, pointing down to the middle of the

great curve of the Anduin. "Is that another city, or what is it?"
"It was a city," said Beregond, "the chief city of Gondor, of which this was only a fortress, for that is the ruin of Osgiliath *on either side of Anduin*, which our enemies took and burned long ago..." ' (RotK, Book V, ch.1, p.36, emphasis ours). It may be worth noting that this story of Osgiliath being taken and burnt - seemingly whilst still a thriving city - does not match with the picture of long slow decline given by Tolkien in the Appendices, where forces from Minas Ithil enter Osgiliath only when it is already a ruin. This is one of several points at which the text of *The Lord of the Rings* seems to preserve a different and perhaps older picture of Osgiliath, as in the reference to 'fords and bridges' there when the course of the wall around the Pelennor is being described, whereas the Appendices are quite clear that there is only one Bridge in Osgiliath.

In the second passage, Guido delle Colonne says that:
'But King Priam, however, for the location of his dwelling and a site for his own mansion ordered the great and famous Ilium, as his great palace was called, to be constructed in a higher place of the city out of the towering native rock in the city. and the master fortress of great security which was hewn by force from this native rock was glorious Ilium. From its foundation to the highest point which roofed it over in the shape of a sphere, its height reached a summit five hundred feet above the tops of the towers not far from it on the ramparts, which were themselves far higher than that same height.' (Colonne/Meek 1974, bk.5, lines 202-211, p.47)
This Trojan citadel 'hewn by force' from the 'towering native rock' is a good match for the citadel of Minas Tirith, perched atop the hill and the 'prow' of rock of which Tolkien says: 'For partly in the primeval shaping of the hill, partly by the mighty craft and labour of old, there stood up from the rear of the wide court behind the Gate a towering bastion of stone, its edge sharp as a ship-keel facing east. Up it rose, even to the level of the topmost circle, and there was crowned by a battlement; so that those in the Citadel might, like mariners in a mountainous ship, look from its peak sheer down upon the Gate seven hundred feet below,' (RotK, Book V, ch.1, p.24)
It is unfortunately not possible to say exactly when this feature entered the description as it is not in any of the relevant passages, nor on any of the maps of Minas Tirith, which are given in the 3 volumes of the HOME series devoted to *The Lord of the Rings*.

The height of Minas Tirith fairly well matches that of Colonne's Ilium; the Citadel is seven hundred feet above the gate, paralleling the towers 'far higher than' five hundred feet in Colonne's account. Tolkien also mentions in the same passage that the White Tower is 'tall and shapely, fifty fathoms from its base to the pinnacle, where the banner of the Stewards floated a thousand feet above the plain.' Fifty fathoms, for those unacquainted with the old British Imperial measurements, is six feet multiplied by fifty, or three hundred feet in total, giving the thousand when added to the seven hundred feet from Gate to Citadel. This is different to Colonne's figure, but reaches a good round number whilst not being wildly unrealistic for any of the components. All the changes to these figures in the course of writing LotR were in the direction of making them more like the dimensions of Troy (*War of the Ring*, HOME vol.VIII, Part 3, ch.II-III). Another difference is that Colonne makes the highest point of Ilium a dome, whereas the highest point in Minas Tirith is the Tower of Ecthelion. This can well be explained by the preference for towers in other medieval 'historical Troy' sources, such as the alliterative 'Destruction of Troy', which does not mention a dome in the parallel passage and says instead:

'Enclosed by a separate wall thickly set all about with towers
perfectly circular like a ring richly made
full five hundred feet was their height.'

(Panton & Donaldson 1968, bk.V, lines 1634-6) [Note 1]

There is no mention of a dome either in the second description of the citadel in book XII, lines 4948-76.

It is worth noting also that on a constrained site such as the Citadel of Minas Tirith (which Tolkien had some visual idea of, since sketches of the city appear in *The War of the Ring* (HOME vol.VIII, Part 3, ch.II & III p.268, 280, 290), a tall tower is far more achievable than a massive dome, especially a half-round European, Classical or Early Byzantine dome (like those of the Pantheon in Rome or Hagia Sophia in Istanbul) with no drum dividing it from the main roof structure and providing extra height, and no outer skin either. St Paul's Cathedral in London, for example, uses both the supporting drum and a lightweight second skin outside and above the real dome, to achieve its total height (the lantern is perched on a brick cone, while the visible dome is nothing but wooden battens and copper sheeting). Tolkien is often oddly realistic, so this choice may be down as much to a consideration of the engineering as to the Middle English sources, or any preference for towers. That Tolkien was willing to have reasonable sized domes is shown by the domed tombs in Rath Dinen in Minas Tirith, such as the House of the Stewards, whose dome is broken by Denethor's funeral fire (RotK, Book V, ch.7).

In this connection it is worth noting as well that the emphasis on tombs and the preservation of the dead in Gondor (and Númenor) is matched by the elaborate embalming of the body of Hector the Crown Prince of Troy, in the medieval accounts. In Guido delle Colonne and in the alliterative 'Destruction', Hector's body is placed in a tabernacle of gold and ebony in the temple of Apollo just outside the Thymbraean gate of Troy (where he can be shown to the people by opening the doors of the enclosure), sitting upright on a throne, fully clothed and preserved by means of continuously flowing balsam (Colonne/Meek 1974, bk.22, lines 35-50, pp.170-1). By comparison, the 'evil' Achilles (as far as medieval versions tell) is burnt upon a pyre - the very thing that happens to Denethor when he attempts to burn Faramir in the houses of the Dead (RotK, Book V, ch.7). Faramir explains to Frodo and Sam in Ithilien that, as Gondor declined: 'Kings made tombs more splendid than houses of the living...' (TT, Book IV, ch. 5, p.286)

The White Tower (or Tower of Ecthelion) itself bears comparison with the medieval towers of Troy. In *The Lord of the Rings*, it is described as 'glimmering like a spike of pearl and silver, tall and fair and shapely, and its pinnacle glittered as if it were wrought of crystals...' This compares with Guido delle Colonne's comment that the panes, piers, capitals and bases of the windows in the citadel of Ilium were all of shining crystal, while the towers were marble (bk.5, lines 215-223, p.47-8), and with the alliterative 'Destruction', which follows him:

'Of well-matched colours to see, all set in courses
Made wholly of marble with carved designs
With sculpture most noble and boldly made
On battlements rightly built and grouped on high
The windows, finely made and regularly set
Shaped most beautifully, all of sparkling stones
Carven into crystal by craft of sculpture
Set into pillars proudly to show
The bases and borders all of bright pearl.'

(Panton & Donaldson 1968, book V, lines 1644-52) [Note 2]

Interestingly, the White Tower of Minas Tirith is at first a recently built or rebuilt structure, fitting with the recent building of the tower of Troy. In the earliest versions of the relevant chapter in LotR the tower is called the Tower of Denethor, an exact match for the Tower of Priam's rebuilt Troy. The name was later changed, but only by one generation to have it built by Denethor's father Ecthelion (*War of the Ring* , HOME vol.VIII, part 3, ch.II-III p.281). Finally in the major changes associated with the writing of the Appendices to LotR, the rebuilding of the White Tower was moved all the way back to 2698 T.A. (a change of some 300 years) and the reign of the newly invented Steward Ecthelion the First. It is still young by comparison with most structures of any significance or beauty in LotR, but the direct comparison with the Tower of Troy has been removed. An indirect link remained, for the name given to the builder, Ecthelion, is a name borrowed from the list of the city's lords in *The Fall of Gondolin* . Moreover, it is a name of strongly Greek form with a possible Greek etymology. The hint of an association with the towers of Troy thus remains.

Both towers and domes appear again in Osgiliath, alongside the dividing river moved from Minas Tirith. Firstly, there is a brief mention in 'The Two Towers', as Sam and Frodo journey through Ithilien to the Crossroads:

'...out of that darkness the long valley came, falling steeply in an ever-widening trough towards the Anduin. At its bottom ran a hurrying stream: Frodo could hear its stony voice coming up through the silence; and beside it on the hither side a road went winding down like a pale ribbon, down into chill grey mists that no gleam of sunset touched. There it seemed to Frodo that he descried far off, floating as it were on a shadowy sea, the high dim tops and broken pinnacles of old towers forlorn and dark.

He turned to Gollum. 'Do you know where we are?' he said.

'Yes, Master. Dangerous places. This is the road from the Tower of the Moon, Master, down to the ruined city by the shores of the River...'

(TT, Book IV, ch.7, p.306)

Regarding domes, in the Appendices to LotR we find that:

'In that siege and burning the Tower of the Dome of Osgiliath was destroyed, and the *palantir* was lost in the waters.' (RotK, Appendix A, section iv)

So the major features of the medieval descriptions of Troy, towers and dome(s), appear in both Minas Tirith and Osgiliath, and the latter city also has a river running through it which further matches those descriptions.

Guido delle Colonne's description of the great hall which Priam builds in his citadel is of interest when compared with Tolkien's palace halls:
'In the inner part of the aforesaid palace, among other structures marvellously vaulted, King Priam established a certain hall which was extremely long and correspondingly broad, the outer surface of which was sheathed in marble slabs; its vaulted ceiling was panelled with wood of cedar and ebony, and diversified materials divided its floor of mosaic work into different colours. The throne of the king was set up at the end of this hall, where the royal table was located, stretched out in its great length, completely constructed of delicate inlays of ivory and ebony. On each side of the table the long rows of benches offered comfortable seats to the dinner guests. At the other end of the hall there was an altar of amazing artistry, covered with jewels and gold, and raised in the name of highest Jupiter, to which easy ascent was made by twenty steps shining with the decoration of mosaic work. At the summit of this altar, accordingly, gleamed a golden image of the god Jupiter which had been placed there; it was fifteen cubits in length and was entirely made of fine gold of inestimable value, which was beautified by the appearance of various jewels, and enriched by pearls placed here and there in various designs.' (Colonne/Meek 1974, bk.5, lines 223-241)

If we turn to Tolkien's description of the hall in Minas Tirith:
' Pippin looked into a great hall. It was lit by deep windows in the wide aisles at either side, beyond the rows of tall pillars that upheld the roof. Monoliths of black marble, they rose to great capitals carved in many strange figures of beasts and leaves; and far above in shadow the wide vaulting gleamed with dull gold, inset with flowing traceries of many colours. No hangings nor storied webs, nor any things of woven stuff or of wood, were to be seen in that long solemn hall; but between the pillars there stood a silent company of tall images graven in cold stone... At the far end upon a dais of many steps was set a high throne under a canopy of marble shaped like a crowned helm; behind it was carved upon the wall and set with gems an image of a tree in flower. But the throne was empty. At the foot of the dais, upon the lowest step which was broad and deep, there was a stone chair, black and unadorned...' (RotK, Book V, ch.1, p.26)
There are a number of similarities - for a start, both buildings are very large, fully vaulted halls. In Minas Tirith, the throne on its high dais replaces the altar of Jupiter. Since there is only royal imagery here, not sacred imagery as well, Denethor's chair can comfortably share the same end of the hall as the throne of Gondor, whereas the throne of Priam and the altar of Jupiter occupy opposite ends of Guido delle Colonne's hall. The tree replaces the gem-studded image of Jupiter and also picks up the marvellous tree of gems and precious metals described as being in the hall by all the medieval sources from Guido delle Colonne onwards, which has been discussed above as the source of the Two Trees of Gondolin.

The obvious differences are the stone-vaulted rather than wood-lined roof, the absence of a table, and the undescribed floor. There is almost certainly a reason for this; wood is the primary material of the hall Meduseld at Edoras in Rohan, which also has a mosaic or at least cut-stone floor:

'The hall was long and wide and filled with shadows and half-lights; mighty pillars upheld its lofty roof. But here and there bright sunbeams fell in glimmering shafts from the eastern windows, high under the deep eaves. Through the louver in the roof, above the thin wisps of issuing smoke, the sky showed pale and blue. As their eyes changed, the travellers perceived that the floor was paved with stones of many hues; branching runes and strange devices intertwined beneath their feet. They saw now that the pillars were richly carved, gleaming dully with gold and half-seen colours. Many woven cloths were hung upon the walls, and over their wide spaces marched figures of ancient legend, some dim with years, some darkling in the shade.' (TT, Book III, ch.6, p.116)

True, a clear statement that the building was wooden would not go amiss. However, the carved and painted pillars of Meduseld, whatever their material, could hardly be more different to the 'monoliths of black marble' at Minas Tirith. The coloured floor of Meduseld has two likely sources. Firstly there is the great Old English poem Beowulf that Tolkien knew so well, where when Grendel arrives while *Beowulf* lies waiting, 'on fágne flór / féond treddode' *the foe stepped onto the painted floor*. Secondly, there is a piece of scholarly work by Tolkien that Shippey cites, a review of the *Introduction to the Survey of Place-Names* , (1926), in which he picks out for praise the etymology of a place called Fawler, ex Fauflor, another *fág flór*, which this time was certainly a Roman mosaic. (Shippey 1992 ch.2, p.30).

It is most likely that Minas Tirith's hall has a plain or at least undescribed floor because it had to be different to Meduseld. In the first drafts of the chapter concerned the floor is mosaic; ' 'But the floor was of shining stone, white-gleaming, figured with mosaics of many colours' ' and 'The floor was of polished stone, white-gleaming, inset with flowing traceries of many colours.'

(*War of the Ring*, HOME vol.VIII, part 3, ch.III, p.281 & 288).

C.J.R. Tolkien says that:

'This was repeated in the following typescript; but in the final typescript , from which the text in RK was printed, the sentence was compressed: '...gleamed with dull gold, inset with flowing traceries of many colours.' Since there is no indication on the second typescript that any change was intended, it seems certain that this was a casual 'line-jumping' error, causing the 'flowing traceries' to be ascribed to the vaulting.' (ibid, p. 288)

A casual error this change may well have been, but it stood uncorrected through all the process of checking proofs (when other more or less significant changes entered, as shown in all the volumes of the 'History of the Lord of the Rings') and even the reworking of the Second Edition. There is therefore a good chance that at some point in that process, J.R.R. Tolkien decided to let this change in the description stand in order to create more difference between Minas Tirith and Meduseld, and perhaps also to differentiate between his hall and Guido delle Colonne's building.

Another echo from the medieval descriptions of Priam's palace is the tree in the court of the fountain in front of the White Tower and the hall in the Citadel of Minas Tirith. Tolkien tells us that:

'Quickly Gandalf strode across the white-paved court. A sweet fountain played there in the morning sun, and a sward of bright green lay about it; but in the midst, drooping over the pool, stood a dead tree, and the falling drops dripped sadly from its barren and broken branches back into the clear water.'
(RotK, Book V, ch.1, p.25)

This tree, like the one inside the hall, echoes the marvellous artificial tree of the medieval Troy-histories. Guido delle Colonne says:

'When they had reached the entry of the spacious court, they marvelled at the buildings of this palace, buttressed with work of such marvellous skill, but they marvelled even more when they saw in the middle of the court itself a certain tree made by magic arts and constructed with clever ingenuity. While its trunk was of gold, slimmer than a lance and twelve cubits in height, at the top of its trunk the tree itself, of an amazing breadth, poured itself out in branches which sheltered the whole court by their length and profusion. In fact, the branches were made partly of gold and partly of silver, as were the leaves and blossoms, while the fruits gleamed, formed of a great diversity of jewels.'
(Colonne/Meek 1974 bk.12, ll.106-16, p.103-4)

Of all the possible medieval sources, Guido delle Colonne's work is the only one so far known to us which explicitly has the tree in the court, rather than 'before the doors' or inside the hall. This makes it all the more regrettable that we have not been able to consult Caxton's *Recuyell*, the most readily available edition of Guido delle Colonne's *Historia* prior to 1936, which is now impossible to obtain outside reference libraries. When the White Tree of Minas Tirith came into being, such objects existed in Tolkien's writings only in Elvish hands, and offshoots or replicas of the original, lightgiving Two Trees could be found east of Valinor only in Gondolin - the White Tree of Númenor is absent from 'The Lost Road', 'The Notion Club Papers' and the accompanying 'Drowning of Anadune'. In authorly rather than invented terms, Nimloth of Númenor is descended from the nameless White Tree of Gondor, not the other way around. The tree in the citadel of Minas Tirith, then, for all its later revisions and crossing influences with the Númenor story, almost certainly took its inspiration from the Trees of Troy and Gondolin.

Indeed, the association of tree and fountain in Minas Tirith most easily matches the description of Gondolin, rather than any possible medieval source we have been able to consult. The two magical trees in the BOLT *Fall of Gondolin* are first said to be 'before the doors of the king's hall', where also 'the fountains that played before the doors shot twenty fathoms and seven in the air and fell in a singing rain of crystal; therein did the sun glitter splendidly by day and the moon most magically shimmered by night.' Again, in the sack of the city the death of Gothmog takes place in something variously called the King's Square, Square of the Palace of Turgon, or Square of the King, which 'had aforetime contained many beautiful trees, both oak and poplar, around a great well of vast depth and great purity of water...'; Turgon's palace seems to stand to one side of this, with the Two Trees in front of the steps leading to the doors. So there is a connection between trees and fountains in Gondolin as in Minas Tirith.

Incidentally, the name of Laomedon, King of Troy and father of Priam, probably gave rise to the province of Lamedon in Gondor, since the Laud Troy Book uses exactly this spelling of Laomedon's name.

Another point worth making is the way in which the archaeological evidence for the relationship of Troy and Mycenean Greece is echoed in Tolkien's description of the links between Gondor and Harad. The distribution of two key pottery types, Grey Minyan ware and matt-painted ware, depicts Troy and the surrounding Troad as a small northern outlier compared to a much larger zone of use to the southwest in Greece. The earliest references we have for this are L.Cotterel 1963 'The Lion Gate' (repr. 1967 ch.5, p.82,), who is citing A.J.B. Wace 1962, A Companion to Homer, Macmillan; but Wace had been excavating in the Aegean and publishing the results since the 1920's, and others as far back as Schliemann and Dörpfeld in the 19th century had made the same point about the relationship between Greece and Troy. Therefore, the information is certain to have been available before the Second World War, in time to influence Tolkien's views. Moreover, there was a not inconsiderable academic struggle going on between the wars, between those archaeologists (such as A.J.B. Wace) who supported the Mycenean Greeks as a people with a creative civilisation of their own, however much influenced by outsiders, and Sir Arthur Evans and his followers, who insisted that all culture and invention in the Bronze Age Aegean sprang from Crete and the Minoans. Whilst usually deeply tiresome for outsiders, such arguments at least ensure plentiful publication and also discussion around college tables. Importantly, Sir Arthur Evans was an Oxford graduate and a former Keeper of the Ashmolean Museum in Oxford, while one of his most vocal opponents was Leonard Palmer, Professor of Comparative Philology at Oxford (according to L.Cotterell, in *The Lion Gate*, 1963, ch.19, p.218). The importance of these two men at Oxford and in the historical debate practically guarantees that one way or another, opinions about Aegean archaeology would have reached Tolkien's ears. This distribution of pots and peoples is a match for the situation of Minas Tirith, capital of the relatively small country of Gondor, in comparison to the much larger Black Númenorean realms in Harad:

'Thus it came to pass in that time that the Númenoreans first made great settlements upon the west shores of the ancient lands; for their own land seemed to them shrunken, and they had no rest or content therein, and they desired now wealth and dominion in Middle-earth, since the West was denied. Great harbours and strong towers they made, and there many of them took up their abode; but they appeared now rather as lords and masters and gatherers of tribute than as helpers and teachers. And the great ships of the Númenoreans were borne east on the winds and returned ever laden, and the power and majesty of their kings were increased; and they drank and they feasted and they clad themselves in silver and gold.

In all this the Elf-friends had small part. They alone came now ever to the north and the land of Gil-Galad, keeping their friendship with the Elves and lending them their aid against Sauron; and their haven was Pelargir above the mouths of Anduin the Great.' (QS, Akallabeth, p.320-1)

'And Sauron gathered to him great strength of his servants out of the east and the south; and among them were not a few of the high race of Númenor. For in the days of the sojourn of Sauron in that land the hearts of well nigh all its people had been turned towards darkness. Therefore many of those who set sail east in that time and made fortresses and dwellings upon the coasts were already bent to his will, and they served him still gladly in Middle-earth. But because of the power of Gil-Galad these renegades, lords both mighty and evil, for the most most part took up their abodes in the southlands far away; yet two there were, Herumor and Fuinir, who rose to power among the Haradrim, a great and cruel people that dwelt in the wide lands south of Mordor beyond the mouths of Anduin.' (ibid, p.353)

V; The Bull Beneath the Earth

One of the most important symbols of the House of the Stewards of Gondor is the horn which Boromir carries. It is the shards of this horn which arrive in Gondor to tell the tale of Boromir's death:

' "I have received this," said Denethor, and laying down his rod he lifted from his lap the thing he had been gazing at. In each hand he held up one half of a great horn cloven through the middle; a wild-ox horn bound with silver.

"That is the horn that Boromir always wore!" cried Pippin.

"Verily," said Denethor. And in my turn I bore it, and so did each eldest son of our house, far back into the vanished years before the falling of the kings, since Vorondil father of Mardil hunted the wild kine of Araw in the far fields of Rhûn." (RotK, Book V, ch.1, p.27)

A little more information about these 'wild kine' is given in Appendix A:

'The wild white kine that were still to be found near the Sea of Rhûn were said in legend to be descended from the Kine of Araw, the huntsman of the Valar, who alone of the Valar came often to middle-earth in the Elder Days. *Orome* is the High-Elven form of his name.'

(RotK, Appendix A, section ii, p.319, footnote)

Boromir's horn seems to appear quite late on in the course of the writing of *The Lord of the Rings*. It is not in any of the early versions of the departure from Rivendell given in *The Return of the Shadow* (HOME vol.VI). In *The Treason of Isengard*, HOME vol.VII, a horn first appears in connection with Boromir in the description of him giving a horn-call, which was added in pencil to fair-copy C of the scene on the Bridge of Khazad-Dûm; this dates to 1940 or later. The Horn as we know it in the published version appeared in May of 1944 or thereabouts, when Faramir was invented. His name is Falborn at this stage, and he says:

'" Then maybe thou canst see it in thy mind's eye: a great horn of the wild ox of the [Eastern wilderness>] East, bound with silver, and written with his name,

[*struck out* : worn upon a silver chain].'
(*War of the Ring*, HOME vol.VIII, Part 2, ch.5, p.146)
So the motif of the Horn appears to have developed alongside the appearance of the Trojan/Gondolin link with the new kingdom of Ond/Gondor.

It is worth noting that while bulls in general are not of symbolic significance in the legends directly concerning Troy, there is one very important piece of Mycenean masonry which *does* carry a depiction of a bull. This is the broken triangular relief taken by Lord Elgin (the same man who purloined the famous Marbles from the Parthenon in Athens) from somewhere in the vicinity of Mycenae, possibly the so-called Tomb of Clytemnestra. Now in the British Museum, these two finely carved fragments could easily have been known to Tolkien. A spectacular silver bull's-head with golden horns was also among the most notable finds made at Mycenae by Heinrich Schliemann. An extensive description of this piece, and a full-page illustration, appeared in C.Tsountas and J.I. Manatt's 1897 book *The Mycenean Age* (ch.V, pp.103-5) - a book with so many passages echoing Tolkien's work as to make one wonder if he owned a copy. It is quite possible that these Mycenean bulls added to the significance of the motif for Tolkien, and the idea is worth adding to our list of correspondences between Trojan/Mycenean culture and Tolkien's writings.

If we are right in thinking that a strictly Trojan version underlay the extant *Fall of Gondolin*, in which the island of Santorini/Thera with its Minoan culture was a vital link in the chain of transmission of the story to the present day, then the appearance of the Horn and the 'wild white kine of Araw' in LotR may echo that early tale. These wild cattle are found near the Sea of Rhûn, and they are white; which parallels the white bull that Poseidon, god of the seas, sent to King Minos of Crete in Greek legend with disastrous consequences (the bull was the father of the cannibal Minotaur). Theoretically, since it was associated with Atlantis as early as 1872 (Friedrich/McBirney 2000 ch.10), a Minoan/Santorini link could also imply a Númenorean link. There does not appear to be any link between bulls and Númenor, but the problem is that there is strong anecdotal evidence that Tolkien's 'Description of Númenor' is a great deal longer than the 'selections' from it which were published in Unfinished Tales to help set the scene for the tale of Erendis and Aldarion. There could be bulls or white cattle in the unpublished sections; it is impossible to say.

VI; Words to the Defenders

The words of Gandalf to the men of the Rammas Echor are very close to what Tuor and Voronwe say to the gate-guards of Gondolin.
Firstly Gandalf:
'Gandalf was speaking to the men that barred his way, and as he listened Pippin became aware that he himself was being discussed.
'Yea truly, we know you, Mithrandir,' said the leader of the men, 'and you know the pass-words of the Seven Gates and are free to go forward. But we do not know your companion. What is he? A dwarf out of the mountains in the North?

We wish for no strangers in the land at this time, unless they be mighty men of arms in whose faith and help we can trust.'
'I will vouch for him before the seat of Denethor,' said Gandalf.'
(RotK, Book V, ch.1, p.20-1)
Now to Tuor and Voronwë:
'Know you not whom you see? I am Voronwë son of Aranwë of the House of Fingolfin. Or am I forgotten in my own land after a few years?...'
'Then Voronwë will remember also the laws of his land,' said the voice. 'Since by command he went forth, he has the right to return. But not to lead hither any stranger. By that deed his right is void, and he must be led as a prisoner to the king's judgement. As for the stranger, he shall be slain or held captive at the judgement of the Guard,...'
Voronwë answered. 'Other shall the wanderer return than as he set forth. What I have done, I have done under command greater than the law of the Guard. The King alone should judge me, and him that comes with me.'
(UT, Part One, ch.1, p.45)
Note that both Voronwë and Gandalf bring a stranger who is not expected and not allowed within - someone not of the race of those who live in that place. They petition that the stranger is judged by the highest authority in the city. Also Voronwë's words describe perfectly the situation for Gandalf as well as himself - the last time Gandalf was in Minas Tirith it was as 'the Grey', he returns having passed through fire and flood as 'Gandalf the White'.
It would seem to us that both the scenes have a common source - this cannot be *The Book of Lost Tales*, as it does not contain the equivalent passage, so we would suggest a Trojan counterpart or antecedent.

VII; Beacons of Hope

One particularly significant detail about the siege of Minas Tirith finds a distinct echo in Homer's *Iliad* . This is the use of beacon fires to send for help. The basic idea is widespread, and the use of beacons for ceremonial occasions if nothing else has continued right up to the 20th century in Britain (beacon chains were lit to mark Queen Victoria's Diamond Jubilee and Queen Elizabeth II's Silver Jubilee, for example). However, the *Iliad* has a specific example of beacons being used at the very last minute, in a desperate attempt to send for help:
'As when the smoke rising from a city reaches the bright sky far from an island that foemen beset, and the day long the contend in grievious strife for their city wall. At sundown the beacon fires blaze in rows and the glare reaches aloft their neighbours to see in the hope that they will come in their ships and ward of their doom.'
(Cotterell 1963, 'Lion Gate', ch.12, p.153, citing Homer translated by E.V. Rieu, *The Iliad*, Penguin 1946)

In *The Lord of the Rings*, Pippin sees the beacons of Gondor lit as he rides with Gandalf from Rohan:
'Then, "What is that?" cried Pippin suddenly, clutching at Gandalf's cloak. "Look!

Fire, red fire! Are there dragons in this land? Look, there is another!"
For answer Gandalf cried aloud to his horse. "On, Shadowfax! We must hasten. time is short. See! The beacons of Gondor are alight, calling for aid. War is kindled. See, there is the fire on Amon Dîn, and flame on Eilenach; and there they go speeding west: Nardol, Erelas, Min-Rimmon, Calenhad, and the Halifirien on the borders of Rohan."
But Shadowfax paused in his stride, slowing to a walk, and then he lifted up his head and neighed. And out of the darkness the answering neigh of other horses came; and presently the thudding of hoofs was heard, and three riders swept up and passed like flying ghosts in the moon and vanished into the West. Then Shadowfax gathered himself together and sprang away, and the night flowed over him like a roaring wind.' (RotK, Book V, ch.1, pp.19-20)
At this point Minas Tirith is not yet under siege; but that follows so swiftly that the errand-riders who follow up the beacons (with the Red Arrow, ibid., ch.3, p.72) are unable to return to Minas Tirith, and in fact are killed as they try to flee back to Rohan; Theoden's riders find them on the road as they make their way to Gondor with the help of the Woses, some chapters later (ibid., ch.5, p.109-10). In this last-minute timing, and the specific use of beacons to call for help, Tolkien seems to be following Homer rather than any other possible source.

VIII; Allies and alliances

The allies who come to help defend a beleaguered city are of great interest in the connected cases of Troy, Gondolin and Minas Tirith. We shall start first with the list of nobles who Pippin sees arriving at Minas Tirith:
'Pippin and Bergil edged their way forward to the front of the crowd and waited....
'Forlong has come,' Bergil answered; 'old Forlong the Fat, the Lord of Lossarnach. That is where my grandsire lives...'
Leading the line there came walking a big thick-limbed horse, and on it sat a man of wide shoulders and huge girth, but old and grey-bearded, yet mail-clad and black-helmed and bearing a long heavy spear. Behind him marched proudly a dusty line of men, well-armed and bearing great battle-axes; grim-faced they were, and shorter and somewhat swarthier than any men that Pippin had yet seen in Gondor....
And so the companies came and were hailed and cheered and passed through the Gate, men of the Outlands marching to defend the City of Gondor in a dark hour; but always too few, always less than hope looked for or need asked. The men of Ringló Vale behind the son of their Lord, Dervorin striding on foot; three hundreds. From the uplands of Morthond, the great Blackroot Vale, tall Duinhir with his sons, *Duilin* and Derufin, and five hundred bowmen. From the Anfalas, the Langstrand far away, a long line of men of many sorts, hunters and herdsmen and men of little villages, scantily equipped save for the household of Golasgil their lord. From Lamedon, a few grim hillmen without a captain. Fisher-folk of the Ethir, some hundred or more spared from the ships. Hirluin the Fair of the

Green Hills from Pinnath Gelin with three hundreds of gallant green-clad men. And last and proudest, Imrahil, Prince of Dol Amroth, kinsman of the Lord, with gilded banners bearing his token of the Ship and the Silver Swan, and a company of knights in full harness riding grey horses; and behind them seven hundreds of men at arms, tall as lords, grey-eyed, dark-haired, singing as they came.

And that was all, less than three thousands full told. No more would come.' (RotK, Book V, ch.1, pp.43-4)

Note that Duilin - italicised above - appears in another list of allies - see below.

One notable point about this is that some of the descriptions of arms and armour are distinctly medieval. 'Mail-clad' (as with Forlong) is not distinctive of date, but the 'full harness' of the knights of Dol Amroth can hardly be other than plate-mail of some description. This is backed up by what happens when Imrahil discovers Eowyn's presence:

'"Men of Rohan!" he cried. "Are there no leeches among you? She is hurt, to the death maybe, but I deem that she yet lives." And he held the bright-burnished vambrace that was upon his arm before her cold lips, and behold! a little mist was laid upon it hardly to be seen.' (ibid, ch.6, p.121)

A 'vambrace' is 'Middle-English *from* Old French, 'avant-bras', 'before the arm', defensive armour for the fore-arm', a term first used in English in 1330 (chronicles of Wace, OED), and its use for anything other than plate-armour is vanishingly rare. Imrahil's action and its result makes it quite clear that he is wearing 'white armour', polished steel plate-mail; perhaps not a full suit, as the few surviving battle armours (and especially those from southern Europe) tend to mix and match for lightness and strength, but certainly some important elements of one. It is most unlike J.R.R. Tolkien to use a word so clearly derived from French, as is well pointed out by C.J.R. Tolkien in a note to one of the chapters of *The Return of the Shadow*:

'The remainder of this part of the text is in very rough pencilled form, with alteration of the last passage in ink preceding it:

'Goodbye, Gandalf!' he cried, and made off into the night. Gandalf remained by the gate for a moment, staring into the dark after him. *'Adieu*, my dear Bilbo,' he said, '- or *au revoir.'* [This was marked with an X; Gandalf would not use French, however useful the distinction.]

(*The Return of the Shadow*, HOME vol.VI, Second Phase, ch.XIV, p.247)

Indeed the only other example of the use of French that survives in the published LotR, the *louver* in the roof at Meduseld, is like 'vambrace' in that it describes a technology for which there is no native English word now surviving, if one ever existed at all.

Moving on, 'men at arms' is another decidedly medieval term, used of well-armed infantry as opposed to both knights on the upper end of the social scale and rabble below (like Golasgil's unfortunate levies). Hirluin's 'gallant green-clad men' sound as if they belong in one or other of Robin Hood's haunts, Inglewood Forest in Yorkshire or Sherwood Forest in Nottingham. 'Bowmen' is not of itself distinctive, but the Rangers of Ithilien certainly carry longbows, a very medieval and for that matter English weapon. Duilin's archers go up against the Oliphaunts at the Battle of the Pelennor Fields, and in terms of sheer military practicality (never to be totally dismissed with the Great War veteran Tolkien) they would have to be carrying either longbows or Central Asian composite bows to do so. Nothing else has the power or the speed in use required - something any practising archer of the day could have told Tolkien if he was interested. So these bowmen from Morthond look as if they are near relatives of the medieval English archers famed for their victories at Agincourt and Crécy.

It is worth noting also that while these new arrivals in Minas Tirith are technically merely 'men of the Outlands marching to defend the City of Gondor in a dark hour', subordinates of the Steward, in practice they have a great deal of freedom of action. All those who do arrive bring less men than expected because of the threat of the corsair fleet, and there is one notable absentee - Angborn of Lamedon, whom Aragorn later finds leading the defence of the coastlands even though his own 'fief' (another distinctively medieval and feudal word!) is wholly inland. In short, these men act like allies of Minas Tirith, not as subordinate lords of Gondor. This matches two patterns in Tolkien's likely sources. First, this is exactly how medieval great lords *would* behave in such a situation, with a weak ruler and their own lands under threat. Secondly, in the medieval Trojan legend, Priam calls on a whole range of allies to help him in his war against the Greeks, and these men are independent rulers who have a choice in what they do when Priam's request for help arrives.

The allies of Gondor from its regions who come to Minas Tirith to help in the defence of the city have a Homeric connection as M.Fenwick pointed out in 1996 (Mythlore 81, 1996, pp.17-23). In the margins of an early draft of the chapter 'Minas Tirith' from LotR, Tolkien scrawled 'Homeric catalogue' next to the description of the Gondorian nobles as they bring in their men for the final defence (*The War of the Ring,* HOME vol.VIII, Part 3, ch.1, p.229)

Incidentally, the swan-ship which is the insignia of Dol Amroth may be another Homeric echo, for 'swanlike' is one of the epithets for ships which appear in the *Iliad* - significantly, once in book XVIII at line 342 (Homer/Fitzgerald 1998, p.330), close to an episode just after the death of Patroclus where Achilles cries out and scares the Trojans in a distinctly Ringwraith-like manner (discussed in more detail below).

If we turn to *The Book of Lost Tales*, it is striking to note the description of the twelve ruling houses of Gondolin assembling before the battle at the walls and on the plain before the city:

'Mighty was the array of the house of the king and the colours were white and gold and red, and their emblems the moon and the sun and the scarlet heart. Now in the midmost of these stood Tuor... and his mail of silver gleamed; and about him was a press of the stoutest of the folk. ... and the emblem of the White Wing was upon their shields. But the folk of Meglin were drawn up in the same place, and sable was their harness and they bore no sign or emblem... and they fought with axes two-headed like mattocks. There Meglin Prince of Gondobar gathered many warriors of dark countenance and lowering gaze about him...

And many other kindreds were there, the folk of the Swallow and the Heavenly Arch, and from these folk came the greatest number and the best of the bowmen... Now the folk of the Swallow bore a fan of feathers on their helms, and they were arrayed in white and dark blue and in purple and black and showed an arrowhead on their shields. Their lord was *Duilin*, swiftest of all men to run and leap and surest of archers at a mark...

There too were the folk of the Pillar and of the Tower of Snow, and both these kindreds were marshalled by Penlod, tallest of Gnomes. There were those of the Tree and they were a great house, and their raiment was green. They fought with iron studded clubs or with slings.... There stood the house of the Golden Flower who bare a rayed sun upon their shield... Behind them came the host of the Harp, and this was a battalion of brave warriors; but their leader Salgant was a craven... a harp of silver shone in their blazonry upon a field of black; but Salgant bore one of gold, and he alone rode into battle.... and he was heavy and squat.'

(BOLT vol.II, ch.3, p.172-4)

Note the presence of Duilin, the comparison between Forlong the Fat and Salgant who is also fat, which goes back to the medieval Trojan version where we have Polidarius who is so fat that he needs a horse to ride to battle just as both Salgant and Forlong (unlike their men) do the same. Note that the men of Forlong are described as grim-faced and swarthy, bearing great battle-axes which compares well with the folk of Meglin who are described as 'grimmest and least good-hearted' and who fight with two-headed axes.

In the medieval Trojan material, the alliterative *Destruction of Troy* gives an exceedingly long list (over a hundred lines of verse) of the kings and lords who come to Troy to help Priam in his war with the Greeks. These men are like the lords of Gondor in that they clearly hold high rank in their own lands - some are even called Kings, just as Imrahil of Dol Amroth is a Prince - but at the same time they are Priam's vassals:

'The kings came thence out of famous lands
That held of him [Priam] as their head-lord.'

(Panton & Donaldson 1968, bk.XIII, lines 5433-4) [Note 3]

The *Destruction* - poet's list, when analysed in detail, names twelve countries as sending help to Troy (the same number as the houses of Gondolin), and twenty-four lords, kings or heroes are named or otherwise identified. This matches the instances in Tolkien's much shorter Gondorian catalogue where more than one person is named for some places (such as Duinhir of Morthond and his two sons) but none for others (as with the captainless men of Lamedon). There is a further correspondence in the numbers involved. At Minas Tirith, 'less than three thousands all told' arrive (a proper count is impossible because Tolkien does not give all the numbers), and as Forlong of Lossarnach passes, the people of the city complain about the lack of men arriving:

' "So few! Two hundreds, what are they? We hoped for ten times the number. That will be the new tidings of the black fleet. They are sparing only a tithe of their strength. Still every little is a gain." ' (RotK, Book V, ch.1, p.43)

So if somewhat less than three thousand arrive, and ten times as many were expected, the tally Denethor was looking for is around thirty thousand. These figures are significant. If we turn to the alliterative *Destruction*, the full tally of men brought by the allies and vassals to Troy is thirty-two thousand (bk.XIII, lines 5537-41) and the commonest number among the groups arriving is three thousand. Thus, both the expected total which is implicit in Tolkien's account and the actual total of men coming to Minas Tirith are very close to the figures given by the anonymous *Destruction* - poet. This makes it very likely that in this case, the alliterative *Gest Hystoriall of the Destruction of Troy* is Tolkien's direct source.

One last point about the lords of Gondor is worth making. Gondor has no King; it is ruled by the Stewards, in defiance of all historical precedent and political logic. There is however one group of texts associated with the tale of Gondolin in which someone called a Steward plays a very prominent part. This is the St Brendan legend, where the saint and his ship's crew of monks meet a man on the Isle of Sheep who is called the *procurator* or steward (Barron & Burgess 2002). The Steward whom St Brendan meets is a very important part of the tale; he provides the saint and his crew with not only food and drink, but an outline of how they are to spend the seven years before God will permit them to find the Promised Land; and when they finally do sail west, it is the Steward who pilots the ship, who escorts them around the Earthly Paradise, and who tells them when it is time for them to leave. While admittedly the Stewards of Gondor have no connection with sheep and Denethor is decidedly un-saintly, the odd coincidence of titles, with no visible reason in any other source, is suspicious and is worth bearing in mind as a possible if slight link.

IX; Sackers of Cities

Another point well worth making is that Minas Tirith is saved by exactly the two forces that destroy Troy; horses and a fleet of black ships.

a; Black Ships

Turning to the second half of this point, we are too prone to assume that the Southron ships are 'black' because they belong to the Bad Guys in the story. Tolkien's colour symbolism is not as simplistic as that; the Citadel Guard of Minas Tirith wear black uniforms, and the banner of the House of Elendil that Aragorn carries is black (in heraldic jargon 'sable, a flowering tree argent encircled by seven estoiles of the second, in chief a crown or'). So it really is worth remembering that one of Homer's favourite epithets for Greek ships is 'black':
'Forty black ships had crossed the sea with these / who now drew up their companies on the flank / Of the Boeotians, and armed themselves.'
(Homer/Fitzgerald 1998 bk II, line 530, p.32),
Likewise, it probably *is* significant that the Greeks like the Corsairs come to the city they attack from the *south*..

b; 'Under the hoofs of wrath'

The destruction of Troy is linked with horses in two ways. Firstly, in the Classical accounts of the matter, the first Sack of Troy is the direct result of a quarrel over horses between the Trojan king Laomedon, and the mighty Greek hero Hercules. Laomedon refused to honour his promise to give Hercules a particular herd of special horses in return for deeds done (something mentioned in passing by Homer in the *Iliad* at Book V, lines 638-58). Understandably annoyed, Hercules summoned a Greek army which took Troy and killed Laomedon and all but two of his children. One son survived, Priam; and Laomedon's daughter Hesione was carried off to Greece and held in dishonour as a slave-concubine. Priam rebuilt Troy and then, fatefully, decided to try to win Hesione's freedom. When negotiation failed he sent his son Paris to raid Greece, leading to Helen being carried off and so the second Fall of Troy, which of course was the direct result of the Trojans being fooled by the famous Wooden Horse and taking it inside their walls.

Since Roman times when the writer Pausanias first pointed this out, it has been repeatedly stated that in reality, the Wooden Horse of Troy must have been some sort of battering ram. Pausanias was blunt;

'Anyone who doesn't think the Trojans were utterly stupid will have realised that the horse was really an engineer's device for breaking down the walls.'
(Wood 1985, ch.7, p.230)

Modern writers (such as Michael Wood - ibid) often associate the Wooden Horse with rams of the Assyrian pattern, sheltered under a wheeled cover of loosely (very loosely, it has to be said) horse-like shape; some descriptions seem to imply that 'wooden horse' is a translation of an Assyrian term for such machines, but none cite a source. There are other more modern items which are called 'horses' that do not resemble one - for instance a horse in a gymnasium for gymnasts to vault over (used also to great effect in a parallel of the Trojan legend by World War 2 POW's escaping a German Prisoner of War Camp by hiding inside it as the Greeks did) and a clothes horse, which is as unhorse-like an object as one can find.

This, of course, is exactly what happens at Minas Tirith, when the main gate of the city is broken by a great battering-ram:

'Great engines crawled across the field; and in the midst was a huge ram, great as a forest-tree a hundred feet in length, swinging on mighty chains. Long had it been forging in the dark smithies of Mordor, and its hideous head, founded of black steel, was shaped in the likeness of a ravening wolf; on it spells of ruin lay. Grond they named it, in memory of the Hammer of the Underworld of Old. Great beasts drew it, orcs surrounded it, and behind walked mountain-trolls to wield it.'
(RotK, Book V, ch.4, p.102)

(One wonders if the wolf-head relates to Snorri Sturlusson's association of the Fenris-wolf with the fall of Troy, as mentioned in ch.1 above).

There is a secondary association here too, for well before Troy fell, the Trojan prince and hero Hector broke the gates of the Greek siege-camp and charged through, just as the Witch-King rides through the gates of Minas Tirith after they are smashed. Hector did not use a ram, but a stone:

'Now Hector picked a boulder that had stood
broad-bottomed, sharp on top, before the gate.
The strongest pair of men in the whole realm
as men are now, could not with ease heave up
this boulder from the ground into a wagon.
Lightly Hector handled it alone,
for Zeus, the son of crooked-minded Cronos,
made it a trifling weight for him. A shepherd
will carry easily, in either hand
a new-shorn ram's fleece - no great weight for him:
so Hector, lifting up the stone, went forward
to the high double doors of heavy timber
closing the gateway. Two crossbars inside
were rammed in place and one pin fastened them.
He took a stance before the doors and braced
with feet apart, for full force in the blow,
then smashed down at the centre. Hinges cracked
on both sides as the great mass tumbled through,
the doors groaned inward, bars gave way, the planks
were splintered by the impact right and left,
and through the breach in glory Hector leaps,
his visage dark as nightfall, though he shone
terribly from the bronze that he was dressed in, carrying a brace of spears. *No one could stop him*
none but the gods, as he leapt through the gate,
his eyes burning.'

(Homer/Fitzgerald 1998 bk. XII, lines 444-66) (emphasis ours)

Now, as T.A. Shippey points out as a prime example of the way in which philology reconstructs past lives and events, English *hammer* is cognate with Old Slavic *kamy*, stone (Shippey 1992, ch.1, p.13) which gives us a linguistic link with the device that broke the gate of Minas Tirith. For, if the gate of Minas Tirith is broken by a ram called the Hammer of the Underworld, then there certainly can be a relationship linguistically with a scene in the *Iliad* where gates are broken with a monstrous stone. To illustrate this and highlight the similarities, we give the moment when the Witch-King cast down the Gate of Gondor and entered:

'Then the Black Captain rose in his stirrups and cried aloud in a dreadful voice, speaking in some forgotten tongue words of power and terror to rend both heart and stone.

Thrice he cried. Thrice the great ram boomed. And suddenly upon the last stroke the gate of Gondor broke. As if stricken by some blasting spell it burst asunder: there was a flash of searing lightning and the doors tumbled in riven fragments

to the ground.
In rode the Lord of the Nazgûl. A great black shape against the fires beyond he loomed up, grown to a vast menace of despair. In rode the Lord of the Nazgûl, under the archway that no enemy ever yet had passed, and *all fled before his face*.... The Black Rider flung back his hood, and behold! he had a kingly crown; and yet upon no head visible was it set. The *red fires shone* between it and the mantled shoulders vast and dark.' (RotK, Book V, ch. 4, p.102-3) (emphasis ours)
Note above and below in italics in the Homeric lines and Tolkien's quotes that the entering warrior has blazing eyes and that no one could stand against him. Also, when the Witch-King descends upon Theoden at the Battle of the Pelennor Fields:
'Upon it [the winged beast] sat a shape, black-mantled, huge and threatening. A crown of steel he bore, but between rim and robe naught was there to see, save only a *deadly gleam of eyes*; the Lord of the Nazgûl.'
(RotK, Book V, ch.6, p.115) (emphasis ours)

It should also be noted that Tolkien here uses repetition in order to enhance the dramatic rendering of the moment of the Witch-King's destruction of the Gate ('In rode the Lord of the Nazgûl' is repeated) - but this may well indicate a nod in the direction of the original Homeric verses which repeat for aural storytelling effect when performed for an audience, as is explained in the Oxford Worlds Classics translation of the Iliad:
'Homerists had already begun to draw conclusions about Homer's use of repeated phrases when a talented American, Milman Parry, finally demonstrated in 1926 that his [Homer's] style depended on an elaborate system of standardised phrases that could only have been gradually perfected, not by one man but as a result of a whole tradition of aural poetry going back over several generations.'
'Admittedly many modern translators tend to diminish the repetitions in order to reduce this particular problem... Even so, they need to know that the repetitions are there in the Greek, and why they are there.' (Kirk, G.S. Homer The Iliad, Introduction, p.x - xi) Similarly, the above section of LotR is one of the most effective passages for recitation aloud.

So firstly, the horse/ram equation is close enough for Tolkien's version to be an acceptable transformation of the motif of the Wooden Horse, and secondly, his description of the ram and the entry of the Witch-King echoes another scene of gate-breaking in the *Iliad*.. When we consider this association of horses and battering rams, it is worth remembering that throughout LotR, Tolkien generally follows the medieval 'pseudohistorical' line and plays down the marvellous and the supernatural in favour of realistic explanations wherever possible. Even Galadriel's Mirror does not show what *will be*, only what might be; it works by probability rather than true foresight. Most medieval works that were considered romances at the time are far freer with their marvels than is 'The Lord of the Rings'. Indeed, most modern fantasy writers are far more prone to introduce the marvellous and the magical than Tolkien was - one point among many at which the modern fantasy genre departs sharply from the trail that Tolkien blazed.

X; Conclusions

To summarise the points we have made in this chapter;

The breaking of the gate of Minas Tirith by a ram probably relates to the Fall of Troy, through the longstanding belief that the Wooden Horse was actually a battering-ram or similar device.

Minas Tirith is saved by the same two forces that destroy Troy, horses and a fleet of black ships.

The significance of the number seven in levels in the cities and number of gates links Minas Tirith to the historical Troy and to Gondolin in the 1950's version.

The appearance of Minas Tirith with its wide streets and high quality masonry where the older parts are the better built corresponds with the historical site of Troy.

The geographical setting of Minas Tirith on a hill at the end of a mountain range by a river with a fertile plain before it matches Troy specifically and also a number of important Mycenean Greek sites.

The sheer scale and power of 'cyclopean masonry' (i.e. seemingly not built by mortal men) is present in both Minas Tirith and Troy (and Mycenean Greek city ruins).

The position of Gondor geographically versus the Black Númenorean colonies in Harad matches the geographical juxtaposition of Troy against Mycenean Greece.

The importance of symbolism of bulls in the line of the Stewards (Boromir's horn) matches the importance of the symbolism of bulls in Minoan culture, which was contemporary with Troy, which were linked by trade.

The name of Minas Tirith meaning Tower of Guard is an exact match for one of the seven names of Gondolin in the Book of Lost Tales. This provides us with a linguistic link between Gondolin and Minas Tirith.

There are a whole series of points at which Tolkien's descriptions of Minas Tirith match medieval descriptions of Troy: these include the White Tower, the height of both the tower and the citadel, the Tree in the court of the fountain, the Great Hall, the presence of domes and the importance of tombs.

Singly, any of these points could be coincidence; set together, we would submit that is unlikely in the extreme that all these resemblances could occur by accident. We believe that in all probability Tolkien deliberately used the Trojan story, perhaps refracted through the Tale of Gondolin, as the most important source for the section of LotR which centres on Minas Tirith.

We may also draw some further general conclusions as well.

Inversion of existing motifs is perhaps Tolkien's commonest strategy in adapting old material to create new stories. A use of inversion which only seems straightforward appears in 'On Fairy-Stories': 'Of course, fairy-stories are not the only means of recovery, or prophylactic against loss. Humility is enough. And there is (especially for the humble) *Mooreeffoc*, or Chestertonian Fantasy. *Mooreeffoc* is a fantastic word, but it could be seen written up in every town in

this land. It is Coffee-room, viewed from the inside through a glass door, as it was seen by Dickens on a dark London day; and it was used by Chesterton to denote the queerness of things that have become trite, when they are seen suddenly from a new angle.'
(Tolkien 1988 (orig. written 1938, published 1947, 1964), 'Tree and Leaf', Unwin Hyman; part 1, On Fairy-Stories, p.54).
We may not be far wrong if we look to the medieval Trojan legend, with its inversion of Homer's story, as the single most important lesson on the usefulness of this strategy available to Tolkien.

Tolkien probably went to a variant of the Gondolin stories because by the time he reached Minas Tirith, he was well aware of the pitfalls in borrowing from earlier material into the ongoing LotR. Having Fëanor make the Rings, as suggested in an outline written as Tolkien worked his way past Lórien, would have nearly sunk the Silmarillion; he would not repeat that mistake. So he decided to borrow from an alternative version - but it is a variant in turn that comes to have a major impact on the 'later Tuor' *because* Tolkien had picked up some of its ideas and developed them. It is possible that this 'variant' derived directly from the pre-Gondolin Trojan story whose existence seems so probable, since it appears to have drawn far more distinctly on the real setting and appearance of Troy than does *The Fall of Gondolin* in *The Book of Lost Tales*. This variant may also have already appeared in *The Hobbit*. For a start, the appearance of Glamdring and Orcrist, swords made for the Goblin-wars around Gondolin, has long puzzled students of Tolkien's works. There are no wars around Gondolin in the 1977 *Silmarillion* version, and not really any in BOLT either. So where does this come from? Perhaps a 'more Trojan' version, with something more like the ten-year siege would be the best place to seek it. Following on shortly after this, the scene where Bilbo, Gandalf and the dwarves reach Rivendell at dusk, picking out the white marker stones along the way, coming down hill to be greeted by singing elves, bears a marked resemblance to the scene in the alliterative *Destruction* where the people of Colchis come out to greet Jason and the Argonauts - a scene that also affected the welcome of Tuor and Voronwë by the elves of Gondolin in BOLT:
'It was indeed a much wider land from the ford to the mountains than ever you would have guessed. Bilbo was astonished. The only path was marked with white stones, some of which were small, and others were half-covered with moss or heather. Altogether it was a very slow business following the track, even guided by Gandalf, who seemed to know his way about pretty well.
His head and beard wagged this way and that as he looked for the stones, and they followed his lead, but they seemed no nearer to the end of the search when the day began to fail. Tea-time had long gone by, and it seemed supper-time would soon do the same. There were moths fluttering about, and the light became very dim, for the moon had not risen. Bilbo's pony began to stumble over roots and stones. They came to the edge of a steep fall in the ground so suddenly that Gandalf's horse nearly slipped down the slope.
'Here it is at last!' he called, and the others gathered round him and looked over

the edge. They saw a valley far below. They could hear the voice of hurrying water in a rocky bed at the bottom; the scent of trees was in the air; and there was a light on the valley-side across the water.
Bilbo never forgot the way they slithered and slipped in the dusk down the steep zig-zag path into the secret valley of Rivendell.' (The Hobbit, ch.3, pps. 49-50)
In the alliterative *Destruction*, when Jason comes to Colchis he crosses a fair land to reach the city:

'About the circle of the city there was indeed a plain
Full of flowers freshly decking the ground
With leafclouds on high both pleasant and fair
To refresh those who came fainting with heat
With arbours under vines against strong sunshine
There welled up a wealth of most pure water
In each part of the plain were abundant streams
[That] with a murmuring and a sweetness swept over the ground
And all birds in their feathers were there to be seen
That are well-known to dwell upon riverbanks
Small birds above in the shining leaves
Sang loud songs among the bright boughs
A most noble noise of melody to hear
Through mirth and music made upon high
To this royal city that yet was far off
Jason went with his noble companions
Stepped on a street straight to the gate
As they went by on the roadway the people saw [them]
Wondered at the men and eagerly desired
To know more of those who came and understand why [they were there]
Who were so royally arrayed and [made such a] merry company
It was wondrous to see such fair men walking
So young and so well-dressed, generous of disposition,
People soon inquired of those noble warriors
Of what country they had come [from] and the reason why [they were there].'

(Panton & Donaldson 1968, bk.I, lines 335-59) [Note 4]
Compare this with the account of Tuor and Voronwë's arrival in Gondolin in *The Book of Lost Tales*:
'Then Tuor and his companion fared over the plain that was of a marvellous level, broken but here and there by boulders round and smooth which lay amid a sward, or by pools in rocky beds. Many fair pathways lay across that plain, and they came after a day's light march to the foot of the Hill of Watch.... Then did they begin to ascend the winding stairways which climbed up to the city gate; nor might any one reach that city save on foot and espied from the walls. As the westward gate was golden in the last sunlight did they come to the long stair's head, and many eyes gazed upon them from the battlements and towers...

Even so they came to the gates, Tuor in wonder and Voronwë in great joy that daring much he had both brought Tuor hither in the will of Ulmo and had

himself thrown off the yoke of Melko for ever. Though he hated him no wise less, no longer did he dread that Evil One with a binding terror...
Now there is a sally from the gates of Gondolin and a throng comes about these twain in wonder, rejoicing that yet another of the Noldoli has fled from Melko, and marvelling at the stature and the gaunt limbs of Tuor, his heavy spear barbed with fish bone and his great harp...

Behold the armed guardians of the gate pressed back the thronging folk that gathered about the wanderers, and one among them spake saying: "This is a city of watch and ward, Gondolin on Amon Gwareth, where all may be free who are of true heart, but none may be free to enter unknown. Tell me then your names."
But Voronwë named himself Bronweg of the Gnomes, come hither by the will of Ulmo as a guide to this son of Men; and Tuor said: "I am Tuor son of Peleg son of Indor of the house of the Swan of the sons of the Men of the North who live far hence, and I fare hither by the will of Ulmo of the Outer Oceans." '
(BOLT vol.II, ch.3, pp.158-60)

Gondolin is 'a day's light march' from the tunnel and guards, just as Colchis is 'far off' to those crossing its plain. Both plains are smooth and fertile, and in both cases the people of the city are eager to know more of the strangers coming through their gates. Jason merely 'steppit up to a strete' whereas Tuor and Voronwë climb a considerable hill by stairs, but the general idea of progress up a defined path is there in both cases.

The various crossings of the Bruinen all appear to reflect crossings of rivers at Troy, either episodes which certainly exist (such as the ford on the Scamander at which Achilles nearly drowns when the river rises in anger, an event considered in detail in the next chapter) or which could well do so. The idea of a narrow and hence defensible bridge appears in *The Hobbit* and in *The Lord of the Rings*, and it could well derive from some version of the Trojan legends in which there was a bridge across one of Troy's rivers, the Simois and Scamander, which was likewise intended to be defensive because it was not easy to pass.
'On they all went, leading their ponies, till they were brought to a good path and so at last to the very brink of the river. It was flowing fast and noisily, as mountain-streams do of a summer evening, when sun has been all day on the snow far up above. There was only a narrow bridge of stone without a parapet, as narrow as a pony could well walk on; and over that they had to go, slow and careful, one by one, each leading his pony by the bridle.
The elves had brought bright lanterns to the shore and they sang a merry song as the party went across.
'Don't dip your beard in the foam, father!' they cried to Thorin, who was bent almost on to his hands and knees. 'It is long enough without watering it.' '
(The Hobbit, ch.3, pps. 51-52)
This is hardly a practical crossing, but in the context of *The Hobbit*, it could well be an exaggeration of something Tolkien had already invented and used elsewhere. The same idea could lie behind the bridge which Turin has constructed across the

River Narog before the gates of Nargothrond, 'the bridge of their pride', which is crossed by Glaurung the Golden when the city falls - which could well be a golden dragon substituting for a bronze horse coming to the Scaean Gate of Troy. The Bridge of Khazad-Dûm may also be a further reflection of this idea:
'Suddenly Frodo saw before him a black chasm. At the end of the hall the floor vanished and fell to an unknown depth. The outer door could only be reached by a slender bridge of stone, without kerb or rail, that spanned the chasm with one curving spring of fifty feet... They could only pass across it in single file.' (FotR, Book II, ch.5, p.343)
This is very close indeed to the bridge at Rivendell in *The Hobbit*.

This same 'variant version of the Troy/Gondolin story could also account for the descriptions of Minas Tirith, which as we have seen strongly resembles the hill of Hissarlik 'unpacked' and reassembled to give seven gates in vertical sequence. Just as the scene where Bilbo first comes to Rivendell may run parallel with the 1950's scene where Tuor and Voronwë have to come from a tunnel up and over a high pass to reach Gondolin, so the scene where Gandalf and Pippin enter Minas Tirith may run parallel with a scene where Tuor and Voronwë enter Gondolin and climb up into the city. After the simple hill-ring of BOLT with no specified gates, this would represent an intermediate stage with a climb up and over a pass, then a journey through seven gates inside a city, which finally develops to a tunnel followed by a climb up a pass and passage through seven gates outside a city, the situation in the 1950's Tuor printed in Unfinished Tales. This is speculation, but it fits the known patterns of Tolkien's work and could be proved or disproved by reference to the appropriate papers - though since a 'Trojan version' might well not have been kept with the rest of the *Silmarillion* papers, some care in research would be needed.

Herein we give the original Middle English texts of the poems:

Note 1:

'Closit with a clene wall crustrit [properly clustrit] with towres
Euyn round as a ryng richely wroght -
ffyue hundrith fete fully the heght; -'

(Panton & Donaldson 1968, book V, lines 1634-6)

Note 2:

'Of crafty colours to know, all in course set,
Made all of marbyll with mason deuyse,
With ymagry full honest openly wroght.
In cornols by course clustret o lofte.
The windows, worthely wroght in a mesure,
Shapyn full shene all of shyre stones,
Caruen into Cristall by craft of Entaile,

Pight into pilers prudly to shewe
The bases and bordours all of bright perle.'

(Panton & Donaldson 1968, book V, lines 1644-52)

Note 3:

'The kynges there come out of kyde londes,
That holdyn were of hom, as there hede lordes.'

(Panton & Donaldson 1968, book XIII, lines 5433-4)

Note 4:

'Umbe the sercle of the Citye was sothely A playne
fful of floures fresshe fret on the grounde
With lefsales uppon loft lustie and faire
ffolk to refresshe for fainting of hete
With voiders under vines for violent sonnes
There was wellit to wale water full nobill
In yche place of the playne with plentuis stremes
With a swonghe and a swetness sweppit on the grounde
And all fowles in ffethir fell thare uppon,
ffor to reckon by right that to ryver haunttes
Small briddes above in the bright levys
With shrikes full shrill in the shire bowes
The noise was full nobill of notes for to here,
Thurgh myrth and melody made uppon lofte
To this souerayne citté that yet was oloft
Iason aioynid and his iust freres
Steppit up to a strete streght on his gate
As they past on the payment the pepull beheld
Haden wonder of the weghes, & wilful desyre
To know of there coming & the cause were
That were so rially arait and a rowte gay
So faire frekes uppon fote was ferly to se,
So yonge and so yepe, gynerous of wille,
ffolk fraynide fastat tho fre buernes,
Of what cuntre thai come and the cause why.'

(Panton & Donaldson 1968, book I, lines 335-59)

Chapter Six:

Heroes and villains; Achilles and his counterpart.

I; The Witch-King and the Myrmidons

Once Tolkien brings his tale to Gondor, the previously vaguely outlined character of the Witch-king comes into sharper definition:

'Yet now under the Lord of Barad-Dur the most fell of all his captains is already master of your outer walls,' said Gandalf. 'King of Angmar long ago, Sorceror, Ringwraith, Lord of the Nazgul, a spear of terror in the hand of Sauron, shadow of despair.' (RotK, Book V, ch.4, p.92)

At this point he acquires new associations from a very unexpected direction, but one which is logical since there seem to be so many signs Tolkien was using the medieval Trojan legends in creating this section of his story. The Greek prince Achilles, son of Peleus the King of Thessaly and leader of the Myrmidon people, stands at the heart of Homer's *Iliad*. The greater story of the Greek expedition against Troy is strung around the lesser tale of the wrath of Achilles, his withdrawal from battle as a result of perceived insult from the Greek commander Agamemnon, his return after the death of his best friend Patroclus (who went out wearing Achilles' armour), his killing of the Trojan prince Hector and finally, his decision to allow the aged Priam, king of Troy, to ransom the body of his son. Achilles is already an ambiguous figure in the *Iliad*, a hero whose actions can be both barbaric (as when he kills twelve Trojan prisoners as sacrifices over the grave of Patroclus) and civilised (as in his gentle reception of Priam). In the pseudohistorical Troy tradition, Achilles' reputation sinks markedly, and more so in the normally pro-Greek Dictys than in Dares. It is Dictys who has Achilles set up an ambush when he hears of Hector riding out with only a small company; in the following fight Achilles not only kills Hector but has all save one of his companions slaughtered as well, and compounds his sins by cutting off the hands of the lone Trojan whom he spares to carry the news home (Frazer 1966, Dictys, p.79).

If we turn to the medieval versions of the Trojan story, Achilles comes off even worse. He is depicted as being cruel, treacherous and cowardly - a leader, but no hero. This steep descent of Achilles' reputation may well account for why, before the walls of Minas Tirith, the Witch-king takes on a number of distinctively Achillean attributes.

Firstly, there is one instance in the *Iliad* itself where Achilles has a markedly Ringwraith-like effect on his enemies:

'...Moving from parapet
to moat, without a nod for the Achaeans,
keeping clear, in deference to his mother,
he halted and gave tongue. Not far from him

Athena shrieked. The great sound shocked the Trojans
into tumult, as a trumpet blown
by a savage foe shocks an encircled town.
so harsh and clarion was Achilles' cry.
The hearts of men quailed, hearing that brazen voice
Teams, foreknowing danger, turned their cars
and charioteers blanched, seeing unearthly fire,
kindled by the grey-eyed goddess Athena,
brilliant over Achilles. Three great cries
he gave above the moat. Three times they shuddered,
whiling backward, Trojans and allies,
and twelve good men took mortal hurt
from cars and weapons in the rank behind.'
(Homer/Fitzgerald 1998 book XVIII lines 219-35, pp.326-7)

In this instance, Achilles' cry resembles the voices of the Ringwraiths:

'Suddenly as they talked they were stricken dumb, frozen as it were to listening stones. Pippin cowered down with his hands pressed to his ears; but Beregond, who had been looking out from the battlement as he spoke of Faramir, remained there, stiffened, staring out with starting eyes. Pippin knew the shuddering cry that he had heard: it was the same that he had heard long ago in the Marish of the Shire, but now it was grown in power and hatred, piercing the heart with a poisonous despair.' (RotK, Book V, ch.4, p.82)

And also:

'Then the Black Captain rose in his stirrups and cried aloud in a dreadful voice, speaking in some forgotten tongue words of power and terror to rend both heart and stone.

Thrice he cried. Thrice the great ram boomed. And suddenly upon the last stroke the Gate of Gondor broke.' (ibid, p.102)

Three times the Witch-king cries aloud to break the Gate - as did Achilles above the moat as cited above.

A minor but significant point is that in one place in the Appendices to LotR, Tolkien reverses a motif from the *Iliad* 's account of Achilles. Homer's Achilles receives the Trojan king Priam courteously and allows him to ransom the body of his son Hector for proper burial. In contrast, look at what happens with the Witch-king's challenge to the last king of Gondor, Eärnur, who rides out to Minas Morgul and is never seen again - no body is ever recovered:

'He [Eärnur] rode with a small escort of knights to Minas Morgul, but neither he nor his company were ever heard of again.... Since his death was not certain Mardil the Good Steward ruled Gondor in his name for many years.'
(*The Peoples of Middle-earth*, HOME XII, Part 1, ch. VII, pp.201-2).

This is Tolkien inverting the run of story in the *Iliad* to fit his purposes.

There is another point at which Achilles and the Witch-king look very much like each other. In Book Twenty-One of the *Iliad* , to summarise a long story, Achilles is leading a Greek attack and has reached a point half-way between Troy and the Greek camp. At this place the road passes a ford on the River Scamander;

Achilles cuts off a number of fugitive Trojans and drives them into the river, where he slaughters them mercilessly. Finally, the angry river-god can hold back no longer (his own son by a Trojan maiden is among the numerous dead), and he unleashes a flood that nearly drowns Achilles:
'...The deep
and swirling river then addressed Apollo:
'All wrong, bow of silver, child of Zeus!
You have not worked the will of Zeus. How often
he made you free to take the Trojan side!
You could defend them until sunset comes,
till evening darkens grain-land.' As he spoke
the great spearman Achilles in a flash
leapt into midstream from the arching bank
But he, the river, surged upon the man
with all his currents in a roaring flood...'
(Homer/Fitzgerald 1998, book XXI, lines 230-40 selected from pp.364-74)
The Greek hero survives only thanks to divine intervention, Poseidon and Athena lifting him back to his feet amid the rush of waters while Hephaestus drives the river off with fire.

In the same way the Witch-King and his fellow-wraiths could be said to survive only through 'supernatural intervention' when they fall foul of the Ford of Bruinen (in much the way Achilles does in the river) as they chase Frodo on Glorfindel's horse:
'There were Nine Riders at the water's edge below, and Frodo's spirit quailed before the threat of their uplifted faces...
Suddenly the foremost Rider spurred his horse forward. It checked at the water and reared up. With a great effort Frodo sat upright and brandished his sword...
... and immediately their leader urged his horse forward into the water, followed closely by two others....
Then the leader, who was now halfway across the Ford, stood up menacing in his stirrups, and raised up his hand. Frodo was stricken dumb... His sword broke and fell out of his shaking hand. The elf-horse reared and snorted. The foremost of the black horses had almost set foot upon the shore.
At that moment there came a roaring and a rushing: a noise of loud waters rolling many stones. Dimly Frodo saw the river below him rise, and down along its course there came a plumed cavalry of waves. White flames seemed to Frodo to flicker on their crests and he half fancied that he saw amid the water white riders upon white horses with frothing manes. The three Riders that were still in the midst of the Ford were overwhelmed: they disappeared, buried suddenly under angry foam. Those that were behind drew back in dismay...
The black horses were filled with madness, and leaping forward in terror they bore their riders into the rushing flood. Their piercing cries were drowned in the roaring of the river as it carried them away.' (FotR, Book I, ch.12, p.226-7)
Later on in Rivendell, Gandalf explains this turn of events to Frodo:
'Caught between fire and water, and seeing an Elf-lord revealed in his wrath,

they were dismayed, and their horses were stricken with madness. Three were carried away by the first assault of the flood; the others were now hurled into the water by their horses and overwhelmed.'
'And is that the end of the Black Riders?' asked Frodo.
'No,' said Gandalf. 'Their horses must have perished, and without them they are crippled. But the Ringwraiths themselves cannot be so easily destroyed...'
(FotR, Book II, ch.1, p.236)
And:
'We can't start until we have found out about the Riders.'
'I thought they were all destroyed in the flood,' said Merry.
'You cannot destroy Ringwraiths like that,' said Gandalf. 'The power of their master is in them, and they stand or fall by him. We hope that they were all unhorsed and unmasked, and so made for a while less dangerous; but we must find out for certain...' (FotR, Book II, ch.3, p.286)
There is another inversion of plot here, for whereas the Ringwraiths were driven into the river by Glorfindel with fire, in the Iliad the river is driven off to save Achilles by the use of fire (by Hephaestos).

If we return to Homer again, we find that at one point in the Trojan War, Achilles allows his close friend Patroclus to borrow his armour, and lead the Myrmidons into battle whilst wearing it. Patroclus is killed by the Trojan hero Hector, who takes the armour for himself. Achilles, distraught, appeals to his mother, the sea-nymph Thetis, for help, and she goes to the smith-god Hephaestus to have a new set of armour made for her son. When Achilles kills Hector, he is wearing the new armour. Compare this with the situation at the Ford of Bruinen, where the Ringwraiths are forcibly deprived of their horses and clothes by the rushing floodwater, and some of what they lose is taken as evidence of their troubles by the Elves of Rivendell:
'In no region had the messengers discovered any signs or tidings of the Riders or other servants of the Enemy. Even from the Eagles of the Misty Mountains they had learned no fresh news... Three of the black horses had been found at once drowned in the flooded Ford. On the rocks of the rapids below it searchers discovered the bodies of five more, and also a long black cloak, slashed and tattered. Of the Black Riders no other trace was to be seen, and nowhere was their presence to be felt. It seemed that they had vanished from the North.
"Eight out of the Nine are accounted for at least," said Gandalf. "It is rash to be too sure, yet I think that we may hope now that the Ringwraiths were scattered, and have been obliged to return as best they could to their Master in Mordor, empty and shapeless.
"If that is so, it will be some time before they can begin the hunt again. Of course the enemy has other servants, but they will have to journey all the way to the borders of Rivendell before they can pick up our trail. And if we are careful that will be hard to find. But we must delay no longer." ' (FotR, Book II, ch.3, p.287-8)

The essential similarities here are that just as Achilles cannot rush straight out to seek vengeance for the death of Patroclus, but must wait, because he has no armour, so also the Ringwraiths cannot continue their hunt for the Ring at once. They have to wait until they are reclothed. Like Achilles, they cannot do this for themselves; there is no question of creeping off to Bree and stealing whatever fits from the nearest washing-line! Instead the Witch-king and his fellows have to go all the way back to Mordor - a volcanic country, and Hephaestos' Roman equivalent was Vulcan, patron of volcanoes as well as smithing and fire-crafts - and seek help from a supernatural father-figure, just as Achilles was helped by a supernatural mother.

The names of the rivers of Troy offer us yet more unexpected links here. Firstly, there is the Simois, also called Xanthus, which can plausibly be linked with Tolkien's River Bruinen, where the Witch-king comes so badly unstuck in *The Fellowship of the Ring*.. In Greek, *xanthus* is fair, bright, blond, covering a much wider range than in modern English combinations based upon Greek, where it is treated as meaning simply 'yellow' (OED s.v. xantho-) - something a philologist like Tolkien would certainly have known. Not only did he study Classics in general and Greek philology in particular, but the same pattern is found across all the Indo-European languages. 'Yellow' and its relatives have meanings circling around 'light, bright'; in Old English it is *geolu*, 'yellow', while Old Irish *gel* (Modern Scottish Gaelic *geall*) is 'white' and Welsh *golau* is 'light, bright, shining' (OED s.v. yellow; Ordnance Survey 1981). None of this seems to offer any connection to a river whose name looks as if it develops from English *bruin*, bear. However, there is more to this than meets the eye.

'Bruin' came into English as a loan from Middle Dutch, a word meaning 'brown in colour' (brune, bruyn in Caxton's version) which was used for the name of a bear - a European Brown Bear, *Ursus arctos*. If we follow 'brown' back through its Germanic analogues, we find an extraordinary word. Old High German *brûn* can mean either 'glänzend', shining (and so is close to the *yellow* group and *xanthos*) or 'dunkel-farbig', dark-coloured, brown in the modern English sense (OED s.v. brown). The same pair of meanings appear in Medieval Latin 'brunire', to polish. This process makes things both brighter, because shinier, and darker, because they reflect other objects rather than scattering light as a grainy, unpolished surface does. Likewise, a white wall appears lighter in colour than a mirror. The concept lies hidden in modern English *burnish* (which ought to be *brunnish* if post-medieval English would allow the combination). So, given all this, Tolkien's river-name *Bruinen* can actually be a straightforward Germanic/Sindarin pun, with a first real-world meaning of 'the shining (burnished, gleaming) river' which is a good parallel to *Xanthos* , 'shining, bright, fair'.

Tolkien's river-name Bruinen also has a second plausible 'real-world' derivation. The name of the Roman fort Bremenium, derived from a stream-name, was shortened in Medieval Welsh to Breuoin or Brewyn, both pronounced roughly *Broin* or *Bruin*. The straightforward meaning of the original is 'the loud or roaring one' (Rivet and Smith 1979 s.v. Bremenion) - and the translation of Bruinen is Loudwater, as Aragorn explains to Meriadoc Brandybuck in book I, chapter 12 (The Flight to the Ford) of *The Fellowship of the Ring*. So close a parallel between sound and meaning is highly unlikely to be coincidence. Indeed, a fast-rushing and 'loud' river or stream will pick up mud and stones and run brown, as will fast-flowing water over peat run brown in colour. We will be following this up in detail in our next book, for it points to another important and unexpected strand in Tolkien's writing in general and *The Lord of the Rings* in particular.

Secondly, there is the Scamander, *Scamandros* in the Greek original. If, following Geoffrey of Monmouth, the British are taken as Trojan descendants, then this word can be investigated through known British place-name elements, just like Bruin-en/Bremenion. The first syllable immediately suggests a common river-name, Isca, found in modern Welsh as Usk, in Gaelic-influenced Scotland as Esk, and in English names as Exe or Axe (with the middle consonants switched round, -ks- for -sk-). The same element also occurs in a number of 'German' river names, such as the Isch (a tributary of the Saar, whose first recorded form is *Isca*) and the Ischl (a tributary of the Traun, first recorded as *Iscala*). The second element of the Trojan river's name then becomes mand-ros/er or something similar. Going back to British and related languages, **mandu* - signifies small horse, pony, in placenames and personal names (Rivet and Smith 1979 s.v. Isca and Manduessedum). The word was adopted into Latin at an early date as *mannus*, which would give a perfect parallel to a Greek reworking which misread the second half of 'Scamander' as 'andros', man. Words tend to be changed in ways which seem to make them meaningful when they move between languages, so a change from **Iscamandus* to *Scamandros* is perfectly plausible. Furthermore, the **mandu* - element is said by at least one authority to be 'Illyrian', that is, from a language spoken by a non-Greek people whose country reached from the Adriatic coast in what is now southern Albania to the borders of Greece and Macedon, which brings it right into the area of Greek and Trojan legend. All this kitchen philology turns the meaningless Scamander into an **Iscamandus* with a meaning, horse-river, which is absolutely appropriate for Troy. In Homer's *Iliad* one of the Trojan people's recurring epithets is 'horse-breaking', and the country of Ilios within which Troy is set is called 'of the fine horses' (Wood 1985 ch.5, p.166). In context, these horses can only be chariot-ponies, because Homer's heroes never ride. Therefore, the Celtic/'Illyrian' word **mandus* - , small horse, pony, is exactly right. The meaning 'horse-river' is also extremely appropriate for the Bruinen, where white horses are conjured amidst the flooding waters by Gandalf. (FotR, Book I, ch.12, p.227).

So we can say firstly that there is good reason to think that the name of the river Bruinen holds hidden parallels with one of the two rivers of Troy, the Xanthos or Simois, and secondly that the motif of the magical horses in the water could well link the Bruinen to the other river of Troy, the Scamander. Taking these relationships of the River Bruinen into account, together with the other evidence for what Tolkien was doing with the scene of the Black Riders at the Ford, we think that it is justifiable to regard this section as a first incursion of Trojan material into *The Lord of the Rings*. Moreover, it is a development associated with the most clearly 'Homeric' character in LotR, the Witch-King. There are other resonances to the name of Bruinen that draw in another important strand within Tolkien's own writing, but we will be dealing with these in the next book.

Tolkien introduces the idea that the Witch-king is very hard to kill right from the early phases of the writing of LotR - for even in the first versions of the Ford of Bruinen, the flood does not actually destroy any of the Ringwraiths, and in the published text only eight drowned horses are found, leaving open the chance that the Witch-king himself has escaped. The Witch-king can however be slain under certain conditions (Gandalf mentions that if the Lord is destroyed then so his servants will fall). It appears that the notion of no man being able to kill the Witch-King was a late development in the writing. In a similar fashion, Achilles is only half-mortal, the son of King Peleus of Thessaly and 'silvery-footed' Thetis, a sea-nymph. His mother tried to make him invulnerable by dipping him in one of the rivers of the Underworld (usually the Styx, more rarely but possibly more accurately the Lethe - a stream of the same name actually rises near an important Mycenean site in northern Greece (L.Cotterel 1963, 'Lion Gate', ch.23). However, Thetis has to hold the baby somewhere, and so fails to immerse Achilles' heel in the protecting water. As early as the sixth century BC Achilles appears on painted vases, identified by a written name and shown lying dead with an arrow through his heel. Later writers varied, some making the heel the vulnerable point, others the more general ankle or calf (M. Scherer 1963, ch.3, The Fall of Troy, p.99). In adapting this motif to the Witch-king, Tolkien retains the idea of the character being hard to kill, but switches from one common legendary motif (that of someone only having one vulnerable spot, as with Achilles and Sigurd) - to another common motif, the idea that someone can only be killed under specific circumstances (Macbeth in Shakespeare's play being both a well-known example and the recipient of the same double-edged prophecy as the Witch-King, that no man of woman born can kill him).

At the same time, Tolkien keeps the motif of a blow to the leg being crucial to his downfall:

'But suddenly he too stumbled forward with a cry of bitter pain, and his stroke went wide, driving into the ground. Merry's sword had stabbed him from behind, shearing through the black mantle, and passing up beneath the hauberk had *pierced the sinew behind his mighty knee.'*

And again:

'No other blade, not though mightier hands had wielded it, would have dealt that foe a wound so bitter, cleaving the undead flesh, *breaking the spell that knit his unseen sinews to his will.'*

(emphasis ours; both quotes RotK, Book V, ch.6, p.117 and p.120)

Now, there are two things of interest here. The first is the blade that Merry uses to stab the Witch-King. It is one of the blades from the barrow on the Barrow-downs, which were first described as:

'bronze swords, short, leaf-shaped and keen'

(*The Return of the Shadow*, HOME vol.VI, ch.VII, p.128)

In the published text written some ten years later the same blades are described as:

'For each of the hobbits he chose a dagger, long, leaf-shaped, and keen, of marvellous workmanship, damasked with serpent-forms in red and gold.'

(FotR Book I, ch.8, p.157)

Leaf-shaped blades 'damasked in red and gold' and possibly of bronze have only one parallel in European archaeology or history. This is with Mycenean Greek weapons, made of bronze and decorated with figures and animals in yellow gold, white silver, red copper and black paste inlay. The best-known examples of such swords and daggers are those found by Schliemann in the first Grave-Circle at Mycenae itself, in the tombs which the German archaeologist wrongly thought were those of Agamemnon and his kinsfolk. While most Mycenean blades are not noticeably 'leaf-shaped', the swords carved on the grave-markers at Mycenae are very distinctly of this form (as shown in Tsountas and Manatt 1897, ch.V, p.92, plate XI; their Chapter VIII has good illustrations and descriptions of inlaid swords). So the sword which alone can harm the Witch-king itself hints at Homeric origins for this scene. Tolkien emphasised this connection from the earlier version to the later one, so this is deliberate. Interestingly, it has long been suggested (R. Atkinson, Stonehenge (3rd Ed.), 1979) that one of the carvings of daggers on the stones of Stonehenge which appears to date from the Bronze Age is distinctly Mycenean Greek in shape. This gives us the connection that allows Tolkien to have his hobbits finding Mycenean Greek swords in the home of the Barrow-wight, which is very clearly a Bronze Age English barrow like those on the Downs near Oxford, and also the barrows near Stonehenge with their rich treasures.

Secondly, what brings down the Witch-King is having his Achilles tendon cut, which is not coincidence. This both saves Eowyn from the Witch-king's blow and makes him fall so that she in turn can rise and strike - probably not killing him (for Tolkien says only that the Witch-king 'was not heard again in that age of this world', which lasts only another year or two!) but certainly sending him out of action for the meantime.

It is worth noting further that in the Classical works, Achilles dies after a battle when yet another ally has come fruitlessly to the aid of Troy - this time Memnon, King of Ethiopia, son of the dawn goddess Eos. The motif of dawn being involved is repeatedly echoed in the descriptions of the attack of the Rohirrim, one of whose most immediate results is the Witch-king's death. When Théoden leads the first great charge: 'His golden shield was uncovered, and lo! it shone like an image of the Sun, and the grass flamed into green about the white feet of his steed. For morning came, morning and a wind from the sea, and darkness was removed, and the hosts of Mordor wailed, and terror took them, and they fled, and died, and the hoofs of wrath rode over them.'

(RotK, Book V, ch.5, p.112-3)

In the next chapter and the battle itself, the same motif recurs when, 'The new morning was blotted from the sky' by the fell beast's wings as the Witch-king attacked Théoden. Thus, just as it is the battle with the son of Eos/Dawn that leads to the death of Achilles, so it is a battle at dawn, with a king who is transfigured into a veritable solar hero of true myth rather than Tolkien's usual legend, that leads to the death of the Witch-king. Memnon's Ethiopians appear on the opposite side, in the shape of the Southrons and Easterlings supporting the Witch-king. The precise catalogue of these exotic peoples at the Battle of the

Pelennor Fields probably owes a great deal to medieval Arthurian literature, as we will be showing in a later book. It is very possible, however, that the idea of non-European peoples being there at all is drawn from the association of Ethiopians with the death of Achilles in the medieval Trojan legends.

Incidentally, it may be worth noting that all the constellations named by Homer as being on the shield of Achilles (Pleiades, Hyades, Orion and the Great Bear) have seven main stars, or are most often represented that way, and seven stars feature on the banner of the house of Elendil that Aragorn unfurls at the Battle of the Pelennor Fields shortly after the disappearance of the Witch-King (Homer/Fitzgerald 1998 book XVIII, lines 486-9, p.334).

The death of Achilles in various writers' versions contains a number of ideas which are most important for Tolkien's possible use of the character. Alluded to by the dying Hector in the *Iliad*, the scene was elaborated by the anonymous writer of one of the so-called 'Epic Cycle' poems, the *Aethiopis*. It also appears in Ovid's *Metamorphoses*, as follows:

He pointed to Achilles laying low
The troops of Troy, and turned the bow on him
And guided the sure shaft with deadly aim.
This, after Hector, was a thing to make
Old Priam glad. And so Achilles fell,
Victor of mighty triumphs, vanquished by
The craven ravisher of that Greek wife:
If in a woman's fight he had to fall,
He'd have preferred the Amazon's double axe.

And now that terror of the ranks of Troy,
The grace and guardian of the name of Greece,
Achilles, prince unconquerable in war
Had burned upon the pyre. The selfsame god
Had armed him and consumed him in the end.
Now he is ashes; of that prince so great
Some little thing is left, hardly enough
To fill an urn. (Ovid/Melville/Kenney 1986, bk.XII, lines 590-617)

Firstly, this encounter may contain the germ of the encounter between Gandalf and the Witch-king inside the broken Gate of Minas Tirith, for it takes place *inside* the Scaean Gate of Troy; Achilles had rushed into the city on the heels of men seeking refuge there after defeat in the field. Secondly, the deadly dart aimed by a god which kills Achilles is very close to the arrow, believed to have been loosed by a Ringwraith, that brings down Faramir; this is a typical reversal of a motif by Tolkien to create a new incident. Thirdly, the lines about 'If in a woman's fight he had to fall/ He'd have preferred the Amazon's double axe' refer to Achilles' duel with Penthesilea and prefigure the death of the Witch-king at the hands of Eowyn, a woman warrior if not exactly an Amazon, whose stroke moreover appears to *behead* the Witch-king - just like an axe-blow. This also fits with Ovid's abrupt jump from Achilles on the battlefield to Achilles in his urn, since the Witch-king's body disappears and only his clothes are left.

II; Horse-riding Heroines Unmasked

As we have just seen, there is a potential link between the Rohirrim and the Trojan story, which runs through Tolkien's Eowyn of Rohan on the one hand and the Classical character of Penthesilea, Queen of the Amazons ('Queen of Femynye' to Chaucer (Knight's Tale) and in Lydgate's Troy Book - Benson 1980 p.107) on the other. Amazons are mentioned in the *Iliad*, but do not take part in the fighting as depicted in that work. They do occur in the related poem *Aethiopis*, of possibly 8th century BC date, preserved only in a 2nd-century AD summary. This poem described how Penthesilea, Queen of the Amazons, led her people in an attempt to relieve the Siege of Troy; after showing great prowess, the queen was killed by Achilles and buried by the Trojans, while the remnant of her army fled. Achilles was said not to have known he was fighting a woman until he pulled the mortally wounded Penthesilea from her horse and took off her helmet; he fell in love with her on the spot and was stricken with remorse for killing her. Seeing this reaction, a Greek called Thersites insulted Achilles and was promptly killed by him (M. Scherer 1963 p.96-7 and relevant Notes; s.v. Aethiopis under 'Epic Cycle' in Appendix I).

By the time Tolkien reached the Minas Tirith chapters the Rohirrim were already well-established as a 'horse people'. When first we meet the Rohirrim at Meduseld there are strong overtones of Germanic legend about them, drawing on both the Old English poem *Beowulf* and legends about the Goths. But then the story (and the Rohirrim) move from the Mark towards the 'kingdom of Men' that Tolkien had envisaged early in the writing of the New Hobbit. As soon as he began to use the Trojan/Gondolin material as a source for the development of the as-yet-unexplored southern kingdom of 'Ond', the horsiness of the Rohirrim would strongly tend to draw in similar aspects of the Trojan legends to suit the purposes of the story. Firstly, Homer regularly associates horses and Trojans; one of the people's recurring epithets is 'horse-breaking', and the country of Ilios within which Troy is set is called 'of the fine horses' (Wood 1985, ch.5, p.166). Secondly, Troy is almost saved by a horse-people, the Amazons, and despite all the epithets, there is no other considerable cavalry force among the Trojans themselves or their allies when fighting the Greeks. The momentum of the developing plot of LotR would have strongly pushed the Rohirrim towards taking up some version of the Amazons' role in the next section of the story as they moved from Rohan into Gondor. Indeed, there is a definite difference between the Rohirrim when they are in Rohan and when they move into Gondor, a change emphasised by the passage through Drúadan Forest (RotK, Book V, ch.5, p.104-109). When Théoden and his men are led through the woods by the Woses, it seems like a journey through a timeless realm, for just as with Lórien, the enemy are evaded. An army waits for them on the open road, but the Rohirrim travel secretly and safely through the forest. Tolkien himself more than once referred to the Rohirrim as 'heroic "Homeric" horsemen'. (Letters, No.131, p.159)

The 'renewal' of Théoden may well also have drawn the Rohirrim towards the medieval Tale of Troy. That group of stories associated the beginnings of the

Trojan War with the Quest of the Golden Fleece, and in his History of the Fall of Troy, Guido delle Colonne says of Aeson, father of Jason, that he;
'... lived a long time after the reign of this Peleus, so that, failing on account of his great old age, his eyes dimmed and the vigor of his body dwindled away in old age. The same Ovid, in the same book, the *Metamorphoses*, says he was afterwards renewed to the flower of his youth and his youthful vigor, so that a young man was made from an aged shadow by the healing remedy and magic power of Medea...' (Colonne/Meek 1974, bk.1, lines 34-40, p.4)
Théoden is called Ednew, the Renewed, and while his transformation is less dramatic than Aeson's (in the book - the Jackson film comes much closer to that scale of change), this is another potential link drawing the Rohirrim towards taking some suitable role in the 'Trojan' scenario which we believe forms the framework for the whole Gondor episode.

More speculatively, Tolkien already appears to have been considering some sort of far-ranging link between the Trojan legends and Northern European, 'Germanic' tales. As we saw in chapter 4, the hero Tuor's connections to both swans and (in BOLT) bears may well link him to a range of Northern stories about heroes who come from the water in time of need. In one of the early versions of his famous paper 'Beowulf: the Monsters and the Critics', Tolkien makes an extremely odd throwaway remark:
'This is not a military judgement - we are not here asserting that that, if the Trojans had employed a Northern king and his warriors, they would have driven Agamemnon and Achilles and all the Achaeans into the sea more decisively than the Greek hexameter routs the alliterative line (though this is highly probable).' (Drout 2002, ' 'Beowulf' and the Critics', version B, p.119)
Tolkien is definitely letting his heart rule his head here - nobody short of the very greatest 'Germanic' kings such as Eormanric the Ostrogoth or maybe Aelfwine of the Lombards could really have challenged Agamemnon, Homer's 'King of Men' and commander of all the Greeks before Troy. Anyway, this idea distinctly prefigures the arrival of the Rohirrim (loosely 'Anglo-Saxons' and in any case 'Northern') to help Gondor (Troy) in *The Lord of the Rings*. Perhaps the southward movement of the Rohirrim to the aid of 'Ond'/Gondor, (which may well already have been thought of by Tolkien as an older and more sophisticated country), and their half-Gothic, half Anglo-saxon nature, was one factor moving Tolkien towards using his 'Trojan' stories as a basis for the southern realm. A people like the Rohirrim, part-Gothic and part-Anglo-saxon, could have had a real existence - as Tolkien would have known well - only in very early times when the Primitive Germanic peoples had not yet split into eastern (Gothic) and western (Anglian, Saxon) groups, and such an era might well coincide with the time of the Trojan War, c.1200 BC.

It should be pointed out that in the pre-Drúadan Forest scenario, the Rohirrim seem to operate in small bands of warriors, and the lords seem to be as important as the King (e.g. Erkenbrand), very much along the lines of the Angles and Saxons. By contrast, in the post-Drúadan Forest setting, the Rohirrim appear as a well-organised mass of mounted troops, an army from a mobilised nation led by its king, very much in the style of Aelfwine's Lombard host or the armies described in the medieval Trojan legends.

It is worth mentioning that this Northern-Southern link, as seen in the coming of the Rohirrim to Gondor, may have sparked another event in LotR. It appears that Tolkien had already decided in *The Book of Lost Tales* that such a Trojan/Germanic connection inevitably involved the 'hero from the sea' stories. This idea finds a clear echo in *The Lord of the Rings* in the arrival of Aragorn at the Pelennor Fields in the nick of time *by boat*, rather than in any other fashion.

In the medieval versions of the Tale of Troy, it is emphasised that the Amazons arrive in Troy's darkest hour; all the city's heroes are dead, and the people are cowering behind their famous walls, refusing to fight (Benson 1980 part 2, ch.IV, p.74). The situation is not quite as dramatic in Dictys and Dares, but in both versions the Amazons' arrival occurs after Hector has fallen, and is effectively the last hope for Troy (Frazer 1966 Dictys p.79-80, 87-8; Dares p.162-3). In Dicty's version, news of the Amazons' imminent arrival brings about Hector's death, as the Greeks learn that the Trojan prince is setting off with a few companions to meet her, and Achilles lays an ambush for them. Hector and all his companions save one luckless son of Priam are killed; the sole survivor is sent home to carry the news with both hands cut off - a parallel to the fate of Gelmir son of Guilin of Nargothrond before the Fifth Battle, Nirnaeth Arnoediad, in QS: 'Then the Captain of Morgoth sent out riders with tokens of parley, and they rode up before the outworks of the Barad Eithel. With them they brought Gelmir son of Guilin, that lord of Nargothrond whom they had captured in the Bragollach; and they had blinded him. Then the heralds of Angband showed him forth, crying: "We have many more such at home, but you must make haste if you would find them; for we shall deal with them all when we return even so." And they hewed off Gelmir's hands and feet, and his head last, within sight of the Elves, and left him.' (QS, ch.20, p.230)

The Amazons finally reach Troy during Hector's funeral:

'During the funeral, Penthesilea (whom we have mentioned above) arrived. She brought a huge army of Amazons and other neighbouring peoples. On being informed of Hector's death, she was very upset and desired to go home. But Alexander [Paris] gave her much gold and silver, and finally prevailed upon her to stay.'

Similarly, when the Rohirrim arrive outside Minas Tirith it is the city's darkest hour. The walls are surrounded by hordes of foes; the First Circle is ablaze; the men of the garrison have either fled the walls or are trapped there without hope. Minas Tirith's closest thing to a prince, Faramir, is believed to be dying or dead, and in fact is almost killed by his own father, the Steward Denethor. He is the ruler of Minas Tirith, but like Priam he has given up all pretence of command or of will to fight.

> *'Priam, for sorrow over his fine sons,*
> *Had no will to fight, nor to pass the walls*
> *He determined to wait for two months before taking any action*
> *[And] swiftly commanded that the gates be straitly guarded.*

The Trojans in that time, as the book says,
[Went with] much sorrow in the city, sobbing piteously
[They] had no hope of their safety; then their hearts failed
And they slipped down into despair as if they would die.
Agamemnon sent word to the great [Priam] by [the hands of] skilled men
Often, in truth, in that same time,
[And] told him to send forth his soldiers, assemble on the field
And make ready for battle, or yield up his city
The noble [Priam] would not answer, for fear of what might happen
He had fallen into deep dread of taking risks since his fate seemed bleak
[and feared] that his people in battle should finally be destroyed.'

(Panton & Donaldson 1968, book XXVII, lines 10788-804) [Note 1]

The people of Troy were as disheartened as their King and feared they would eventually be brought down by hunger, which Tolkien also mentions as a long-term threat to Minas Tirith in *The Lord of the Rings*.

'Now the Trojans in grief and anger, all the town gates
Guarded very carefully, with great sorrow in their hearts
They believed they were without hope of any help from within
Or of any aid to be sent [to them] out of far lands.
All the walls of the city were broad and very high
[And] sentinels they chose, watches to keep
Of trusty men in [the] towers, lest others plan treason,
[And] To save the city from the assaults of her foes.
So huge was the height of the tall towers
With ditches most deep dug on every side
That no warrior might take it until the world's end
Save through lack of food, that brings weakness to the people. '

(Panton & Donaldson 1968, book XXVIII, lines 11151-62) [Note 2]

This exactly matches Tolkien's words:

'At first men laughed and did not greatly fear such devices. For the main wall of the City was of great height and marvellous thickness, built ere the power and craft of Númenor waned in exile; and its outward face was like to the Tower of Orthanc, hard and dark and smooth, unconquerable by steel or fire, unbreakable except by some convulsion that would rend the very earth on which it stood. 'Nay,' they said, 'not if the Nameless One himself should come, not even he could enter here while we yet live.' But some answered: 'While we yet live? How long? He has a weapon that has brought low many strong places since the world began. Hunger. The roads are cut. Rohan will not come.' (RotK, Book V, ch.4, p.96)

Both Troy and Minas Tirith are ringed by great walls, tall and broad, impenetrable to assault; but both fear hunger and expect no help from 'far lands'. It is worth noting also that Tolkien's suggestion that the walls of Minas Tirith could not be broken 'except by some convulsion that would rend the very earth on which it stood' looks like a double Trojan reference; to Poseidon the Earthshaker, who built the walls of Laomedon's Troy, most of which were still standing to face the Greeks a second time; and to the mid-20th-century theory that it was an earthquake which broke the walls or gates of Troy and so allowed the besieging Greeks inside. So the arrival of Penthesilea and her Amazon cavalry in an hour of desperate sorrow and apparently inevitable defeat, accompanied by the funeral of a prince, matches the situation of the arrival of Eowyn and the Rohirrim in an hour of despair and nearly unstoppable defeat, accompanied by the near-death of Faramir.

Dictys continues the story by telling what happened when Penthesilea led her women out to do battle with the Greeks:

'Several days later she drew up her forces and made an attack, without any help from the Trojans, so great was her trust in her people. She arranged the archers on the right flank, the foot soldiers on the left, and the cavalry, to which she herself belonged,
in the centre. Our men were drawn up to meet her... Thus the two armies, having drawn up their forces, joined battle. The queen slaughtered many, using her bow, as did Teucer for us... Achilles found Penthesilea among the cavalry and, hurling his spear, hit the mark. Then - no trouble now that she was wounded - he seized her by the hair and pulled her off her horse...' The Greeks find Penthesilea still alive after driving off the rest of the Amazon army; a vote is taken, and she is drowned in the River Scamander - 'It goes without saying that this was a very cruel and barbarous act. But thus the queen of the Amazons, having lost the forces she brought to aid Priam, died in a way that befitted her foolhardy character.'

In Dares' version, things go rather differently:
'On the next day Agamemnon drew up his army in front of the gates and challenged the Trojans to come out and fight. But Priam stayed in the city, increasing his fortifications and waiting for Penthesilea to come with her Amazons.

When Penthesilea arrived, she led forth her army against Agamemnon. a huge battle arose. It raged for several days, and then the Greeks, being overwhelmed, fled for their camp. Diomedes could hardly prevent Penthesilea firing the ships and destroying all the Greek forces.

After this battle, Agamemnon kept his forces in camp. Penthesilea, to be sure, came forth each day and, slaughtering the Greeks, tried to provoke him to fight. But he, following the advice of his council, fortified the camp, strengthened the guard, and refused to go out to battle - until Menelaus arrived.

When, on Scyros, Menelaus had given Neoptolemus the arms of his father, Achilles, he brought him to join the Greeks at Troy. And here Neoptolemus wept and lamented above the tomb of his father.

Penthesilea, according to her custom, drew up her army and advanced as far as the camp of the Greeks. Neoptolemus, in command of the Myrmidons, led forth his forces. And Agamemnon drew up his army. Greeks and Trojans clashed head-on. Neoptolemus wreaked great slaughter. Penthesilea, having entered the fray, proved her prowess again and again.

For several days they fought fiercely, and many were killed. finally Penthesilea wounded Neoptolemus, and fell at his hands; in spite of his wound, he cut her down. The death of Penthesilea, the queen of the Amazons, caused all the Trojans to turn and flee in defeat for their city.'

Medieval writers generally followed Dares and had Penthesilea killed by

Achilles' son Neoptolemus/Pyrrhus, preferring to restrict the love of Achilles himself to the Trojan princess Polyxena.

Two loose parallels in Virgil's Aeneid are also worth mentioning here. At the end of Book 7, in the list of the forces ranged against Aeneas and his Trojan refugees, and their Latin allies:

'Last of all came Camilla, the warrior maiden of the Volsci, leading a cavalry squadron flowering in bronze. Not for her girlish hands the distaff and wool-basket of Minerva. She was a maid inured to battle, of a fleetness of foot to race the winds. She could have skimmed the tops of a standing crop without touching them and her passage would not have bruised the delicate ears of grain. She could have run over the ocean, hovered over the swell and never wet her foot in the waves. Young men streamed from house and field and mothers came throning to gaze at her as she went, lost in wonderment at the royal splendour of the purple veiling the smoothness of her shoulders, her hair weaving round its gold clasp, her Lycian quiver and the shepherd's staff of myrtle wood with the head of a lance.' (Virgil trans. West 1990/2003, Bk.7, p.164)

In early versions Eowyn rides openly to battle:

'Eowyn says that the women must ride now, as they did in a like evil time in the days when Brego son of... Eorl's son, when the wild men of the East came from the Inland Sea into the Eastemnet.' (*The War of the Ring*, HOME Vol. VIII, Part 3, ch.2, p.243)

'Theoden leaves Edoras Feb. 11 with Eomer and Eowyn... Reach battle Feb. 15... Siege relieved by the Rohirrim and the allies of Lebennin... Theoden slain and Eowyn slays the King of the Nazgul and is mortally wounded. They lie in state in the white tower.' (ibid, p.255-6)

This is very significant, because Penthesilea is killed by Neoptolemus/ Pyrrhus in the battle before Troy (Dares and Dictys), something we discuss in detail elsewhere in this chapter.

Later of course Tolkien has Eowyn take on the persona of Dernhelm and hide herself (as well as bring Merry with her). Eowyn ends up bearing a closer resemblance to Penthesilea in this regard in the Battle of the Pelennor Fields, because her female identity is hidden, just as Penthesilea is not recognised as a woman at first.

The importance of the Amazon cavalry, their own major arm and the best part of the army, should be noted here in comparison to Tolkien's Rohirrim. Penthesilea's role in Dares and Dictys ends up being split by Tolkien; the royal leader who is killed after a fall from a horse is Théoden, but involved alongside him is an 'Amazon', or at least a woman who fights, in the shape of Eowyn. In the varying versions of the Trojan episode, it is consistently either Achilles or his son Neoptolemus (also called Pyrrhus) who is responsible for the downfall and death of Penthesilea. In Tolkien's story, it is the Witch-King, who seems to occupy much the same space in the story as Achilles and to derive some important attributes from the Greek hero (as detailed above), who kills Théoden and nearly slays Eowyn.

Having two characters instead of one queen to work with, Tolkien can raise the tension far more than either the Classical writers or their medieval successors could. Théoden falls mortally wounded and is left with no defence against the Witch-king but a woman and a hobbit, creating a point of crisis. Reversing the fortunes of the fight as described by Dares, Tolkien has Eowyn suffer injury but kill the Witch-king. Like Achilles, the Witch-king has no idea he is fighting a woman until he sees her without her helmet; but whereas in the Classical versions Achilles makes the discovery and Penthesilea has nothing to do with it, Tolkien has Eowyn reveal herself with considerable dramatic impact. Indeed, Tolkien almost duplicates the motif, having Imrahil of Dol Amroth make the same mistake as Achilles until he looks more closely at the unconscious Eowyn. As we have seen, another motif that Tolkien picks up on is the arrival of the Amazons in Troy's darkest hour. There can be few arrival scenes more powerful than the coming of the Rohirrim, in the darkness before dawn when Minas Tirith is burning and all seems lost. For a while it looks as if the Rohirrim will have no better luck in saving Minas Tirith than the Amazons had in saving Troy, but this situation is overtaken by the great reversal of fortunes as Aragorn arrives in the Corsair ships. Indeed, Imrahil shows how the presence of one woman warrior (Eowyn) could be transformed by rumour into an army of Amazons (RotK, Book V, ch.6, p.120-1).

An incident somewhat like that of Théoden's fall occurs in the *Aeneid*, at the end of Book 10, when Mezentius faces Aeneas in single combat. Mezentius up to this point is the most thoroughgoing villain of the Italian section of the poem, an impious, cruel and tyrannical ruler hated as much by his own people as his enemies. In the last battle, though, he acquires some nobility, accepting the gods he has long scorned, fighting fairly; saved by his own son at the cost of the boy's life, he goes back out to the fight even though already wounded, speaking to his horse - 'his glory and his comfort' - before he does so. The audience's sympathies, therefore, are divided at this point in time:

'Then, weary of all the delay, weary of plucking javelins out of his shield and hard-pressed in this unequal battle, Aeneas, after turning many plans over in his mind, at last burst forward and threw his spear, catching Mezentius' warhorse in the hollow between its temples. Up it reared thrashing the air with its hooves and throwing its rider. Then as it came down with all its weight, dislocating its shoulder, it fell head first on top of Mezentius and pinned him to the ground.' (Virgil trans.West, 1009/2003, Bk.10, p.236)

Knocked unconscious in the fall, Mezentius recovers and is able to speak to Aeneas, asking for a decent funeral, before the Trojan hero kills him.

If we compare the above with the death of Théoden it can be seen that it is very similar indeed in many respects:

'Then Merry stooped and lifted his hand to kiss it, and lo! Théoden opened his eyes, and they were clear, and he spoke in a quiet voice though laboured.

"Farewell, Master Holbytla!" he said. "My body is broken. I go to my fathers. And even in their mighty company I shall not now be ashamed. I felled the black serpent. A grim morn, and a glad day, and a golden sunset!"

Merry could not speak, but wept anew. "Forgive me, lord," he said at last, "if I broke your command, and yet have done no more in your service than to weep at our parting."
The old king smiled. "Grieve not! It is forgiven. Great heart will not be denied. Live now in blessedness; and when you sit in peace with your pipe, think of me! For never now shall I sit with you in Meduseld, as I promised, or listen to your herb-lore." He closed his eyes, and Merry bowed beside him. Presently he spoke again. "Where is Eomer? For my eyes darken, and I would see him ere I go. He must be king after me. And I would send word to Eowyn. She, she would not have me leave her, and now I shall not see her again, dearer than daughter."...
But Eomer leaped from the saddle, and grief and dismay fell upon him as he came to the king's side and stood there in silence. Then one of the knights took the king's banner from the hand of Guthlaf the banner-bearer who lay dead, and he lifted it up. Slowly Théoden opened his eyes. Seeing the banner he made a sign that it should be given to Eomer.
"Hail, King of the Mark!" he said. "Ride now to victory! Bid Eowyn farewell!" And so he died...' (RotK, Book V, ch.6, p.117-9)
Like Mezentius, Théoden is crushed beneath his horse when it falls to a dart. Neither is killed outright, both are able to leave instructions. But in a characteristic reversal, Tolkien has Théoden speak to his legitimate heir whereas Mezentius can only speak to his deadly foe.

It should be noted that Virgil's 'Amazon', Camilla of the Volsci, is not found in close proximity to this scene. She has not been mentioned earlier in Book 10 and by the time she appears in Book 11, events have moved on a considerable distance. The chances are, therefore, that if Virgil is any influence on Tolkien at all, rather than the motif being independently evolved from both men's knowledge of riders' mishaps, then the idea has been imported casually, perhaps almost unconsciously. We should remember that Tolkien was educated at a good grammar school before the First World War, where he showed uncommon aptitude for Classical studies; since Virgil's poem was a central text for school Latin studies, it is not unreasonable to suppose that Tolkien had once known Virgil's *Aeneid* very well indeed, and might have 'quoted' without realising where an idea had come from. The very small number of possible parallels between Tolkien's writings and the *Aeneid* would suggest some such slight and sidelong influence, rather than active use of the poem as a source. The death of Penthesilea in the Trojan War, especially as described in the medieval versions, is a far clearer model for the scene where the Witch-king falls.

It is worth noting also Imrahil's words when he sees Eowyn being carried towards Minas Tirith:
'Then the prince went from his horse, and knelt by the bier in honour of the king and his great onset; and he wept. And rising he looked then on Eowyn and was amazed. 'Surely, here is a woman?' he said. 'Have even the women of the Rohirrim come to war in our need?'
'Nay! One only,' they answered. 'The Lady Eowyn is she, sister of Eomer, and we

knew naught of her riding until this hour, and greatly we rue it.' '
(RotK, Book V, ch.6, p.120-1)
The men of Rohan may deny that any woman save Eowyn has accompanied them, but as we have said before, it takes no great imagination to see how Imrahil's question could lead to a rumour that an army of women came to Minas Tirith. We have been shown just such a process of misunderstanding and exaggeration shortly before. Peregrine Took's arrival in Minas Tirith with Gandalf causes a chain of rumours to develop:
'There had already been much talk in the Citadel about Mithrandir's companion and his long closeting with the Lord; and rumour declared that a Prince of the Halflings had come out of the North to offer allegiance to Gondor and five thousand swords. And some said that when the Riders came from Rohan each would bring behind him a halfling warrior, small maybe but doughty.'
(RotK, Book V, ch.1, p.40)
If one Hobbit can be multiplied into an army, so can one Amazon. We should remember that Tolkien intended all his stories to be set not in a nebulous 'fantasy world' but an unrecorded chunk of real prehistory. Looked at from this angle, the half-remembered and much misunderstood story of the Ride of the Rohirrim to Minas Tirith could be attached to the historical event of a mainly-cavalry group arriving as allies of Troy, transforming them in turn into Amazons.

III; One Ring to Bind Them All...

As a last point, relevant to the Witch-king insomuch as he is a Ringbearer, it is well worth mentioning that invisibility in general, and specifically rings which grant the ability to pass unseen, occur in a number of the possible sources for Tolkien's ideas. One of these is mentioned in the medieval 'historical Trojan' material, where a ring which can grant invisibility is one of the items which Princess Medea of Colchis gives to Jason to help him in his attempt to gain the Golden Fleece. Guido delle Colonne says of this ring that:
'Then she gave him a certain ring in which there was a stone of such great virtue that it would attack any poison and turn aside its noxious force, and by its virtue it would preserve anyone who had perhaps been infected by a maddening poison, just as if he had taken something harmless. *There was also in this same stone another very great virtue, so that if anyone carried this stone held tight in his hand, with the result that the stone itself stuck to the skin of the person carrying it, he would immediately become invisible, with the result that while he was carrying it in his hand, the means of seeing him would appear to no-one.'* (Colonne/Meek 1974, bk.3, lines 156-166, p.25, - emphasis ours)
Admittedly, in the alliterative 'Destruction of Troy', this ring is less impressive:

'Then she took to him a ring with a precious stone
So that no poison could injure him, for such was its power
And if it were carried in battle on his bare skin
He should slip away cunningly and not be killed.'

(Panton & Donaldson 1968, book III, lines 786-9) [Note 3]

The point is still interesting, however, as another example within Tolkien's likely source-set of this motif.

Guido delle Colonne has another passage which may be relevant to Tolkien's conception of the One Ring. Having rebuilt Troy after its first destruction, King Priam sends an embassy to Greece to try to obtain the return of his sister Hesione, who had been captured in the sack of the city and given to the Greek prince Telamon, in whose household she remained as a slave and a concubine. Faced with Priam's request, as carried by the trusted Trojan lord Antenor, Telamon reacts badly:

'Friend, whoever you are, I am stirred with great wonder at the lack of seriousness of your king, since I am not joined to him nor he to me by any signs of friendship, and for that reason it is not my desire to hear his entreaties. For your king knows that to avenge a certain crime, certain other Greek nobles and I with an army, attacked king Laomedon, the perpetrator of the crime, and that I shedding not a little of my blood, was first to enter the Trojan city by force of arms. On account of this, and by the assent of the whole army, Hesione was handed over to me as the reward of victory, to do with her as I wished. I think this was no *trifling* gift, since she is endowed with extreme beauty, distinguished by much learning, and lovely in the possession of praise-worthy virtues. It is not for me to give back as a *trifle something that precious*, obtained at that much peril to my life. Therefore tell your king that he will not be able to obtain Hesione except at the point of a slaughtering sword. Furthermore, I think you showed yourself a great fool when you volunteered to assume the burden of such a mission, since you should have known that in doing so you were subjecting yourself to obvious peril and to the power of those who persecute you and those like you with hateful insults. Depart then quickly from this land. If you do not do this instantly, I would have you know that you will without doubt be risking your life.'

(Colonne/Meek 1974, bk.5, lines 370-391, pp.51-2) Emphasis above ours.

There are two ways in which this speech about Hesione, the victim of one Trojan War and the cause of another, is echoed in *The Lord of the Rings*, both in the Council of Elrond. Firstly, there is Gloin's account of the messenger from Mordor who comes to the Lonely Mountain:

'Then about a year ago a messenger came to Dáin, but not from Moria - from Mordor: a horseman in the night, who called Dáin to his gate. The Lord Sauron the Great, so he said, wished for our friendship. Rings he would give for it, such as he gave of old. And he asked urgently concerning *hobbits*, of what kind they were, and where they dwelt. "For Sauron knows," said he,"that one of these was known to you on a time."

At this we were greatly troubled, and we gave no answer. And then his fell voice was lowered, and he would have sweetened it if he could. "As a small token only of your friendship Sauron asks this," he said: "that you should find this thief," such was his word, "and get from him, willing or no, a little ring, the least of rings, that once he stole. It is but a *trifle* that Sauron fancies, and an earnest of your good will. Find it and three rings that the Dwarf-sires possessed of old

will be returned to you, and the realm of Moria shall be yours for ever. Find only news of the thief, whether he still lives and where, and you shall have great reward and lasting friendship from the Lord. Refuse, and things will not seem so well. Do you refuse?"
At that his breath came like the hiss of snakes, and all who stood by shuddered...'

It is blindingly obvious that this is no 'least of rings' that Sauron seeks - to be worth three dwarf-rings and the realm of Moria (probably not actually in Sauron's power to give, but never mind that just now!) this seeming trinket must actually be of the greatest importance. So also Telamon twice describes Hesione as 'no trifle' within as many sentences - 'I think this was no *trifling* gift, since she is endowed with extreme beauty, distinguished by much learning, and lovely in the possession of praise-worthy virtues. It is not for me to give back as a *trifle* something that *precious*, obtained at that much peril to my life.' This is mirrored in Tolkien's words as given to the horseman from Mordor (FotR, Book II, ch.2, p.254).
Secondly, there is Gandalf's report of Isildur's scroll, given during the Council of Elrond:
'But for my part I will risk no hurt to this thing, of all the works of Sauron the only fair.It is precious to me, though I buy it with great pain.' (ibid, p.266)
Here Isildur's words parallel Telamon's, '...something that *precious*, obtained at that much peril to my life.' Hesione's beauty and distinction also match the 'fair' seeming of the Ring.

IV; Conclusions

To summarise the points we have made in this chapter;

The Witch-King in this section is very probably affected by the character of Achilles in the Trojan story.

The fall of the Witch-King at Eowyn's hands draws on aspects of several versions of one event during the Trojan war, the killing of the Amazon queen Penthesilea by Achilles or his son Neoptolemus/Pyrrhus.

Many of the turns of battle mirror the Pelennor Fields and what occurs to the main protagonists.

Any one of these parallels could be construed as coincidence; taken all together however, we suggest that is highly improbable that all these similarities could have come together by accident. We suggest that in all likelihood Tolkien deliberately utilised the medieval Trojan legend, probably reinterpreted through the Tale of Gondolin, as the dominant source for the episodes in LotR which focus on the Witch-King.

Hereto we give the original Middle English texts of the poems:
Note 1:

'Priamus, for pité of his pure sons
Hade no wille for to weire, nor the wallis pas.
Two monethis with might, er he meue wold,
The yates to yeme he yepely comaundit.
The troiens in the tyme, as the text sais
With myche sorow in the Cité, sobbyng vnfaire,
Hade no hope of there hele: than there hert failet,
And thai drepit in dole, as thai degh shuld.
Agamynon, by graith men, to the gret sent
Oft-sythes, for sothe, in the same tyme,
Bade him send furth his soudiouris, assemble to feld,
And buske vnto batell, or his burgh yelde.
The noble hym denyet for noy that might happon,
He drede him full depely for desteny feble,
Lest his folke in the feld were fynally destroyet...'

(Panton & Donaldson 1968, book XXVII, lines 10788-804)

Note 2:

'Now the troyens, with tene, all the toun ȝatys
Keppit full cloyse, with care at hor hertes;
Withouten hope of any helpe holdyn hom with-in
Or any socour to be send out of sere londys.
All the burgh is full bigge, ouer the brode allis,
Wacchemen for to wale, wacches to kepe,
Of trewmen in towres, for treason of other,
The Cité to saue from saute of hor fos.
ffor the heght is so hoge of the hegh touris,
With dykes so depe drâghen a-boute,
That no werriour hit win may to the worldes end
But thurgh ffailyng of fode, that fainttes the pepull.'

(Panton & Donaldson 1968, book XXVIII, lines 11151-62)

Note 3:

'Than ho raught hym a ring with a riche stone,
That no poison empaire might, the power is soche;
And if it borne were in batell on his bare flesshe
He shulde slyde forth sleghly and vnslayne worthe.'

(Panton & Donaldson 1968, book III, lines 786-9)

Chapter Seven:

What It Isn't; Gondolin & Famous Fallen Cities.

It is fairly easy to look at J.R.R. Tolkien's writings and find parallels with possible 'sources', especially if you keep to short sections of stories or to limited extracts. Some very strange comparisons have been made over the years by this method and we would not wish to fall into a similar trap ourselves. Can we be sure that something else does not fit the Tale of Gondolin even better than the Tale of Troy?

Firstly, this study is conducted, as we have seen, with no small scale comparison of short sections or single motifs, no limited extract analysis. The Troy-Gondolin comparison embraces the whole Tale of Gondolin and extends into the Tale of Eärendel, and it explains on levels of linguistic, narrative character and descriptive connection why these two stories are linked. Any competing hypothesis has to account for just as many aspects of these two stories if it is to be seriously considered, and if it is to oust the Tale of Troy from its place as probable source it has to account for even more of what Tolkien writes than the theories put forward in this volume. The Tale of Troy also provides a whole series of plausible reasons for why Tolkien wrote what he did, when he did - a biographical layer of explanation that fits. This too has to be overtaken by any other source-tale if that is to be taken seriously. That is a tall order. Nonetheless, let us see if there is any real competition for the Tale of Troy as a source for the Tale of Gondolin. What we won't do in our study is to ignore other possible ideas for the sake of our own - as many so-called academic investigations sadly very often do.

We will start where Tolkien himself suggests we should, with the list of famously destroyed cities to which the fall of Gondolin is compared in *The Book of Lost Tales* version: 'Nor Bablon, nor Ninwi, nor the towers of Trui, nor all the many takings of Rûm that is greatest among men, saw such terror as fell that day upon Amon Gwareth in the kindred of the Gnomes: and this is esteemed the worst work that Melko has yet thought of in the world.'
These are noted under Changes to Names in *The Fall of Gondolin*:
Bablon, Ninwi, Trui, Rûm The original text of *Tuor A* had *Babylon, Nineveh, Troy* and (probably) *Rome*.' (BOLT II, ch.3, pps.196 & 203)
So we know which cities to look at first to find some links to rival those we have described in the previous chapters. Can Babylon, Nineveh or Rome compete with Troy as a source for *The Fall of Gondolin*?

I; Cities of the Plain

a; Babylon

The single biggest problem with comparing Babylon to Gondolin is that whilst the city had a long and chequered history, it survived everything thrown at it for over two thousand years with remarkable resilience, surviving all manner of problems from ecological and economic collapse (during the fall of the House of Hammurabi in 16-1700 BC), through raids and occupations (the Elamites in 1157 BC or thereabouts) to a major destruction by the irate Assyrian king Sennacherib in 689 BC after one rebellion too many. Every time, the Babylonians picked themselves up and rebuilt their city. At the best-known change of hands, the one described in the Bible when Belshazzar is warned of impending doom by a hand writing on the wall when he and his courtiers are feasting (OT Daniel 5), Babylon was not actually taken and sacked. The city was conquered by the Persian king Cyrus in 539 BC and lost its place as a capital, but it was not destroyed or even damaged. That is made clear by a chronicle written at the time:

'In the month of Tashritu (September-October)... The sixteenth day, Gubaru, the governor of Gutium, and the army of Cyrus entered Babylon without a battle. Afterwards, Nabonidus was arrested in Babylon when he returned (there).

In the month of Arahsamnu (October-November), the third day, Cyrus entered Babylon. Great twigs were spread in front of him. The state of 'peace' was imposed on the city. Cyrus sent greetings to all Babylon...'

(Nabonidus Chronicle, cited in Roux 1992, ch.23, p.387)

In fact, no-one in Babylon wanted to risk defying the Persians, and someone showed them how to get past the defences via the bed of the River Euphrates, which then ran through the city. It was a useful treachery, for as G. Roux explains, not only the city but the whole realm was well-treated:

From the first day of Persian occupation (12 October 539 BC), care was taken not to offend the Babylonians in any way, and every effort was made to resettle them in their homes, to enforce law and order throughout the country. The gods of Sumer and Akkad, whom Nabonidus had brought into Babylon during the war, were reinstalled in their chapels, 'the places which make them happy', and even the gods of Assyria, once taken captive by the Medes, were returned and their temples rebuilt. Cyrus made it known that he considered himself the successor of the national rulers, that he worshipped Marduk and 'praised the great godhead joyously'. Indeed, we can believe the Persian conqueror when, in an inscription written in Akkadian on a clay cylinder, he declares that the Babylonians accepted his rule with enthusiasm: *'All the inhabitants of Babylon, as well as of the entire country of Sumer and Akkad, princes and governors, bowed to him (Cyrus) and kissed his feet, jubilant that he had received the kingship, and with shining faces happily greeted him as a master through whose help they had come to life from death and had all been spared damage and disaster, and they worshipped his name.'*

Proclamations like that deserve to be taken with more than a pinch of salt, but it is clear, firstly, that the previous rulers of Babylon, Nabonidus (Nabû-na'id) and his son-cum-regent Belshazzar (Bel-shar-usur) were deeply politically inept and definitely unpopular, and secondly, that Cyrus did a much better job than some later conquerors of what is now Iraq. He was well-known for integrating his conquests into his realm and ruling justly and wisely. Babylonian opinion was against war with Persia to the extent that border garrisons mutinied and towns revolted when Nabonidus tried to lead his people to battle. Afterwards, Cyrus imposed a rule which was seen as legitimate and not oppressive, and was generally welcome.

Babylon remained a major city for a considerable time after the Persian conquest; three attempts at getting loose from Persian rule resulted only in battles outside the walls, and though Xerxes did some damage to the city as punishment, it bounced back. It was still one of the foremost cities in the world when Alexander the Great arrived there in 331 BC, though trade and culture were both faltering. What followed afterward was a long, slow decline. It was not war but economics that finally reduced Babylon to a heap of ruins. Babylon was not the capital of Alexander's successors in Mesopotamia, the Seleucid kings, and it faced stiff competition from a new Greek colony-city, Seleucia-on-Tigris, to which much of the population of Babylon was actually transferred by the king. Sporadic efforts were made to revive Babylon, but the city was slipping inexorably downwards. By 140 BC another Iranian dynasty, the Parthians, had taken over. There was a short revival in Babylon, but this was accompanied by a massive influx of new settlers which effectively swamped what little was left of the city's ancient culture and language. Babylon twice fell into the hands of Rome, but on the first occasion the Emperor Trajan found it hardly more than a village and by 199 AD, Septimus Severus found the place entirely deserted when he came to offer sacrifice to the spirit of Alexander the Great. Babylon faded 'with a whimper' and did not 'go out with a bang' as was the case with both Troy and Gondolin.

So the comparison of Babylon with Gondolin falls at the first hurdle. There was no single occasion on which Babylon was conclusively destroyed. Furthermore, Babylon bore no physical resemblance to Gondolin. It lay on the flat plain of the Euphrates with the river running through it, and the only elevation in sight was the man-made hill of the *zigurrat* at the temple of Esagila, whereas Gondolin stands on a hill in a small plain encircled by mountains. Babylon had a double ring of walls with eight gates in the inner defence and an unknown number in the outer ring, which was close to the inner on north and south and created two 'garden suburbs' to east and west, whereas Gondolin appears to have had one main gate in the city proper, and a variable number elsewhere. Whereas Babylon was built almost entirely of brick and timber, Gondolin is a city of white marble.

No tale of flight of survivors carrying knowledge or stories was attached to Babylon; indeed, if there were any stories at all about the great city, they have not survived. In fact, the only claim to fame that the Babylonians have is a Biblical connection with the Tower of Babel, something that helped to sow confusion throughout the world (Genesis 11, 1-9). Nor did the history of Babylon link it with the sea in any straightforward manner. The city was a great river-port with wide-ranging connections by water and land, but all the evidence for seaborne commerce comes from the southern cities of old Sumer. So there is nothing that could develop into a link with the firmly sea-centred Tale of Eärendel. It might be objected that the story of Sindbad and his seven voyages comes from much the same area, being retold in *The Thousand and One Nights* as a story set in the Baghdad of Caliph Haroun al-Rashid. Baghdad is definitely not Babylon, however. The two cities do not overlap geographically (there is a hundred kilometres or more between them) or chronologically - Baghdad was founded in 762 AD, by which time Babylon had been a deserted ruin for over five hundred years. In any case Sindbad's resolutely commercial voyages cannot be considered the primary source for the Tale of Eärendel with its political/mystical goals, even if Tolkien might have been thinking about using some of the Sindbad material - a debatable point, given how little we have of the Tale of Eärendel.

Beyond all this, Babylon lies in an area for which we have no evidence of Tolkien taking any interest until the early 1940's when mentions of Mesopotamia begin to turn up in the writings on Númenor (*Sauron Defeated*, HOME vol.IX, 'The Notion Club Papers'). That is nearly thirty years after *The Fall of Gondolin* was written as the first story of what would become *The Book of Lost Tales*. A good deal of important evidence about Babylon in particular and Mesopotamia in general was also not available until after Gondolin had been invented; the Babylonian Chronicles quoted earlier were not published until 1923, seven years after *The Fall of Gondolin*.

Therefore, since the two differ at all the major points, Babylon cannot possibly be a source for Gondolin. There is perhaps a faint chance that the long decline of Babylon was the model for the decline of Osgiliath, as shown in the Appendices to *The Lord of the Rings*, but even that is fairly unlikely. Other cities have also declined over a long period.

b; Nineveh

The one-time capital of the Assyrian kings from about 1700 BC onward, Nineveh lies in what is now northern Iraq, just across the River Tigris from the modern city of Mosul. It is mentioned in the Bible (Old Testament, books of Ezekiel, Nahum, Zephaniah, Kings and Chronicles, etc.) as the original luxurious city inhabited by an aggressive, imperialist people famed for their wide-ranging and often brutal conquests, who frequently interfere in Jewish affairs. The Assyrian empire suddenly fell into major difficulties around 630 BC, and by 612 BC the Babylonians and Persians were besieging Nineveh. After a three-month siege, the city was taken in *Ab* , July-August; plundered and burnt, its people dead, fled or carried off, Nineveh became 'a ruin-mound and heaps of debris' according to a contemporary chronicler in Babylonia (Roux 1992, ch.23, pp.372-7, ch.25 p.4,16). Nineveh really was abandoned for several hundred years after this (it revived as a prosperous village under the Greek Seleucid kings in the last two centuries BC), and so is if anything closer to Gondolin at first inspection than is Troy. That city was rebuilt and destroyed at least once more in the chaos that engulfed the Aegean between 1200 and 1100 BC, depending which version of the archaeology you take as 'Homer's Troy', and it struggled on as a village until it was abandoned around 800 BC. There was also a later refoundation in which some of the people, judging by their pottery, may have been true Trojans and not Greek colonists (Wood 1985, ch.8).

However, we must not put too much faith in archaeology unless Tolkien gives us reason to believe we should. There is only one episode in *The Fall of Gondolin* and its related stories, as given in *The Book of Lost Tales*, that appears to draw on the real history of Troy. This is the episode in one of the outlines for the Tale of Eärendel has him returning to Gondolin, to find men living there in miserable camps and orcs hunting for gold in the ruins - a fair picture of the real, archaeological, fate of Troy. This idea was fairly certainly discarded as the story changed. The vast majority of what Tolkien wrote in *The Book of Lost Tales* clearly draws on the legend, and not the reality, of Troy - and according to those legends, there was no rebuilding. If anything survived at Troy, it was of no note compared to the dispersal of the survivors. The same is true of Gondolin - out of the survivors came Eärendil who bore a Silmaril into the skies and brought about the downfall of Morgoth, and out of his progeny came the first king of Númenor and the line of its kings thereafter. Tolkien does not appear to make major use of the Trojan archaeology until much later, and then not - so far as we can tell from published work - in direct relationship to Gondolin. This archaeological Trojan and Mycenean material can be seen in *The Lord of the Rings*, and ideas derived from this then turn up, much changed, in the 1950's 'Of Tuor and his Coming to Gondolin'. So by itself, the catastrophic destruction of Nineveh is not enough. There would have to be much more than this to justify calling it the primary source for Gondolin - and there is not.

For a start, we know the approximate date of the fall of Nineveh, July/ August, and it does not match with the date of the fall of Gondolin at 'the Gates of Summer', which on any reckoning has to be before the summer solstice. Secondly, the Bible gives us no *story* of Nineveh - only the fact of its glory and its fall. There are faint traces of the existence of something fictional about Assyria and Nineveh in later Greek romances, probably under the title of 'Ninus and Semiramis', but it has survived only as scraps of papyri. Two of these were known to exist from 1893 and were published as text and translation in 1916 - but only as part of a Loeb Classical Library volume whose main text was Longus' romance *Daphnis and Chloe.* Tolkien's reading taste could be surprising, but this pastoral romance with a sweet-and-sour centre (translated by C. Gill in Reardon 1989) is neither the sort of thing he could remotely be expected to like nor the visible ancestor of anything in his writing. Moreover, it appeared at a time when he was deeply involved with military matters and chronically short of cash. On both counts there would be little chance of Tolkien running across the second text in the book. Even if he did, it would not seem to have made any impression on him. The 'Ninus' story as we have it centres on the problems of two young lovers, the lady's name not surviving, and bears no resemblance to anything in *The Fall of Gondolin* ('Ninus' in Reardon 1989). This lack of story means that we have no characters or incidents to compare between Nineveh and Gondolin, whereas such a comparison is possible (and fruitful) with the Tale of Troy. Nor is there anything in the setting or appearance of Nineveh that matches what we are told about Gondolin. Like Babylon, Nineveh was a city of brick, fired or unfired; stone seems to have been mostly used indoors, since much of it was soluble gypsum. The low *tell* of Nineveh cannot compare with the high platform of Gondolin, nor are there any hills or mountains nearby. Sporadic excavation does not appear to have given us any clear plan of the city; no source available to the authors gives anything as basic as the number of gates, though the city was clearly walled - as were almost all cities pre-Industrial Age.

Most important of all, despite its position next to the Tigris, Nineveh was much less of a port than Babylon. Apart from the short Book of Jonah, no story connects Nineveh with the sea, and that biblical tale makes it quite clear that the voyage-episode has nothing to do with the city. Jonah is trying to head in the opposite direction, to Tarshish in the west, but has to turn back and go to Nineveh in obedience to God. Even given Tolkien's use of reversal to create new motifs, it would take some doing to convert this into the voyages of Eärendel; and it seems pointless to try when there are models which are clearly better as they stand. 'Occam's Razor', the principle of the simplest explanation being the best, works as well in literary criticism as it does in science. Nor does the reaction of the people of Nineveh, who repent when they hear Jonah's message, correspond to the refusal to heed a warning which is a major motif in the plot of the Tale of Gondolin and which *can* be matched in the Tale of Troy. Finally, like Babylon, Nineveh lies in an area which there is no reason to believe Tolkien was interested until the early 1940's. We can be certain Tolkien knew his Classics, since as we have pointed out, he was accepted at Oxford to study the subject as an undergraduate; we have no evidence for him taking an interest in Mesopotamia until the *Notion Club Papers* - and these are late in his career when the *Silmarillion* material had been worked out. So once again, Nineveh may have been famous in its destruction, but it does not resemble Gondolin in anything like enough ways to begin to challenge Troy as a source for the Tale of Gondolin.

II; Heart of the Empire

a; Rome

The problem of lack of story and characters for comparison with Tolkien's Gondolin surfaces immediately with Rome too. There have indeed been 'many takings' of the city, but none have generated any specific story that we could discover. Nor do any of the Falls of Rome correspond with the Fall of Gondolin. The occupation of Rome by Gauls under Brennus in 390 BC is an event whose historical nature is much debated by scholars. This certainly would not put Tolkien off, but there are other problems with it. The Gauls met the Romans in pitched battle eleven miles from the city and inflicted a huge defeat on them, one of the worst that Rome's forces would ever suffer. They then marched on the defenceless city, most of which was burnt; an archaeological destruction layer of broken tiles and burnt debris is often dated to this time. Possibly the fortress on the Capitol Hill held out; certainly the story of the faithful geese which cackled a warning of climbing Gauls while the dogs slept is pure invention. So too, probably, is the story of Brennus throwing his sword into the Gaulish side of the scales on which the city's ransom was being weighed out when the Romans quibbled. None of the famous stories about this event match anything in the Tale of Gondolin, and neither do any of the characters (Grant 1978, ch.3, p.44). Since as first written Gondolin was built and flourished after the Battle of Unnumbered Tears, the sequence of battle and immediately following sack at Rome can hardly be a match either. So this first recorded Fall of Rome will not do as an alternative to Troy as a source for the Tale of Gondolin.

Rome next succumbed all of eight hundred years later in 410 AD, to Alaric the Visigoth, an event which sent shockwaves throughout the western world. It should not have done; the successful siege was Alaric's third attempt, and he had twice been bought off. Rome could not afford a third payment and Alaric was in too precarious a political position to accept one even if the city had produced the cash. In actual fact, while the psychological impact was immense (the theory that abandoning the old gods and turning Christian had caused the disaster provoked Saint Augustine of Hippo to write one of the most influential books of western Christianity,*The City of God*) the practical effect was negligible. Rome was under siege for a short while, was taken on 24th August, and was then given over to the Gothic soldiery for three days. Loot and hostages were taken, some fires were started, and no doubt it was an exceedingly unpleasant experience for the Romans. Yet so far as we can tell, the city kept going exactly as it had before and the imperial regime was totally unaffected, as R. Collins points out:
'...in less than a year after the Sack of Rome, Honorius's forces sent from Italy were restoring imperial control in at least the southern part of Gaul... Whatever the psychological reverberations of the Visgothic looting of the Eternal City the imperial regime in Italy displayed remarkable resilience and activity once the threat of a barbarian domination of the state was lifted.' (Collins 1991, ch.4, p.57)
Not one single anecdote about the event appears to have survived; no-one at the time wrote poems on the subject; and if it inspired any modern writer, they were the sort whose works are obscure past easy retrieval. Beyond this, Tolkien's allegiances in that particular case might be expected to be split, since the attackers were speakers of a language he loved and found inspirational from the early days of his linguistic invention, Gothic. So, since it was practically ineffective and we can be fairly confident Tolkien's sympathies would be divided if not outright with the attackers, and since there is a total lack of associated story, the 410 AD Fall of Rome would appear to be a non-starter as far as comparison with Gondolin goes (Collins 1991, ch.4, p.55-7; Grant 1978, ch.20, p.326).

Attila the Hun in 452 AD marched into Italy, ravaged the Po Valley in the north and intended to advance on Rome. Pope Leo the first met him before he had moved out of the Po basin, and somehow persuaded him to back off. All manner of reasons from an epidemic in the Hun army to Leo pleading utter poverty and the inability of Rome to support or reward an invading army have been advanced; none really seems to account for Attila's retreat. He died the following year, making all arguments over what might have happened next irrelevant

(Collins 1991, ch.4, p.55-7; Grant 1978, ch.20, p.329). So Rome never did face an attack by the most thoroughgoing villain in the whole era of the Fall of the Western Empire, a man whose reputation has been comprehensively blackened. Unless, that is, like Tolkien you read medieval German and Scandinavian romances; in a number of them (including the well-known Nibelungenlied and the less familiar cycle of tales associated with Dietrich von Bern), Attila is portrayed as a noble ruler with a great court of heroes, a man almost on a par with King Arthur... (Gerritsen and Van Melles 1998, s.v. Attila). Huns may well have played a part in the formation of Tolkien's picture of Orcs; the 'black propaganda' against the Huns, from Late Roman writers to William Morris's romance *The Roots of the Mountains*, looks very orcish indeed. But for all the damage he did and all his terrible reputation (not wholly deserved; Attila didn't kill the Byzantine ambassador whom he discovered was plotting to have him murdered!) Attila the Hun never sacked any Western city in circumstances that generated much comment, let alone legend. So again, this is a dead-end in the search for possible sources for the Tale of Gondolin.

Next, the Vandals attacked Rome in 455 AD, after an agreement with the Western Empire was broken when the ruler with whom it had been made was murdered. A Vandal fleet sailed from North Africa, landed unopposed and took Rome without a blow being struck; apparently no attempt was made to defend the city. The Vandals were far more thorough than the Visigoths; they stayed for two weeks, extracting an immense plunder and carrying off thousands of captives (Collins 1991, ch.6, p.84-5; Grant 1978, ch.20, p.329). For all that, again there is a total lack of anything but the briefest of historical notices of this Fall of Rome, and again the city staggered back to its feet and carried on. So once more, there is nothing to compare with Tolkien's Tale of Gondolin.

There was not another really notable conquest and sack of Rome until 1527, which is much too late for it to be at all likely to have influenced Tolkien. To summarise the possible comparisons of Rome with Gondolin, the site - seven hills on two sides of a river - is wrong; the nature of the place as capital of an empire is wrong; there is no sign of any real or legendary organisation like the twelve lordships of Gondolin. The circumstances of all the sieges and sacks are wrong, and none of them had catastrophic consequences for the city. Nor did any of these incidents result in the flight of known refugees carrying information or stories. Also, none of them produced any story or characters which can be compared to the Tale of Gondolin, much less to the linked doublet of Gondolin/ Eärendel. Overall, then, it does not look at all likely that Rome could have been used as the model for Gondolin.

b; Constantinople

At first sight Constantinople looks like a much better comparison for Gondolin than does Rome. The fall of the capital of the Eastern Roman Empire was an ideologically charged conflict, with Muslim Turks on one side and Christian Greeks (and some Europeans) on the other, apparently matching the conflict between Melko/Morgoth's orcs and the Elves of Gondolin; the main reason for the fall of the city was the Turks' skilful use of artillery, which could be reinterpreted as fire-breathing dragons; the fall of the city led to a sack of appalling proportions, seeming quite the equal of 'the worst work of Melko'; it also led to the flight of many Greek scholars with their books, carrying a priceless cargo of Classical knowledge to Renaissance Italy. The lack of story could easily be counterbalanced by the greater detail of history, which gives real characters. Alas, all these good points are either outweighed by bad ones, or dissolve on closer examination.

For a start, Constantinople fell in 1453 AD, and it would be astonishing if something this late in date had inspired J.R.R. Tolkien. Nor is there any reason why Tolkien should have taken an interest in these events. During his lifetime, the Byzantine Empire was held up as a good example of how *not* to run a country in English historical studies (the word being used as an adjective to describe state bureaucracy run riot), and (despite Lord Byron and his romantic feelings for oppressed underdogs) modern Greece was often viewed as an unworthy heir to its Classical glories, a poor relation to northern European states. Indeed, in a letter of 1944 to his son Christopher (Letters, No.94) one can pick up a suggestion of this: 'And the great Greek states, esp. Athens at the time of its high art and power, were rather Dictatorships, if they were not military monarchies like Sparta! And modern Greece has as little connexion with ancient Hellas as we have with Britain before Julius Agricola...'

There would have to be very good reason indeed for Tolkien to take an interest in a part of history so disregarded, and we can find no such reason mentioned anywhere in his published works and correspondence, or any of the reliable biographies. By contrast, we know for certain that Tolkien knew his Classics inside out, since that was his original undergraduate course at Oxford and, unlike rich students, he had to win his place against stiff competition. There are also hints from letters that Tolkien was interested in the Minoans and thus in the archaeologically-attested historical background to any Trojan War. No such clear interest or even hints exists which would create a link to the Fall of Constantinople. The setting of Constantinople on a peninsula between the Sea of Marmara and the Golden Horn inlet is totally unlike that of Gondolin, with no mountains and no hill and citadel. Details such as the number of gates do not appear to match. The orcs/Turks link falls down in short order when we see that most people in what little was left of the Byzantine Empire at its end were more in favour of peace with the Turks, than of reconciliation with Western Europe. There was some hope of maintaining their cultural and religious independence as a 'client state' of the Ottomans, but the West wanted Byzantium to give up its Orthodox faith and act like a proper Catholic country, and had broken promises of military support more than once before. In fact, it was Western European armies which had first broken the walls of Constantinople, conquering and looting the city and empire in the redirected Fourth Crusade of 1204, so it was hardly surprising that Catholic Christendom was viewed with as much if not more distrust in Constantinople as the Turks. Above all, Constantinople was not destroyed by the Turks, but was restored, reinvented and renamed - it is now Istanbul - and went on to become the capital of the Ottoman Empire (Ostrogorsky 1968, ch.VIII, section 4).

The greater detail of history which we have for Constantinople does indeed provide us with characters, but not with anyone who can be compared to those who figure in Tolkien's story. The brave and tireless Emperor Constantine XI, who died in the fighting as the Turks broke through, bears no resemblance to Turgon of Gondolin, retreating to his tower and refusing to rule in the face of the siege and sack of his city. Again unlike Turgon, Constantine had no direct family, and those of his relatives who escaped (such as his niece who later married the Russian Tsar) were not involved in the siege (she and her father lived in the Peloponnese in southern Greece). Nor is there anyone who can be compared to characters like Tuor and Maeglin. The only major arrival before the fall of the city was the Genoese captain Giustiniani, who was not married to a Greek, arrived only weeks before the siege began in earnest, and died on the final night, fighting shoulder to shoulder with the Emperor - and therefore will not bear comparison to Tuor. So far as can be told, once the Turks began their blockade in earnest no-one escaped from Constantinople itself, Those who reached the West either fled earlier, or had come from outside the city, especially the Peloponnese where there had been something of a revival of Greek culture and learning. Thus these people cannot be compared to the survivors of Gondolin. Beyond this, no story or history of such a flight leading to great sea voyages or even long pilgrimages exists, even though coincidentally Constantinople only fell thirty-nine years before Columbus discovered America. Therefore, a Constantinople-inspired Gondolin would have no obvious or even obscure link to the Tale of Eärendel, whereas taking the line that Troy lies behind Gondolin does create a series of clear connections. So, overall, the few good points of comparison with Gondolin which Constantinople has to offer are much outweighed by the differences.

We have looked at three of the cities that Tolkien himself names in comparison to Gondolin, Nineveh, Babylon and Rome, and at one which thought of itself as a 'second Rome', Constantinople (now Istanbul). All four have proved to be dead ends. None of them explain anything like as many points about the Tale of Gondolin itself as the Trojan hypothesis does. Most of them have major negative factors that rule them out almost at once. Nor do any of them offer any way in which a story based on them could be linked to the Tale of Eärendel, which we know Tolkien was working on before he invented Gondolin, and again, the idea of influence from the Trojan legends in their medieval form offers precisely such a link. So thus far, the Trojan hypothesis is still by far the best candidate.

III; Other Possibilities

Two more cities are worth considering in some detail as possible rivals for Troy as a source for the Tale of Gondolin. These are Jerusalem and Carthage, the former a very important place for Christian European culture, the latter a city whose brutal destruction at the hands of the Romans would be known to anyone who studied the Classics as Tolkien did.

a; Jerusalem

Jerusalem is a city often destroyed and as often rebuilt, a place sacred to three religions which all entwine religion and politics; and therefore, it is cursed with a political importance that has brought disaster time and again. The Babylonians destroyed Jerusalem in 587 BC after the king of Judah made one political mistake too many; most of the population of the city and townlands were deported to Babylon. From 537 BC onwards under the Persian Empire, a painfully slow rebuilding and repopulation took place. By the second century BC, Jerusalem was caught up in international Hellenistic Greek politics. The Seleucid kings of Syria initially made a peaceful takeover, but were confronted with political, cultural and religious intransigence on the part of the Jews. In 169 BC, what began as riot-control ended with the city being nearly destroyed. It was not rebuilt while the ensuing Maccabean Revolt lasted. After this, there was a brief period of peace under the Hasmonean dynasty, descended from the last of the Maccabees.

The Romans captured Jerusalem not once but several times over. In 63 BC, one side in a Jewish civil war called for Roman help, leading to the appearance of Pompey the Great and his army before the walls of Jerusalem. Relatively little damage was done because the people of the city were split between the two factions, and one side opened the gates; the Temple Mount was held by the other side and suffered a full-scale siege and sack. Local politics led to two sieges and sacks in short order thereafter, the first and less destructive in 40 BC when the Hasmonean prince Mattathias Antigonus reclaimed the throne of Judea from Herod, the son of the ruler whom Pompey had left in place, the second and far more serious one shortly afterwards in 37 BC, when Herod (father of the New Testament Herod) reclaimed Judea with Roman help. A far more thorough destruction took place in 70 AD (nine years before the massive eruption of Vesuvius that destroyed Pompeii and Herculaneum) when the city was laid waste and the Second Temple destroyed by the Romans under Titus son of Vespasian; this was during the First Jewish Revolt of 69-73 AD. Slow rebuilding thereafter took place until 130 AD, when the Emperor Hadrian visited the area. Finding Judea still restive under Roman rule and far more religiously rigid than the Jewish Diaspora, Hadrian responded with a mixture of anti-monotheist measures and moves designed to promote Romanisation; of the latter, the most important was the planned conversion of Jerusalem into a Roman colony. This led to a ferociously-fought and equally ferociously suppressed revolt in 132-5 AD, led by Bar Kochba, who was backed by the greatest Jewish scholar of the day, Rabbi Akiba. After the fall of Jerusalem, Hadrian levelled the site and built a new city named Aelia Capitolina, of determinedly Graeco-roman culture and religion.

The next major disaster was another Persian attack by a completely different dynasty in 614 AD (seventeen years after St Augustine landed in Kent), when the mostly Christian population of Jerusalem were foolish enough to accept terms and then rebel spectacularly, massacring the Persian garrison and the Jews of the city. Returning, the Persian army broke in after a month-long siege; three days later, hardly a building in Jerusalem was left standing, the most important Christian holy relics were seized as spoils, and most of the population was killed. Rebuilding began under Persian occupation and was continued when the city was peacefully returned to Byzantine control in 629 AD. Jerusalem had however barely begun to recover when Islam exploded onto the international scene as the faith of a seemingly unstoppable army of Arabs. The city was besieged, but negotiations led to a peaceful surrender. In 1099 the next major event took place, the capture of Jerusalem by the Crusaders; there seems to have been little physical damage, but there was a serious massacre. Just under a hundred years later in 1187 Salah ad-Din appeared before the city with his army, but the city surrendered twelve days later. This was the last occasion before the First World War when Jerusalem was in any sense in the front line of military action; and in 1917, the city surrendered without resistance to the British, whose commander General Allenby chose to walk into the city as a gesture of humility. This last event can be discounted as influencing Tolkien in regards to Gondolin as he had by then conceived of his city.

As we have seen, several of the destructions of Jerusalem were followed by long periods of near-desertion, so the continuing existence of the city is not by itself grounds to reject it as a possible source for Gondolin. Nor is religion a barrier, even though since the state of Israel was founded, there has been much slanting of history to emphasise the Jewishness of Jerusalem (as in Kolley and Pearlman 1968). Firstly, when Tolkien first invented Gondolin, the Western European picture of Jerusalem was primarily as a Christian city. Secondly, Tolkien himself seems to have been free of anti-Jewish prejudice in any case. The following quote comes from a letter sent to Stanley Unwin on 25th July 1938. A German translation of 'The Hobbit' was being negotiated for, and the German publishers wrote to Tolkien asking if he was of 'arisch'/Aryan origin. This was necessary for them because at that time, publishing a book by someone of Jewish descent would have led to the book's being banned and the company concerned receiving serious censure. Tolkien was seriously unhappy about receiving such a request, as his comments to Sir Stanley Unwin reveal;

'Personally I should be inclined to refuse to give any *Bestatigung* (although it happens that I can), and let a German translation go hang. In any case I should object strongly to any such declaration appearing in print. I do not regard the (probable) absence of all Jewish blood as necessarily honourable; and I have many Jewish friends, and should regret giving any colour to the notion that I subscribed to the wholly pernicious and unscientific race-doctrine.'

('Letters', no. 29)

So neither the course of Jerusalem's history nor its religious associations would prevent Tolkien using it as a source.

What does conclusively rule Jerusalem out is the lack of any series of incidents or characters connected with any of the destructions of the city which can be compared to the Gondolin story in the way that the Trojan story can. To select a few examples, Maeglin's treachery is at once more thoroughgoing (in the BOLT version) and less so (in the *Silmarillion* versions) than that of the city-dwellers who opened the gates of Jerusalem to Pompey. The prophetic warnings of what could happen to Jerusalem when faced with the Assyrians and Babylonians focus on religion, ethics and morals, not political or military action, as in Ulmo's recommendations to Turgon; and importantly, those warnings are the work of men believed to be inspired by a single all-powerful god, not a semi-deity with defined responsibilities. None of the stories feature the escape of a family, and the propagation of both knowledge and actions through that family; Tuor, Idril and Eärendil have no counterparts in any story of a Fall of Jerusalem. Since in the *Orendel* romance, Jerusalem is specifically said to survive, it cannot make the Eärendel/Gondolin link, which requires a city to fall and refugees to take to sea-voyaging. So, even by selecting incidents from various Falls of Jerusalem, it is not possible to find a match for the Gondolin story associated with this city. Therefore, Jerusalem cannot be a source for Tolkien's tale.

b; Carthage

The Phoenician city of Carthage (now in Tunisia in North Africa, close to the capital Tunis) was founded in the late 8th century BC as a colony from the Near Eastern city of Tyre, intended to control the western sea-routes to the rich metal deposits of Spain, Sardinia and Etruscan Italy, and the agricultural riches of Sicily and coastal North Africa. Carthage gradually freed itself from its ties to the mother-city Tyre, and developed a considerable realm of its own. Position and interests meant that Carthage and Rome were on an almost inevitable collision-course. In the First Punic War (264-241 BC), Carthage was conclusively defeated; in the Second (218-205 BC, most famous for the Italian campaign of the Spanish-Carthaginian commander Hannibal and his crossing of the Alps with elephants) initial successes were followed by grinding attrition and finally, defeat in North Africa itself. The Third Punic War of 150-146 BC saw the destruction of Carthage (a demolition so comprehensive that the levelled ruins were sown with salt to prevent anything worthwhile growing there, although a great deal remained underneath for archaeologists to find).

One reason why Tolkien might *not* take an interest in Carthage can be conclusively demolished at once. The Phoenicians were a people to whom all the bad characteristics foisted onto modern European Jews could readily be attributed, living at a time when real Jews could not be attacked because they were in the middle of writing the Old Testament, an integral part of Christianity and thus European culture. As a result, the Phoenicians were on the receiving end of much pseudohistorical hysteria from late 19th and early 20th century writers, both academic and popular. As we have already seen, Tolkien's own words make it certain that he was no anti-Semite, and therefore he would be highly unlikely to be anti-Phoenician. Furthermore, anti-Phoenicianism was never as common or as virulent in the British Isles - for whom the 'tin-trading Phoenicians' represented an important connection to the Biblical and Classical worlds - as in some other European countries. So on both personal and general grounds, Tolkien *could* have taken an interest in Carthage. He might also have done so from a philological basis, examining the possible influences of the Semitic languages (of which Phoenician is one) upon the Indo-European languages; a notion beset with major controversy in the philological community at the time.

The problem is that there is absolutely no evidence that Tolkien did so. There is no evidence of any 'Semitic' component in any of his languages until the 1940's and Adunaic. At that point it is fairly clear that firstly, it is Akkadian that is involved, the language of Babylon and Assyria, not Phoenician or any closely related tongue; and secondly, that this unusual material appears for a good reason in connection with Númenor and the Atlantis legend. There is no mention anywhere, in Tolkien's letters or in reliable biographies, of him taking an interest in North Africa, Carthage, the Phoenicians or the Near East, at a date before the writing of *The Fall of Gondolin*. Turning to Carthage itself, the setting is not implausibly far out for a match to Gondolin (certainly no worse than Troy). However, there is no tale of survivors fleeing from Carthage (those who lived through the siege and sack were enslaved); neither Carthage, the victim, nor Rome, the aggressor, were monarchies; the provocation of the Third Punic war was straightforwardly political without even lip-service to any oracle or warning from the gods on either side; the specific causes of the fall of the city were all wrong (it was starved until unable to defend itself and only then taken by assault); and there are no parallel characters or incidents on either side of the fight. Indeed, the Carthaginians are mere ciphers in the surviving accounts of the war. It is a point well worth mentioning that of all the falls and sacks of famous cities discussed here, only Troy was eventually to have a history written by the losers - an idea which is absolutely central to *The Fall of Gondolin*.

So, once again we have seen that possible alternatives fail to fit the bill as a source for *The Fall of Gondolin*. Carthage falls on its inappropriate government, its lack of survivors, and its lack of characters and incidents paralleling those of Gondolin.

c; Any Other candidates?

Could some more obscure event be a possible source for the Fall of Gondolin? It appears unlikely to the authors that this could be the case. For this to be even a remote possibility, a number of criteria would have to be satisfied. Firstly, it has to be possible that J.R.R. Tolkien would have known of the event. Secondly, it has to be likely that Tolkien would have been interested in it. So far as our knowledge of Tolkien goes, that practically rules out any city not in geographical Europe or North Africa - that is, west of the Urals-Caucasus-Zagros line, and north of the Sahara. India and Iran, as areas where Indo-European languages are spoken, might be exceptions to this rule, but it would need unequivocal evidence of interest from Tolkien in the place and event concerned before such an idea could be introduced, evidence which so far we do not have. Thirdly, the event concerned has to have happened at a time in which Tolkien is either likely to have taken an interest, or for which, again, there is new and unequivocal evidence. Broadly, this means that anyone supporting an event from 1000-1500 AD would have to work hard to prove their case, and any falls of cities dating to after 1500 can practically be ruled out.

Fourthly, the event being put forward as a source has to provide explanations for more events, descriptions and characters in *The Fall of Gondolin* than does our 'Trojan source' hypothesis in order to supplant it. It also has to provide as many points of connection to the 'Eärendel' material as that hypothesis does, and to provide a reason why Tolkien would have used that particular event when *The Fall of Gondolin* was written. So far, we are aware of nothing that could fit these criteria sufficiently well to challenge let alone supplant the hypothesis that one major source for *The Fall of Gondolin* was the Tale of Troy.

IV: Conclusions

We have looked a number of cities whose history might be taken as making them potential sources for Tolkien's story *The Fall of Gondolin.* Three are cities which Tolkien himself named in that story; Rome, Babylon and Nineveh. Three more are famous cities which for various reasons might be considered relevant; Constantinople/Istanbul, the 'Second Rome'; Jerusalem, the most famous city in Judeo-Christian culture; and Carthage, whose involvement with the Romans ensured that it would be known to generations of Classics scholars. Some of these cities have a few points at which their story either does parallel that of Gondolin, or could be argued to do so. None, however, has anything like the sheer number of points of comparison which exist between Troy and Gondolin. Nor do any of these cities provide a clear set of connections which could create the overarching pattern of the Gondolin-Earendel pair of stories as set up by Tolkien, whereas Troy does. Again, none of the cities considered here has a history or story which can both be proved to be known to J.R.R. Tolkien, and which he would have reason to use as the basis for a new story in the particular circumstances of 1916. We have also considered if any less-well-known city might be relevant. None appears to be, but we have in any case set up a list of criteria which would have to be fulfilled for any such example to warrant serious consideration. After this consideration of alternatives, it still looks certain to us that Troy and the Trojan legend, especially in its medieval European form, was an extremely important source for Tolkien's Tale of Gondolin.

There is a further point to be made here - that of the re-use of the same material in *The Lord of the Rings* to establish Minas Tirith. When cross-referenced in this fashion with the Gondolin information, Troy comes out as pretty well the only possible match with Tolkien's cities that circle around the number seven.

Chapter Eight:

Eärendil's Fellow Voyagers.

The character of Eärendil in Tolkien's works represents one of the most complex, frustrating and fascinating studies that one can find in all the writings. Christopher Tolkien tells us:
'The matter is complicated, however, as will be seen in a moment, by my father's also making the *Nauglafring* the first part of the *Tale of Eärendel.*
But the great tale was never written; and for the story as he then conceived it we are wholly dependent on highly condensed and often contradictory outlines. There are also many isolated notes; and there are the very early Eärendel poems. While the poems can be precisely dated, the notes and outlines can not; and it does not seem possible to arrange them in order so as to provide a clear line of development.' (BOLT vol.II, ch.5, p.252)
The version that appears in the *Silmarillion* is a condensed and rather unsatisfactory account; the voyages only account for a page and a half and the arrival in Valinor and enthronement on the ship in the sky a further two and a half pages. Seeing as Christopher Tolkien described this as a 'great tale' above, we are clearly missing much:
' 'It is a mighty tale, and seven times shall folk fare to the Tale-fire ere it be rightly told; and so twined is it with those stories or the Nauglafring and of the Elf-march that I would fain have aid in that telling...'
If the six parts following the Tale of the Nauglafring were each to be of comparable length, the whole Tale of Eärendel would have been somewhere near half the length of all the tales that were in fact written; but my father never afterwards returned to it on any ample scale.' (ibid, p.252-3)
We have calculated that the length of all the tales that were written is some two hundred and sixty six pages of text. Half of this would come to one hundred and thirty three pages. By the other calculation, if Nauglafring at twenty pages is one seventh of the whole Eärendel tale's length, then in total it would come to one hundred and forty pages. This is amazingly close correspondence and just shows what a 'great tale' Eärendel might have been had it been tackled in ample scale.

In this chapter we shall examine the connections from the medieval world of literature to the character that became Eärendil. This will range widely, and consider the analogues to both Eärendel and Elwing, touches on their offspring, and includes a study of the ship Vingilot upon which he sailed to Valinor and thence among the stars in the heavens. In our long and complex journey, we shall be going to Denmark and the North Sea, Ireland, Iceland and the Atlantic Ocean crossing towards America, the Adriatic, Aegean and the Black Seas, and the Arabian and Indian Oceans and the South China Seas. Truly Eärendel can be said to have led us like a 'Merry Mariner' upon a voyage right around the world.

I: Eärendel & His Philological Cousins

a: Return to Orendel

Returning to the hero Eärendil, under the heading 'Orendel', Gerritsen and Van Melles 1998 cite a number of references. Setting aside the possibly 12th-century romance of *Orendel*, which was discussed in relation to the story of Tuor in Chapter 4, what they have to say runs as follows;

'The appendix to the Strassburg Heldenbuch (15th century) names King 'Erentheil' of Trier as the earliest of the heroes. Saxo Grammaticus in his *Gesta Danorum* (c.1200) mentions one 'Horwendillus' as the father of 'Amlethus' (=Hamlet). The name is also found as a personal name among the Lombards ('Auriwandalo') and in Old High German ('Orentil'). Partly because of this, it has been thought that there must have existed an older epic about a hero called Orendel. The king's name has been linked to the Old English word 'earendel' (daybreak, morning star, beam of light') and with the Old Norse 'Aurvandill', the name of a semi-mythical figure. This, however, is extremely problematic.'

Gerritsen and van Melle cite two earlier works that discuss 'Orendel' in detail; an edition of the poem printed in Darmstad in 1976 by W.J. Schröder, 'Spielmannsepen vol.II, Sankt Oswald, Orendel, Salman und Morolf'; and a study by Michael Curschmann, printed in Stuttgart in 1968, 'Spielmannsepik: Wege und Ergebnisse der Forschung von 1907 bis 1965'. The latter reference suggests that much of the discussion of 'Orendel' goes back to a point in time where it could have influenced Tolkien. Parts of this material have already been amply discussed in connection to the Tale of Tuor, but it is well worth going over the ground again in this context to see how different aspects of the story emerge in Tolkien's account of Eärendil.

Setting aside the question of dates, Gerritsen and van Melles' other remarks have a fair amount to offer in themselves. The 15th-century German Strassburg 'Heldenbuch' to which they refer is one of a number of compilations of heroic tales made around this date, which often preserve the sole surviving copies of much earlier material. The writer of the Foreword (not Appendix, judging by the ref. in Gillespie 1973) to the Strassburg 'Heldenbuch' almost certainly made a closer association between his 'Ernthelle' or 'Erentheil' of Trier and the 'Orendel' of the romance than Gerritsen and van Melle seem to realise. We can say this because the wife of Ernthelle is called Brigida, the full form of the Irish name which also appears in short form as Brîde, the name of Orendel's princess (a name which was adopted into German use from the 8th century onwards according to Gillespie 1973, who also provides the link between the two women under s.v. Brigida). The 'Heldenbuch's listing of 'King Erentheil of Trier' as the earliest of the heroes connects neatly with the Classical belief that the Trojan War marked the start of 'history' in the sense of being the first securely recorded and datable event (as noted by E.J. Kenney in his Introduction to Ovid/Melville 1986, p.XXVI note 21). Nobody before the generation that took part in the Trojan War could be safely regarded as a real or a fully human person; too little was known about them. This also explains why Tolkien placed Eärendil's story at the end of the First Age in all the versions from *The Book of Lost Tales* to the 1977 *Silmarillion*. However much Tolkien altered and developed the chronology of his stories, the Gondolin/Eärendil story marks a fundamental change in the type of events being told. It is the last tale set in the 'Elder Days', when the Valar and the Elves were more important than Men. In *The Book of Lost Tales* and the following versions up until the 1930 *Quenta Noldorinwa* there is *much less time* between the end of the First Age and the beginning of recorded history than is the case later in Tolkien's writings, and especially after the writing of LotR. In our first book (Lewis and Currie 2002, 'Uncharted Realms'), it was pointed out that Tolkien during the writing of the Appendices to LotR extended each Age of the Sun to last for approximately three thousand years. Therefore, in the 'framework' of the early versions, names from the very end of the First Age could be expected to be remembered with greater accuracy and to appear in real rather than feigned legend. Later, Eärendil still retains his position as chronological marker, even if only for a change of Age in a more complex picture. At this early stage, Tolkien would not have foreseen the Second Age and the history of Númenor, much less the Third Age and the history of the Rings, as periods of time separating the era of Eärendil and Gondolin from the start of recorded history at the time when the Dominion of Men began.

The medieval German romance of *Orendel* also suggests that its hero, like Tolkien's Eärendil, is only half human. G.T. Gillespie points out that 'In *Orendel* (12th cent.?) the hero's father is named *Ougel* .' (Gillespie 1973 s.v. Eugel). This name occurs only once elsewhere, in the late 'Lied vom hürnen Seyfrid' (Song of Scaly Siegfried), where Eugel/Ougel is the name of a dwarf who is nonetheless the son of the human Nibelunc, and so the brother of the luckless princes who run foul of Siegfried and lose their treasure, lands and lives to him. Defeated by Siegfried, Eugel is spared and helps him to conquer the dragon of the Trachenstein mountain; but the dwarf loses the treasure that rightfully belongs to him and his kin, which they hid when the dragon first arrived, only to have it find the gold and lair atop it. This is a faint link but it does suggest the possibility of Orendel/ Eärendil being not wholly human. The story of Ougel and Siegfried hints at Túrin's interaction with the dwarf Mîm. It also prefigures the tale of Nargothrond when Hurin comes to find the lair of Glaurung where the treasure is piled, and *The Hobbit* where Smaug is resident at the Lonely Mountain.

b: A Quest Shipwrecked

Orendel is shipwrecked whilst sailing to the Holy Land to search for his princess. By comparison, in the BOLT version of the Tale of Eärendel, shipwreck plays a major part but in a by-now familiar pattern, the cause of Eärendel's voyages has been inverted - rather than searching for his wife, the early travels are apparently undertaken in search of his father and not Elwing (as she is dead in the early versions - i.e. Scheme B). There appears to be an influence from The Odyssey in this part of the story, for Telemachus goes looking for news of his father Odysseus:

'But now let me have a rapid ship and a crew of twenty to make the voyage out and back; I mean to go to Sparta and sandy Pylos to seek for news of my father's homecoming he has been away from us too long.' (Odyssey, Shewring, 1980, Book II, p.17)

Later in the Scheme C BOLT version Eärendil is searching for his wife, and they are already married rather than him being in quest of a bride as is Orendel - here she has dived into the sea to escape Melko and his orcs. At this point, she had the Nauglafring though it is lost together with the Silmaril when she turns into a sea-bird. Presumably, in this version, this Silmaril finds its long home in the sea. (BOLT Vol. II, ch,5, pps.252-5)

'Eärendel departs all the same and is wrecked by the treachery of Osse and saved only by the Oarni (who love him) with Voronwë and dragged to Falasquil.'

The Oarni are mermaids/ sea-nymphs. (ibid, p.254)

Odysseus himself is also shipwrecked in his journeys - brought to grief by Poseidon who hates him for blinding the Cyclops, but is saved by Calypso - a nymph-goddess, daughter of Atlas. (Odyssey, Shewring, 1980, Book V, p.56)

c: 'What is woman that you forsake her?' - Eärendil's family

There are three possible influences on Tolkien's depiction of the fate of Eärendil's family whilst he is away at sea. Firstly, there is Saxo Grammaticus's reference to 'Horwendillus' as the father of 'Amlethi'/Hamlet which may be reflected in Tolkien's depiction of Eärendil's troubled family life, with his wife and sons suffering deprivations while he is away at sea. Secondly, there is the episode in the 13th-century Norse story *Thidhrekssaga*, where the giant Vadi (Wade), son of a king and a sea-spirit, apprentices his son Velent to two dwarf smiths, who are more skilful than any human smith and the best in the whole world at smithing iron. They become jealous of Velent when they see how good a pupil he is and plot to kill him if Vadi does not collect the boy on the agreed day. Vadi does not arrive, having been killed in a landslide on the way there, but he has already hidden a sword for Velent to use at need. When Velent realises his father is dead, he takes the sword, kills both dwarfs, and escapes with their treasure and his tools (E.B. Haymes 1988, The Saga of Thidrek of Bern, Garland; section 57-61 p.40-2). It is worth noting that the Fëanorians are renowned for their skill in smithcraft, just as the dwarves are - and that it is one of the sons of Fëanor who befriends and fosters the sons of Eärendil. A third possible influence is, again, the Odyssey, and the troubles that Penelope and Telemachus faced whilst Odysseus was embroiled in his long return from Troy.

The trials and tribulations of the sons of Eärendel with the Fëanorians are not mentioned in BOLT vol. II. The people who attack the Havens are the forces of Melko in those versions - and indeed Eärendel has no children at this point. In a note, Christopher Tolkien cites his father as writing:

'Eārendel weds Elwing before he sets sail. When he hears of her loss he says that his children shall be "all such men hereafter as dare the great seas in ships".'

(BOLT vol. II, ch.5, p.264)
In the later versions of this story in *The Silmarillion*, Eärendil's distant kinsmen Maedhros and Maglor take the 'Hamlet's Uncle' role and bring up Eärendil's sons Elros and Elrond:
'Great was the sorrow of Eärendil and Elwing for the ruin of the havens of Sirion, and the captivity of their sons, and they feared that they would be slain; but it was not so. For Maglor took pity upon Elros and Elrond, and he cherished them, and love grew after between them, as little might be thought; but Maglor's heart was sick and weary with the burden of the dreadful oath.' (QS, ch.24, p.298)

II: Wade

It is sometimes thought that there is a significant connection between the mysterious medieval legendary character Wade, and J.R.R. Tolkien's Eärendil. Two early discussions mention Wade in connection with Tolkien's writing. The first is Tom Shippey in 'The Road to Middle-earth', where he says:
'Who is the powerfully described 'Man of the Sea' in the passage discussed above? Clearly one answer is Ulmo, the sea-god of Tolkien's mythology, as is hinted in BLT 2, 319-20. But another answer must be that he is 'Wade', the mythical sea-giant dimly mentioned in the furthest reaches of Old English tradition and still remembered by Chaucer but otherwise entirely forgotten*.'
*The original Note 3 refers the reader to R.M. Wilson's *Lost Literature of Medieval England.* (Shippey 1992 ch.9, p.271)
This links Wade and Ulmo, but says nothing about Eärendil. How by this reasoning is he connected to Wade?

Secondly and far more importantly there is C.J.R. Tolkien, commenting on a fragment of verse in *The Lays of Beleriand* :
'The reading of line 7 as first written (it was not struck out, but *Tûr the earthborn was tried in battle* was added in the margins:

But Wade of the Helsings wearyhearted

is remarkable. It is taken directly from the very early Old English poem *Widsith*, where occurs the line *Wada Hælsingum*, sc. *Wada [weold] Hælsingum*, 'Wada ruled the Hælsingas'. One may well wonder why the mysterious figure of Wade should appear here in Tuor's place, and indeed I cannot explain it; but whatever the reason, the association of Wade with Tuor is not casual.' (*Lays of Beleriand*, HOME III, Part II section 2, p.143)
After explaining something of the very obscure evidence for Wade and his story, C.J.R. Tolkien goes on to say:
'Most interesting, however, is the fact that in Speght's annotations to Chaucer (1598) he said:

> Concerning Wade and his bote *Guingelot*, as also his strange exploits in the same, because the matter is long and fabulous, I passe it over.

The likeness of *Guingelot* to *Wingelot* is sufficiently striking; but when we place together the facts that *Wingelot* was Eärendel's ship*, that Eärendel was Tuor's son, that Tuor was peculiarly associated with the sea, and that here 'Wade of the

Helsings' stands in the place of Tuor, coincidence is ruled out. *Wingelot* was derived from Wade's boat *Guingelot* as certainly, I think, as was Eärendel from the Old English figure (this latter being a fact expressly stated by my father, II. 309).

Why my father should have intruded 'Wade of the Helsings' into the verses at this point is another question. It may conceivably have been unintentional... this possibility in no way diminishes the demonstrative value of the line that *Wingelot* was derived from *Guingelot*, and that there was a connection of greater significance than the mere taking over of a name - just as in the case of Eärendel. *In which he undertook 'fabulous exploits'. It is conceivable that there was some connection between Eärendel's great world-girdling voyage and the travels of Wade as described by the 12th-century English writer Walter Map, who tells how *Gado* (sc.Wade) journeyed in his boat to the furthest Indies.' (ibid., p.144)

We have explored this possible link between Wade and Eärendel as thoroughly as we can in order to satisfy ourselves that no line of enquiry has been omitted, but as shall be shown, this specific link becomes both less likely and less significant as the investigation progresses, whereas the Tuor connection does appear to hold some importance, as we have mentioned in Chapter Four.

a; The Medieval Evidence

What R.M. Wilson actually says of Wade (in the first chapter of his book) is that references to him are commoner in Middle English sources than either earlier or later. Wilson also points out that many Continental mentions of this character are also from high or even late medieval rather than early medieval works. At this time Wade was also linked with other characters of Northern European legend. In the probably mid-13th-century Norse work *Thidrek's Saga af Bern*, (Haymes 1988, Garland), for example, Wade/Vadhi is the son of King Vilkinus and a sea-wife or mermaid, and the father of Weland/Velent. As far as the surviving evidence goes, the medieval Wade had two major facets to his reputation. Firstly, Wade had a reputation as a great warrior. He appears in this guise in the middle section of the early 13th-century German romance *Kudrun*, and in the Arthurian legends, where Wade appears as a standard of valour and prowess not only in the alliterative *Morte Arthure* (in the episode of the Giant of Mont St. Michael), but also in Malory (bk7, ch.9). This was an addition by the printer and publisher Caxton and so editions based on the manuscript rather than the printed book will not have this reference. Secondly, Wade is associated with love-trickery, as in Chaucer's *Troilus and Criseyde* and in 'The Merchant's Tale' in the *Canterbury Tales*. There were also a number of minor associations of Wade. In the first third of *Kudrun*, he has as much power to heal as to wound. The Middle English romance *Bevis of Hamton* links Wade with Bevis as both are dragonslayers. His name appears in a list of notable fictional heroes (with whom the true tale of Troy is contrasted) in the *Laud Troy Book* . Wade is said to be in 'Elvelond' in a fourteenth-century Latin work of uncertain nature, the *Fasciculus Morum* where he is linked with Unwen son of Eastgota (all R.M. Wilson 1970, ch.1). None of these attributes of Wade have any bearing that we can see on either of Tolkien's characters, Eärendil and Ulmo.

b; Lord of the Waves

The idea of Wade as a sea-giant or sea-god comparable to Tolkien's Ulmo probably goes back to R.W. Chamber's 1912 book on the Old English poem *Widsith*. Although this piece says firmly that 'Wada ruled the Helsings' and contains no other definitely mythological as opposed to legendary figure, Chambers interprets the scanty evidence in mythological terms. He forgets that Wade comes from the southern North Sea, where - unlike Scandinavia and Iceland - myth survives only if attached to later heroes. Already when Chambers wrote, it was beginning to be accepted that Arthur (to take only one example) was a real man who had inherited parts of the myths once attached to the Celtic god Lugos - myths that could only survive in a Christian world if they were recycled and therefore neutralised. To regard a figure like Wade as a one-time deity without clear evidence, when this is intrinsically unlikely and so much material has been lost (where are the legends of Hengist or the tales of Ida the Burner? Who now can tell of the deeds of Penda of the March?), is somewhat dubious to say the least of it.

The idea of Wade as a giant appears to owe much to modern Northern English folklore. 'Wade and his wife Bell' were apparently held responsible for many landscape features around Whitby in North Yorkshire, and a number of familiar tales were told of them - how they built two castles, tossing their only hammer back and forth; how Bell's apron-strings gave way while she was carrying stones, creating moorland cairns; how Wade built a road, raising mounds, digging hollows and laying paving, in order to help his wife milk their gigantic cow, whose rib was once proudly displayed by a local gentry family (www.mysteriousbritain.co.uk).

A number of standing stones in the same district are still called Wade's Stone, and there were once more of them. The 'pebble' which Wade and Bell's equally enormous son tossed at his mother to get her attention was dented when it struck her, and the enormous boulder with its inexplicable hollow on one side was pointed out on Sleights Moor until broken up for roadstone in the 19th century (www.northernearth.co.uk). All of this is late and general - the sort of stories which can be attached to almost anyone from Arthur downwards. None of it should be taken as any evidence for Anglo-saxon myth or legend about Wade.

The evidence for Wade as a sailor is only found in the 15th-century works of Chaucer. By then Wade and his boat were evidently proverbial, but given the considerable development and change in many figures of early legend who survived as characters in medieval story, it is exceedingly dangerous to project this concept backwards. Criticism of all these points has a long history, so there is good reason to think that J.R.R. Tolkien could have taken a very cautious attitude to the evidence for Wade as a 'sea-giant'. There is also another source for a sea-god figure which could well have affected the picture of Ulmo - but more of that later.

c; The Name of the Ship

The only clear link between Wade and Eärendil is the name of Wade's boat, Guingelot, which with the common medieval gu/w alternation (think of French Guillaume versus William) is virtually the same as Tolkien's Vingilot. However, we rapidly run into trouble on closer inspection. The name is mentioned only by Chaucer's 16th-century editor Thomas Speght in the famous quote: 'Concerning Wade and his bote called Guingelot, as also his strange exploits in the same, because the matter is long and fabulous I passe it over.' This name actually appears in two different forms. G.T. Gillespie (1973, note 10 on p.138) has: 'The name Gringalet given to Wade's boat by Speght in his edition of Chaucer's works in 1598 is that of Gawain's horse: this horse-name occurs in O[ld] Fr[ench] in the 12th cent[ury]., and is probably of Celtic origin; cf Cymric gwyngalet, 'white-hard' (Flutre, 97)

The reference is to the formidably-titled *Table des noms propres avec toutes leurs variantes figurant dans les romans du Moyen Age écrits en français ou en provençal et actuellement publiés ou analysés* of Louis-Fernand Flutre, Poitiers 1962. This should not be taken as the earliest publication of the point in question. Since Flutre was working from published pieces, there is a good chance that the *Guingelot/Gringalet* connection could have been spotted by someone writing early enough for Tolkien to pick it up. In the Welsh 'Triads', Gawain's horse is usually called Meingalet but in the Black Book of Carmarthen version, the horse is named Kein Caled and 'This is the original of Guingalet, Gringolet, the famous horse of Gawain in the French romances...' (Bromwich 1961 no's 46 & 42, note c). It is highly probable that information about the name of Gawain's horse would be in J. Rhys and J.G. Evans, 'The Text of the Mabinogion and Other Welsh Tales from the Red Book of Hergest', Oxford 1887, which includes the Triads.

All of this has two consequences. Firstly, why did Speght give this name for Wade's boat in the first place? Is he really a trustworthy witness to traditions about Wade; or is he working from a source (such as an Arthurian romance) which had already gotten confused as to who owned what and the names of the animal or object concerned; or did he know that Wade's boat had a name, failed to remember the right one and substituted the first suitable name that came to mind? Secondly, does any of this affect Tolkien's use of this name? It is probably impossible to answer any of these questions in the current state of the evidence, but the questions are worth setting down. What we can say is that the various medieval forms are all close to but not identical with Tolkien's versions. In BOLT vol. II, Eärendel has two ships - Earum/Earámë (meaning eagle-pinion), which is wrecked on one of Eärendel's northern voyages, and then he builds Wingelot/Vingilot with which he sails to Valinor, and which is hallowed and set to sail in the skies. In *The Silmarillion* Eärendil only has one ship, Vingilot and Eärrámë (meaning sea-wing) is Tuor's ship.

Just to confuse matters further, in the 13th-century Scandinavian *Thidhreks Saga af Bern*, it is Velent/Wayland, the son of Vadi/Wade, who has the marvellous boat, a veritable submarine constructed from a tree-trunk and equipped with glass portholes which carries him, his treasure and his tools to safety overseas after he has killed the treacherous dwarfs who meant to murder him before he could leave them and display the skills in which he, the apprentice, surpassed them, the masters. (Haymes 1988, section 61, p.42)

In the matter of names, then, the jury is out. The coincidence is remarkable, but even if Wade's boat did lend its name to Eärendil's ship, this is a very slight connection leading to an area of medieval storytelling which appears appears to have been otherwise unused by J.R.R. Tolkien.

d; Walter Map and Wade

One possible link between Wade and Eärendil which is worth looking into is found in the account of the 12th-century writer Walter Map, where Wade/Gado is the hero who returns beyond all hope, just in the nick of time, to save a British kingdom from invasion. However, if we actually look at the story, it does not resemble Tolkien's tales of Eärendil at all. Gado is not British, but 'the son of the king of the Vandals', a Germanic people nowhere to be found in Tolkien's work whether as themselves or in fictional guise. A great hunter and fighter, speaker of many languages (though with only 'a sufficient knowledge of letters'), Gado 'was reputed to know everything, and though a whole mass of armed men could hardly withstand the sword of his right hand, he was an eminent lover and defender of peace, and went about the world taking part in every notable contest, yet always inquiring into the claims of both sides, so that he might be the putter down of wrong and the champion of right.'

This singularly competent and scrupulous knight-errant is very far indeed from Tolkien's voyaging messenger. Eärendil is specifically half-elven from *The Book of Lost Tales* onwards, but Gado is explicitly of pure human blood:

'Though not a monster himself like Hercules, in gigantic height, nor like Achilles, by fairy descent, he deserves to be no less exalted than they; nay, he seems even to have excelled them in worth and strength.'

In the actual structure of the story, Gado's first visit to Britain is accidental; he befriends the King, Offa; he leaves for India in response to a plea for help; the Roman emperor, Offa's father-in-law, promptly hatches a long-planned plot and invades Britain; Gado comes to the rescue and solves the problem after one small battle. Theoretically, knowing that Tolkien's favourite device is inversion, the latter part of this story could be made to look like the Eärendil story. Gado is summoned by messages; Eärendil therefore by reversal carries a message; the Havens of Sirion are attacked in his absence just as is Britain. However, there are too many discrepancies. In the earliest versions, Eärendil is *not* a messenger - Ulmo wants him to go to Valinor with news but Eärendil persists in looking for his father and mother. Moreover, even when Eärendil is actually made to arrive in Valinor, until the later 1930's he still carries no message, for the Elves have already left for the Great Lands before he appears. Furthermore, there is nothing magical or significant about Gado's ship, as is sometimes suggested; he is simply blown off course to Britain. The Sons of Fëanor, who attack Eärendil's lordship at the Havens of Sirion, are not nearly as closely related to Eärendil as the Roman Emperor is to Offa, and Eärendil does not return to defeat them, but to lead the Valar and Valinorean Elves to defeat Melko (Gillespie 1973 s.v. Wate (1), p.138; Map/James 1983 distinction II, chapter 17). In our view the chances are, then, that Walter Map's work is not a source used by Tolkien.

e; Conclusions about Wade

The links between Wade and J.R.R. Tolkien's writings which have previously been put forward appear to come down to two points. Firstly, Wade as a 'sea-giant' is an Anglo-Saxon figure comparable to Tolkien's sea-Vala Ulmo. The trouble with this is on the one hand that the evidence for Wade actually having a maritime connection is poor and could have been known to Tolkien as such, and on the other hand that the Welsh and Irish sea-god Manannan is much more like Ulmo than any real or theoretical description of Wade that we have been able to find (Rhys, 1901, Celtic Folklore: Welsh and Manx, ch.9, p.549). Secondly, the name given to Wade's 'bote' is virtually the same as the name Tolkien uses for the ship of Eärendil. This may well be a real link. The trouble with this is that on the one hand the name is a more complicated affair than has been realised by previous writers on Tolkien, and on the other hand that it is an isolated piece of information. No other Wade-element seems to us to be visible in the outlines of the Tale of Eärendil which have thus far been published. There is of course always the potential for surprises; 'Wada of the Haelsings' may yet turn up in the as-yet-unpublished *The Fall of Arthur*, or somewhere similarly unexpected. On the currently available evidence, however, we believe that the enigmatic and changeable figure of Wade had only a very slight impact on J.R.R. Tolkien's published writings.

III: Saint Brendan the Navigator

a; Promised Lands and Earthly Paradises

In contrast to the tangled and unclear associations of Wade, there can be absolutely no doubt that Tolkien was using the story of the Irish Saint Brendan, nicknamed the Navigator, from a very early date and in wide-ranging ways. It appears certain to us that it was the medieval 'Voyages of St Brendan' that provided Tolkien with a number of key concepts. These are: the Earthly Paradise across the sea to the West, not across land to the East (as in most writers of the Middle Ages); zones of supernatural darkness and storms surrounding that Paradise; the unearthly continuous brightness and equable climate of the country; the gemstones on the shore of the Earthly Paradise; the few but beautiful people of the country; the possibility of reaching the Earthly Paradise by long and difficult sea-voyaging; the need to be worthy to actually land on the shores of the Paradise; and the presence of islands near that country on which live people who have come from Ireland (the 'real world') but who know the Earthly Paradise (the 'otherworld') well. Other important points either coming from the St Brendan legend or reinforced by it are the North as the abode of the Devil and the place of perils, including fiery mountains, dragons and burning demons which look like near relatives of Tolkien's Balrogs. St Brendan will be covered in more detail in a later volume of studies.

Here we will be concentrating on the possible links between Brendan and Tolkien's Eärendil. Brendan's story appears in the *Navigatio Sancti Brendani*, a bestseller among medieval saint's lives, which was translated into many languages besides its original Latin. Versions can be found in Middle English and Middle Dutch among others. In essence the tale is simple; Brendan is an Irish abbot who hears from another monk of a third man who regularly voyages to the Promised Land or Earthly Paradise. At once, Brendan wants to go there; he chooses a crew, builds a boat and sets out; after seven years and many adventures in God's marvellous ocean, they finally reach the Promised Land and spend some time there, after which they return to Ireland and Brendan dies at peace with his Lord. Incidentally, since Tolkien's day, the noted explorer-historian Tim Severin has proved that the *Navigatio* may well be the record of a series of Atlantic voyages made by Irish monks in search of ever more remote hermitages, by reconstructing the type of boat the saint's life speaks of and successfully reaching North America in it from Ireland along a route which produced practical answers to virtually every problem the story offers. Severin's adventures are recounted in his exceedingly interesting book, 'The Brendan Voyage' (Severin 1978, 'Brendan Voyage'). What is of interest here, though, is the medieval tale and its relationship to J.R.R. Tolkien's writings.

b; Brendan and Eärendil

So far as we know, Tolkien never actually wrote a coherent version of the Tale of Eärendil - a fact remarkable in itself, since this after all is the character who is at the root of the whole endeavour. What we do have is the beginnings of Eärendil's life in *The Fall of Gondolin*, and an assortment of summaries and notes.

The 'Isle of Seabirds' which appears in several of the outlines for the Tale of Eärendel and to which 'all the seabirds of the world repair at times', echoes the island of the Birds' Paradise which Brendan discovers. It is not impossible that Tolkien was already influenced by modern editions suggesting that St Brendan did cross the Atlantic, and that the Paradise of Birds might be in the Faeroe islands with their great seabird-colonies.

The original version of this episode appears explicitly in Tolkien's poem 'Imram' or 'The Death of St Brendan' (printed in *Sauron Defeated*, HOME vol.IX, Part 2, section 4, pps.295-9) as the tree laden with white elf-birds. Seemingly exotic, this idea is in fact a straight borrowing:

'By the well stood a tree : very broad and round
Birds most white and fair were on every branch
so that scarcely any leaf : might he see there
that was much joy and bliss : to look on such a tree'

These birds are angels sent down from heaven at the time of the fall of Lucifer:

'And we also fell down : but for no sin it was
For we did not agree with his foul unrighteousness
Rather it was only to show our sweet Lord's power'

They fly about the earth and skies, and

'And on Sunday, which is the day of rest, such forms we take
The shape of white birds : as you may see
And honour the god who made us : here on this broad tree'

(Horstmann 1887 ch.36, from lines 179-210) [Note 1]

The connections between Brendan and Tolkien's Eärendil also revolve around names. These points are all small, but this is a matter of cumulative significance, so they are worth recording as pieces in the jigsaw. Firstly, the saint's 'Life' tells us that St Brendan's mother was named either Cara or Broinngheal, the former being a straight Romance 'beloved' even if it also has an Old Irish explanation, and the latter name meaning 'bright or shining breast'; when he is a year old, Brendan is fostered with the nun Saint Ita (Barron & Burgess 2002, Introduction). Eärendil's mother's name has the consistent Gnomish/Sindarin form Idril, while in Quenya it is Irildë, later Itaril/Itarillë (the change being very late indeed, sometime after 1968 - intro. to The Shibboleth of Fëanor, HOME vol 12). In the very early linguistic material associated with the Lost Tales *idril* is a Gnomish word meaning sweetheart, beloved, and therefore paralleling *Cara* (BOLT vol.II, Appendix on names, p.343). The early Quenya form means 'mortal maiden' (ibid) changed to 'wise' by 'The Lost Road' (Etymologies); the late Quenya form is of interest as it expands Ita's name and means 'shining, sparkling' (*Peoples of Middle-earth*, HOME XII, Part 2, ch.XI, p.363, note 42), corresponding to one element in *Broinngheal*. Even at this late date, consciously or otherwise Tolkien seems to be drawing on his original sources to enrich his tale with fresh layers of imagery and meaning.

The connection between Brendan and Eärendil is greatly improved by the fact that in the original Latin of the *Navigatio*, Brendan is seeking the *terra repromissis sanctum*, the Promised Land of the Saints; Eärendil is like Brendan heading West to find a 'holy land'. His near-nameksake Orendel in his tale is trying to get to Jerusalem, in the Promised Land of the Jews. In the early outlines of *The Book of Lost Tales*, Eärendil is an old man when he sails west (BOLT vol. II), and this fits well with the Brendan legend, as Brendan died shortly after his return from the Earthly Paradise.

c; Brendan and Sindbad

To complete the investigation for possible links from Brendan that could have influenced the Eärendil story, we ought to at least consider Sindbad the Sailor, famous from the Arabian Nights.
Strange as this may seem, the Early English Text Society in the footnotes to the South English Legendary suggest that Brendan legends are connected to the Sindbad stories:
'... this embodies part of the story of Sindbad.' (EETS Laud 108, Ed. C.Horstmann, 1887, v.) There is however no elucidation on this matter in the document.
If we turn to a major study of 'The Arabian Nights', M. I Gerhardt's 1963 book *The Art of Story-Telling, a Literary Study of the Thousand and One nights*, we find that Gerhardt discusses the possibility of links between the St Brendan and Sindbad story-groups, only to dismiss the idea:
'De Goeje has attempted to fix the terminus ante quem [date before which Sindbad must have been written] by demonstrating SINDBAD's influence on the European *Saint Brandan*. But to my mind, the motifs of *Saint Brandan* that recall SINDBAD (the island-fish Jasconius, the stone-throwing devils from the 'smithy of hell') may well come from a ubiquitous oral tradition, and do not necessarily point to the actual story.'
(Gerhardt 1963, ch.IV, part III, section 2, p.241)
The reference is to MJ de Goeje, De Reizen van Sindebaad in De Gids, issue 53, 1889. This section in Gerhardt's book is preceded by an interesting footnote, referring to the comment that:
'It is generally admitted that SINDBAD originated in Baghdad, or perhaps in the great seaport of Basra*, a meeting-place of sailors, merchants, travellers and foreigners from all parts of the then known world.
*As suggested by J.Oestrup 1925, Studien über 1001 Nacht, trans. O.Rescher, p.35 [ref expanded] (his view about the Indo-European origin of the story cannot be maintained) and probably after him, Elisséeff 1949 p.41.' (ibid)

The idea of an Indo-European origin for the Sindbad stories would allow for bringing some of Sindbad's adventures into Eärendil's orbit as part of a wider ranging mythology (which we shall discuss more fully elsewhere). However, on closer consideration there really seems to be very little connection between the *Sindbad* and *Saint Brendan* stories as we have seen above. This would make it unlikely that J.R.R. Tolkien would borrow from *Sindbad* as a model for the voyages of Eärendil. When one closely examines the Sindbad stories there is something central to them which would also make them unusable: their resolutely mercantile atmosphere. Sindbad is no explorer or mystic (unlike Eärendil and Brendan); he is a trader first and foremost, and trade is the object of all his voyages - even if all he has to sell are the logs of the raft he has just escaped on in the tale of the 7th voyage. He encounters fabulous beasts on his journeys, but so do almost all medieval travellers - and Sindbad's interest in these creatures is purely mercenary - i.e. what profit he can make out of them. It would be possible to lift some of his adventures entirely out of context and rework them into the voyages of Eärendil, but there would seem little reason for Tolkien to have plundered *Sindbad* in this way. It appears all the more unlikely since as far as we can see there is no visible echo of the Sindbad material anywhere in Tolkien's known works. The *St Brendan* motifs, in contrast, are relatively frequent and significant. So the attractive idea of a connection between the Seven Voyages of Sindbad and the wanderings of Eärendil must be given up, unless evidence to the contrary should emerge.

d: Brendan's Fellow-Voyagers

We shall touch briefly on a voyager who shares some characteristics with Brendan, but yields little to help us understand Eärendil any the better.
Bran Mac Feabhail is a fictional character of an 8th century text known as an *imrama*, or 'rowing voyage'. The story goes as follows: An otherworld woman with a silver branch came to the palace of Bran. The branch emitted beautiful music, and she revealed that it was from an apple tree in the realm of Eamhain... she further disclosed that this was a far away island, and she described its wonders and invited Bran and his men to row there. She then disappeared from sight, and Bran set out on the sea with thrice nine for a crew. When they were two days on their journey they encountered Manannán, who described the sea as his estate and gave them instructions on how to reach the island of Eamhain before sundown. Coming to that island, Bran rowed around it and saw a crowd of people staring and laughing at his crew. One of his men went ashore, and immediately he began to stare and laugh like the rest. They next encountered the Island of Women, the inhabitants of which invited them ashore. They remained there in great delight and joy for what they thought was a year, though it was in fact many years. Bran returns with his crew, one of whom steps ashore and withers away - so he tells of his voyages and then disappears. (O' hOgain 1990, 'Myth, Legend and Romance', s.v. Bran mac Feabhail)

'The Voyage of Bran' appears to have no connection to the Eärendil story from what we have shown above, though it does have a fine summary of the nature of elves in one verse;

We are from the beginning of creation
Without old age, without consummation of earth [the grave]
Hence we expect not that there should be frailty
The sin has not come to us. [Note 2]

The previous quatrain may have supplied the first hint for Lothlórien:

A wood with blossom and fruit
On which is the vine's veritable fragrance,
A wood without decay, without defect,
On which are leaves of golden hue. [Note 3]

(Kuno Meyer ed. & trans, 1895, The Voyage of Bran, verses 43 (2nd quote) & 44; cited from the 1994 Llanerch reprint (pp.20-23) which does not contain Alfred Nutt's essay, 'Upon the Irish vision of the Happy Otherworld, &c'; we have not been able to obtain a copy of the book including this, and therefore cannot say if the essay contains anything relevant.)

Another Irish *immrama* is the voyage of Maol Dúin, in which the hero sets sail to seek vengeance and ends up in the otherworld instead. He and his crew come across many islands which surpass each other in fantasy... they have encounters with massive ants and birds, demon horses, and a monstrous cat which guards treasure. They come to an island of women who become their lovers in an ageless realm, but eventually Maol Dúin's men prevail on him to set out for home... they run across an island of apple trees with beautiful golden apples and wondrous pigs which disappear underground at night. On another island they come to a lake which restores youth to those who bathe in it, and which also restores health to the sick and injured. They also come to an island surrounded by a revolving wall of fire, which wall has one open doorway. Each time this doorway passes them they catch a glimpse of all within - handsome people with beautiful clothes drinking ale from goblets of gold, with wondrous music being played for them. We are not told if Maol Dúin and his crew ever make it back home.
(O' hOgain 1990, 'Myth, Legend and Romance', s.v. Maol Dúin)
Again, there are no recognisable elements from Eärendil's voyages in this story.

Readers might perhaps be forgiven for feelings of 'deja vu' when reading stories such as these. There are strong Classical antecedents to all the above. Jason and the Argonauts, perhaps? The island of women (the island of women that Jason and his crew visit?); massive birds (harpies?); monstrous cat guarding a treasure (hydra and the golden fleece?); the lake with supernatural properties (the golden fleece itself? Perhaps mixed with elements of the island with the golden apples?); the revolving wall of fire (the clashing rocks?). One can do exactly the same with the Odyssey: Bran and the island of women (Circe, maybe?).

Even the scholars admit that these *immrama* have strong Classical sources. Irish scholars believe that the St. Brendan voyages are the first of the *immrama* (J.M. Wooding, 2000, The Otherworld Voyage) which were developed out of it. They are therefore based on Christian and Classical material even more than Irish tradition. There have been trading links between the Roman empire and Ireland from pre-Christian days, and though Ireland never became part of the Roman Empire as Britain did, once Christianity was imported, the Classical stories re-imagined came along too. Sea-voyage stories would be especially 'relevant' as Ireland is an island and the sea plays a prominent part in the lives of its people (much as it did, say, for the Classical Greeks). Classical tales were being re-cast in terms of the lives of saints by Christian writers, much in the same way as Snorri was doing with the Trojan legends and the northern mythologies. This allowed tales of wonder to survive into a modern Christian world with its rules of morality and censorship. Such saints lives and adventures would have been embellished and changed to suit the character of the country into which they were brought; thus stories of Jason and Odysseus which had been turned into the lives of, say St. Thomas, St. George, or St. Anthony, perhaps - would then have been retold and transformed into the *immrama*. So now we can turn our attention to the

Classical voyagers from whom Eärendil might have drawn some of his elements.

IV: The Greek voyagers and Eärendil

a: Jason

The legend of Jason and the Argonauts is older than Homer: 'In the Odyssey Homer refers to 'celebrated Argo' which managed to evade the Wandering Rocks when 'homeward bound from Aeetes' coast'. And in the Iliad he wrote of Euneos, Jason's son by Queen Hypsipyle on Lemnos. As Homer is our oldest surviving source of Greek mythology, this means that the ancestry of the Argonaut story is established as far back as records exist. Quite how far back that ancestry goes, we have no way of knowing...' (Severin, 1985, The Jason Voyage, Appendix 1). It becomes clear at once that there are elements of Jason's voyages in the Eärendil story - the most obvious one is the 'named' ship which is in some way special. Jason has the best ship ever built and it is called the Argo after its builder. Indeed, the crew are known as the Argonauts. In the best known Classical texts no other ship has a name. Of its construction, it is said: '... Apollonius Rhodius had written about Jason's boat. He had said that the first Argo carried a very special piece of timber in her prow - a bough cut from a sacred oak at the holy shrine of Dodona. This timber was some sort of lucky talisman, a charm, and according to Apollonius it gave the boat the power of speech. At special moments... the first Argo had cried out in a human voice.' (ibid, ch.2, p.53) Similarly, Eärendil's ship has a name and is 'hallowed' by the Valar. In the early versions Wingilot is special even at the point of its construction:

'Ulmo bids him build a new and wonderful ship of the wood of Tuor from Falasquil. Building of Wingilot.' (BOLT vol. II, ch.5, p.254)

In the 1930's-written *The Silmarillion*, Eärendil's ship is constructed with the aid of a special shipwright, Cirdan:

'With the aid of Cirdan Eärendil build Vingilot, the Foam-flower, fairest of the ships of song; golden were its oars and white its timbers, hewn in the birch-woods of Nimbrethil, and its sails were as the argent moon.' (QS, ch.24, p.296).

The idea of the specialness of this ship is carried forward into LotR as Bilbo tells:

'Eärendil was a mariner
That tarried in Arvernien;
He built a boat of timber felled
In Nimbrethil to journey in;
Her sails he wove of silver fair,
Of silver were her lanterns made,
Her prow was fashioned like a swan,
And light upon her banners laid.'

(FotR, Book II, ch.1, p.246)

Jason undertakes perilous voyages into unknown regions and he has a definite quest - as does Eärendil (though his quest was the search for his father Tuor). He also succeeds in his quest to bring back the Golden Fleece, and this is achieved only with the help of his 'wife' Medea - in the same way as Eärendil only manages to sail to Valinor when Elwing his wife is with him.

There is an early outline for Eärendel's voyages that appears to follow in part the course of Jason's voyages:

'Mediterranean (loses his boat (travels afoot through wilds of europe?)) or Atlantic.' (BOLT vol. II, ch.5, p.261)

In the best known version of the story of Jason and the Argonauts they return home by sailing up the Danube and down into the Adriatic. This is impossible practically, but fits well with the idea of the loss of a ship and having to walk home - if one were to try and carry out such a journey.

b: Odysseus

The evident links between the medieval Troy stories and Tolkien's 'Fall of Gondolin' raise another possibility of connections, for the most famous voyager in Greek legend after Jason was an important figure in the Trojan War before he sailed for home and ran into trouble. This is of course Odysseus (the Latinised Ulysses). Like Eärendil, Odysseus has left behind him a ruined city (Troy which he helped to sack, as opposed to Gondolin from which the former fled) and both encounter adventure and shipwreck on their way 'home' - home in Odysseus' case is his palace and in the case of Eärendil might be taken to mean the 'long home' of the Silmaril which he bears. Both voyagers are reunited with their wives. The island of Circë where Odysseus and his crew are stranded for a long time in what seems to be a place outside time could equate with the Magic Isles that bar the way to Valinor. The Sons of Fëanor making off with Eärendil's two sons could be seen to match the unwanted suitors of Penelope who caused his son Telemachus such problems. Odysseus' return to his homeland begins with his arrival at a remote location and he travels inland on foot - which compares well with Eärendil's arrival in Valinor and walking through a deserted Tirion.

Both of the Greek voyagers have successful outcomes to their journeys, unlike the voyagers of the *immrama* whose journeys' ends are not always as fruitful - which parallels the outcomes of the voyages of Eärendel (who does not succeed) and Eärendil (who does). There is also another point to be made: Jason's voyage is a round trip as are most of the *immrama* - i.e. they all end up returning to where they started from. Odysseus in the Odyssey on the other hand starts out from Troy and ends up on Ithaca. When one compares this to the matter of Eärendil/ Eärendel, there are two differing patterns that emerge - with the earlier mariner he makes at least one round trip before voyaging into the sky (like Bran who after his round trip then vanishes) whereas in the later Eärendil versions once he sets sail from the Havens of Sirion, he never returns there - much as Odysseus never returns to Troy.

V: The Messenger's Arrival

The whole purpose of Eärendel/Eärendil's journey changed dramatically from the time of its original conception to the time when the *Silmarillion* was being developed. Basically, Eärendel was a failure and Eärendil a success. It is remarkable that in the early versions Eärendel is a traveller who carries no message and whose ostensible errand is a failure. In the meeting between Ulmo and Tuor in BOLT vol. II, the sea-God says: 'Yet maybe thy life shall turn again to the mighty waters; and of a surety a child shall come of thee than whom no man shall know more of the uttermost deeps, be it of the sea or of the firmament of heaven.' (BOLT vol. II, ch.3, p.155)

Christopher Tolkien picks up on this in his discussion of *The Tale of Eärendel*:

'In these very early narrative schemes there is no mention of Eärendel's speaking to the Valar, as the ambassador of Elves and Men (QS, ch.21, p.249), and we can only conclude, extraordinary as the conclusion is, that Eärendel's great western voyage, though he attained his goal, was fruitless, that he was not the agent of the aid that did come out of Valinor to the Elves of the Great Lands and (most curious of all) that Ulmo's designs for Tuor had no issue. In fact, my father actually wrote in the 1930 version of 'The Silmarillion':

'Thus it was that the many emissaries of the Gnomes in after days came never back to Valinor - save one: and he came too late.' The words 'and he came too late' were changed to 'the mightiest mariner of song', and this is the phrase that is found in *The Silmarillion*, p.102') (BOLT vol.II, ch.5, p.257)

The text that C.J.R. Tolkien is referring to is the *Quenta Noldorinwa*, published in *The Shaping of Middle-earth* /HOME vol IV, which dates to 1930. The sentence in question appears in §6, after the description of the Hiding of Valinor; the alteration from *he came too late* to *the mightiest mariner of song* is footnoted but not marked as a 'late change'. Following Christopher Tolkien's notes on this matter, this suggests the alteration occurred in the first layer of alterations to the *Quenta Noldorinwa*, and therefore not long if at all after its writing - some things which are alterations in the early part of the text are taken up into the text itself later on. Further into the story, §17 tells the story of the voyage of Eärendel, and exists in two versions. In the first, Eärendel wants to bring a message to Valinor but fails:

'Two thoughts were in his heart blended as one: the longing for the wide sea; and he thought to sail thereon following after Tuor and Idril Celebrindal who returned not, and he thought to find perhaps the last shore and bring ere he died a message to the Gods and Elves of the West, that should move their hearts to pity on the world and the sorrows of Mankind.'

But in the event:

'He came too late to bring messages to the Elves, for the Elves had gone.'

Footnoted to this section is an original note 'written very quickly and faintly in pencil' which says:

'Make *Eärendel* move the Gods. And it is said that there were Men of Hithlum repentant of their evil in that day, and that so were fulfilled Ulmo's words, for by

Eärendel's embassy and the aid of valiant Men the Orcs and Balrogs were destroyed, yet not as utterly as might have been.'
(*The Shaping of Middle-earth*, HOME vol. IV, Part III, §17, pps.149-151)

The second version seems to be very close in date to the first, according to Christopher Tolkien's description in the Introduction to the whole piece. In this 'QII' account, Eärendel's role is shifting in line with the previous footnote, and is for the first time foreshadowed:
'In Valinor Ulmo spoke to the Valar of the need of the Elves, and he called on them to forgive and send succour unto them and rescue them from the overmastering might of Morgoth, and win back the Silmarils wherein alone now bloomed the light of the days of bliss when the Two Trees still were shining.... The Quendi have said that the hour was not yet come, and that only one speaking in person for the cause of both Elves and Men, pleading for pardon upon their misdeeds and pity on their woes, might move the counsels of the Powers...'
Eärendel is still 'restless' in general, 'and his voyages about the shores of the Outer Lands eased not his unquiet'. The same two purposes drive him to sail, making two voyages westward. The first is unsuccessful and Eärendel turns east in haste, driven by a premonition of the assault of the Sons of Fëanor on the Havens of Sirion. Now Elwing arrives in bird-shape aboard Wingelot, only to assume her own form in Eärendel's arms, and together they sail west, this time succeeding. The arrival at Valinor and events there are as in the 1977 *Silmarillion*; as might be expected, for this version of that period of time was the last one J.R.R. Tolkien actually wrote, an astonishing fact.

In the 1950's *Unfinished Tales*, when Tuor meets Ulmo, the sea-God says: 'But it is not for thy valour only that I send thee, but to bring into the world a hope beyond thy sight, and a light that shall pierce the darkness.' (UT, Part One, ch.1, p.30) This foretells the birth of Eärendil and his success as a messenger.

Tolkien was drawing from many sources for his Eärendel/Eärendil legends - and we have shown that primarily this has to have been the Classical and the later Classically-inspired Irish legends as well as the medieval retellings of Trojan legends such as Orendel.

VI; Elwing

In almost all the accounts of Eärendil's voyages from *The Book of Lost Tales* to the 1977 *Silmarillion*, Elwing is strongly connected with the sea and with flight. The central concepts are her attempt to kill herself by leaping into the sea rather than face capture, her temporary transformation into a seabird, her dwelling in a tower in the North which all the seabirds of the world visit, and her continuing to fly either by changing shape or on constructed but clearly magically effective wings.

a; Ladies Transformed; Elwing and Classical Legend

The Roman poet Ovid has some thought-provoking passages to offer in connection with the theme of transformation - which in the Greek form *Metamorphoses* , is the title of one of his longest and best-known works. In the lead-in to the tale of 'Pyramus and Thisbe', one of the daughters of Minyas, wondering which story to tell her sisters as they sit spinning (a bad idea; they should be out taking part in a festival to Dionysus, and for this mistake are about to be transformed themselves), considers but rejects:

'Or of her daughter, who grew wings and spent
Her final years upon a tall white tower' (Ovid/Melville 1986, bk.IV, lines 45-6)

The lady in question is Semiramis daughter of Dercetis of Babylon, who was turned into a white dove. This is slight but potentially important nonetheless because Elwing, who was once a white bird and later wears wings in the dove-colours of white and silver-grey (QS, ch.24, p.301) is quite consistently said to dwell in a tower, and no other possible source contains this detail.

Ovid also mentions a transformation into a white bird within the Trojan royal lineage itself:

'Antigone she pictured too, who once
Challenged the royal consort of great Jove
And Juno changed her to a bird, and Troy
Availed her nothing nor Laomedon
Her father - no! with snowy feathers clothed
In self-applause she claps her stork's loud bill.'
(Ovid/Melville 1986, bk VI, p.124, lines 93-8)

There is also is the unfortunate fate of Aesacus son of Priam, King of Troy:

'Then from a clifftop that the booming waves
Had eaten out below he flung himself
Into the sea. In pity as he fell
Tethys received him gently, and as he swam
clothed him with feathers; thus the golden chance
Of death so much desired was never given.
The lover, outraged to be forced to live
Against his will, to find his soul that longed
To leave its lamentable home restrained,
With new wings on his shoulders flew aloft
And once more launched himself into the waves.
his feathers broke his fall. In fury then
Poor Aesacus dived down into the deep
Trying endlessly to take the road to death.
Love made him lean; his jointed legs are long,
And long his neck, and long his head extends.
He loves the sea; that name of his he keeps,
A diver, for he dives into the deeps.'
(Ovid/Melville bk., p.272-3, lines 782-95)

This is important because, like Elwing, Aesacus was trying to commit suicide but was transformed instead; he was turned into a seabird by the seagoddess Tethys as Elwing is transformed by the sea-Vala Ulmo; as a Trojan prince he is in the right legendary family to be adopted and adapted in a story about the royal lineage of Gondolin, which as we have seen has so many Trojan connections. No birdwatcher, Ovid leaves uncertain the species that Aesacus was turned into, but 'divers' in modern ornithological parlance are sub-arctic freshwater birds, and the only diving seabird that might be expected in the Mediterranean is the gannet. Gannets are large birds, long-necked, long-legged and long-beaked just as Ovid describes, which are mostly white; they are extremely strong flyers that wander far and wide across the North Atlantic. In short, this is a very suitable shape for Elwing to take when flying in search of Eärendel. Even the description of Elwing as '... a pale flame on wings of storm' (QS, ch.24, p.298) fits neatly with the black tips to a gannet's otherwise white wings. By sheer coincidence it is this bird that a number of artists illustrating the transformed Elwing have chosen to show, most notably Roger Garland on the first paperback cover of *The Shaping of Middle-earth*.

Not a transformation but still of interest as connected to Troy and involving white waterbirds is the well-known legend of Leda, queen of Sparta, who was seduced by Zeus in the shape of a swan; she had four children as a result, Helen of Troy, Agamemnon's wife Clytemnestra, and the twin heroes Castor and Pollux who became gods. All of them were hatched from eggs, a detail that would only really make sense if Leda herself had been transformed into a swan, rather than sleeping with a god in the shape of one (Ovid/Melville 1986, bk.VI, p.124 lines 112-3). Elwing is never described, whereas Helen was fatally beautiful, but it is still Elwing who makes a decision that leads to the destruction of a settlement, just as Helen's decision to run off with Paris led to the fall of Troy. Elwing's refusal to hand over the Silmaril leads to the attack of the Sons of Fëanor and the destruction of the Havens of Sirion, which - sitting near or in the swamps of Arlisgion/Lisgardh, which as we have seen is a name with definite Trojan links - occupy a geographical position definitely related to that of Troy. This is an idea in which Tolkien altered and strengthened the possibly Trojan elements over time. From being attacked by orcs (derived from Greeks attacking Troy) in the early Tale of Gondolin (BOLT vol. II), the Havens came to be attacked by the sons of Fëanor (in QS). They, as quarrelsome and dangerous cousins, occupy the position that Ajax Telamonius, son of Hesione daughter of Laomedon of Troy, occupies in relation to Hector and the other sons of Hesione's brother Priam in the Trojan legends. The tragedy and futility of the killing of kinsfolk at the Havens of Sirion is a clear echo of the tragedy and futility of the Trojan War as depicted by medieval writers, particularly Guido delle Colonne. That Maedhros and Maglor foster Elros and Elrond, the sons of Eärendil, as if they were their own children, parallels the way in which the Trojan royal lineage (for which read that of Gondolin) takes over from the rightful Greek line of descent (the House of Fëanor) in Thessaly, the kingdom where in the medieval Trojan legends all the trouble between Greece and Troy began. Returning to swans, in *The Fall of Gondolin* proper, Tuor of course is linked with these birds, and as the wife of Tuor's son, Elwing may have picked up the 'white waterbird' motif by association. There is a further reason why Elwing, the granddaughter of Lúthien Tinúviel and Beren, should be associated with swans, but that is best dealt with in a full-length examination of that story in a later volume of studies.

b; Elves, Seabirds and St Brendan

The idea of a northern island visited by all the seabirds of the world probably derives from the *Voyages of St Brendan*, where the Paradise of Birds is one of three islands that are regularly visited by the saint and his crew of monks. St Brendan's birds are 'neutral angels' (elves, in British and Irish folklore) who turn into great white birds on Sundays to honour their creator. All the attempts to relate St Brendan's voyages to the real world have identified the Paradise of Birds as one of the Faeroe Islands, with their vast seabird colonies, and it seems likely that in some such identification we find the root of Tolkien's Isle of Seabirds. So also the idea of 'elves' turning into white birds may well have helped reinforce if it did not spark the notion of Elwing's transformation.

c; Parted lovers

As a rule Elwing and Eärendel are together at least part of the time, but this rule is broken twice. This happens first in *The Book of Lost Tales*, when they are separated from the sack of the Havens to the Faring Forth of the Elves to try to rekindle the Magic Sun. Secondly and far more importantly, in the 1930 *Quenta Noldorinwa* there are two versions of what happens to Elwing and Eärendel. First: 'Eärendel was their guide; but the Gods would not suffer him to return again, and he built him a white tower upon the confines of the outer world in the northern regions of the Sundering Seas; and there all the seabirds of the earth at times repaired. And often was Elwing in the form and likeness of a bird; and she devised wings for the ship of Eärendel, and it was lifted even into the oceans of the air.'

This is satisfactory enough in its own way, but at an uncertain later date, Tolkien rewrote it:

'In those days the ship of Eärendel was drawn by the Gods beyond the edge of the world, and it was lifted even into the oceans of the air. Marvellous and magical was that ship, a starlit flower in the sky, bearing a wavering and holy flame; and the folk of earth beheld it from afar and wondered, and looked up from despair, saying surely a Silmaril is in the sky, a new star is risen in the West. But Elwing mourned for Eärendel yet found him never again, and they are sundered till the world endeth. Therefore she built a white tower upon the confines of the outer world in the Northern regions of the Sundering Seas; and there all the seabirds of the earth at times repaired, And Elwing devised wings for herself, and desired to fly to Eärendel's ship But [?she fell back]...'

(*The Shaping of Middle-earth*, HOME vol.IV, ch.III, pps. 154 & 156)

By comparison, Odysseus is parted from Penelope his wife and wishes to return to her, Jason finds on his journeys Medea and marries her - but the likes of the voyager monks such as St Brendan are by definition unmarried.

d; Star-followers

Elros son of Eärendil follows the Star of Eärendil to the Island of Númenor which echoes Aeneas and his son Iulus sailing west to Italy and founding the city of Alba Longa, from which their descendants found Rome - a great imperial power just as Númenor is. It looks like Tolkien in developing the Eärendil story has been following Classical sources once again.

Hereafter we give the original texts:
Note 1:
'Bi the welle stod a treo ; brod and round ynou3
Foweles white & faire ynou3 ; were in euerech bou3
that unnethe eni leef : hi mi3te thereon iseo -
ther was ioye & blisse ynou3 : to lokie on suche o treo'

These birds are angels sent down from heaven at the time of the fall of Lucifer:
'& we fulle also a-doun : ac for no synne hit nas,
for nothing that we assentede : to his foule vnri3t,
Bote solement forto schewe : ore louerdes suete might.'

They fly about the earth and skies, and
'& sonedai, that it dai of rest : such forme we taketh:
the forme of suche white foweles : as thu mi3t iseo
[&] honoureth god that ous makede : her on this brode treo.'
(Horstmann 1887 ch.36, from lines 179-210)Note 2:
Fil dún ó thossuch dúle
cen áiss, cen foirbthe n-úre
ni frescam de mbeth anguss
nintaraill int immorbus
(Kuno Meyer ed. & trans, 1895, The Voyage of Bran, verse 44; cited from the 1994 Llanerch reprint (pp.20-23)

Note 3:
Fid co m-bláth ocus torud
forsmbi fine firbolud
fid cen erchre, cen esbad,
forsfil duilli co n-órdath.
(Kuno Meyer ed. & trans, 1895, The Voyage of Bran, verse 43; cited from the 1994 Llanerch reprint (pp.20-23)

Chapter Nine:

Quenya - the Concept.

It has been a revelation and delight to uncover the many links back to the world of Homeric Greece in Tolkien's writings (specifically *The Fall of Gondolin* and the tale of Eärendil), through of course the viewing lens of the medieval tradition as he applied it. We are asking a lot of readers to take us 'on trust' in this - though we have of course set ourselves very rigorous ground-rules to prove our many points. In terms of story and episodic content we feel we have proven the linkage completely. We have so far only touched upon the full import of the meaning of the word as and where it impacted directly upon the story-lines.
However, the most severe test of our theories would surely be: 'Tolkien is about language above all else; he himself said as much: language came first and then story. So, if the world of Homer and the Trojan Wars were so important to the development of two of his main stories, how does that relate to his languages?'. That is a fair point, and we decided to proceed with an investigation into his earliest language available to us - Quenya, or Qenya. This is the 'language of the Eldar', the most ancient of the elvish languages, and also the first one Tolkien devised for his race of immortals in the time before Tolkien's involvement in the First World War. It is also the earliest invented language we have evidence for that we have available to study. It is always suggested that Quenya is 'based upon Finnish' and that Sindarin is 'based upon Welsh'. For instance, Carpenter suggests: 'He [Tolkien] never learned Finnish well enough to do more than work through part of the original *Kalevala*, but the effect on his language inventing was fundamental and remarkable. He abandoned neo-Gothic and began to create a private language that was heavily influenced by Finnish. This was the language that would eventually emerge in his stories as 'Quenya' or High-elven.' (Carpenter 1977, Part Two, ch.5, p.67)
Tolkien himself however was less specific about the connection in a 1955 letter to W.H. Auden:
'I gave up the attempt to invent an 'unrecorded' Germanic language, and my 'own language' - or series of invented languages - became heavily Finnicized in phonetic pattern and structure.' (Letters, No.163, p.214)
So, we cannot be certain that the language Tolkien discusses above which he was altering in around 1913 before his Hons Mods. is the same as Quenya, which emerges in around 1915 as shown by Christopher Tolkien in the introduction to the Appendix on names in BOLT vol. I. Therefore the connection between Finnish and Quenya is really no more than an assumption, and one that in the case of Quenya seems to be quite wrong. Finnish certainly never affected the vocabulary of any of Tolkien's languages as far as we can tell (see Table B below). To the best of our knowledge, no other researcher has looked into this area of linguistic comparison to come to any definite conclusions. Finnish is not an Indo-european language, and has little in common with them apart from loan words.

We can confirm that in a straight comparison of word-form, phonetics and of meanings, Quenya is almost certainly based upon ancient Greek. That is, more precisely, upon a form of Greek that is probably older than Classical Greek of the 5th century BC onwards. The Greek of the Homeric epic or earlier.

In the analysis we were limited by a lack of decent reference material - and were forced to utilise several Classical Greek dictionaries which are meant for school students - one of the authors used Lidell and Scott's dictionary to study Classical Greek when he was at school. They are far from comprehensive, have much missing and do not cover more ancient forms than are expected to be found by school students studying Classical Greek for O and A Levels. Tolkien, having studied Greek Philology and having been allowed at King Edward's school to look into the history of the Classical Greek language, would have had access to at least the full unabridged version of Lidell and Scott and most likely several other specialised dictionaries. His results at school (he did win an Exhibition to study Classics at Oxford after all) and thereafter at University (he scored an alpha + at Greek Philology for his Hons. Mods.) means that he knew the Greek language to a very deep level, and in very great detail as far as the development of ancient Greek from the Homeric and even pre-Homeric level right up to its Classical and eventually New Testament variants.

How close is Quenya/Qenya to Classical Greek? We give below in tabulature the exact comparisons of words from BOLT vol. I - our earliest source - and with some comparisons with the Etymologies in *Peoples of Middle-earth*. Quenya turns out to be a very close match to Classical Greek. We chiefly used the word lists from BOLT vol. I, as those of BOLT vol. II contain mostly words of 'Gnomish' origin. However, those Quenya roots given (under QL) in BOLT vol. II have been analysed as well.

Of the 220 word and root forms Christopher Tolkien listed in Table A, only 6 cannot be found counterparts for both phonetically and in terms of meaning with Greek, and of the 97% plus of words, 31% have straight one for one analogues. The others are in meaning so close that it usually takes a lesser philologist than Tolkien to make the very simple connections required. This is perhaps as strange and revolutionary a discovery as that in the 1950's that Linear B - a script that was asserted by Sir Arthur Evans, the leading authority of the early 20th Century in the Minoan civilisation, to have nothing to do with Greek - was indeed an old way of writing Greek. The Linear B code was 'cracked' when a pair of researchers challenged the prevailing wisdom. In a very analogous way, we have shown that Quenya/Qenya is indeed based on Greek - to a greater than 97% confidence level. Since, from what we have said, Finnish has few roots in common with Greek, as can be seen from Table B, it looks most unlikely that a correlation can be made between that language and Quenya/Qenya. Basically, for comparison, we have here something that quacks and has feathers, webbed feet and a bill - and we are proposing that it is a duck!

The intriguing idea for us is that Kenia/Kwenia can be rendered as 'concept' in Greek (see Table A), which is very appropriate for what this language was to Tolkien in the scheme of things. Also, and just as interestingly as far as we are concerned, there is a suspicion growing that because of the K- KWE shifts that Tolkien utilises, since these turn up in Linear B, perhaps Tolkien had already worked out some of the links between Linear B and Greek for himself, some 30 years before the people who are credited with 'cracking the code'. This is not something that anyone can prove - it is just a feeling one has from studying the Greek roots of Quenya/Qenya. However, we shall in a future volume of research compare the symbol shapes and meanings between Linear B, Linear A and the Angtheras and Tengwar, as well as the usual northern runes. We can for this volume go so far as to say that with its 60 symbols, the Angtheras resembles as a concept Linear B with 88 symbols, far more than it does the runes which have between 16 and 24 symbols. The connections and implications of this shall be investigated and discussed in a future volume of Tolkien research.
One might be moved to ask 'why?' - and an intriguing possibility would be that Tolkien was trying to piece together a Trojan language. During Tolkien's lifetime it was thought that the Trojans spoke some form of language akin to Greek, perhaps even a dialect. Tolkien may have been trying to 'reconstruct' this language through Quenya.

To list all the 220 words would be overkill - and also hard work for those not as interested in these areas as the linguists. We have a full listing and are happy to discuss it with researchers. Here in Table A we give some of the more obvious word connections (we are not just emphasising the 31% analogues but giving a broader selection), plus the 6 'no shows' cited above. The Greek word meanings are mostly taken from Lidell and Scott's abridged Classical Greek dictionary, but from elsewhere as needed.

Table A

Quenya/Qenya root	meaning	Greek word	meaning
Ainur	Pagan God	Αινη (Ainu)	praise
akairis	a bride	ακκω (ako)	a vain woman
	also:	κορη (kore)	young woman
alda	spread (growth)	αλδαινο (aldaino)	to grow/nourish
alkwi	swan	αλκυων (alkion)	kingfisher
amu	upwards	ανα (ana)	upwards
angaino	tormentor	αναγκαζο (anangazo)	great force/torture
austa	summer	αυσταλεος(austaleos)	sunburnt, parched
aute	prosperity	αυξω (auxo)	to grow, increase
dana	day	δαν (dan)	for a long while
dome	dusk, gloom [1]	τομα (toma)	sacrifice for oaths
drond	race, course, track	δρομος (dromos)	race, course, track
Earendel/Iarendel [2]	eagle/holy	ιαραξ/ ιερος (ierax/ieros)	hawk/ holy
Eldamar/ Eldar (from)	egla -far away	ελδωρ/ελδομαι (eldor/eldomai)	longing

Quenya/Qenya root	meaning	Greek word	meaning
Eriol (er)	(alone)	ερıμos (erimos)	loneliness, desert
Falasse	surf	θαλασσα (thalassa)	the sea
fantur/ fana	sleep or death	φαντασμα (fantasma)	phantom/ dream
Feanaro (phay)	fiery spirit	φαινω (faino)	shine, give light
fion	goblet, bowl	φιαλη (fiali)	bowl
gumlaith	grief	γουναζομαι (gounazomai)	to fall down
Here	rule, have power	χαιρ (haer)	hand
hise/histe	dusk	ησυχos (isichos)	still, quietness
Iluvatar - atar-	father	πατηρ (pater) [8]	father
Ilwe	heavens/sky	ηλιos (ilios)	the sun
Inwe/ ini-	small	ινις (inis)	a child
kale/ kalwa [3]	morning/beautiful	καλλι (kalli)	beautiful
kauka	crooked/bent	κακos (kakos)	evil, ugly, wicked
kele/kelu	flow	κελλο (kelo)	run a ship ashore
kemi	earth/soil/land	χομα (homa/koma)	earth, ground
kosomot - moko-	hate	κοσμεω (kosmeo)	order/arrange
	also:	κοτos (kotos)	ill will, wrath
kuru	magic	κυρos (kuros)	power, authority
linde/liri	song/sing	λυρικos (lirikos)	to sing to the lyre
loko	twist, curl	λοξos (loxos)	crosswise, oblique
mala	crush	μαλα (mala)	far too much force
makar/ maka	slay	μαχη (mahi)	battle, combat
mir	one/ gem	μυριos (mirios)	countless
mornie	black grief	μωρωs (moros)	heavy, doom
	also:	μοιρα (moira)	goddess of fate
nand	field	ναιω (naio)	dwell, inhabit
mele	love	μελω (melo)	to be object of care
nyehe	weep	νυκτos (nictos)	gloom, night
nekte	honey	νεκταρ (nektar)	drink of the Gods
Nol	to know	νωμα (noma)	a thought, design
olore	dream	ονειρos (oneiros)	dream
ork	monster, demon	ορκos (orkos)	swear an oath
oro	hill/ mountain	ορos (oros)	mountain
osta	homestead	ο σταθμos (o stathmos)	the abode
qala	die	καλεω (kaleo)	to summon
Quenya/Qenya [3]	language/speech?	κενω/κενια (keno/kenia)	know/concept
querkaringa [3]	first element obscure	κερκos (kerkos)	tail of a beast [4]
chill gulf twixt Helkaraxe & Great Lands		κερκουρos (kerkouros)	a boat [4]
pelekko	axe	πεκκω (pekko)	to shear, clip
Poldorea (Tulkas) [5]	power	πολυ–δωρos (polydorus)	many gifted (This could be an epithet for a God)
ringil	cold, chill	ριον (rion)	peak of mountain
ronta	tube	ρομβos (rombos)	something turns
Sahora (saha)	the south (be hot)	ισα ορα (isa hora)	midday (heat)
sari/ sa	fire	σειρos (seiros)	scorching, hot
sarko	flesh	σαρκοω (sarko)	to make flesh

Quenya/Qenya root	meaning	Greek word	meaning
sulp	lick	θυλασσο (thulasso)	suckle
Teleri/ Telu	finish, end	τελος (telos)	the end, to finish
tereva	boring/piercing	τρημα/ τρεπω (trema/trepo)	bore/pierce
Tintiltha [6]	twinkle	εις αντηλλα (eis antille)	near the sun
Tirith/tir-	guard	τηρος (tiros)	watch/ guard
		also: τυρσις (tirsis/tirthis)	tower, bastion
Tolos	boss of shield, centre	θολος (tholos)	circular vault
Tuile/tulu	spring/ bear	τυλη (tule)	swelling of buds
turu	be strong	τυραννος (turanos)	absolute ruler
ungwë [7]	spider	νγολιαθ (ngoliath)	sea monster
uru	fire	πυρ (pur/pyr) [8]	fire
usu	escape	υσιος (usios)	straight (path)
vaima	robe	βαιτη (baite)	coat of skins
vondo/ yondo	son	Ios (ios)	son

We shall now give the six word parts that seem to have no connection at all with Classical Greek, with any possible Latin analogues given after the words:
a. Ilverin - heart?; (viscera - heart, verus - truth, reality; Latin: also Greek root βεβαιως (Bebaios/Vebaios - firmly)
b. kulu - gold; (- culullus - goblet - Latin: also Greek - κυλιξ (kulix) - drinking cup)
c. gwini - glint; - no match to anything.
d. Taha - lofty; - no match to anything.
e. telpe - silver; - no match to anything.
f. winge - foam; - no match to anything. It is likely to be (w)i(n)gë, but this does not yield any comparable roots in Latin, Greek or English as far as we can see.

Two of the six have some elements that link to the Latin, and a less firm connection to Greek where the sense as well as sound is comparable.
An important limitation in the above analysis is the very basic Latin dictionary available at the time - far smaller than even the Classical Greek dictionaries we have utilised in the rest of this chapter.

We shall now move onto Finnish and its lack of phonological or semantic similarity to Quenya/Qenya. For this word-list we have relied upon the Liverpool University online Finnish dictionary to search for words, and to whom thanks are extended for providing such a useful 'Freeware' resource:

Table B

Quenya/Qenya root	meaning	Finnish word	meaning
Ainur	Pagan God	Jumala	god
alda	spread (growth)	kasvaa	grow
		tulla joksikin	grow
		viljella	grow
austa	summer	Kesä	summer

Quenya/Qenya root	meaning	Finnish word	meaning
aute	prosperity	kasvaa	grow
		tulla joksikin	grow
		viljella	grow
dome	dusk, gloom	hämärä	dusk
drond	race, course, track	tie	road
Earendel/Iarendel	eagle/holy	kotka	eagle
		??	holy
Falasse	surf	meri	the sea
		valta, meri	ocean
lin-	pool, mere	järvi	lake
Iluvatar - atar-	father	isä	father
Ilwe	heavens/sky	taivas	sky
kauka	crooked/bent käryä		bent
kele/kelu	flow	virrata	flow
		joki	river
kopas	harbour	satama	harbour
		gloppet	bay, inlet
linde/liri	song/sing	laulaa	sing
nekte	honey	hunaja	honey
oro	hill	vaara	hill
oro	mountain	vuori, tunturi	mountain
		karki	peak
osta	homestead	vuokrata maata	farm
		vuokrasopimus	farm
		maati	farm
palurien pala-	flatness	laakea	flat
		ta saineri	flat
sarko	flesh	liha	flesh
sil	white, moon	kuu	moon
Taniquetil, taha-	lofty	tähti	stars
Tirith	guard	vartioida	guard
Tolos	shieldboss, centre	hauta	tomb
Tol	island	saari	island
turu	be strong	mestari, isäntä	master
		voimakas	
strong			
uru	fire	tuli	fire
vaima	robe	puku	robe
vondo/ yondo	son	poika	son

Out of 29 roots above, one might accept perhaps one - the taha/ tähti root as being vaguely similar, although it is stretching the bounds of credence to do so - and one has to take into account the closer meaning of the Finnish word below

that has no connection whatsoever. Similarly, uru- and tuli are hard to reconcile, as the 't' at the start is 'hard'.
We shall now examine the six word parts that seemed to have no connection at all with Classical Greek, with any possible Finnish analogues:

a. Ilverin - heart;	- not found.
b. kulu - gold; - kulta (gold)	(this is a match).
c. gwini - glint;	- not found.
d. Taha - lofty; - korkëa (high)	(not a match).
e. telpe - silver; - hopea	(not a match).
f. winge - foam; - vaahto	(not a match).

Only one of the six has elements that link it to Finnish, although there is a very similar word in Latin (see above p.240). This alternative route to the word has to be taken seriously, when there are obvious southern loan-words in Finnish such as meri (sea) and hunaja (honey).

Thus from Tables A and B above, it is quite clear that Quenya/Qenya is far more closely matched to Greek than to Finnish. Even on the point which Tolkien himself suggests, the phonology (sound) of the language, Quenya/Qenya and Finnish do not seem to resemble each other to any degree. Although Tolkien mentions Finnish influence of the grammar of some of his languages, no one at present can discuss this sensibly since we do not have any of the Quenya/Qenya grammar to investigate. We have also done a check of the above words against Old Norse (Arthur, 2002) and found no matches.

Note 1:
The English word 'gloom' is unlikely to be derived from the domë- root as gloom comes from either 'glome', muddy, foggy, or 'gloaming', afterglow. If domë- leads instead to the English word 'doom', then from OED, we have a link back to a Greek root θεμις (themis) 'to place'. However, the Greek root τομα / τομιος (toma/ tomios) which means the part of a sacrifice used for taking solemn oaths, seems a far more likely candidate to us. This helps to explain the shift phonetically from a word in Quenya to its near-relative in English. From the other end, domë- relates in terms of meaning 'gloom' very well with the Celtic roots dubno- and dumno- which mean 'dark, black, deep, hidden'.

Note 2:
Christopher Tolkien gives Iarendel as an early alternative spelling of his father's for Earendel in BOLT vol. I.

Note 3:
The introduction of the 'w' sound is very suggestive of the forms in Linear B. Classical Greek does not have this, but it was expected that it would be found -

and it duly was once Linear B was cracked. We have as yet not been able to ascertain the chronology of the 'w' form's acceptance to compare to when Tolkien was utilising it in his invented languages.

Note 4:
The first element of the word is not as obscure as Christopher Tolkien has suggested if Greek is invoked; the same word element, meaning both a tail and a boat. See the shape of the sea where the land meets the ice to the north at Helcaraxe and it could be so described - tail of ocean and needing a boat to cross it.

Note 5:
Poldorea, Polydorus - who is said to be the youngest son of Hecuba and Priam of Troy. In Virgil's *Aeneid*, Polydorus is sent to Thrace to keep him safe from the Greeks, but the king of Thrace kills him. Snorri Sturluson says that Thor was originally 'Tror', grandson of Priam who was fostered by the rulers of Thrace but killed them when he was aged only 12. This links Polydorus with Thor, who shares many attributes with Tulkas. A second god, the Celtic 'Lugh', has a name which is an exact match in meaning for Polydorus and that is 'samildanach', one skilled in all the arts. Like Tulkas, Lugh is a late-comer among his divine kin and he is a defender against evil (including Balor who has one blazing eye).

Note 6:
This is a complicated combination of word elements, but one which solves a few strange story ideas. Tintiltha, twinkle most closely resembles the Latin word scintilla, sparkle - which has Greek roots of the same meaning. The only way to 'create' the word scintilla in Classical Greek is to conflate two words: eis + antille = to antilles, the isles opposite the sun, magical isles where the statues of the Gods reside. The elements 'ant' (near to or opposite) + 'Ilios' (the sun) mean that the isles would be bathed or soaked in pure light. This gives the strange picture of a wayfarer landing upon the antilles, and becoming imbued with light. This is exactly the scene when Earendil comes to Tirion and his clothing picks up diamond dust and he sparkles. The presence of diamond dust is not mentioned elsewhere concerning Valinor, but as part of this concept it fits in perfectly. The wayfarer and his ship would become imbued with light and launch into the void to become a star. Perhaps this is the projected 'fate' of Iarendel, the version of the wayfarer with a Greek-influenced name, that Tolkien developed.

Note 7:
The ungwë- root is a formidably complex one to follow. We know that words formed from this root such as Ungoliante represent monsters or bad things - in this case, a gigantic spider. The connection is made through assuming that the ng- sound is an ancient form of straight 'g' in Classical Greek as it is in Sindarin. Thus, 'ngoliant' could be expressed as 'goliant', where the final 't' can also become a theta, or 'th'. This yields 'golia(n)th'. The gol- root in Classical Greek comes in as kol- as in κολαση (kolase) which is a term for hell or the underworld - again an

abode of monsters and somewhere bad. If for a moment we pause to consider a possibility that the old word was infact 'angoliant' - the ang- root is a very significant one; it comes in a Classical Greek word ανανκε (ananke) or need/ succour. The nk- and ng- forms are interchangeable. This Classical Greek word includes the prefix an- which reverses the meaning of the element that follows. Thus we might rightly ask what anke- is. A reasonable guess would be 'woe' or ill fortune. This would chime in well with the overall meaning of a monster such as 'angoliant'. The name 'Goliath' comes to us from the Old Testament in the chieftain of the Philistines who was defeated by David (I Sam. xvii). However, in another passage it is said that Goliath of Gath was slain by a certain Elhanan of Bethlehem (II Sam. 21: 18-22). It is thought that this is a transcriptural error as in the parallel I Chron. 20:5 the contradiction is avoided by saying: 'Elhanan slew Lahmi the brother of Goliath.' Where did Goliath come by his name? The OED gives no Hebrew root or parallel. If he struck fear in all who saw him (which he did, because he was a giant of a man), he might have taken on the name of a famous monster to raise his reputation. Most such creatures in Greek mythology are sea-monsters (such as Scylla) and in Hebrew mythology Leviathan is a multi headed serpent (and the name also contains the -iath element. According to the OED Leviathan is likely to be derived from a foreign language and not Hebrew - but there is no suggestion as to where it came from). Might both words derive from Mycenean Greek? It is an hypothetical link, but one is drawn to imagine an eight-legged sea-monster (of octopus origins) that comes to land and is so transformed into another eight legged monster - this time, a spider. It may be that ancient people thought of spiders with their eight legs as being related to the octopus. It is also worth noting that octopods and spiders both occur on Minoan vases and seal-stones in forms which can get very close to each other. Also, to judge by their pottery, the Philistines were descended from refugees from the fall of Mycenean Greece (N. Bierling 2002, 'Philistines - Giving Goliath his Due'). Following on from this, Goliath himself has been described as a bronze-clad Greek warrior/hero. If he is angol-iath, then the -iath element means abyss in the elven tongues, which would also take us back to the sea-monster suggestion.

Note 8:
The uru- root gave us considerable puzzlement until we considered the Greek word for fire which gives the English word 'pyre' - and thought about it as a conflation of a preposition and a noun - as in 'up - ur' giving 'pur' over time. The place name 'ipiros' probably is linked to the 'pur' root. The addition of the initial 'p' parallels the case with the atar/ pater root of Iluvatar given above.

Concluding thoughts.

It was when we were drawing together all our work into the chapters of this book that we came across the opening to the Postscript to Garth's biography of Tolkien's early life. It seems very helpful to quote it, as it helps to focus what our book is 'about':
'A pale, drawn man sits in a convalescent bed on a wartime hospital. He takes up a school exercise book and writes on its cover, with a calligraphic flourish; 'Tuor and the Exiles of Gondolin'. Then he pauses, lets out a long sigh between the teeth clenched around his pipe, and mutters, 'No, that won't do anymore.' He crosses out the title and writes (without the flourish): 'A Subaltern on the Somme'. That is not what happened, of course. Tolkien produced a mythology, not a trench memoir. Middle-earth contradicts the prevalent view of literary history, that the Great War finished off the epic and heroic traditions in any serious form.' (Garth, 2003, Postscript: 'One who dreams alone.', p.287)
As can now be readily understood, perhaps Tolkien's original title was somewhat along the lines of the second thought as given above - but we would suggest further that Tolkien incorporated epic and heroic traditions by setting that war experience in the context of the medieval Trojan legends. He then moved to his now well-known title as Garth quoted it, and the Lost Tales were in effect conceived in stages thereafter.

We are fully aware that this volume of Tolkien studies challenges many long held opinions and cherished theories about what, in modern parlance, made Tolkien 'tick' (though to quote Tolkien himself when asked that particular question: 'I don't tick. I am not a machine. (If I did tick, I should have no views on it, and you had better ask the winder.)' (Letters, No.165, 1955, p.218). It would be optimistic in the extreme to assume we shall receive no argument or objection to our wide-ranging ideas. We welcome criticism founded on an objective and rational basis - as we believe that our conclusions are fully able to stand up to any scrutiny. We are happy to consider carefully all suggestions as to how perhaps our theories and conclusions are flawed if they can be shown to be so, or if there is room for improvement or expansion to them. Rational informed discussion is the life-blood of research and is always to be welcomed and encouraged.
What we cannot fight against however is subjective and personal criticism, and we do not intend to do so. If for instance our peers were to level against us the terrible defect that neither of the co-authors of this book hold a current academic position in an august institution of learning, then we would have to hold up our hands and plead 'guilty as charged!'. Does that make our arguments any the less persuasive? Consider that self-made man Joseph Wright and his influence upon J.R.R. Tolkien; he hardly had a conventional academic genteel background, but was ten times the philologist of most in Oxford at the time. Being a 'career academic' or even a 'philologist' is not a prerequisite to being 'allowed' to dedicate yourself to Tolkien research - nor indeed it is the only way to approach the subject.

If we were to be chastised for our arguments not fitting all of Tolkien's writings in all places at all times - we would beg our critic's patience; this is merely the first volume of this current run of Tolkien studies, and much else needs to be discussed and analysed. If we have not talked about some of Tolkien's other works, or other passages within certain works, such as LotR and QS, then it is for a good reason. It is *not* because we are ignoring inconvenient facts that demolish our arguments! We have the next volume all but complete and 'ready to go to press', and that book will cover yet more of Tolkien's works and ideas - and doubtless there will be several more volumes to follow from that one. If our critics decide perhaps to take items out of context, or worse, do not actually read the book and make unfounded statements or put words into our mouths that we did not mean, we would decline entering any debate on such grounds as it would serve no one at all. Another kind of criticism is of a more trivial nature, but still amounts to a 'negative' reaction by default - that is the nit-picking comma counting, indent measuring, typographical error trawling, grammar questioning, reference standard comparing kind. No printed book is perfect; no editor is infallible; no spell checker inexhaustible; no index ever full enough. Our editorial team from *Uncharted Realms of Tolkien* were puzzled that some critics of that first volume seemed to dwell upon those types of flaws more than on the content of the book itself. If you find an error, please let us know - unlike J.R.R. Tolkien when it came to proof-reading the Hobbit, we shall not give two pence for every error found (as he did to his youngest son) (Letter 22, p.28).

This study has looked at *The Fall of Gondolin* and *The Tale of Eärendil* as a linked whole, within an overarching pattern of sources and of the adaptation of material. This is a very different matter to small studies of particular motifs or small sections within tales. Our Trojan/Gondolin hypothesis provides an overarching set of explanations which is far-reaching within the web of Tolkien's stories at any one date, and is also long-lasting in time, for the fragment of the 1950's *Of Tuor and His Coming to Gondolin* shows that Tolkien was still using his old sources some forty years after he began, and after the massive upheaval in the structure of his imagined world which was caused by *The Lord of the Rings*. Our theory illuminates how Tolkien used and transformed his sources to create something at once linked with a very important part of the European literary tradition and yet wholly new. So, in this volume we have shown that Tolkien was no stranger to the Homeric tradition, and that he used it in a particular and original way; his source and inspiration was the medieval Trojan legends. We have shown that this Trojan material was the well-spring of some very important tales - specifically the Tale of Gondolin and the development of the characters of Tuor and Eärendil. It also found a second phase of expression in the Gondorian episodes of Lord of the Rings, Minas Tirith being a second expression of the spirit of Troy.

Following up the Troy-Gondolin hypothesis has taken the authors in many unexpected directions, but we really should not have been as surprised as we were by the results that steadily emerged from our study. Tolkien was a human being, not a plaster statue, and an exceptional human being at that. There is enough evidence of the complexity and wide range of his interests and knowledge to make it clear that if we restrict ourselves to the little boxes that modern academia tends to force students and teachers alike into, we will fail to appreciate the sheer breadth of Tolkien's vision.

We have shown how the unexpected thread of the Tale of Troy runs through the tapestry of Tolkien's work. To do so is by no means to downplay other influences on Tolkien, both those which are well-known and those which so far are almost unknown. The attentive reader will have noticed that in this book we have dealt only with two of Tolkien's 'Great Tales', *The Fall of Gondolin* and *The Voyages of Eärendil*. The *Tale of Tinúviel*,*Túrin Túrambar* and *The Tale of the Nauglamir* and most of the cosmology and 'prehistory' are still to come. In likewise fashion, we have only touched upon episodes within *The Lord of the Rings* (specifically the Ford of Bruinen and Minias Tirith with the battle of the Pelennor Fields and arrival of the Rohirrim). A *very* attentive reader might have spotted that we have not discussed the hypothesis, put forward by Jen Stevens in Jane Chance's 2004 volume *Tolkien and the Invention of Myth*, that the story of Beren and Lúthien is based upon Ovid's tale of Pyramus and Thisbe. This is because there is actually another source which provides an overarching pattern for the *Tale of Tinúviel* with very close fit all the way along, just as the Trojan theory does for *The Fall of Gondolin* and we will discuss this in detail in the next book. Following the thread of understanding through this very Tolkienian labyrinth of tales has at times been a difficult and even exhausting process. Both of us would also like to say that keeping up with Tolkien can be exhilarating, educational and inspirational too. It has been quite a ride so far - and this is only the beginning.

From a linguistic approach, we have shown that Quenya/Qenya is based upon an ancient form of Classical Greek (possibly Homeric). The match is better than 97% on all the many words and roots we have examined, and even some of the 'unmatched' ones (two of the six) could be accepted as being close enough to count as Greek-based. The exact meaning and phonetic matches are around 31%. We have speculated that Tolkien may have been trying to reconstruct the Trojan language which is known to have been very close to the Greek. There has to be some reason for why the elvish languages seem to gravitate towards Greek - and there are in fact two. Firstly, Gerald of Wales said that a priest from St. David's called Elidyr (who claimed to have met the Fair Folk) recounted that they spoke a language like Greek, with Irish and Welsh mixed in with it (Gerald of Wales 1978, Book 1, ch.8, p.135). Tolkien may have been actively trying to model his elvish languages on just such bases. He created many invented languages: there is 'nevbosh' (inspired from his cousins invention of 'animalic'), 'Gautisk' and 'Naffarin' - of which we know very little (apart from Gautisk being perhaps an extrapolation of Gothic which might have been meant to be the tongue of the Geats of ancient Scandinavia (Garth 2003, ch.1, p.17) and Naffarin being Spanish-based, derived from the dictionary belonging to Father Morgan (Carpenter 1977,

Part Two, ch.3, p.45)). We also know that Tolkien was creating his own Greek words from an early age 'for his own entertainment'. However, if we turn to Carpenter, he tells us:
'Realising that he had entered a new phase of his life, Tolkien began (on New Years Day 1919) to keep a diary in which he recorded principal events and his thoughts on them. After starting it in ordinary handwriting, he began instead to use *a remarkable alphabet* that he had just invented, which looked like a mixture of Hebrew, *Greek* and Pitman's shorthand. He soon decided to involve it with his mythology, and he named it 'The alphabet of Rúmil' after an elvish sage in his stories.' (ibid, Part Three, ch. 2, p.107 - also pp. 44- 45) (emphasis ours)
Secondly, and perhaps far more powerfully, Tolkien was utilising an alphabet that embodied Greek - even if he wrote in English with it - from the age of 27 and for the rest of his life on a regular basis for his diary. This means that Tolkien did not 'leave Greek and the Classics behind him' as many perhaps assume when he completed Hons Mods in his second year. He was living with Greek on an almost daily basis from 1919 onwards (indeed, from well before that as our studies have shown) - and this would have been a subliminal and subconscious process as well as an overt one (when puzzling over changes he would make to his invented script). We know that Tolkien also kept with the Latin Mass for the whole of his life (ibid, Part Four, ch.2, p.133) and within that Latin Mass there are many elements of Greek such as the 'kyrie eleison' as well as the major foundation of Greek underlying Latin itself - and these factors might well have been weighed in his scales when considering phonetics as well as word forms and meanings; the existence of the 'Iarendel' form for Earendel for instance (this book, ch. 9, pps. 238 & 241) makes this more than a possibility.

In the end, one might be prompted to ask, what difference does it make whether or not Tolkien drew his inspiration from the medieval Trojan legends and through them from the Classical stories and tales? It matters a great deal. The 'northerness' which many have attached to Tolkien in exclusion of all else does by its nature imply a kind of 'divorce' from the main-stream tradition of the Literature of Western Civilisation. John Garth senses this in his quote given at the start of this section: 'Middle-earth contradicts the prevalent view of literary history, that the Great War finished off the epic and heroic traditions in any serious form.' (Garth, 2003, Postscript: 'One who dreams alone.', p.287) In the light of our research, we can now see that Tolkien was driving that tradition on to new and exciting places. Note the phrase used by W.H. Auden in 1966: 'People seem to divide - they're attracted by either the Northern thing or the Southern thing, by Scandinavia or the Mediterranean.' Tolkien himself rejected that notion forcibly. One always ought to be wary of such stark two way divisions, at any rate - for Tolkien there was not merely Fascism and Communism in the pre-World War 2 years, and he was often irritated by critics who could not envision any of his evil characters in LotR not being 'in league' with Sauron. Tolkien one might suggest, was 'bigger' than the 'things' that Auden tried to shoe-horn him into - his learning and inspiration encompassed all this and more. As we shall discuss and learn in our future volumes of Tolkien research, the full compass of Tolkien's interests is truly astonishing.

By being able to establish the link with the medieval Trojan legends as his source and inspiration for some of his major stories, Tolkien can be seen as fitting into the great Literary Tradition of Europe as one of its most important exponents, indeed we would suggest one of its most successful and original ones. The line stretches from Homer through Vergil via Dante and Milton and through Byron to Tolkien as the 20th century's greatest exponent of recasting the Trojan legends in a more modern format which is relevant to our times. Even Goethe shrank from tackling this material and reinterpreting it - but not Tolkien.

Bibliography.

Anonymous works are listed under the translator or editor and cross-referenced if another description is used in the text. University Press = U.P.

Allen, J., 1978; 'Introduction to Elvish', Bran's Head Books.
alliterative 'Destruction' see Panton and Donaldson 1968
Armstrong, H., (ed.) 1998; 'Digging Potatoes, Growing Trees - 25 Years of Speeches at the Tolkien Society's Annual Dinners, vol.2', Peter Roe Memorial Booklet 6, The Tolkien Society.
Atkinson, R., 1979; 'Stonehenge' (3rd edn.) Penguin.
Arthur, R.G., 2002, English-Old Norse Dictionary, In Parentheses Publications.
Babcock, W.H., 1922; 'Legendary Islands of the Atlantic', American Geographical Society.
Barron, W.R.J., and Burgess, G.S., (eds.), 2002; 'The Voyage of St Brendan; Representative Versions of the Legend in English Translation', Exeter U.P.
Bartlett, R., 1993; The Making of Europe; Conquest, Colonisation and Cultural Change.
Benson, C.D., 1980;'The History of Troy in Middle English Literature', D.S. Brewer.
Bierling, N., 2002; 'Philistines - Giving Goliath His Due', Shangri-La Publications.
Blunden, E., & Taylor, M., 1996; 'Overtones of War', Duckworth.
Britannica 2002; CDROM based encyclopaedia.
Carpenter, H., 1977; 'Tolkien; A Biography', George Allen and Unwin.
1978; 'The Inklings: C.S. Lewis, J.R.R. Tolkien, Charles Williams and their Friends', George Allen & Unwin (Publishers) Ltd.
Carpenter, H., & Tolkien, C.J.R., (eds..), 1981; 'The Letters of J.R.R.Tolkien', George Allen and Unwin (Publishers) Ltd.
Chadwick, H.M., 1912; 'The Heroic Age', Cambridge U.P.
Chambers, R.W., 1912; 'Widsith; A Study in Old English Heroic Legend', Cambridge U. P.
Chance, J., (ed.) 2004; 'Tolkien and the invention of Myth; A Reader', Kentucky U.P.
Child, F.J., 1882-98, repr.1965, 2003; 'The English and Scottish Popular Ballads', orig. pub. Houghton, Mifflin & Co., reprinted Dover Publications Inc.
Coley, J. (trans.), 1986, 'Le Roman De Thebes', Garland Publishing Inc.
Collins, R., 1991; 'Early Medieval Europe 300-1000', 1st edn., Macmillan
Collins, Classical Greek Dictionary, 1995.
Colonne, G. delle, trans. Meek, ME., 1974; 'Historia Destructionis Troiae', Indiana U. P.
Dawood, NJ (trans.), 1973; 'Tales from the Thousand and One Nights', Penguin.
Drout, M.D.C. (ed.), 2002; 'Beowulf and the Critics by J.R.R. Tolkien', Arizona Centre
for Medieval and Renaissance studies
Evans, A.C., 1986: 'The Sutton Hoo Ship Burial', British Museum Press

Evans-Wentz, W.Y., 1911 (reprinted 1990); 'The Fairy Faith in Celtic Countries', Carol Publishing.
www.First World War.com (Arthur Machen, The Bowmen, under Angels of Mons)
Fenwick, M., 1996 'Breastplates of Silk; Homeric Women in The Lord of the Rings ', Mythlore no.81, pp.17-23 (copy kindly provided by the author).
Flieger, V., 1997; 'A Question of Time; J.R.R.Tolkien's Road to Faërie', Kent State U. P.
Flieger, V., 2000, J.R.R. Tolkien & the Matter of Britain, Mythlore 87, Vol.23.1, pps. 47-59
Frazer, R.M., 1966; 'The Trojan War; the Chronicles of Dictys of Crete and Dares the Phyrgian', Indiana U. P.
www.freedict.com/onldict/fin (Liverpool Univ. online dictionary resource)
Friedrich, W.L., trans. McBirney, AR, 2000; 'Fire in the Sea; The Santorini Volcano - Natural History and the Legend of Atlantis', Cambridge U. P.
Fussel, P., 1975; 'The Great War and Modern Memory', Oxford U. P.
Garth, J., 2003; 'Tolkien and the Great War; the Threshold of Middle-earth', HarperCollins
Gerald of Wales, trans. Thorpe, L., 1978; The Journey Through Wales/ The Description of Wales, Penguin.
Gerhardt, M.I., 1963; 'The Art of Story-Telling, a Literary Study of the Thousand and One Nights', E.J. Brill.
Gillespie, G.T., 1973; 'A Catalogue of Persons Named in German Heroic Literature', Clarendon Press.
Grant, M., 1979; 'History of Rome', Faber and Faber Ltd.
Greenman, D., 1992, 'Aeneidic and Odyssean Patterns of Escape and Return in Tolkien's 'The Fall of Gondolin' and The Return of the King', Mythlore 68, pp.4-9
Grotta, D., 1976 (2nd edn. 1978); 'J.R.R. Tolkien; Architect of Middle-earth', Running Press.
Hammond, W., and Scull, C., 1995; 'J.R.R. Tolkien; Artist and Illustrator,' Harper Collins.
Hartland, E.S., 1925 (2nd edn.); 'The Science of Fairy Tales; An Inquiry into Fairy Mythology', Methuen.
Haymes, E.R., 1988; The Saga of Thidrek of Bern', Garland.
Helms, R., 1974; 'Tolkien's World', Thames and Hudson.
Herodotus, trans.Dé Selincourt, A., & Marincola, J., 2003;'The Histories', Penguin.
Hibbard, L.A., 1924; 'Medieval Romance in England; A Study of the Sources and Analogues of the Non-Cyclical Metrical Romances', Oxford U. P.
Homer trans. Fitzgerald, R.,1998; 'The Iliad', Oxford U. P.
trans. Shewring, W., 1980; 'The Odyssey', Oxford U. P.
Homer/Morris see Morris, W., 1912.
Horstmann, C., (ed.) 1887; 'The Early South-English Legendary or Lives of Saints, vol.I, from ms Laud 108, Bodleian Library', Early English Text Society.
Hutton, R., 1999; 'The Triumph of the Moon', Oxford U. P.
2003; 'Witches, Druids & King Arthur', Hambledon & London.

Hymes, S., 1990, 'A War Imagined; The First World War and English Culture', Bodley Head.
Jenkyns, R., 1980; 'The Victorians and Ancient Greece', Blackwell.
1991; 'Dignity and Decadence', HarperCollins.
Jordan, P., 2001; 'The Atlantis Syndrome', Sutton Publishing.
Keegan, J., 1998; 'The First World War'; Hutchinson/Pimlico.
Kinsley, J., (ed.) 1969; 'The Oxford Book of Ballads' (replacing Quiller-Couch, A., 1910) Oxford U. P
Kollek, T., & Pearlman, M.,1968; 'Jerusalem, Sacred City of Mankind; a History of Forty Centuries', Weidenfeld & Nicholson.
Knight, G., 1990; 'The Magical World of the Inklings' , Element.
Laud Troy Book see Wülfing 1902/03
'Letters' see Carpenter and Tolkien 1981.
Liddell & Scott, 1871, reprint 1966, 'Abridged Greek-English Lexicon', O.U.P.

Machen, Arthur see First World War.com
Mallory, J.P., 1989; 'In Search of the Indo-Europeans; Language, Archaeology, and Myth', Thames and Hudson.
'Mandeville, Sir J.' and Seymour, M.C. (ed.. and intro.), 1968; 'Mandeville's Travels', Oxford U. P.
Morris, I., 1964: 'The World of the Shining Prince', Oxford U. P. (reprinted Penguin)
Morris, W., 1912; 'Collected Works of William Morris Vol.13; The Odyssey of Homer done into English Verse', Longmans Green & Co.
Morris, W., 1915; 'Collected Works of William Morris Vol.24; Scenes from the Fall of Troy and Other Poems', Longmans Green & Co.
Morwood, J., Taylor, J., (eds.), 2002, 'The Pocket Oxford Classical Greek Dictionary', Oxford U. P.
Norwich, J.J., 1988; 'Byzantium; the Early Centuries', Penguin.
OED see Oxford English Dictionary
O' hOgain, D., 1990; 'Myth Legend and Romance; An Encyclopedia of the Irish Folk Tradition', Ryan Publishing.
Ordnance Survey, 1981; Place Names on Maps of Scotland and Wales.
Ostrogorsky, G., trans. Hussey, J., 1968; 'History of the Byzantine State', Blackwell.
Oxford English Dictionary 1979 (Compact Edition), Book Club Associates / Oxford U. P.
Panton, Rev. G. A., and Donaldson, D., 1869 & 1874, 2 vols reprinted in 1 in 1968; 'The 'Gest Historiale' of the Destruction of Troy', Early English Text Society.
Reardon, B.P., (ed.), 1989; 'Collected Ancient Greek Novels', California U. P.
Rivet, A.L.F., and Smith, C., 1979; 'The Place-names of Roman Britain', B.T. Batsford Ltd.
Roux, G., 1992: Ancient Iraq (3rd edn..), Penguin.
Sands, D.B. (ed.), 1986; 'Middle English Verse Romances', Exeter U. P.
Scherer, M.R., 1963; 'The Legends of Troy in Art and Literature', Phaidon Press / Metropolitan Museum of Art
Schlauch, M., 1934; 'Romance in Iceland', George Allen and Unwin Ltd.

Severin, T., 1978, 'The Brendan Voyage', Hutchinson.
1985, 'The Jason Voyage', Hutchinson.
1987, 'The Ulysses Voyage', Hutchinson.

Shippey, T.A., 1982 (2nd edn. 1992); 'The Road to Middle-earth', HarperCollins.
2000; 'J.R.R. Tolkien; Author of the Century', HarperCollins.

Spence, L., 1924; 'The Problem of Atlantis', Wm.Rider & Son Ltd.

Stallworthy, J., 2002; 'Anthem for Doomed Youth', Constable/ Imperial War Museum.

Stone, B., 1974, 'Sir Gawain and the Green Knight', Penguin Classics.

Sturluson, S., trans. Faulkes, A., 1987; 'Edda', Dent/Everyman.

Sutherland, E., 1985; 'Ravens and Black Rain; the Story of Highland Second Sight', Constable/Corgi.

Tatum, J. (ed.), 1994; 'The Search for the Ancient Novel', Johns Hopkins U. P.

Todd, M., 1992; 'The Early Germans', Blackwell.

Tolkien, J.R.R., 1937 (4th edn. 1975); 'The Hobbit', George Allen & Unwin.
1954 & 1955 (2nd edn. 1966); 'The Lord of the Rings', George Allen & Unwin.

also: 1st edn.. 1954, 1955 and 3rd edn. 1979

Tolkien, J.R.R., & Tolkien, C.J.R. (ed.), 1977; 'The Silmarillion', George Allen & Unwin.
1980; 'Unfinished Tales', George Allen & Unwin.
1983; 'The Monsters and the Critics and Other Essays'.

The History of Middle-earth Series;
1983; 'The Book of Lost Tales Volume 1', (HOME vol.I), Allen & Unwin.
1984; 'The Book of Lost Tales Volume 2', (HOME vol.II).
1985; 'The Lays of Beleriand', (HOME vol.III).
1986; 'The Shaping of Middle-earth', (HOME vol.IV), Unwin Hyman.
1987; 'The Lost Road', (HOME vol.V).
1988; 'The Return of the Shadow', (HOME vol.VI).
1989; 'The Treason of Isengard', (HOME vol. VII).
1992; 'Sauron Defeated', (HOME vol.IX), HarperCollins.
1993; 'Morgoth's Ring', (HOME vol.X).
1994; 'The War of the Jewels', (HOME vol.XI).
1996; 'The Peoples of Middle-earth', (HOME vol.XII).

Tsountas, C., and Manatt, J.I., 1897; 'The Mycenean Age', Houghton Mifflin & Co.

Wace, A.J.B., 1949, 'Mycenae; An Archaeological History and Guide', Princeton U. P.

Wilson, R.M., 1970 (2nd edn.); 'The Lost Literature of Medieval England', Methuen.

Wimberly, L.C., 1928: 'Folklore in the English and Scottish Ballads', Chicago U. P.

Wood, M., 1985; In Search of the Trojan War', BBC Books.

Index

Achilles 159, 170,179,182
& Amazon queen 191-2
& death of 191
& difficulty to kill 188-9
& River 183-6
& solar heroes 189-90
& comparison to Witch-King 182-90
- see also Witch-King
Ajax Telamonius 59-60, 238
'Alexander'-romance 40
Angtheras (Runes) 243
ANZAC's 89
'Aotrou & Itroun' 118-9
Aragorn & Arwen 12, 33-4
Aragorn & 7 Stars 188-9
Aredhel 57-8
Argos 155-6
Arthur see Fall & Morte
Attila the Hun 209-10
Auden, WH - 241,268
& northerness 2
Axes 95
Babylon 204-6
Balrogs 58-9, 126, 227
Barrow-wight 189
Beacons see Minas Tirith
'Beowulf' 130,162, 191
'Beowulf; Monsters & Critics' 94, 192
Beren & Lúthien 12, 34, 114
Bible n.7 249
Blunden, Edmund 85
& fieldmice 98-9
Boccacio 6
Boromir 165-6
Brendan, Saint - 123-7, 171-5, 226-33, 238
Brigid, Saint 125
Bronze Dragons 62
Brooke, Rupert 84
Carpenter, H - northerness 1
Carthage 215-16
Cassiodorus 11
Celtic -
& languages n.1 247
& gods n.5 248
see also Red Book of Hergest
Censorship 100-1
Chance, Jane 257
Chesterton , GK -
& 'mooreffoc' 176
Churchill, W. 89
Classics, influence of on Britain 24-5
Constantinople 210-2
Copaïs, Lake 39-42,156
'Cottage of Lost Play' 123
Cusp of story 118
Cynewulf (& 'Crist') 106
'Daphnis & Chloë' 207
Dares and Dictys 5, 89,193-5
Dörpfeld, W. 67, 147, 149, 153, 164
Druadan Forest 192
Duck 242
Eärendil 70, 71-72, 97, 102-3, 106, 123, 207, n2, 247, n.6, 248, 256
& Brendan, Saint 228-9
& Earramë 225
as 1st historical hero 220
& Jason 231-3
& Odysseus 233-4,238
& Sindbad 229-30
& success as messenger 234-5
& Wade 222-3, 225
& Elwing 35
& stars 127
Ecthelion & Gothmog 58-9
Elf-human marriages 33-5, 116-7
Elwing -
as bird 236-8
Eowyn -
rides openly to war 196
rides in disguise to war 196-7
& rumour 198
& Witch-King 197

European links
& Aegean 97-8
& Polytheism 27-8
Evans, Sir Arthur 92, 164, 242
Fall/Failure of Cities see Minas Tirith
Fall of Arthur 226
Famous Fallen Cities 37, 203, 217
Faramir 166
Fat Lords -
see Polidarius, Salgant, Forlong
Fenwick, M 1
Finnish 52, 241, 246-7
Flieger, V -
& northerness 4
& time 150-1
Forlong 54, 170-1
Found Manuscripts 89-90, 92, 96
French language see Minas Tirith
Freud, Sigmund 150
Gallipoli 87-8
Gandalf Greyhame 121
& Gondolin 166-7
Garland, Roger 237
Garth, J. 78, 83
85, 90, 91, 101-2, 255, 258
Gate of the Noldor 41
Gawain & the Grene Knight 16
Geoffrey of Monmouth 11, 16, 72
Gilson, R.C. 23
Glorfindel 52
Gondolin -
& abdication 65-6
& date of fall 65
& exiles of 71
& Gandalf 166-7
& geography 39-42, 139
& heraldry 53
& languages 51
& names of lords 51
& Orendel 118-20
& origins of story 93-4
& polarised politics 74
& prophecies of doom 45
& the sea 94-5
& Seven Gates 42-4
& Seven Names 35-6
& story junctions 132-3
& towers 153, 158-9
& tower falling 67
& treachery 60-2
& Troy (see that entry) 256
& 12 Houses 50
& Ulmo 29-33, 38
& women, plight of 68-9
Gondor -
as 'Ond' 144, 236-7, 256
& roads 154
Graves, Robert 85
Greek, ancient language 35-6, 51-2, 90-1, 95, 242
& closeness to Quenya 242-5, 267-8
Grey cloaks -
see Thingol, Gandalf, Ulmo.
Guido delle Colonne 31, 47,58, 61-2, 73-4, 83, 87, 98, 115, 124, 199-200
& Trojan heraldry 53
Guy of Warwick 37, 128, 135-6
Helen of Troy 56-7, 112
Hesione 56-8, 137, 200, 238
Hobbit, The 40, 95, 115, 133-135, 176-9, 220
& Jews 214
Hobbits & rumour 198
Horn of Boromir -
- see Minas Tirith & bulls
Idril
see also Silver Feet
immrama 230-2, 235
Isidore of Seville 124
Jason 107, 177-8, 191-2, 199, 238
& Eärendil 231-3
Jerusalem - 124, 135, 212-5
& Heavenly 49, 54
Jonah, prophet 208
Kalevala 241
Kirk, William 103-4
Lancashire Fusiliers 88

Latin 245-7, 268
Leviathan 124
Lewis, A., -
& Currie, E. 80, 143, 220
& Lacon, R 140
Lewis, C.S. 103, 150
Lindos, Rhodes 36, 145
Linear B script 242-3, n.3, 248
Lisgar(dh)/Arlisgion 38, 237
Lohengrin 131
Lord of the Rings -
as 'new Hobbit' 143
'Lost Horizon' 40, 44
'Mabinogion' 125
Machen, Arthur 103
Maeglin 58, 119-20, 171
Mandeville's Travels 44
Map, Walter 226
Mediation 133-6
Meduseld 162, 197
Minas Tirith -
& beacons 167-8
& bulls 165-6
& geography 155
& compared to Gondolin 144-5
& fall/fail of cities 148-9
& French language 169
& halls 160-2
& lords compared
Troy/Gondolin 168-70
& lords Homeric catalogue 170
& Mycenae 150,152
& names of lords 51-2
& rumour 198
& Seven Gates 42-4, 144-8
& ships, black 172
& Siege 141
& towers Troy/Gondolin 153, 158-9
& Trees 162-3
& compared to Troy 143-174, 176 (numbers)
& Wooden Horse 172-3
'mooreffoc' see Chesterton
Morris, W 21-3, 37, 210
Morte Arthure, alliterative 223-5
Muckle Flugga 138
Mycenae -
& Minas Tirith 150-4
& roads 154
& tholos tombs 44
& decorated weapons 188-9
Newman, Cardinal J.H. 25
Nine Worthies 53-4
Nineveh 206-8
Norse, Old (language) 247
North as home of evil 125-6
Númenor 71-2, 152, 163, 215
Odysseus &Eärendil 233-4, 238
Odyssey 220
ofermod, southern 8, 83
Ond see Gondor
One Ring 199
& trifling gift 200
Orcrist 40
Orendel 106, 108-11, 114, 117-8, 120, 128, 137, 219-22
& geography 111
'Ortnit' 112
Osgiliath 157-8
Otto of Friesing 113
Ovid 29, 55, 68, 191, 257
Quenya 241-7
Palmer, Professor L. 164
Polidarius (fat) 54, 170-1
Polytheism, European links 27-8
Prester John 40, 44
Red Book of Hergest 71, 73
Renault, Mary 92
River-names 186-7
Rohirrim -
& Amazons 191-2
& 'Homeric horsemen' 191
Rome 208-10, 239
& Goths 209
'Rosengarten, Der' 117
Runes see Angtheras
Salgant 54, 170-1

Samothrace 139
Santorini/Thera 90-3, 96, 166
Sassoon, Siegfried 100-1
Saxo Grammaticus 219, 221
Schliemann, H 15, 37, 67, 90, 145-6, 164, 166
Seven Stars 189-90
Severin, Tim 227, 232
Shangri-la 40, 44
Shippey, TA - northerness 1 - 3
ships, black 172
shipwreck 220-1
Silver Feet 55-6
Sindbad & Earendil 229-30
Snorri Sturluson 11-12,16, 27, 50 n.5 248
Sorley, Charles 84
Stevens, J. 257
Stonehenge 189
Stopfel, S. 108, 119-20
Tanks, WWI 64
'TCBS' 79-81, 85, 87
Tengwar see Angtheras
Thebes, Seven Gates 44
'Thidreks Saga af Bern' 116-7, 136, 221, 223, 225
Thingol Greycloak 120-1
Thousand & One Nights 206
Tiryns 151-2, 157
Tol Eressëa 90-93
Tolkien, JRR -
& classics 82-3, 146
& Fall of Gondolin, start 4
& fantastic mode 86-7
& fieldmice 98-9
& Frodo's Dreme/The Sea-Bell 99
& German 'barbarism' 86
& Greece 211
& Happy Mariners 107-8, 123
& Japan 49-50
& languages, early 52, 79, 258
& love for Latin 2
& medieval Trojan legend 72-3
Trees -
& Gondolin, artificial 47-9
& Japan 49
& Minas Tirith 162-3
of the Sun & Moon 40
Trier see Troy
Troilus & Criseyde 20, 223-5
Trojan legend -
& LOTR 143-50
medieval popularity of 10
medieval version 7-9
& Witch-King 201
Troy -
& archaeology 206-7
& Amazons 193-5
& Astyanax the child 70
& Eärendil 127
& exiles of 71
& eucatastrophe 98-9
& futility of war 81-2
& Gondolin 257
& medieval politics 12-14
& northern involvement 192
& Osgiliath 157-8
& Priam's cowardice 65-6
& reality of myth 15
& rivers 185-6
& seven gates 42-4
& treachery 60-2
& Trier 111-2
& Trieste 111-2, 113
& war as 1st historical event 219
& WWI comparisons 84-6, 87-9
Tuor -
& BOLT version 129-32
& Idril 34-5, 133
& Orendel 132
Turin Turambar 220
Uffington, White Horse 64
Ulmo 235-6
& grey cloak 122,140
& patron Gondolin 28-33
& prophecy 42-3

Unwen son of Eastgota 223-5
Vingilot 224-5
- see also Eärendil & Wade
Virgil 6, 33, 67-9, 71-2, 113, 195-7, 198, n.5 248
'Virginal' 113
Volsung stories 116-7, 209, 220
Wade 131, 220
& Earendil 222-3, 225
as medieval hero 223-5
'Waldere' 113
Wayland 17
White Trees -
& Gondor 162-3
& Númenor 114
'Widsith' 224
Witch-king -
& Achilles 182-90
& difficulty of killing 187-8
& Eowyn 197
& Hector 173-5, 184
& rivers Troy 186-8
& solar heroes 189
&Trojan legend 201
'Wolfdietrich' 112, 114-5
Wooden Horse 62, 172-3
World War One -
& Defence of Realm Act 100-1
& eucatastrophe 98-9
& folklore/fantasy 103-4
& futility of war 81-2, 104
&Trojan comparisons 84-6, 87-9
World War Two -
&Trojan comparisons 85-6
Wright, Joseph 255